YA

Ran and the Gray wor
12/04/2019

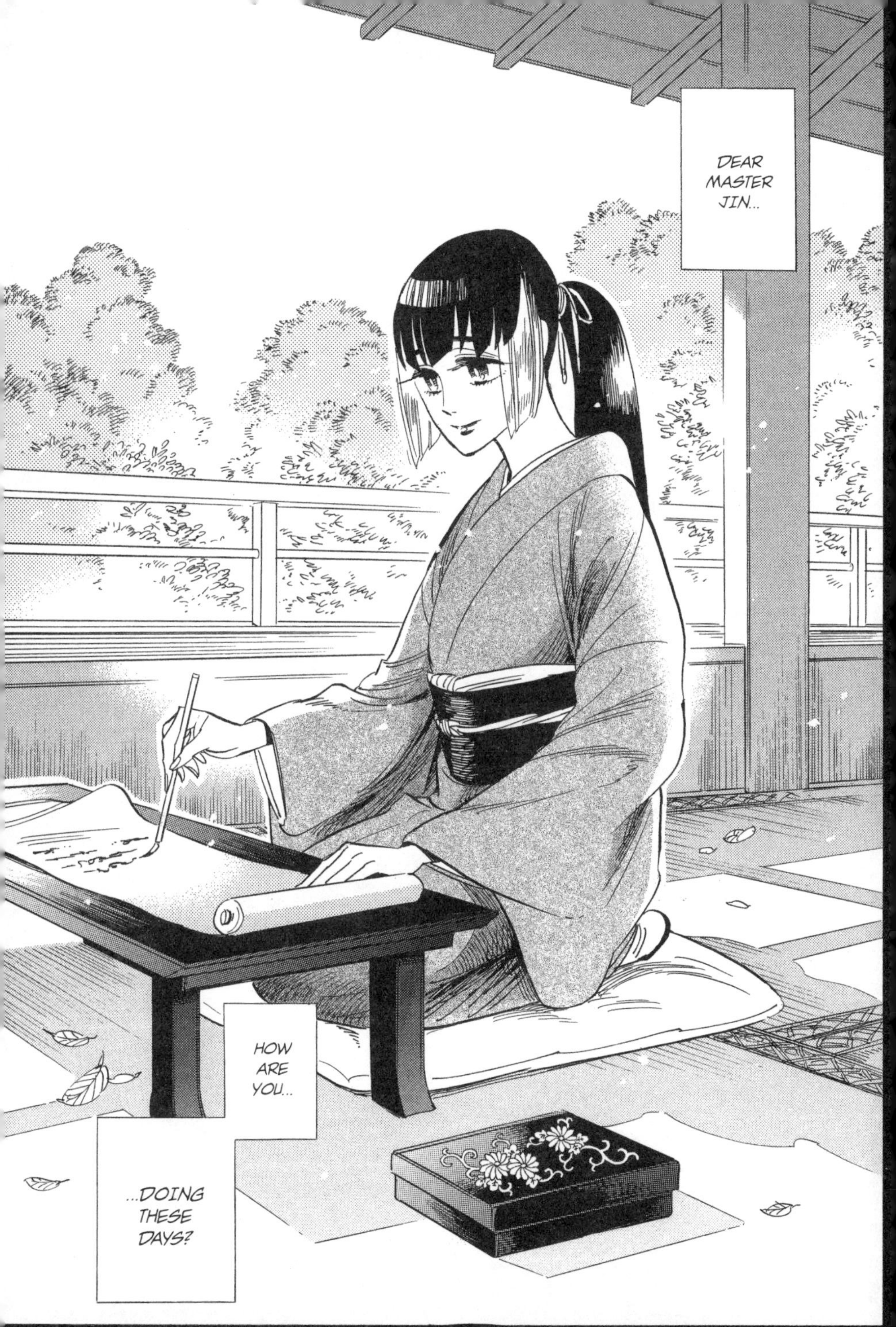
DEAR MASTER JIN...
HOW ARE YOU...
...DOING THESE DAYS?

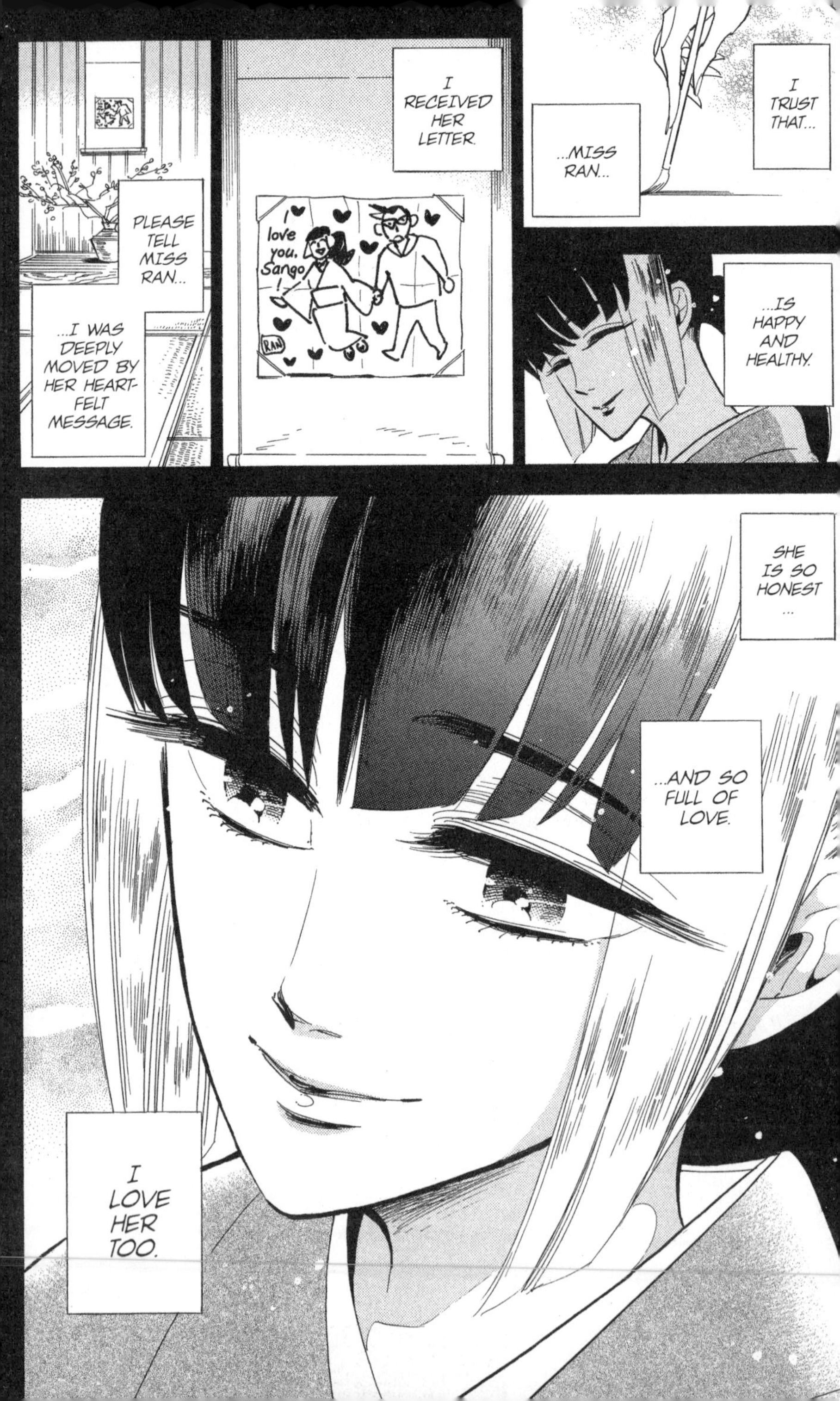
I TRUST THAT...
...MISS RAN...
...IS HAPPY AND HEALTHY.
I RECEIVED HER LETTER.
I love you, Sango!
RAN
PLEASE TELL MISS RAN...
...I WAS DEEPLY MOVED BY HER HEART-FELT MESSAGE.
SHE IS SO HONEST...
...AND SO FULL OF LOVE.
I LOVE HER TOO.

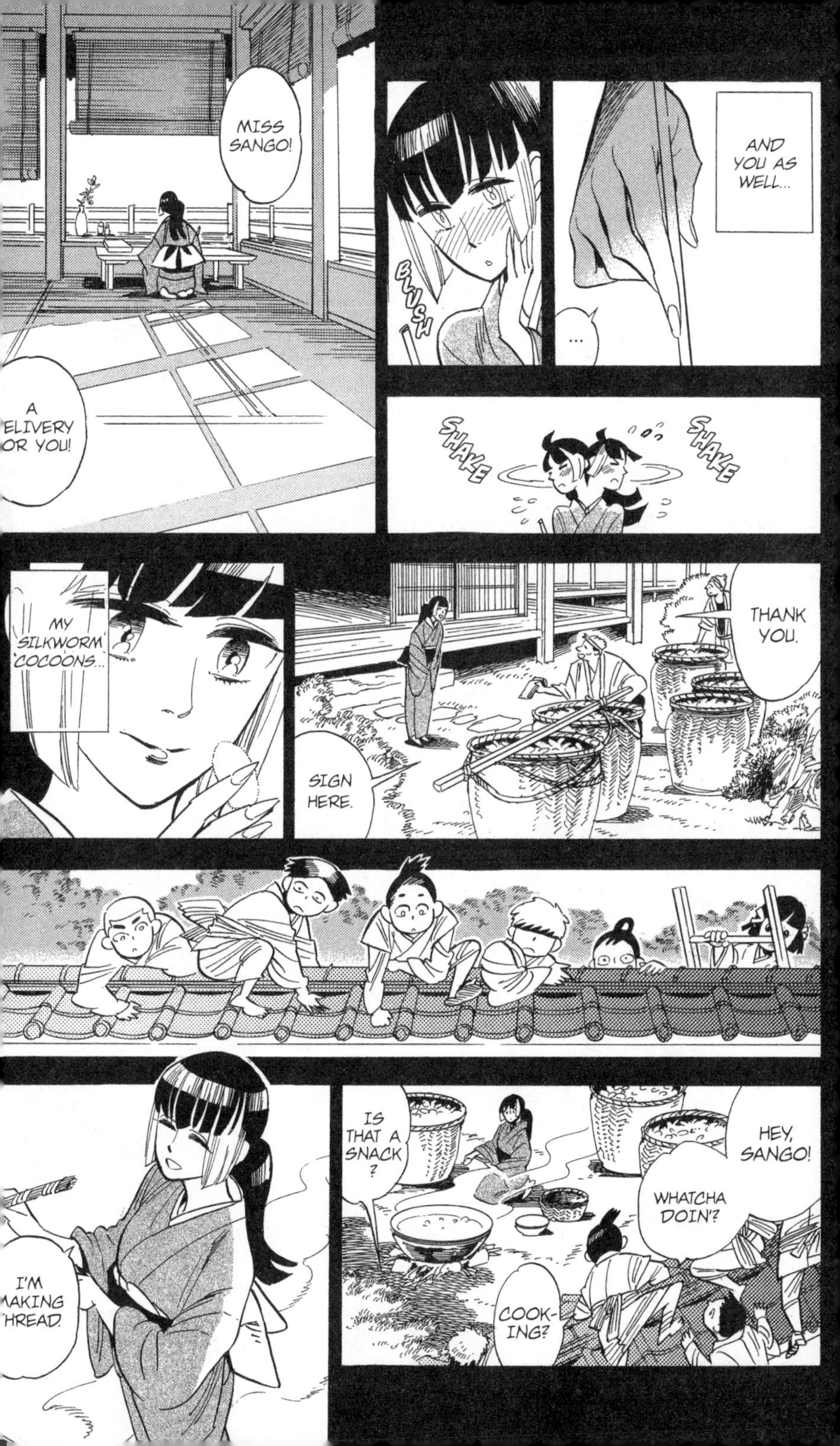
AND YOU AS WELL...
...
BLUSH
SHAKE
SHAKE
MISS SANGO!
A ELIVERY OR YOU!
THANK YOU.
SIGN HERE.
MY SILKWORM COCOONS...
HEY, SANGO!
WHATCHA DOIN'?
IS THAT A SNACK?
COOKING?
I'M AKING HREAD.

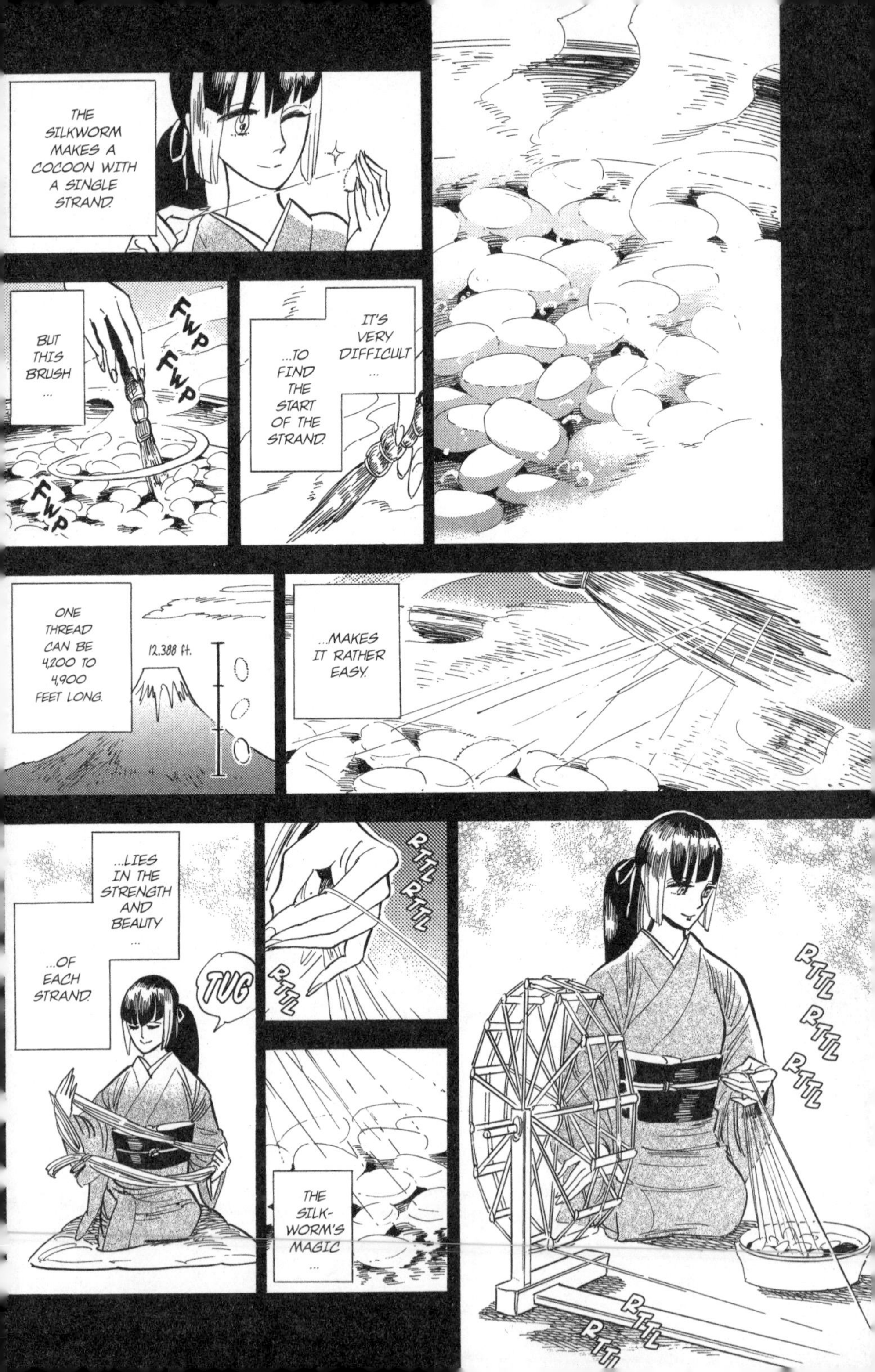
THE SILKWORM MAKES A COCOON WITH A SINGLE STRAND.
IT'S VERY DIFFICULT ...
...TO FIND THE START OF THE STRAND.
BUT THIS BRUSH ...
FWP
FWP
FWP
...MAKES IT RATHER EASY.
ONE THREAD CAN BE 4,200 TO 4,900 FEET LONG.
12,388 ft.
RTTL RTTL RTTL
RTTL RTTL
RTTL RTTL RTTL
THE SILKWORM'S MAGIC ...
...LIES IN THE STRENGTH AND BEAUTY ...
...OF EACH STRAND.
TUG

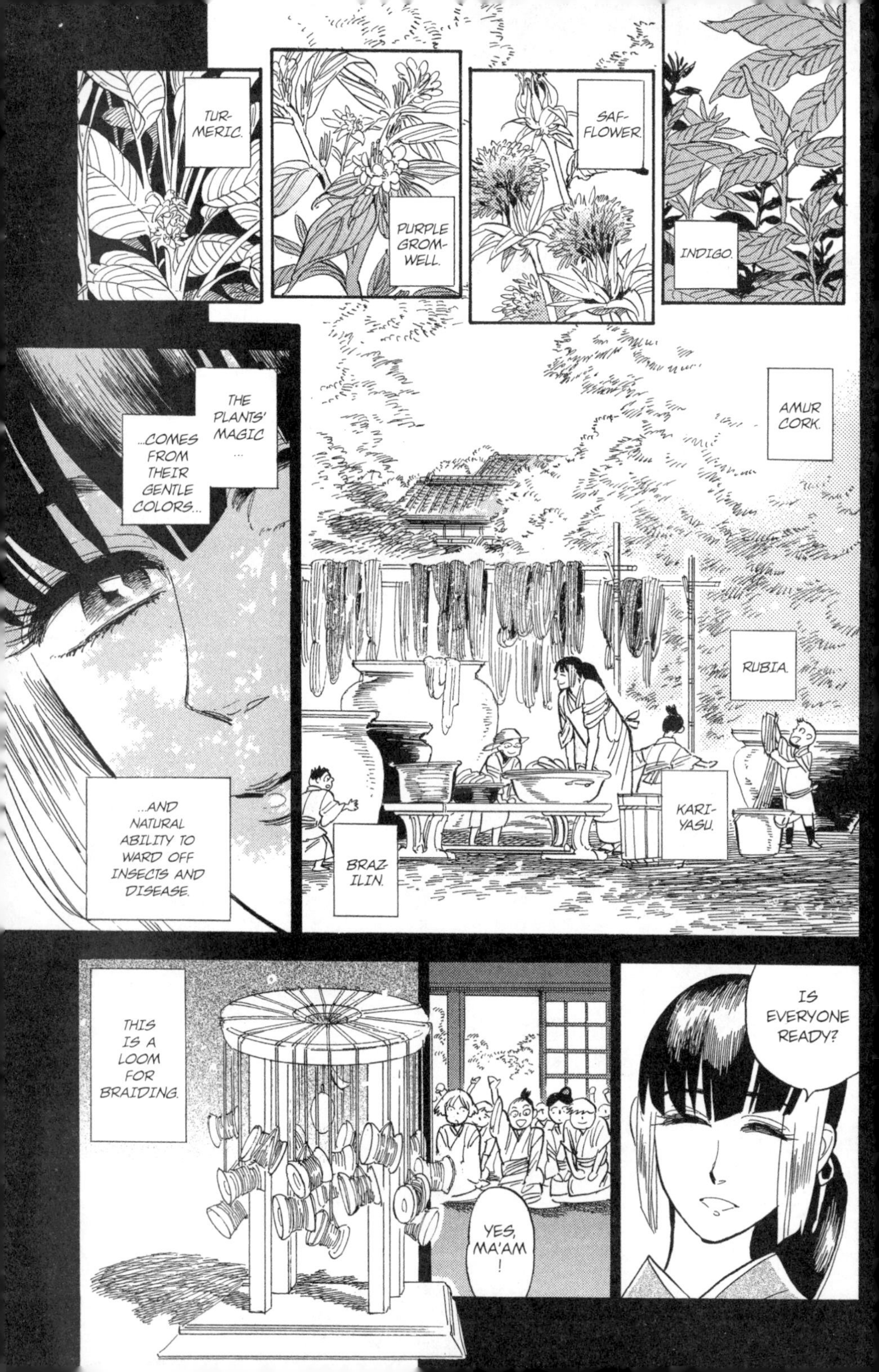
INDIGO.
SAF-FLOWER.
PURPLE GROM-WELL.
TUR-MERIC.
AMUR CORK.
RUBIA.
KARI-YASU.
BRAZ-ILIN.
THE PLANTS' MAGIC...
...COMES FROM THEIR GENTLE COLORS...
...AND NATURAL ABILITY TO WARD OFF INSECTS AND DISEASE.
IS EVERYONE READY?
YES, MA'AM!
THIS IS A LOOM FOR BRAIDING.

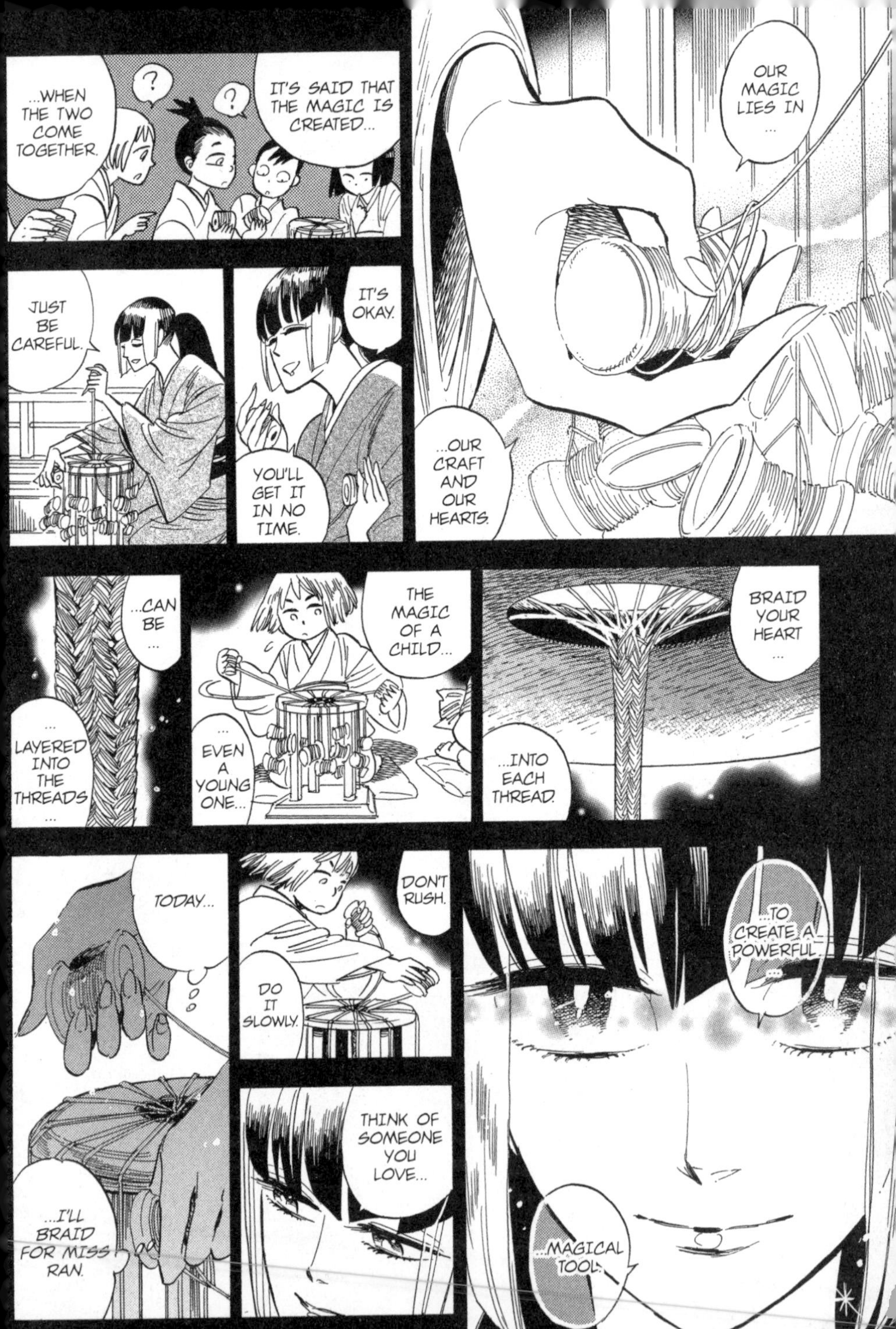
OUR MAGIC LIES IN ...
...OUR CRAFT AND OUR HEARTS.
IT'S SAID THAT THE MAGIC IS CREATED...
?
?
...WHEN THE TWO COME TOGETHER.
IT'S OKAY.
YOU'LL GET IT IN NO TIME.
JUST BE CAREFUL.
BRAID YOUR HEART ...
...INTO EACH THREAD.
THE MAGIC OF A CHILD...
... EVEN A YOUNG ONE...
...CAN BE ...
... LAYERED INTO THE THREADS ...
...TO CREATE A POWERFUL ...
...MAGICAL TOOL.
DON'T RUSH.
DO IT SLOWLY.
THINK OF SOMEONE YOU LOVE...
TODAY...
...I'LL BRAID FOR MISS RAN.

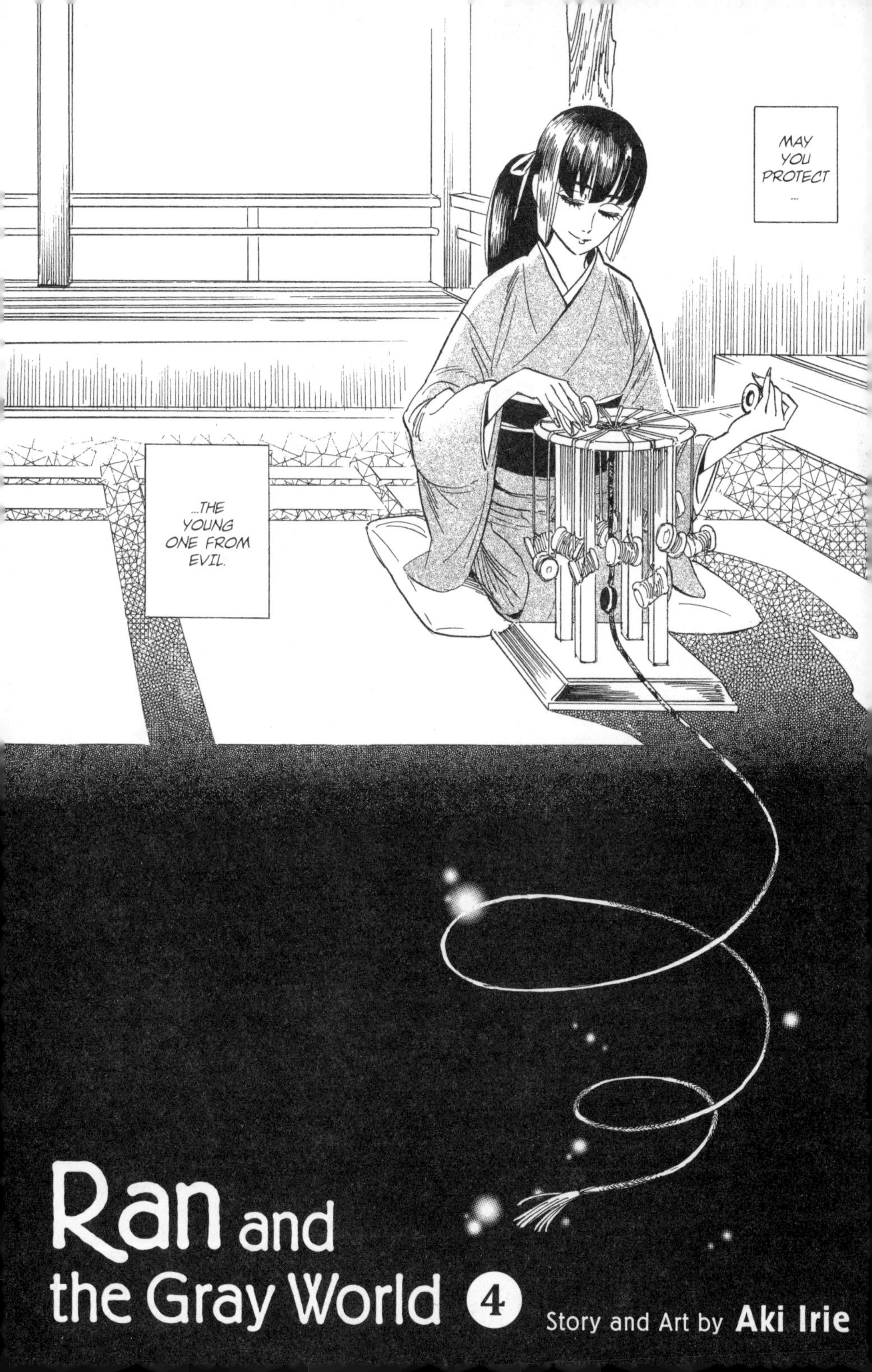
MAY YOU PROTECT ...
...THE YOUNG ONE FROM EVIL.
Ran and the Gray World 4
Story and Art by Aki Irie

Contents

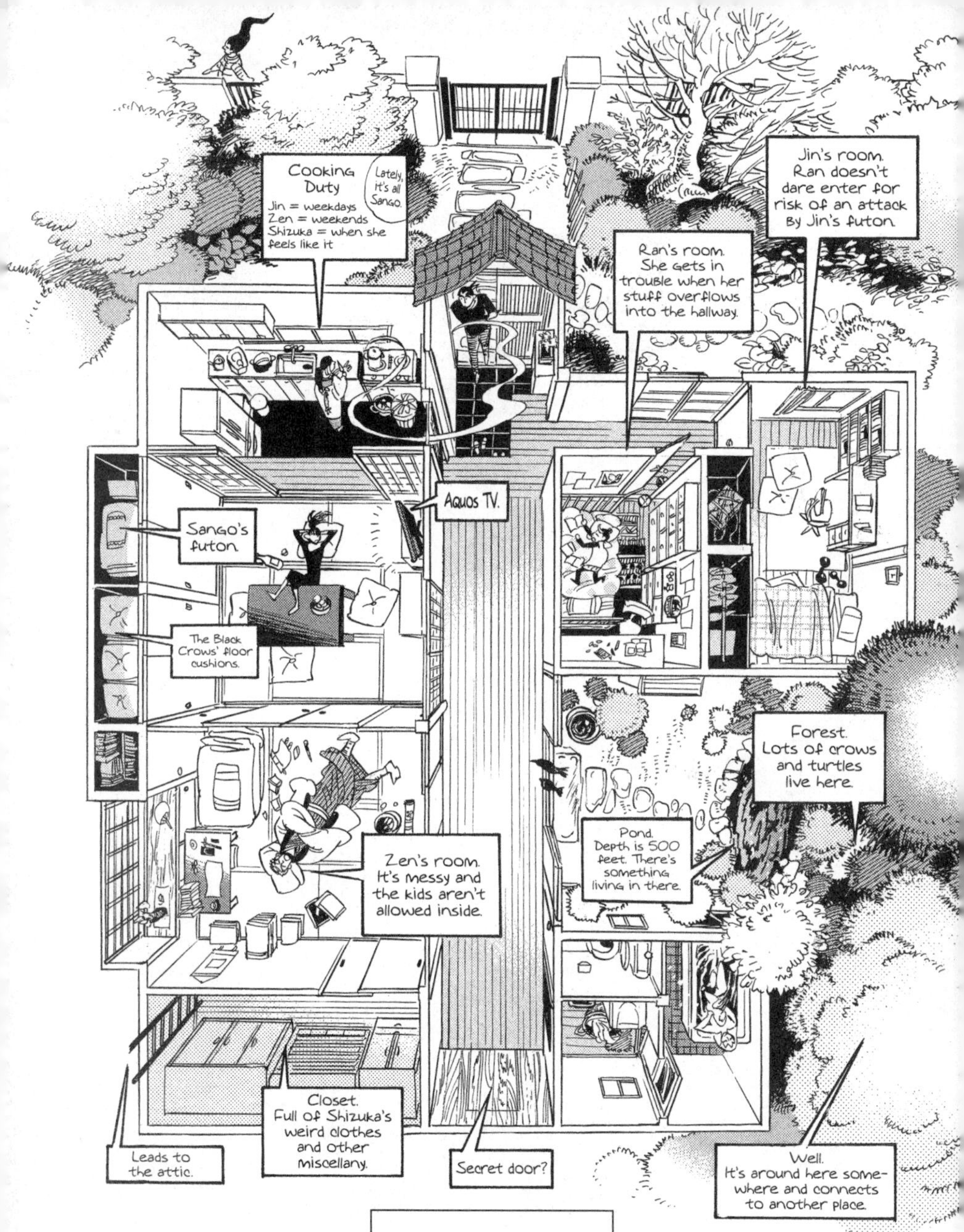
Jin's room. Ran doesn't dare enter for risk of an attack by Jin's futon.
Ran's room. She gets in trouble when her stuff overflows into the hallway.
Lately, it's all Sango.
Cooking Duty
Jin = weekdays
Zen = weekends
Shizuka = when she feels like it
Aquos TV.
Sango's futon.
Forest. Lots of crows and turtles live here.
The Black Crows' floor cushions.
Pond. Depth is 500 feet. There's something living in there.
Zen's room. It's messy and the kids aren't allowed inside.
Well. It's around here somewhere and connects to another place.
Secret door?
Closet. Full of Shizuka's weird clothes and other miscellany.
Leads to the attic.

Chapter 19

Run, Hibi, Run!

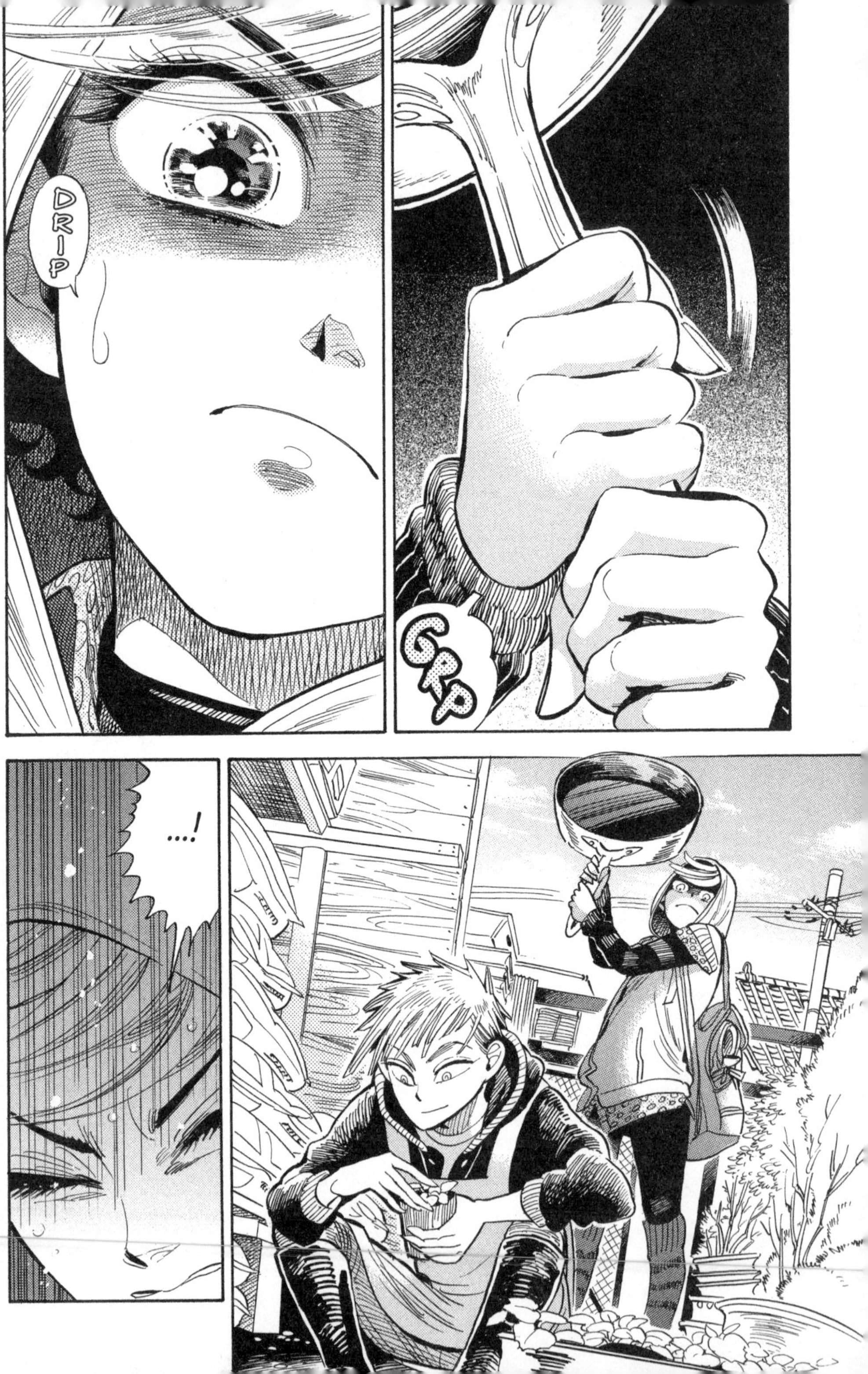
GRP
DRIP
...!

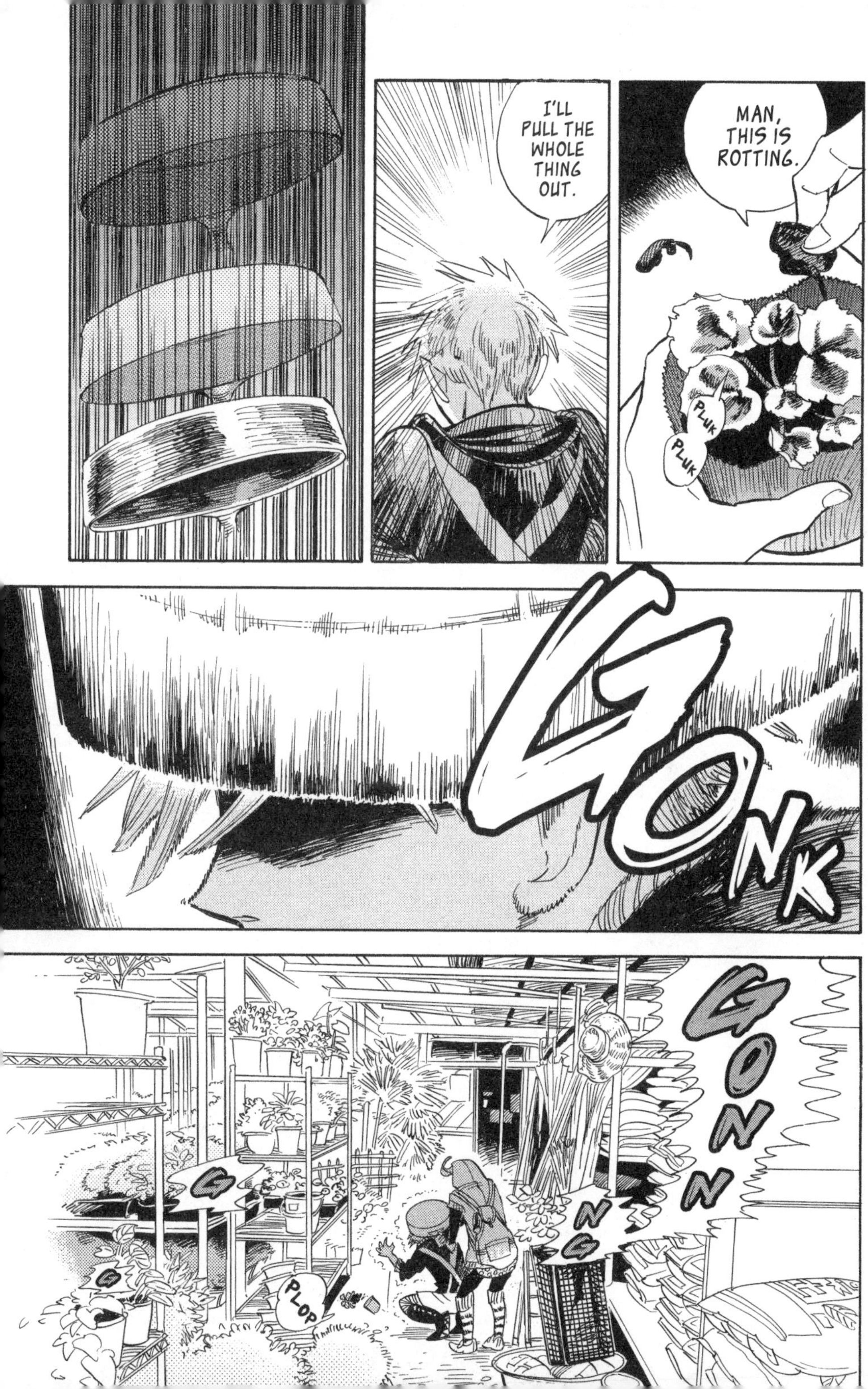
MAN, THIS IS ROTTING.
PLUK
PLUK
I'LL PULL THE WHOLE THING OUT.
GONK
GONN
NNG
G
G
PLOP

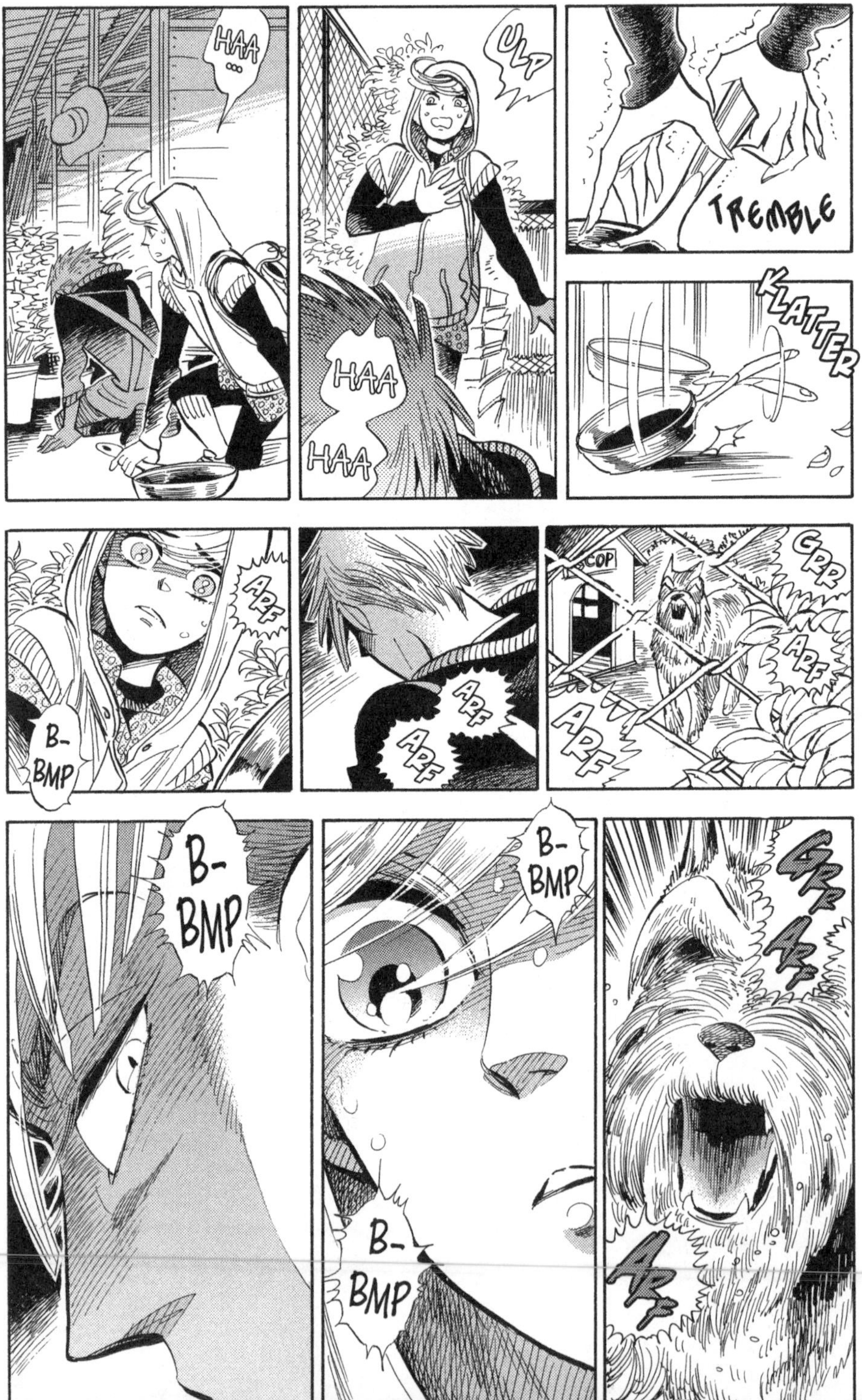
TREMBLE
KLATTER
ULP
HAA
HAA
HAA ...
GRR
ARF
ARF
ARF
ARF
ARF
B-BMP
GRR ARF
ARF
B-BMP
B-BMP
B-BMP

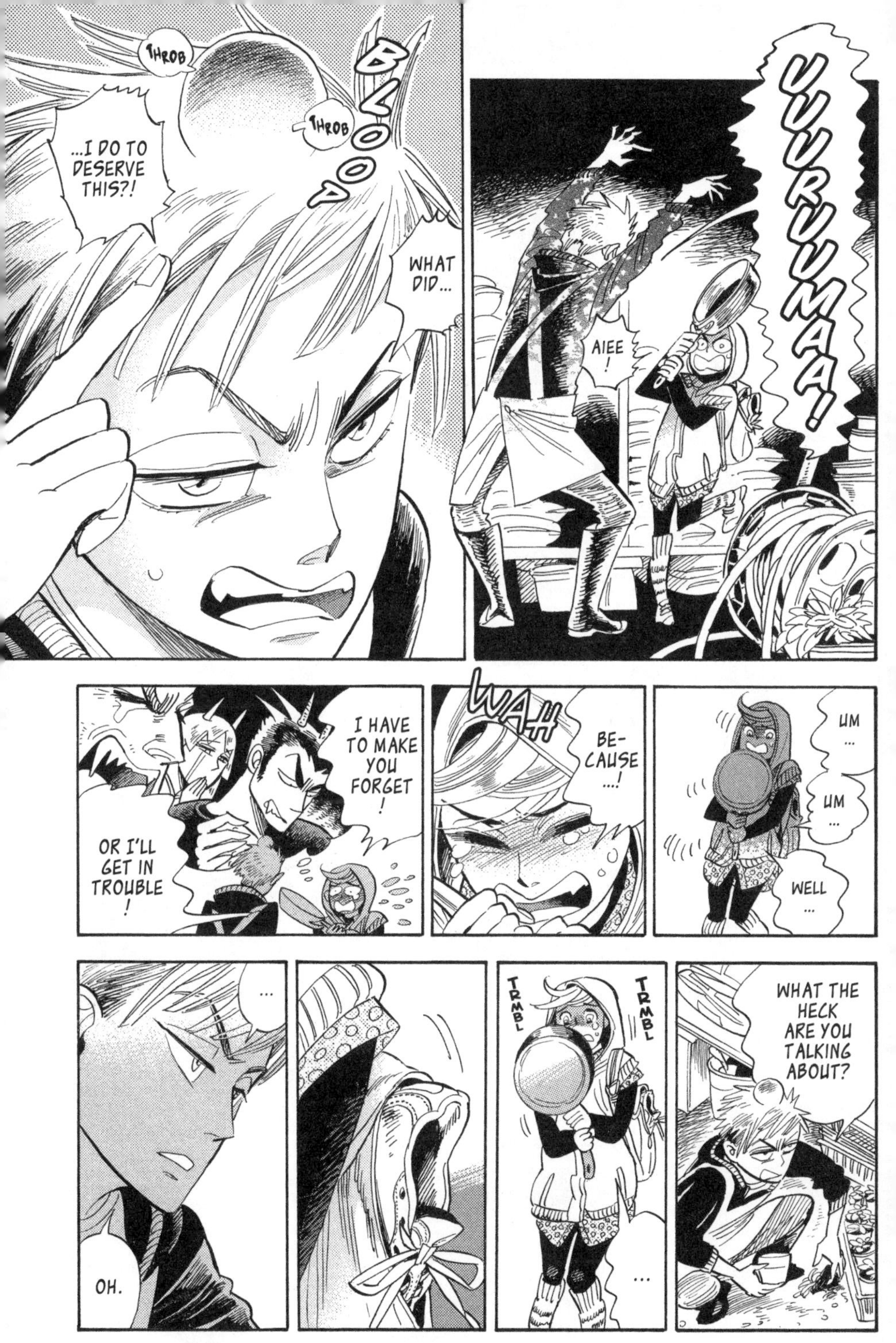
UUURUMAA!
AIEE!
BLOOOP
THROB
THROB
WHAT DID...
...I DO TO DESERVE THIS?!
UM...
UM...
WELL...
WAH
BE-CAUSE...!
I HAVE TO MAKE YOU FORGET!
OR I'LL GET IN TROUBLE!
WHAT THE HECK ARE YOU TALKING ABOUT?
TRMBL
TRMBL
...
...
OH.

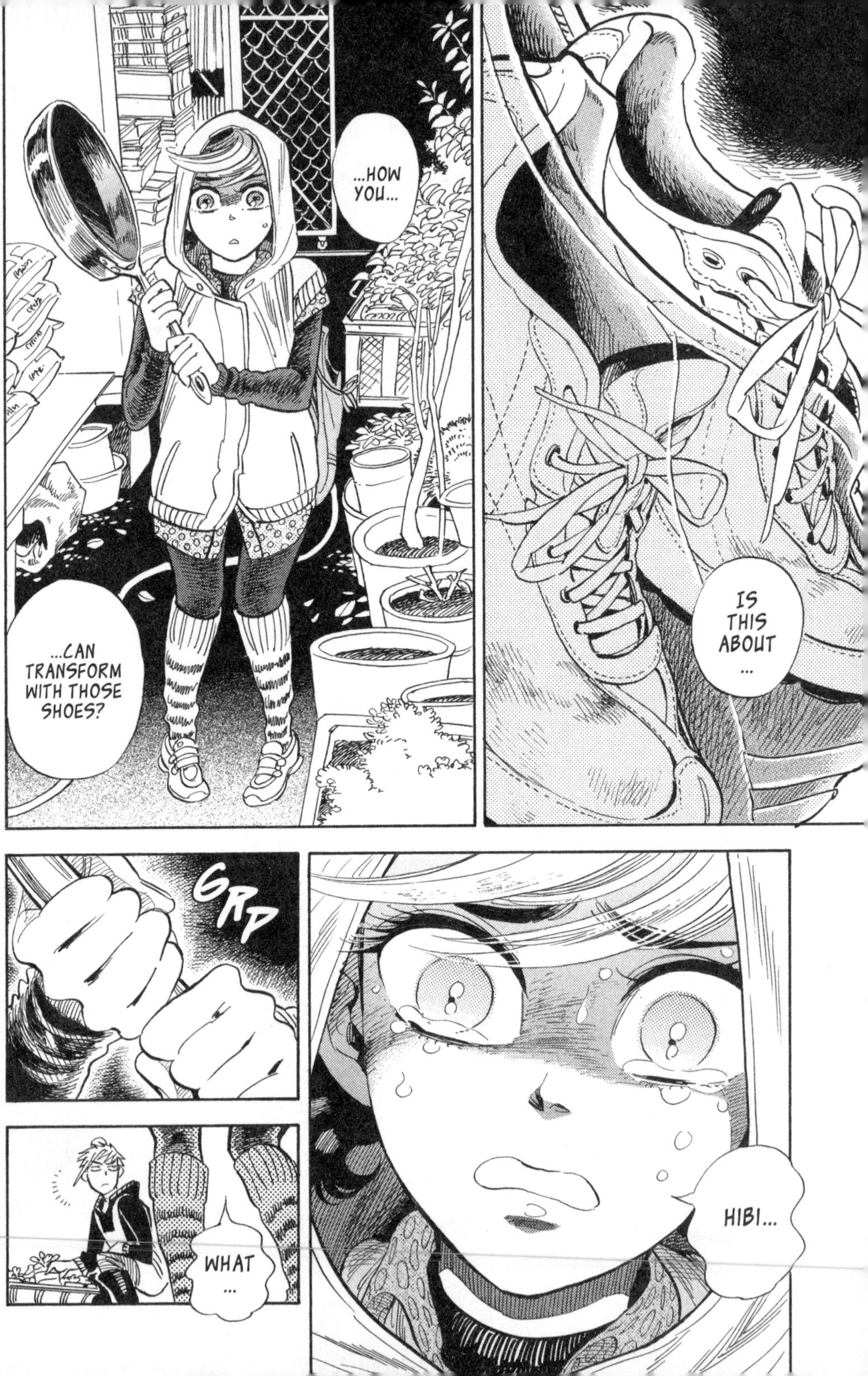
IS THIS ABOUT ...
...HOW YOU...
...CAN TRANSFORM WITH THOSE SHOES?
HIBI...
GRP
WHAT ...

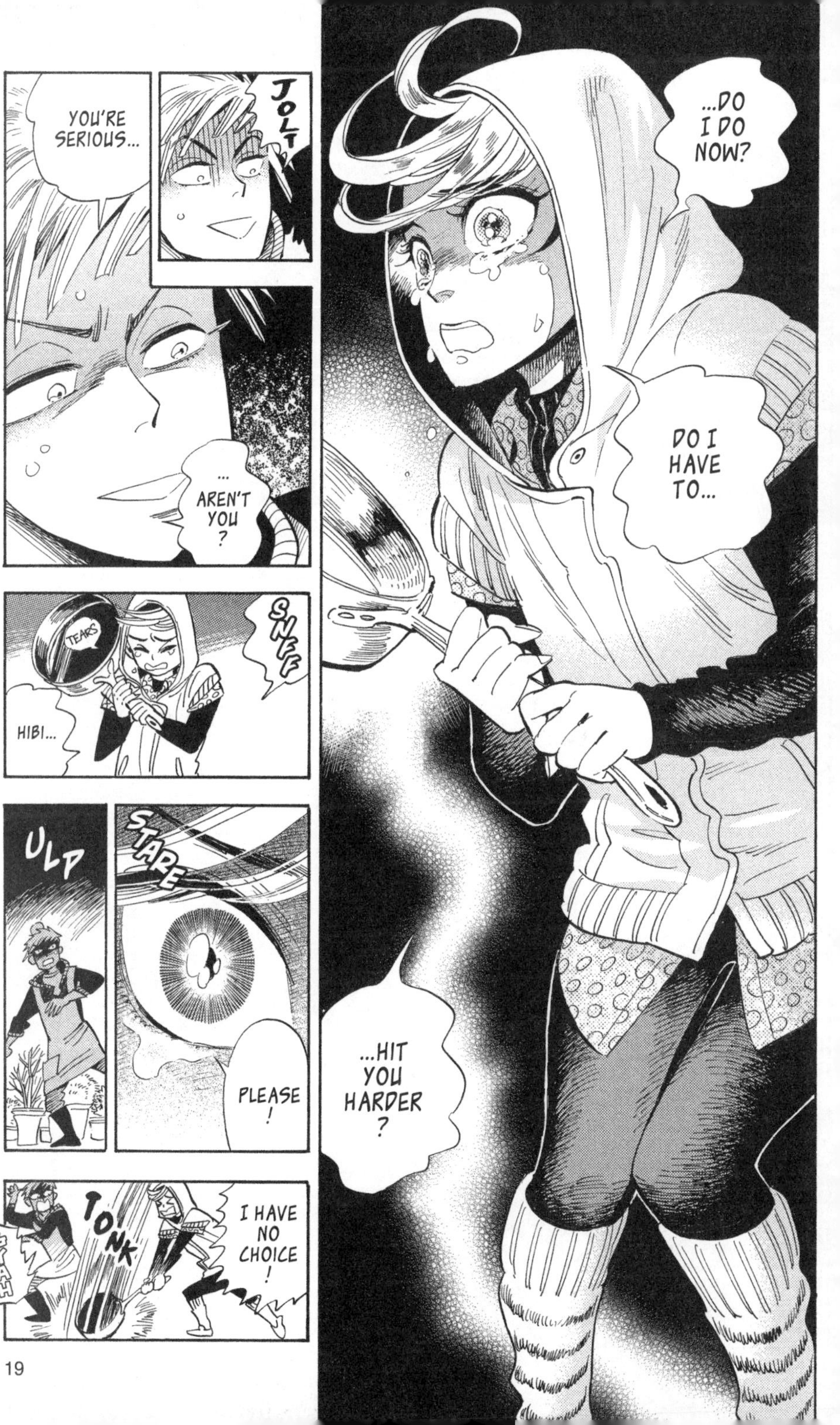
...DO I DO NOW?
DO I HAVE TO...
...HIT YOU HARDER?
JOLT
YOU'RE SERIOUS...
... AREN'T YOU?
SNIFF
TEARS
HIBI...
STARE
PLEASE!
ULP
I HAVE NO CHOICE!
TONK
GYAH

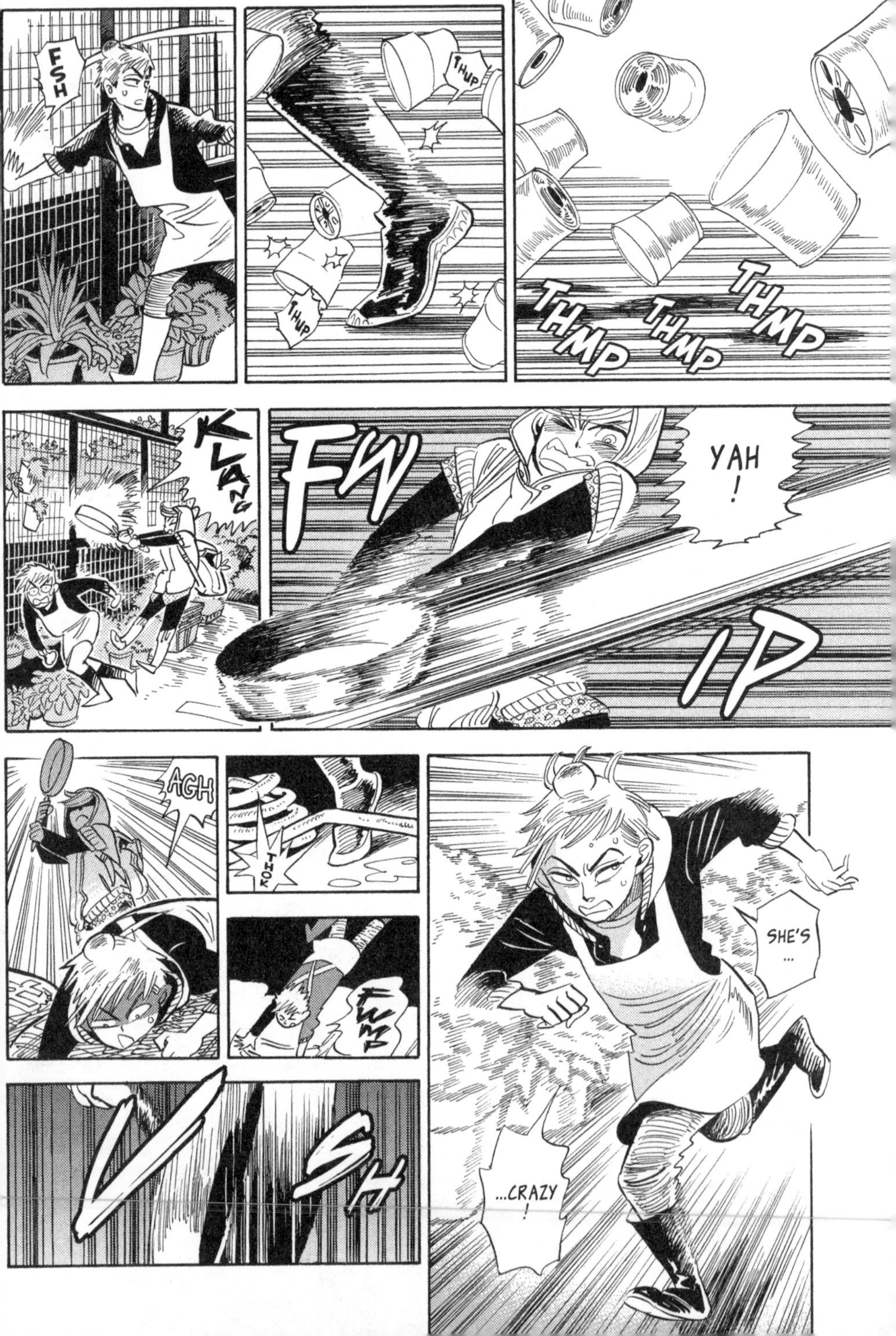
THMP
THMP
THMP
THUP
THUP
FSH
FW
IP
YAH!
KLANG
SHE'S...
...CRAZY!
THOK
AGH
FWMP
VSH

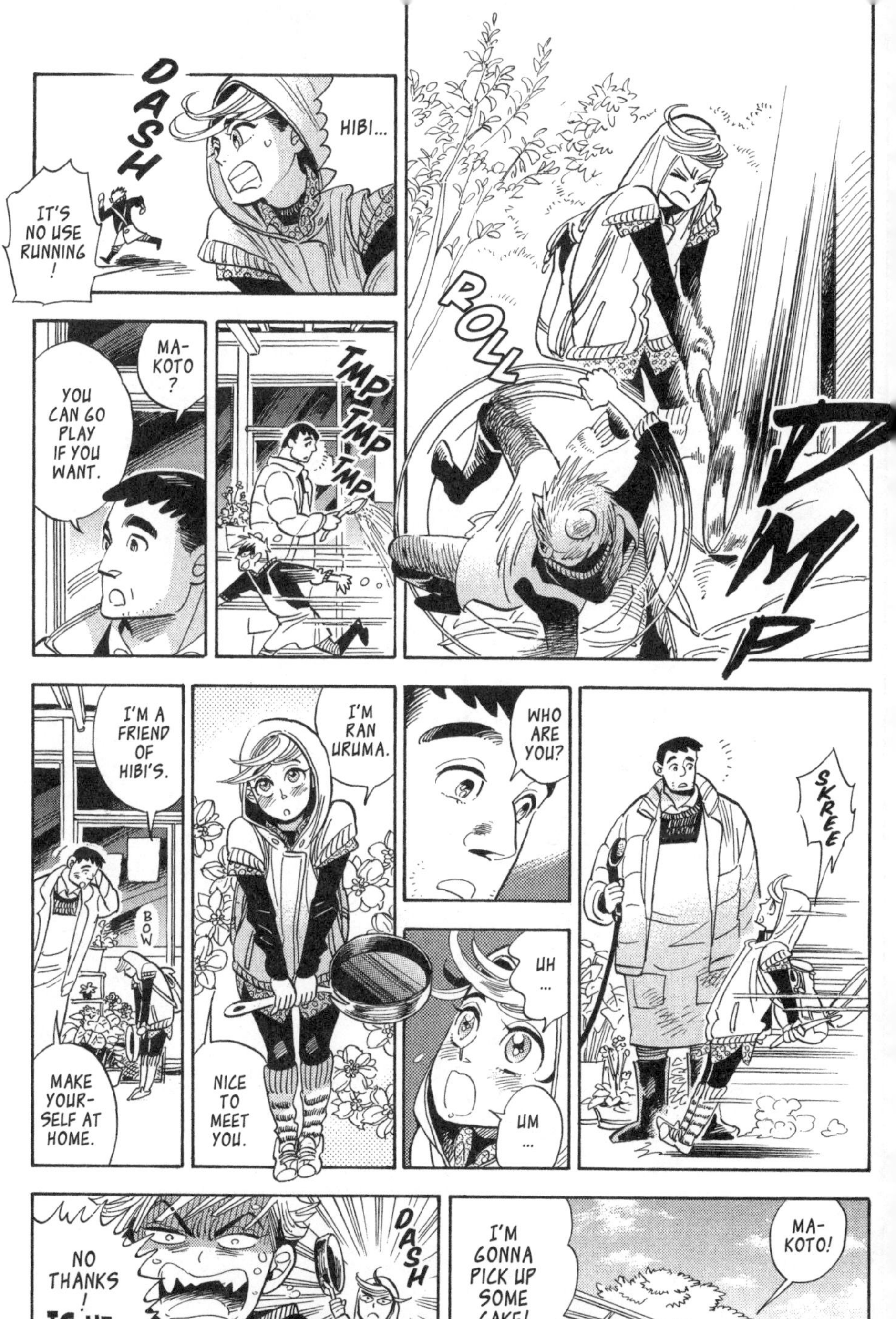
ROLL
DMP
HIBI...
DASH
IT'S NO USE RUNNING!
TMP TMP TMP TMP
MA-KOTO?
YOU CAN GO PLAY IF YOU WANT.
SKREE
WHO ARE YOU?
UH...
UM...
I'M RAN URUMA.
NICE TO MEET YOU.
I'M A FRIEND OF HIBI'S.
BOW
MAKE YOURSELF AT HOME.
MA-KOTO!
I'M GONNA PICK UP SOME CAKE!
DASH
NO THANKS!
IS HE BLIND?!

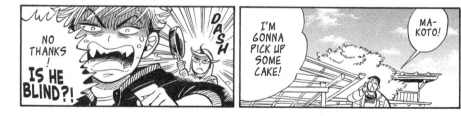

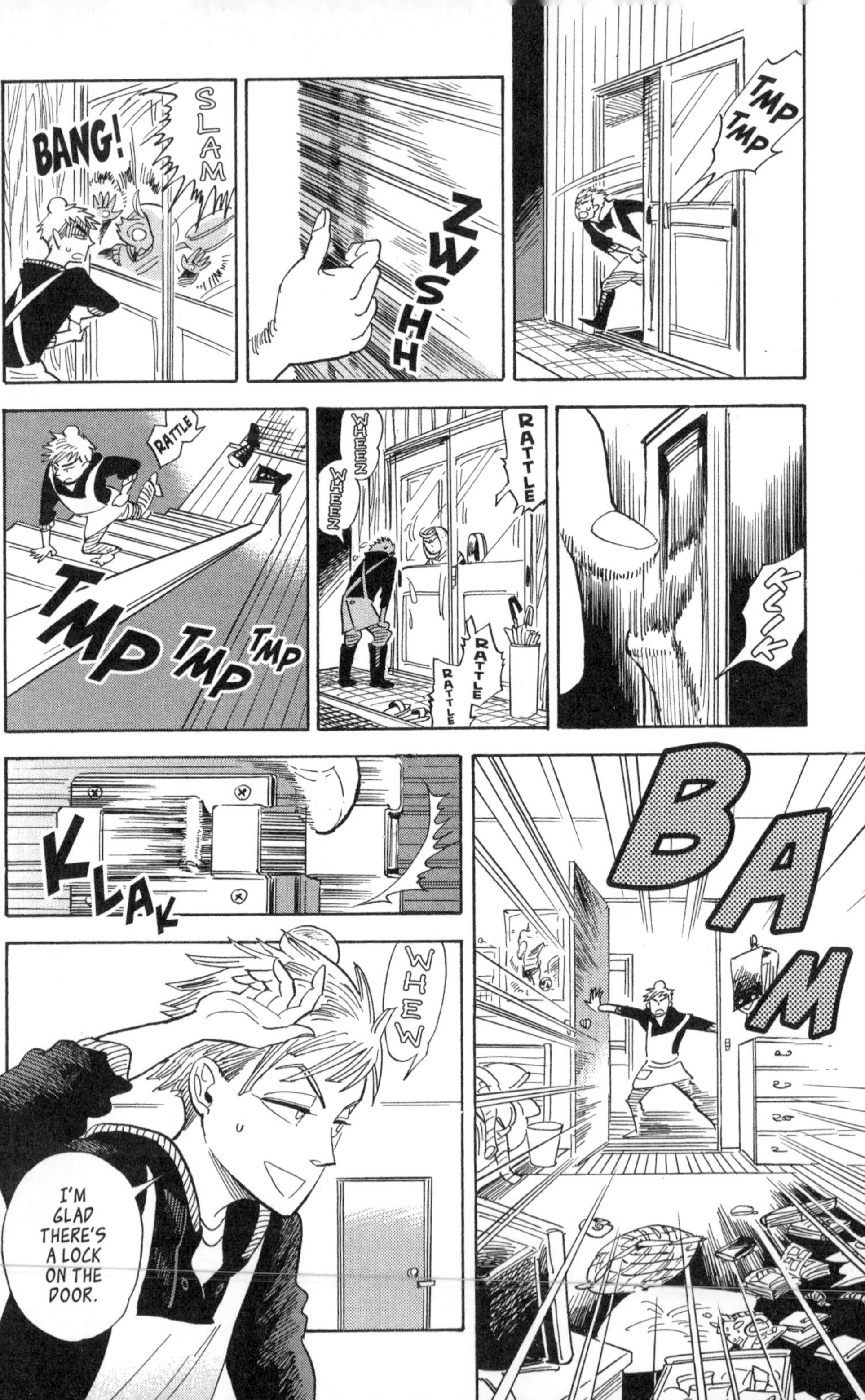
TMP TMP
ZWSHH
BANG!
SLAM
KLIK
WHEEZ WHEEZ
RATTLE
RATTLE RATTLE
RATTLE
TMP TMP TMP
BAM
KLAK
WHEW
I'M GLAD THERE'S A LOCK ON THE DOOR.

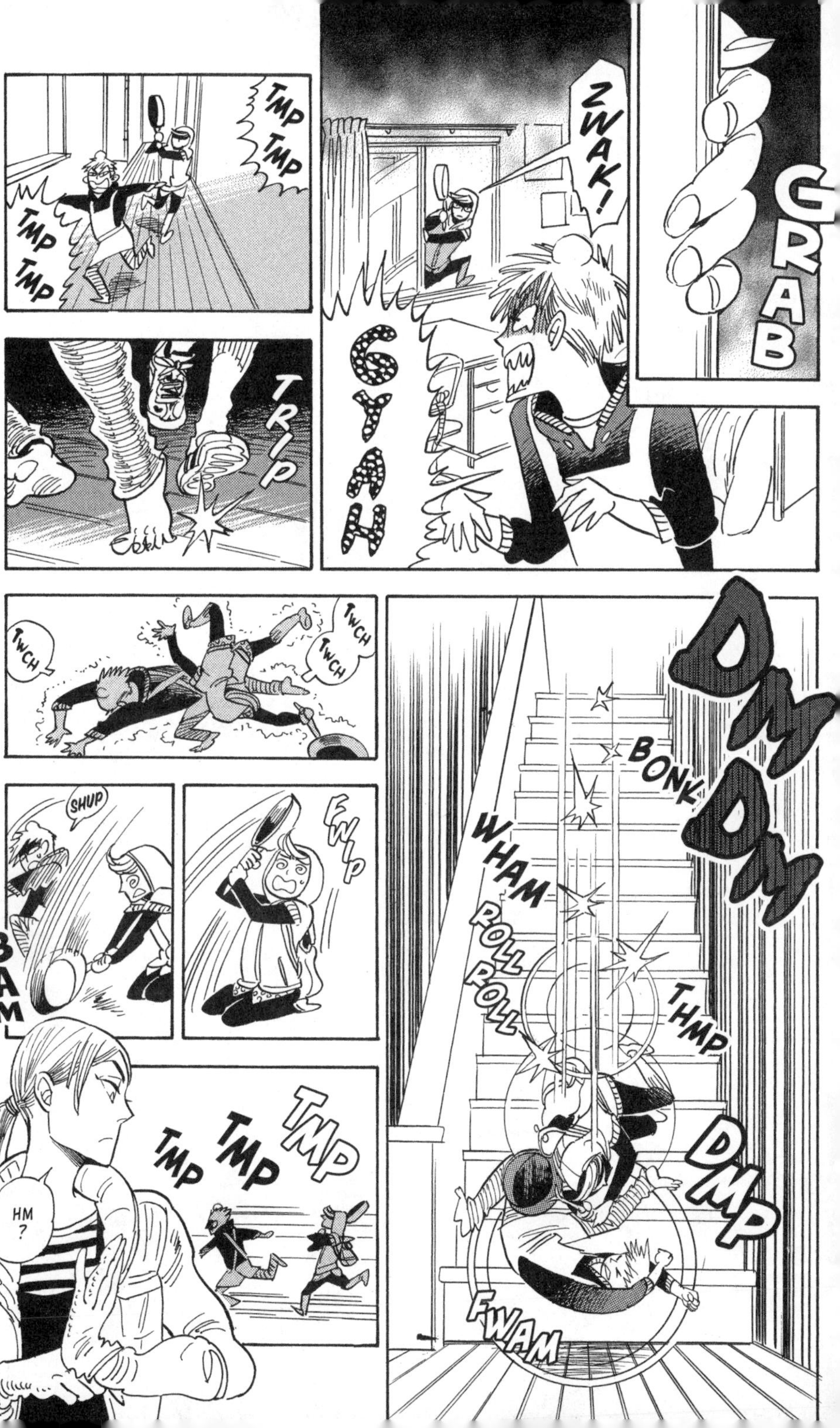
GRAB
ZWAK!
GYAH
TMP TMP
TMP TMP
TRIP
DM DM DM
BONK
WHAM
ROLL ROLL
THMP
DMP
FWAM
TWCH
TWCH TWCH
FWIP
SHUP
BAM
TMP TMP TMP
HM?

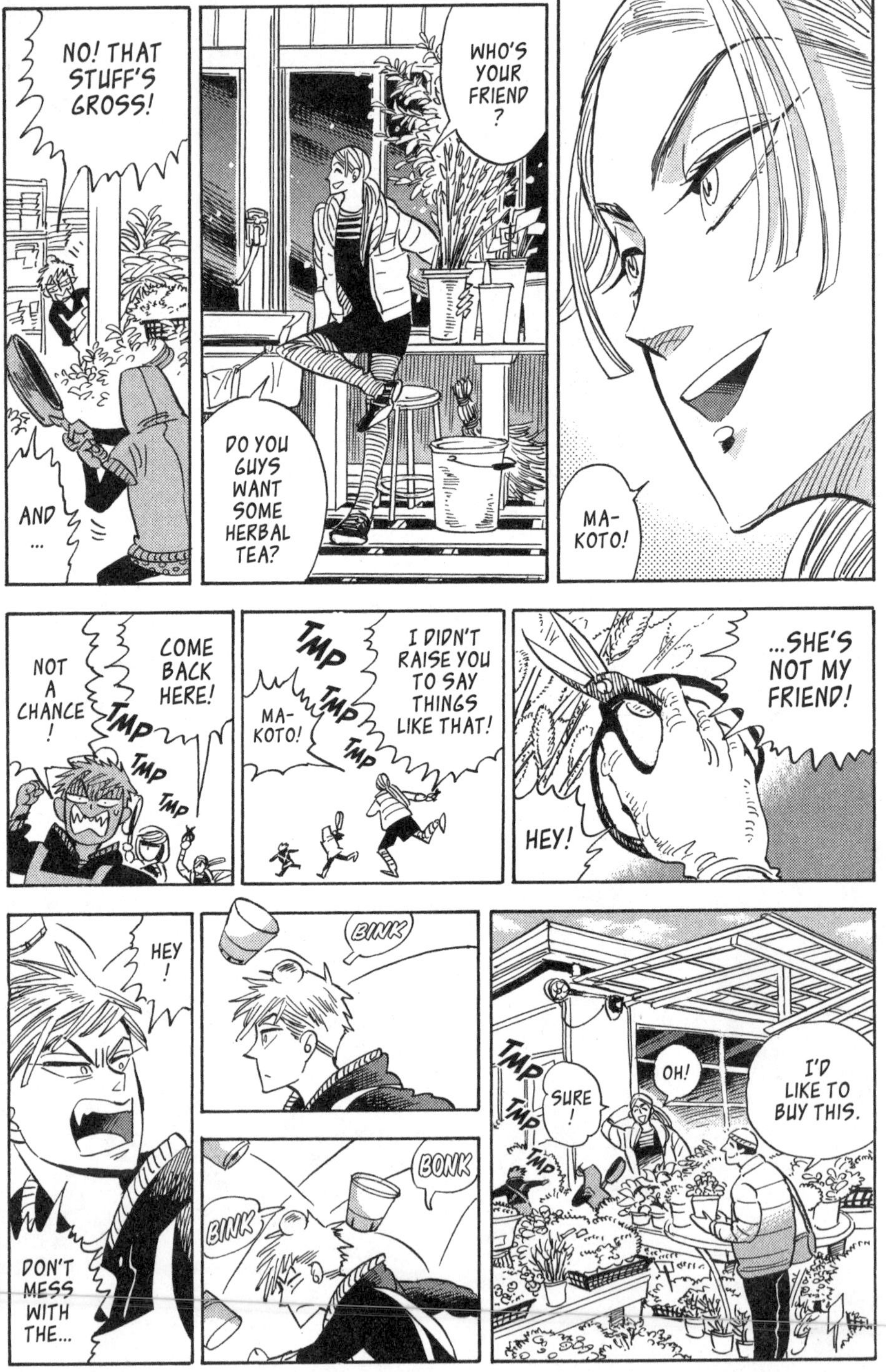
MA-KOTO!
WHO'S YOUR FRIEND?
DO YOU GUYS WANT SOME HERBAL TEA?
NO! THAT STUFF'S GROSS!
AND ...
...SHE'S NOT MY FRIEND!
HEY!
I DIDN'T RAISE YOU TO SAY THINGS LIKE THAT!
TMP
TMP
TMP
MA-KOTO!
COME BACK HERE!
NOT A CHANCE!
TMP
TMP
TMP
I'D LIKE TO BUY THIS.
OH!
SURE!
TMP
TMP
TMP
BINK
BONK
BINK
HEY!
DON'T MESS WITH THE...

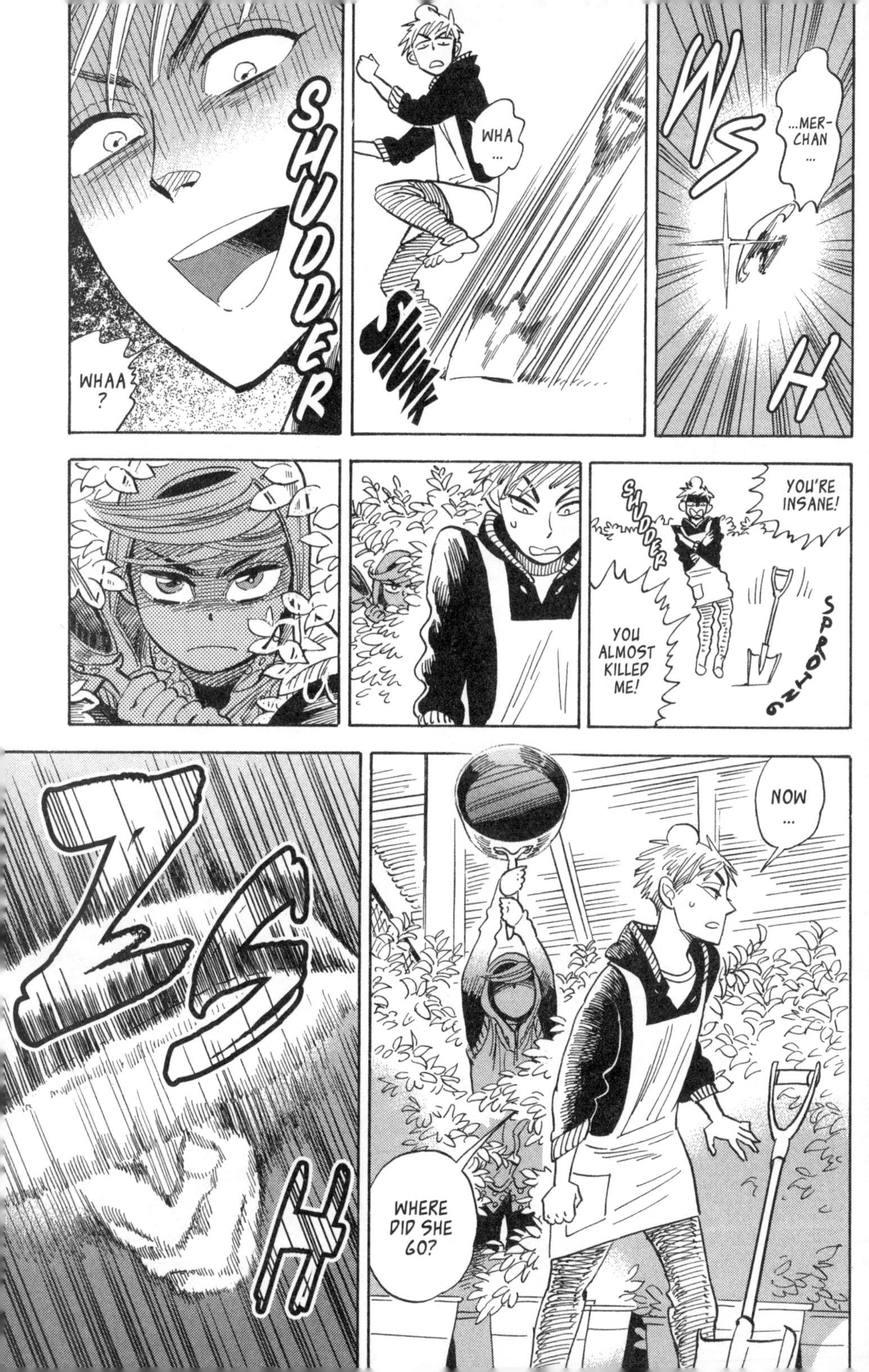
WSH
...MER-CHAN...
WHA...
SHUNK
SHUDDER
WHAA?
YOU'RE INSANE!
SHUDDER
YOU ALMOST KILLED ME!
SPROING
NOW...
WHERE DID SHE GO?
ZSH

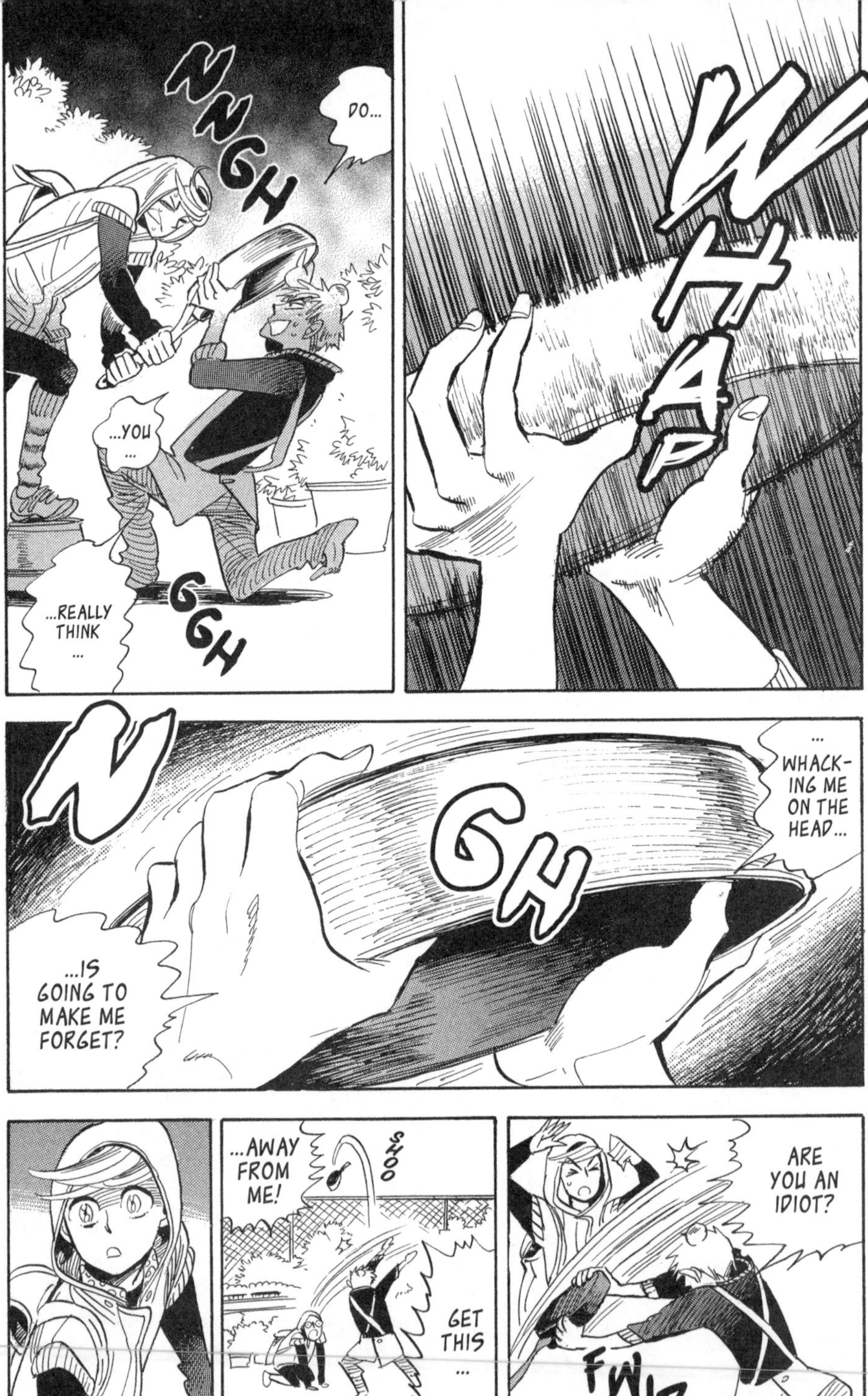
WHAP
DO...
NNGH
...YOU
...
...REALLY THINK
...
GGH
...
WHACK-
ING ME
ON THE
HEAD...
NGH
...IS
GOING TO
MAKE ME
FORGET?
ARE
YOU AN
IDIOT?
FWIP
SHOO
...AWAY
FROM
ME!
GET
THIS
...

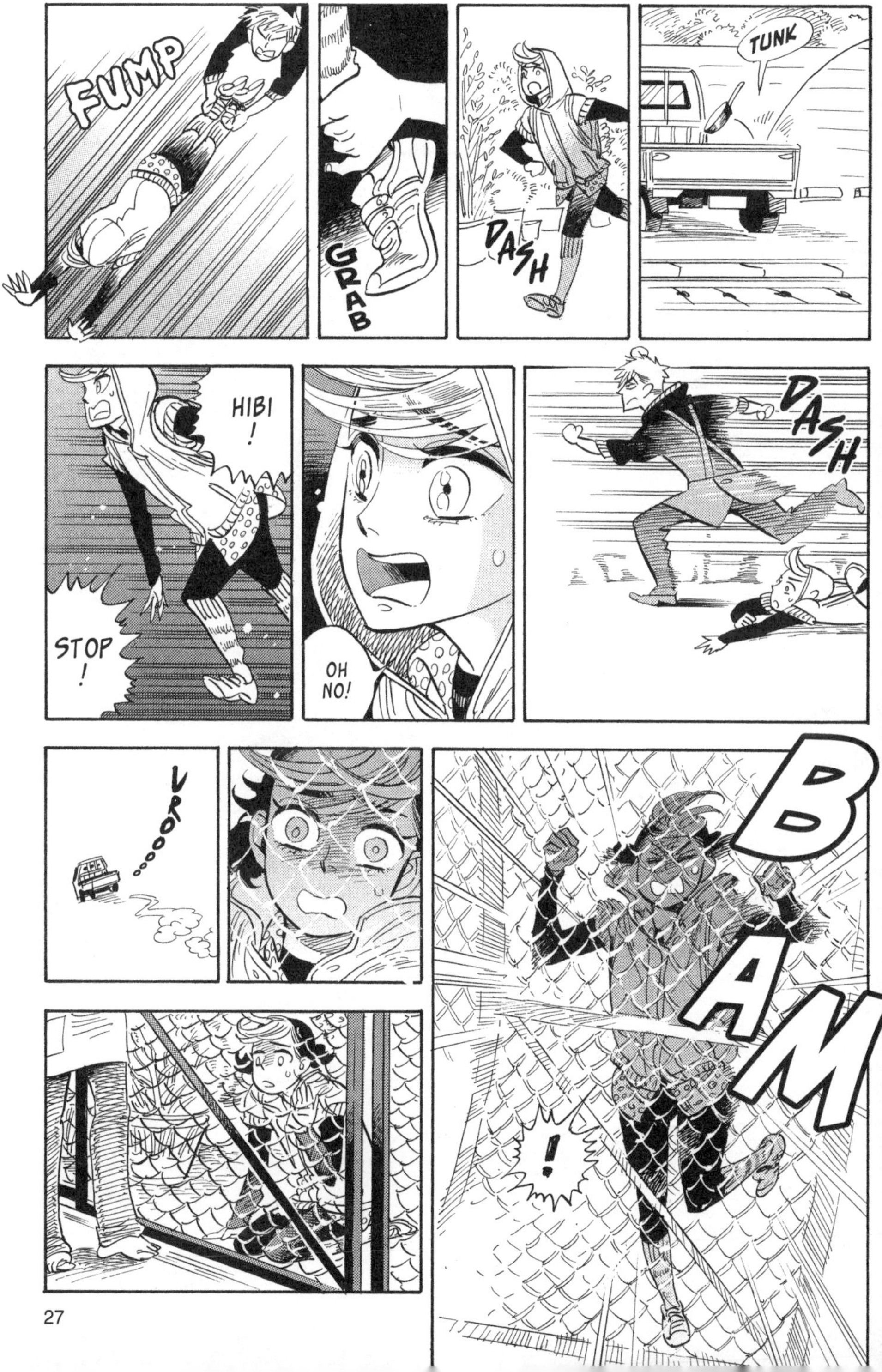
TUNK
DASH
GRAB
FUMP
DASH
OH NO!
HIBI!
STOP!
BAM
!
VROOOOO

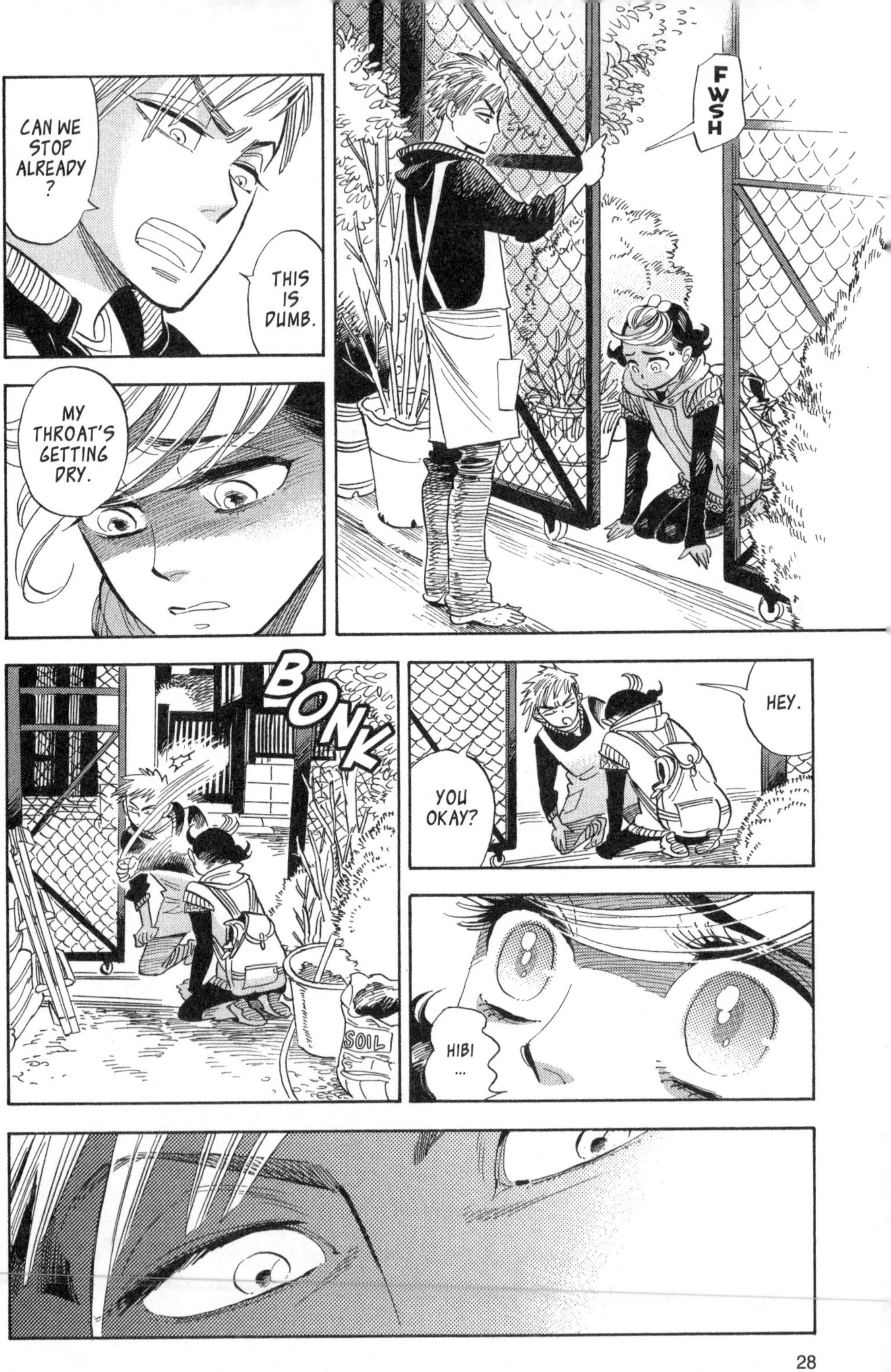
FWSH
CAN WE STOP ALREADY?
THIS IS DUMB.
MY THROAT'S GETTING DRY.
HEY.
YOU OKAY?
HIBI...
BONK

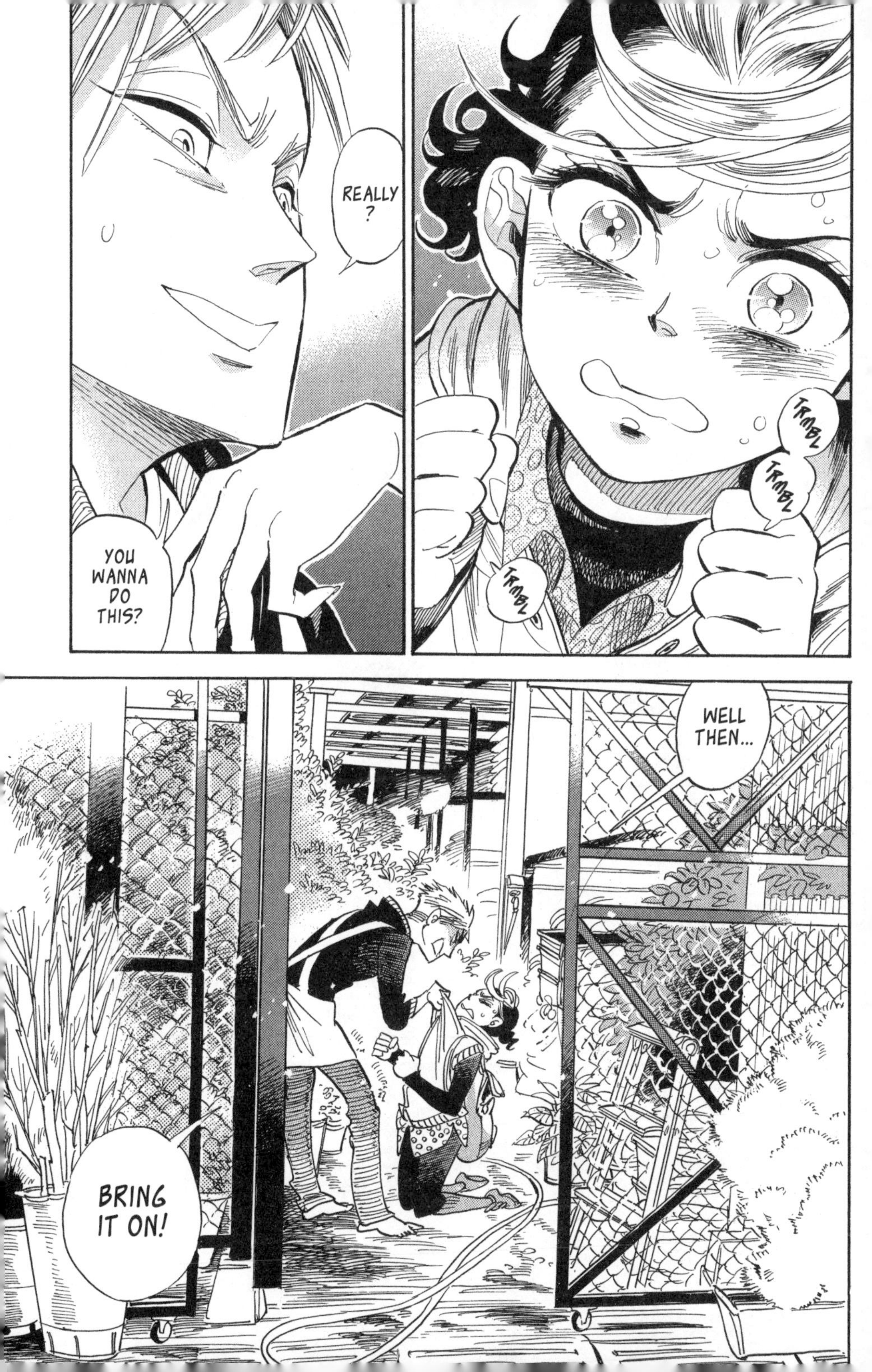
TRMBL
TRMBL
TRMBL
REALLY?
YOU WANNA DO THIS?
WELL THEN...
BRING IT ON!

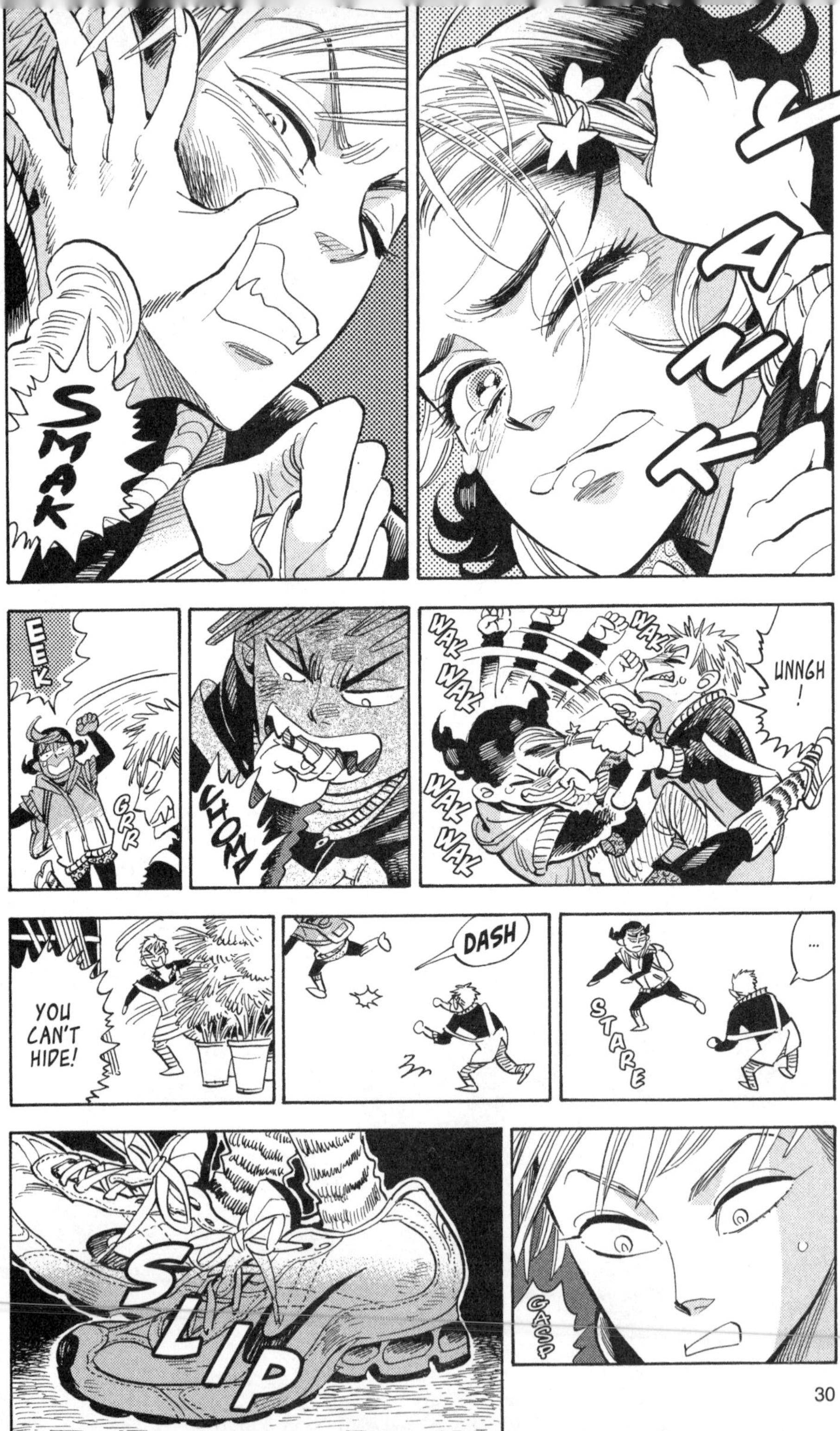
YANK
SMAK
WAK
WAK
WAK
WAK
WAK
UNNGH!
CHOMP
EEK
GRR
...
STARE
DASH
YOU CAN'T HIDE!
GASP
SLIP

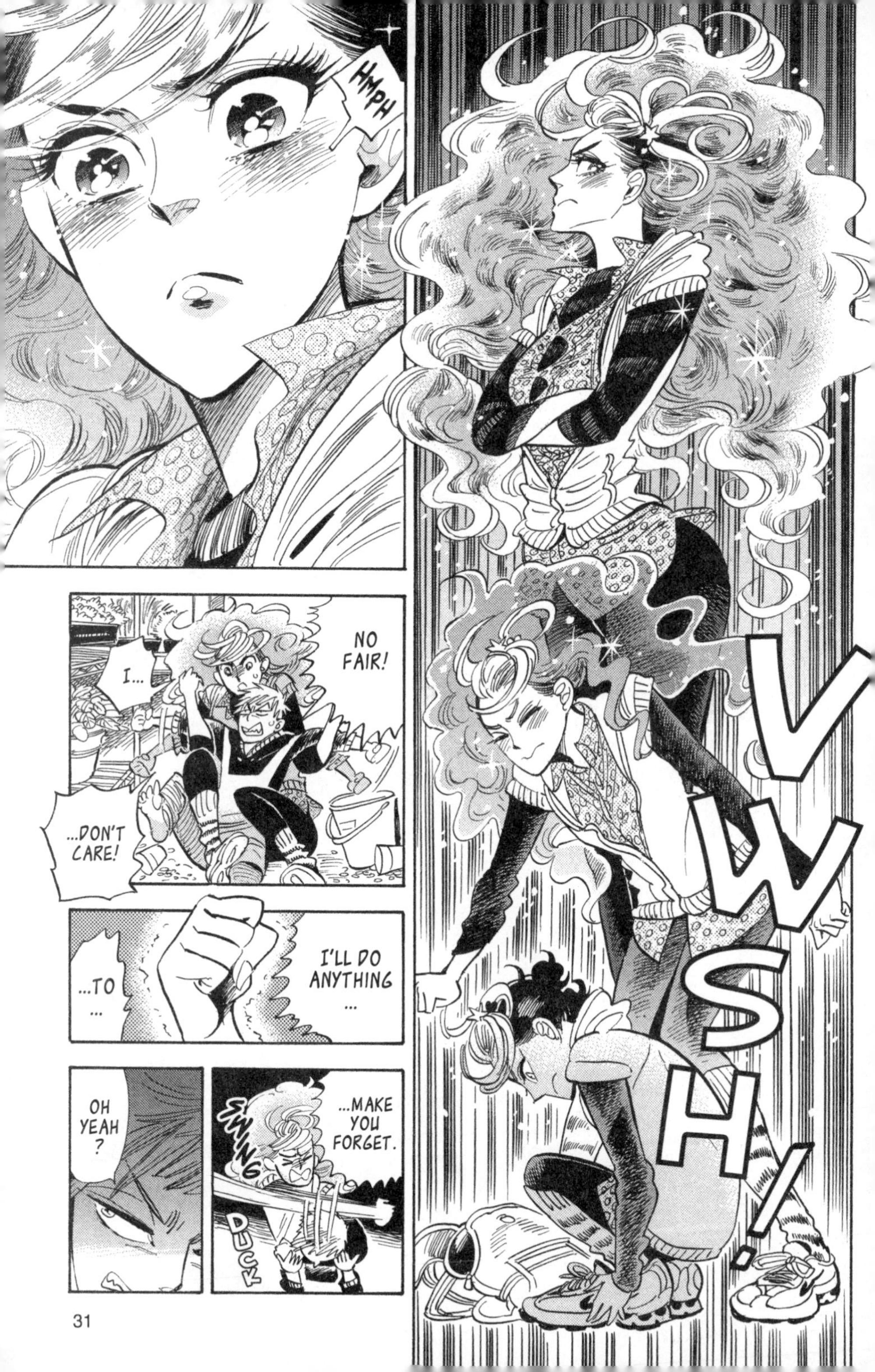
VWSSH!
HMPH
NO FAIR!
I...
...DON'T CARE!
I'LL DO ANYTHING ...
...TO ...
...MAKE YOU FORGET.
SWING
DUCK
OH YEAH ?

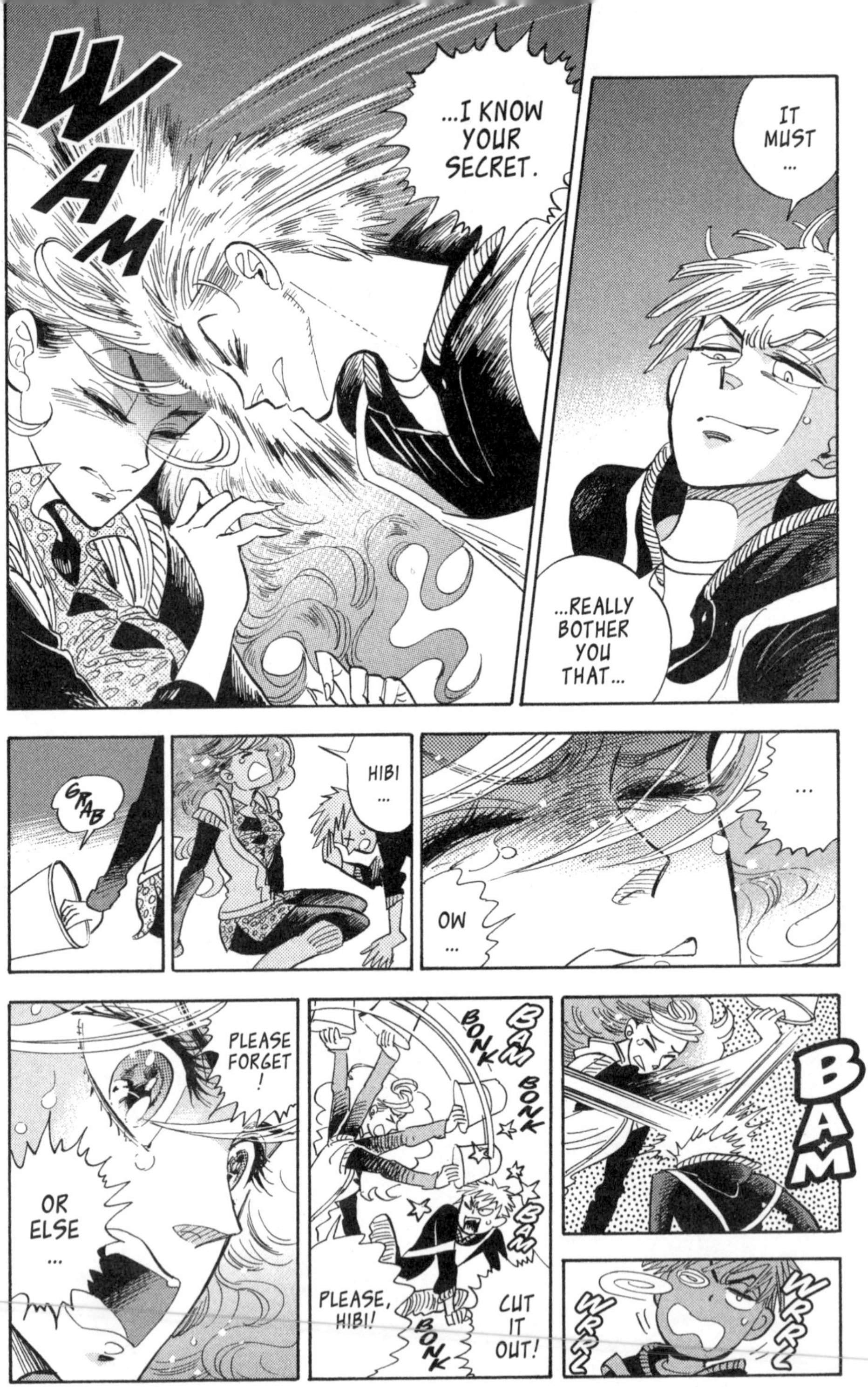
IT MUST ...
...REALLY BOTHER YOU THAT...
...I KNOW YOUR SECRET.
WAM
...
OW ...
HIBI ...
GRAB
BAM
WRRL WRRL
BAM BONK
BONK
BAM
CUT IT OUT!
PLEASE, HIBI!
BONK
PLEASE FORGET!
OR ELSE ...

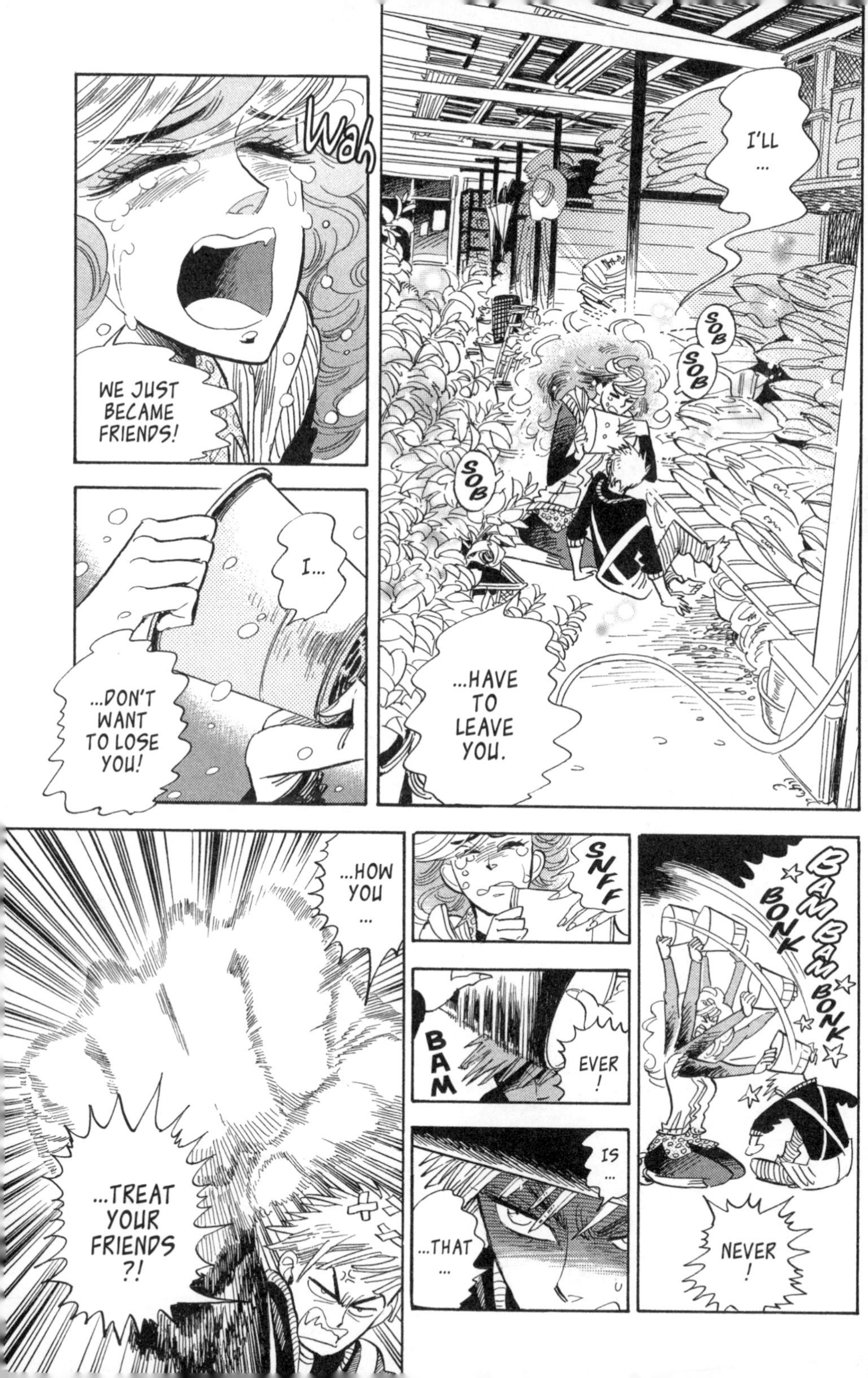
I'LL ...
SOB
SOB
SOB
...HAVE TO LEAVE YOU.
Wah
WE JUST BECAME FRIENDS!
I...
...DON'T WANT TO LOSE YOU!
BAM
BAM
BONK
BONK
NEVER!
SNFF
EVER!
BAM
IS ...
...THAT ...
...HOW YOU ...
...TREAT YOUR FRIENDS?!

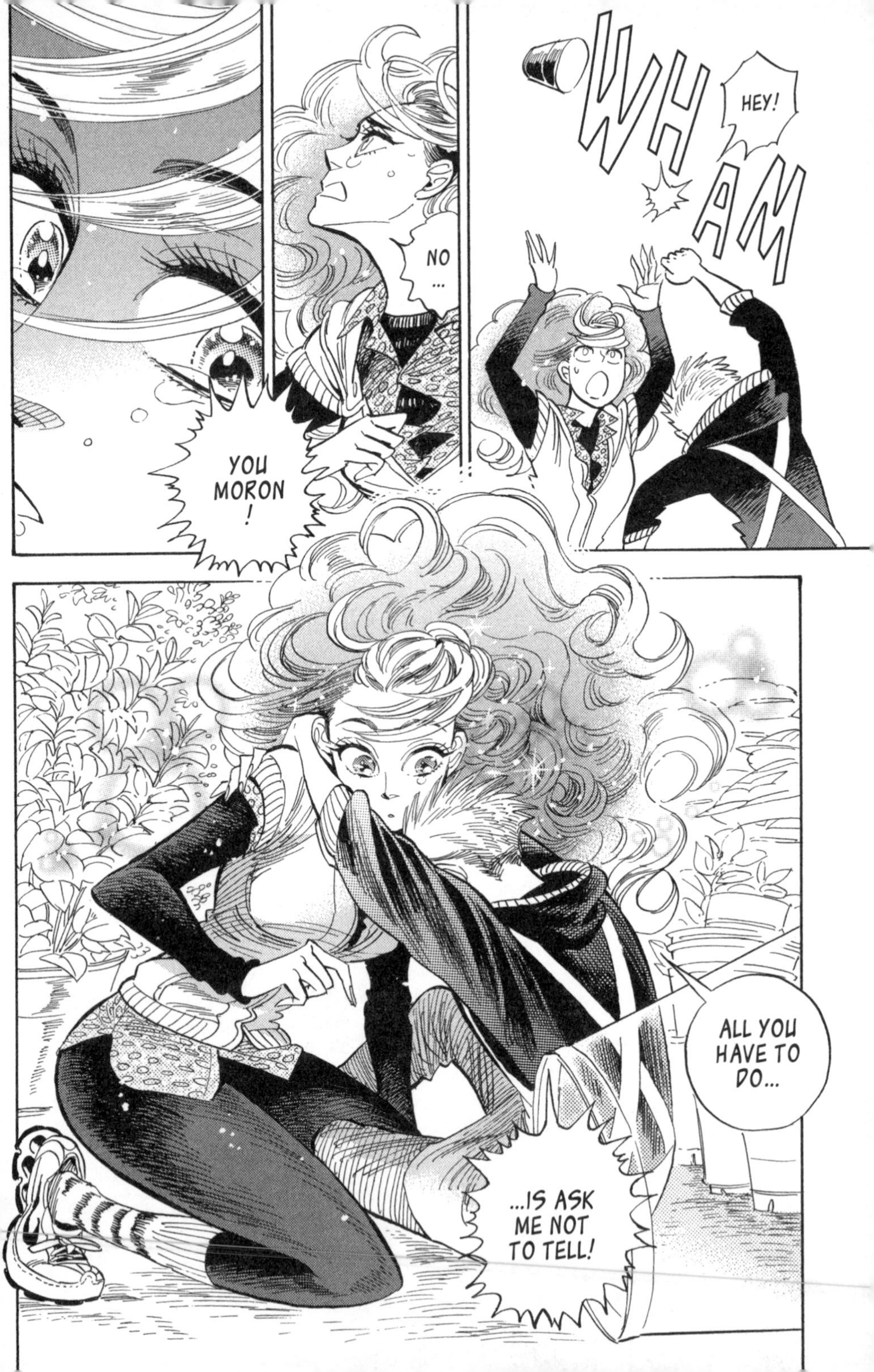
WHAM
HEY!
NO ...
YOU MORON !
ALL YOU HAVE TO DO...
...IS ASK ME NOT TO TELL!

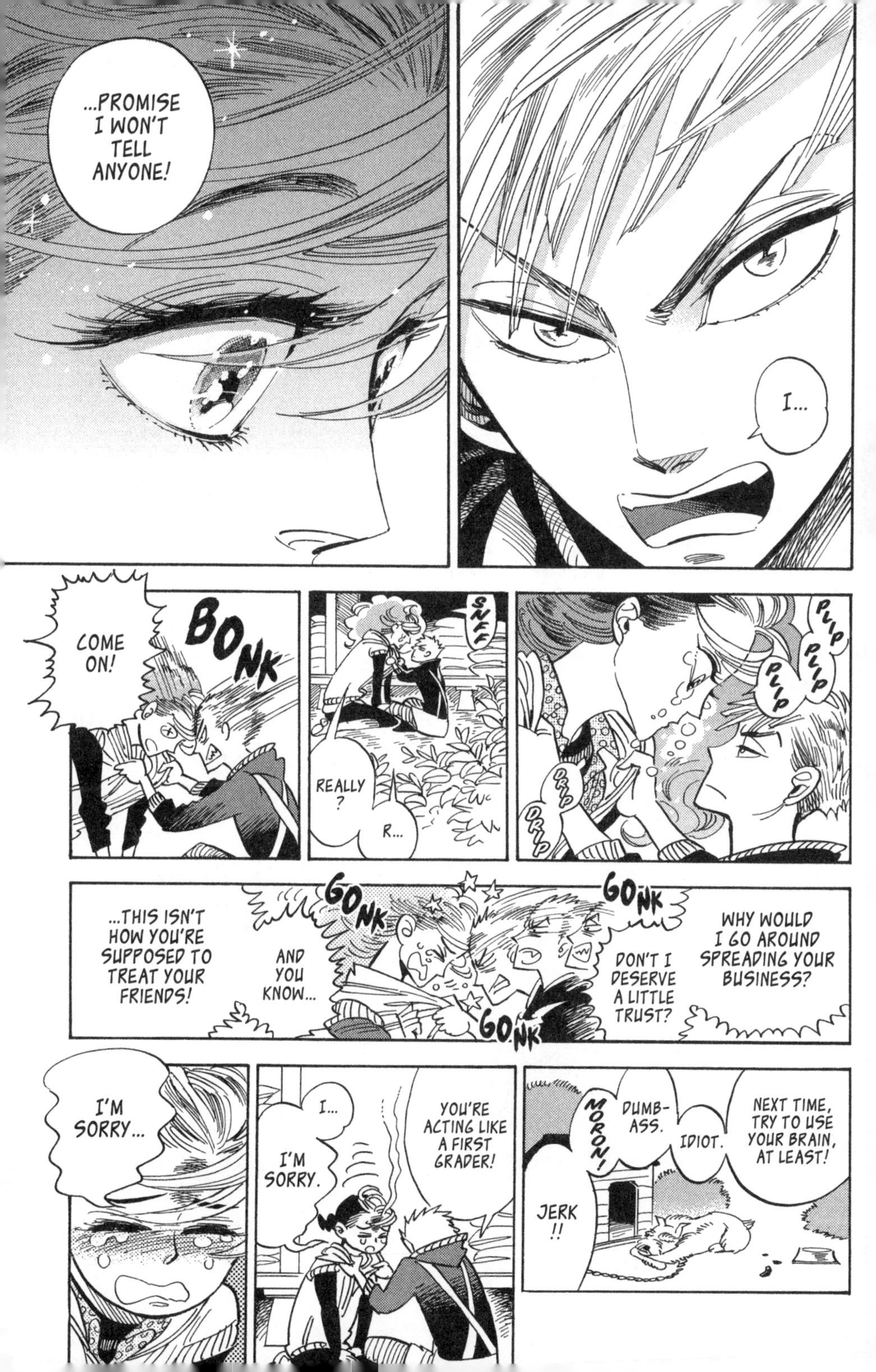
I...
...PROMISE I WON'T TELL ANYONE!
PLIP
PLIP
PLIP
DRIP
DRIP
SNFF
R...
REALLY?
BONK
COME ON!
WHY WOULD I GO AROUND SPREADING YOUR BUSINESS?
GONK
DON'T I DESERVE A LITTLE TRUST?
GONK
GONK
AND YOU KNOW...
...THIS ISN'T HOW YOU'RE SUPPOSED TO TREAT YOUR FRIENDS!
NEXT TIME, TRY TO USE YOUR BRAIN, AT LEAST!
IDIOT.
DUMB-ASS.
MORON!
JERK!!
YOU'RE ACTING LIKE A FIRST GRADER!
I...
I'M SORRY.
I'M SORRY...

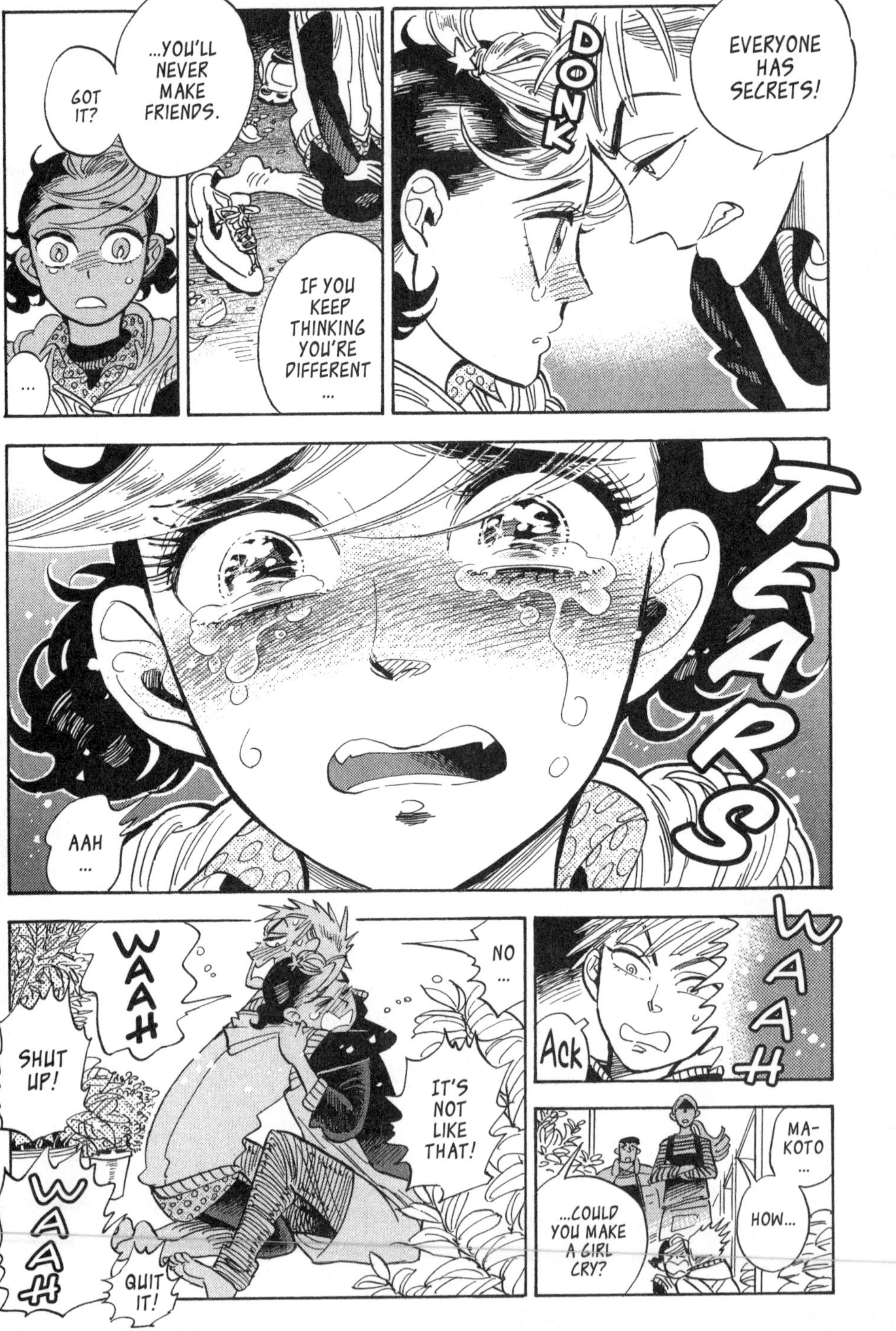
EVERYONE HAS SECRETS!
DONK
IF YOU KEEP THINKING YOU'RE DIFFERENT ...
...YOU'LL NEVER MAKE FRIENDS.
GOT IT?
...
TEARS
AAH ...
WAAH
Ack
MA-KOTO ...
HOW...
...COULD YOU MAKE A GIRL CRY?
NO ...
IT'S NOT LIKE THAT!
WAAH
SHUT UP!
WAAH
QUIT IT!

Chapter 19 / The End

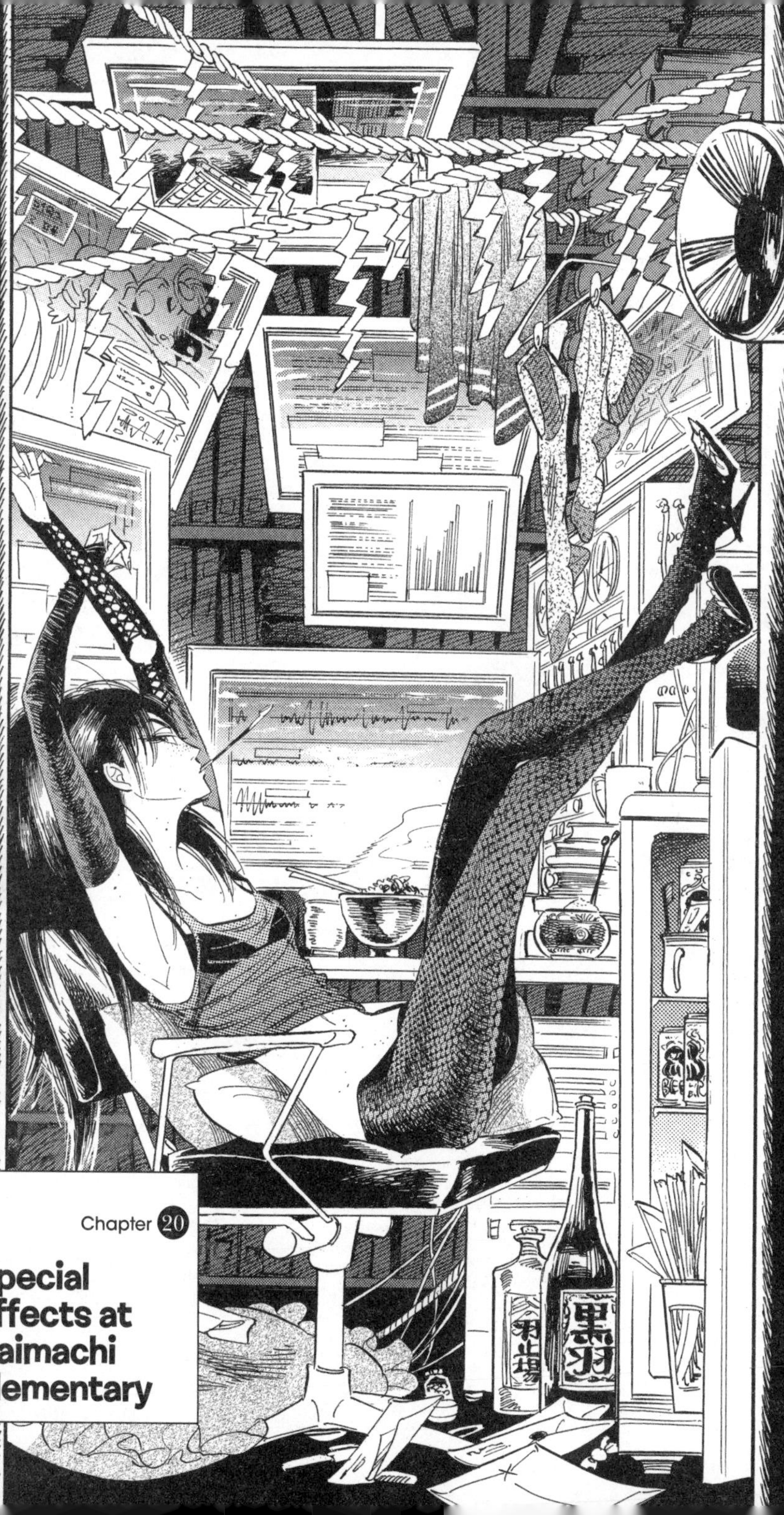

Chapter 20

Special Effects at Haimachi Elementary

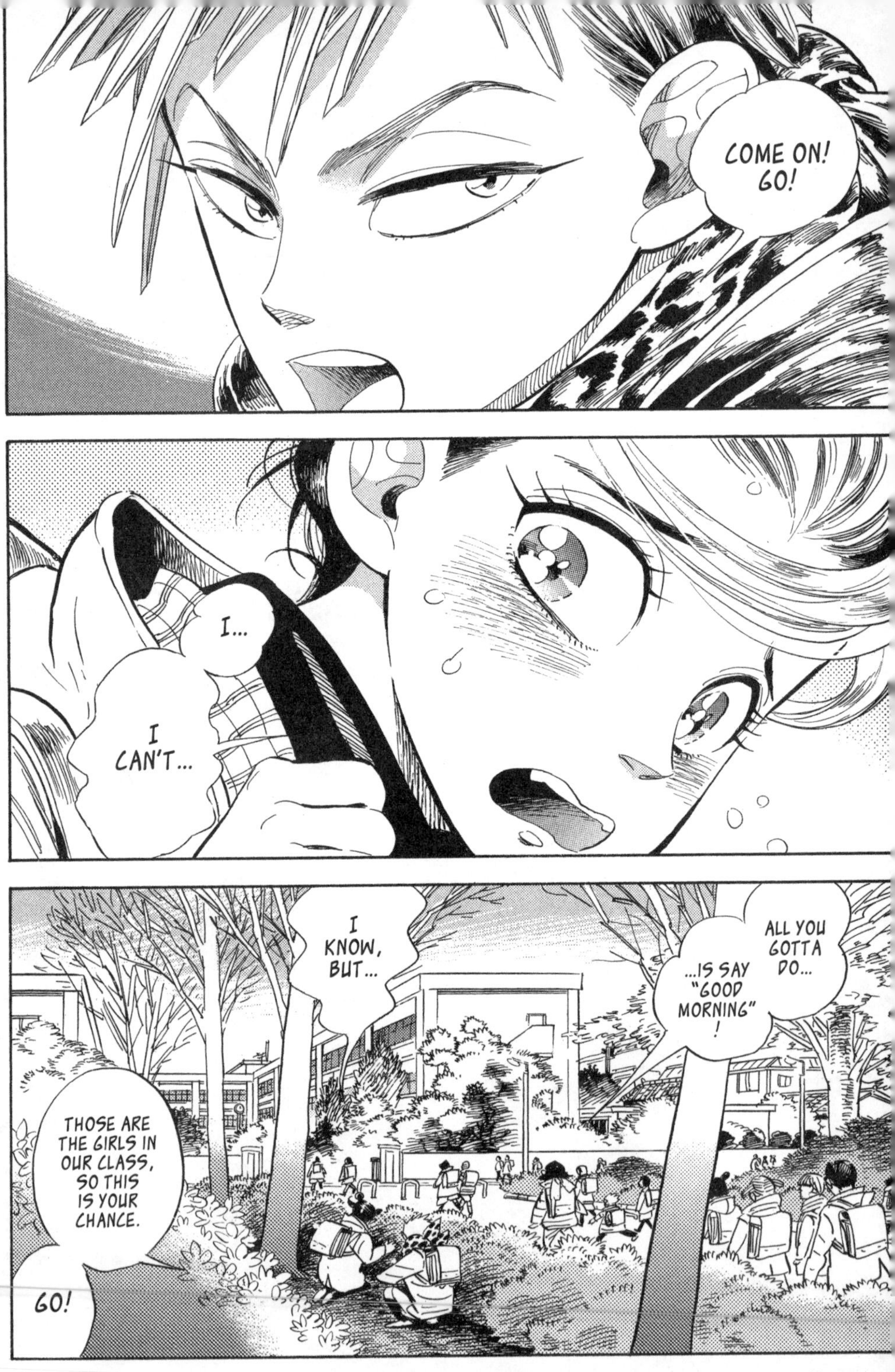
COME ON! GO!
I...
I CAN'T...
ALL YOU GOTTA DO...
...IS SAY "GOOD MORNING"!
I KNOW, BUT...
THOSE ARE THE GIRLS IN OUR CLASS, SO THIS IS YOUR CHANCE.
GO!

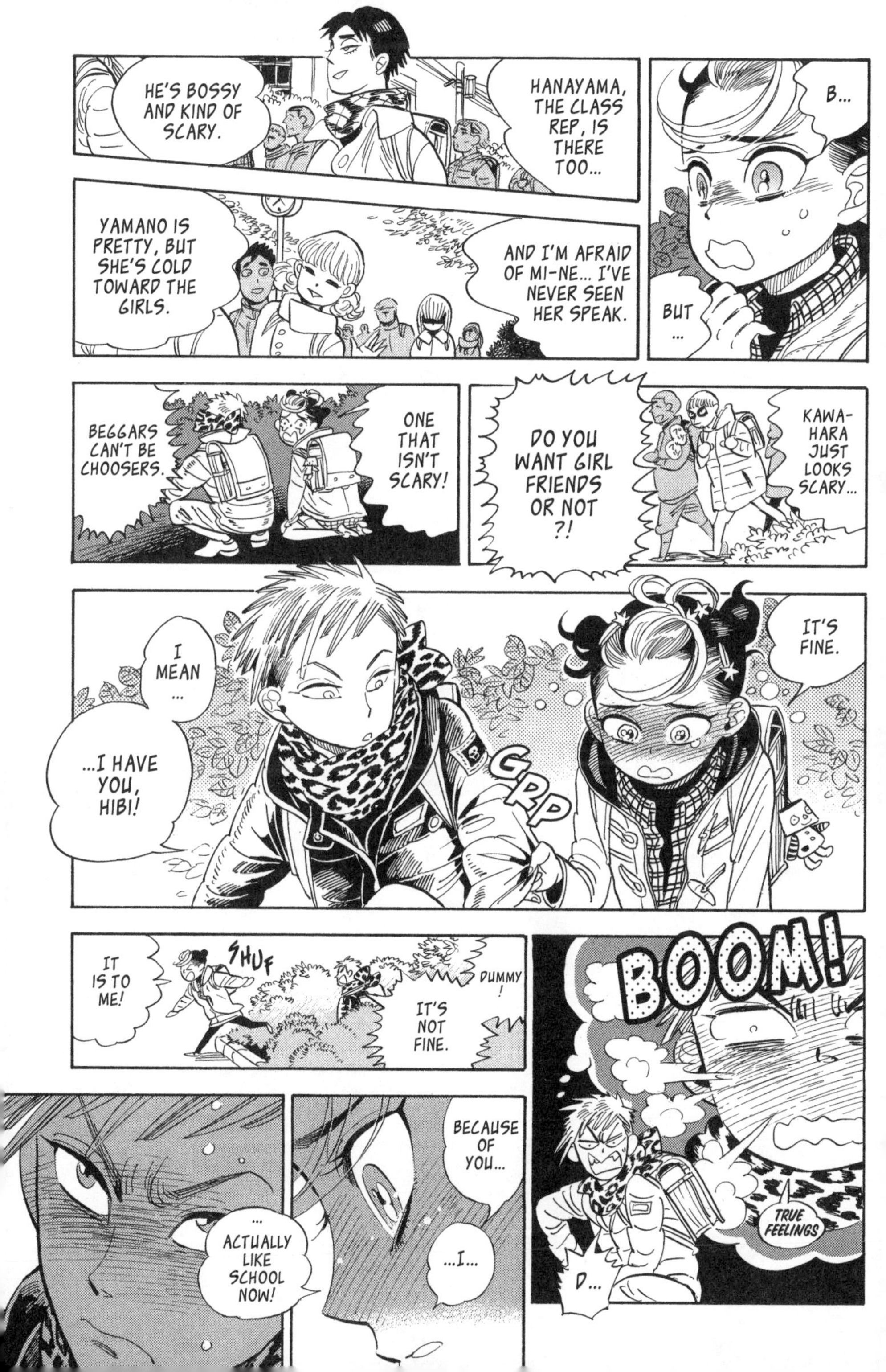
B...
BUT ...
HANAYAMA, THE CLASS REP, IS THERE TOO...
HE'S BOSSY AND KIND OF SCARY.
AND I'M AFRAID OF MI-NE... I'VE NEVER SEEN HER SPEAK.
YAMANO IS PRETTY, BUT SHE'S COLD TOWARD THE GIRLS.
KAWA-HARA JUST LOOKS SCARY...
DO YOU WANT GIRL FRIENDS OR NOT ?!
ONE THAT ISN'T SCARY!
BEGGARS CAN'T BE CHOOSERS.
IT'S FINE.
GRP
I MEAN ...
...I HAVE YOU, HIBI!
BOOM!
TRUE FEELINGS
D...
DUMMY!
IT'S NOT FINE.
SHUF
IT IS TO ME!
BECAUSE OF YOU...
...I...
... ACTUALLY LIKE SCHOOL NOW!

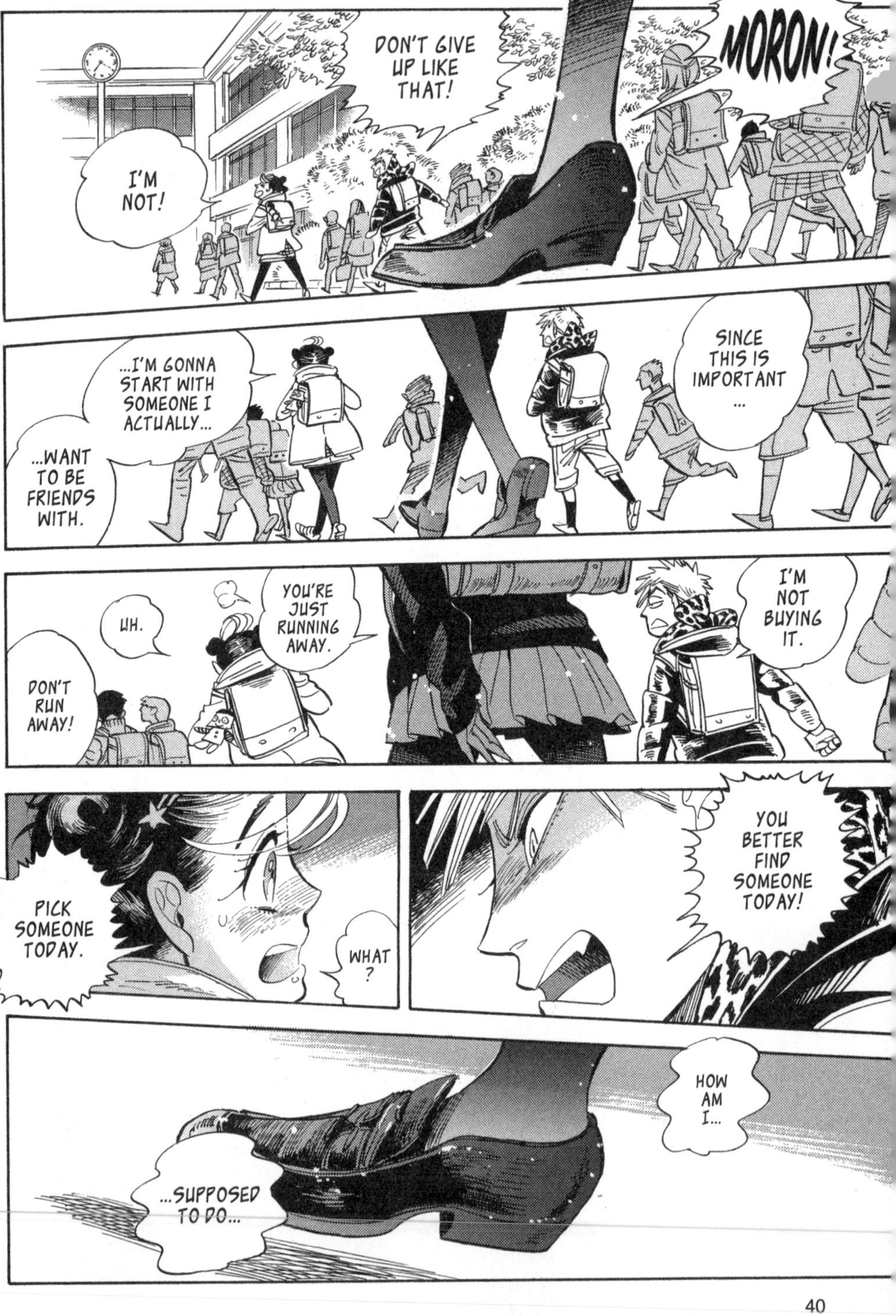
MORON!
DON'T GIVE UP LIKE THAT!
I'M NOT!
SINCE THIS IS IMPORTANT ...
...I'M GONNA START WITH SOMEONE I ACTUALLY...
...WANT TO BE FRIENDS WITH.
I'M NOT BUYING IT.
YOU'RE JUST RUNNING AWAY.
UH.
DON'T RUN AWAY!
YOU BETTER FIND SOMEONE TODAY!
WHAT?
PICK SOMEONE TODAY.
HOW AM I...
...SUPPOSED TO DO...

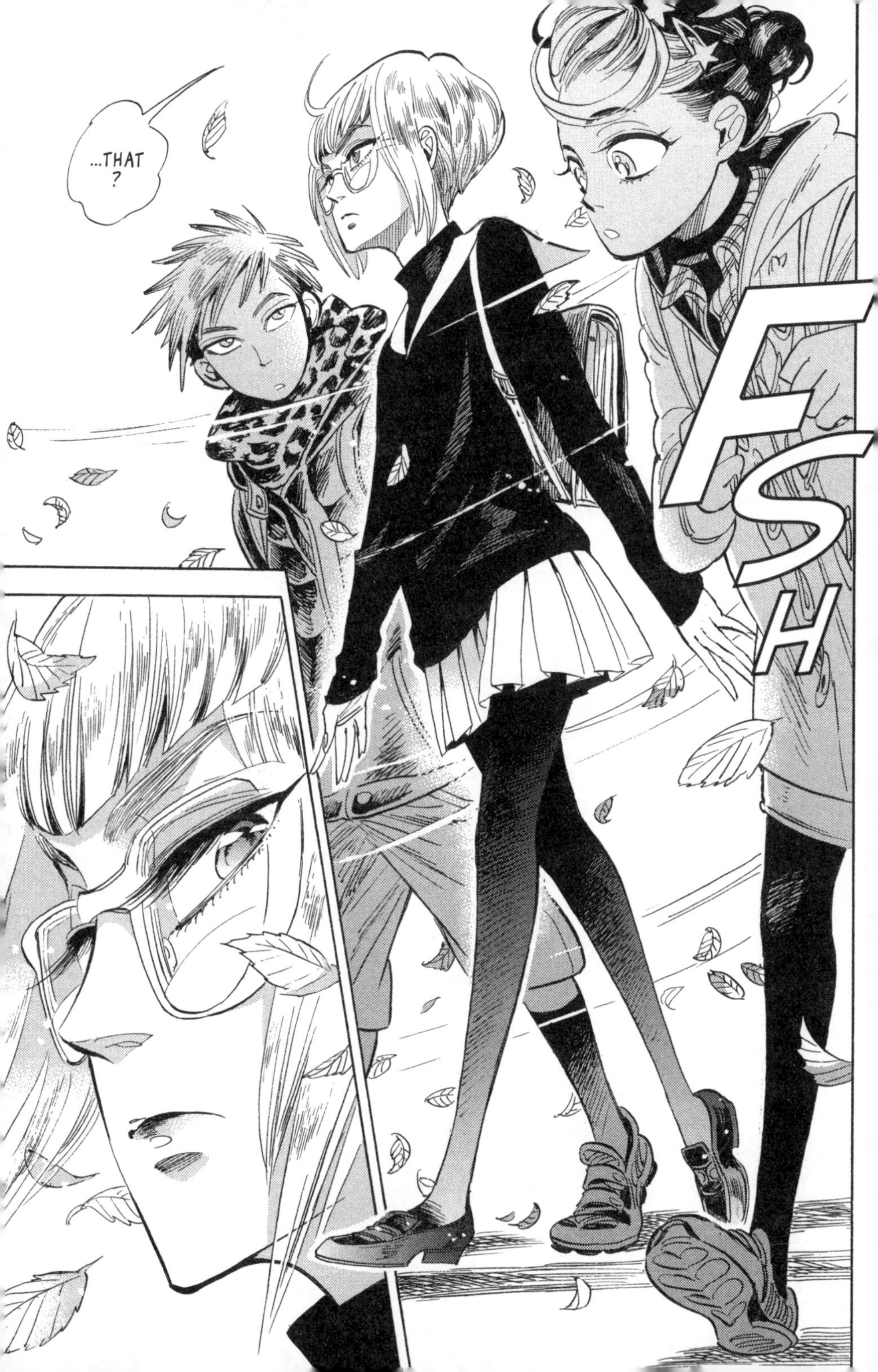
FSH
...THAT ?

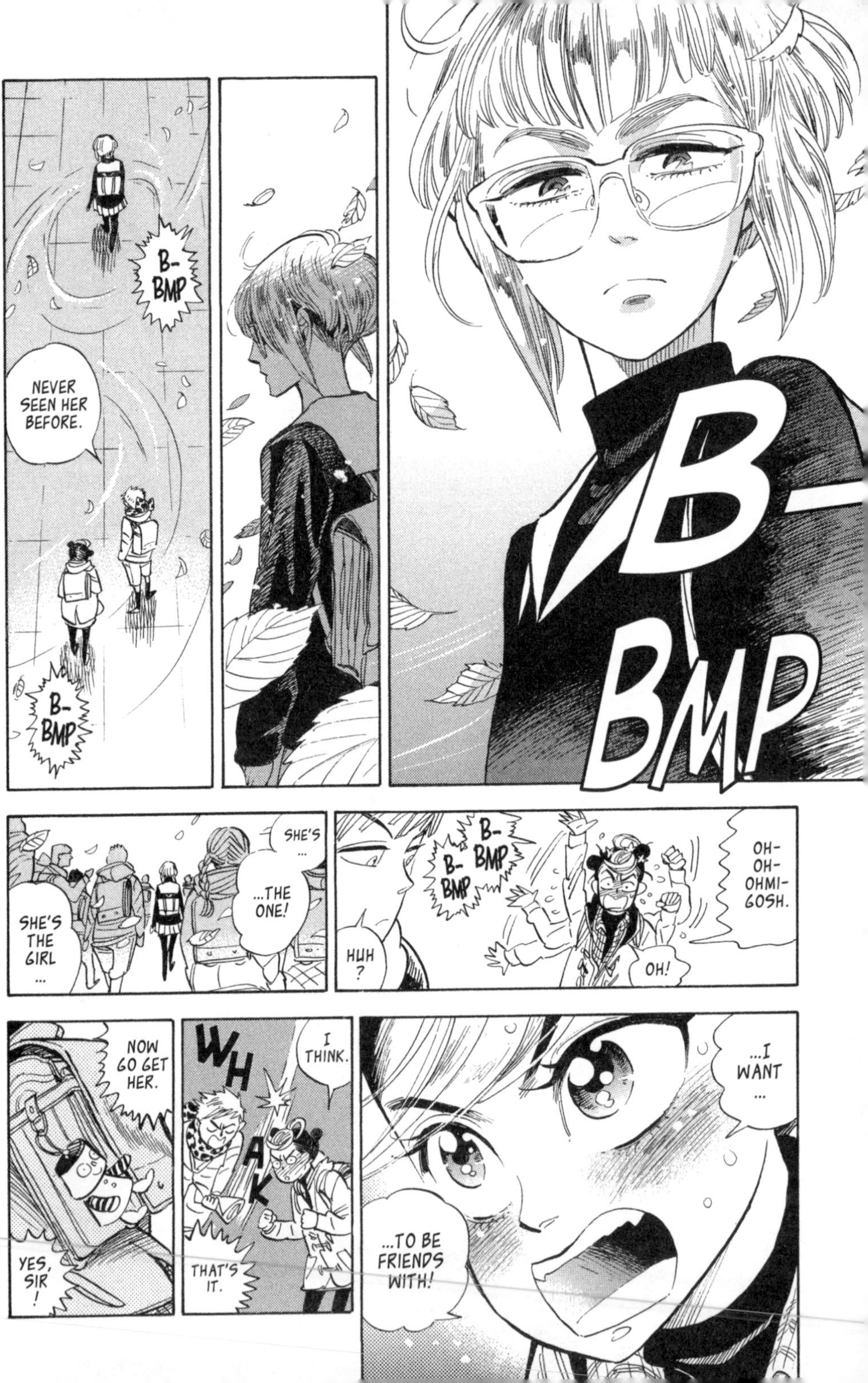
B-
BMP
B-
BMP
NEVER SEEN HER BEFORE.
B-
BMP
OH-OH-OHMIGOSH.
B-
BMP
B-
BMP
OH!
HUH?
SHE'S ...
...THE ONE!
SHE'S THE GIRL ...
...I WANT ...
...TO BE FRIENDS WITH!
I THINK.
WHAK
THAT'S IT.
NOW GO GET HER.
YES, SIR!

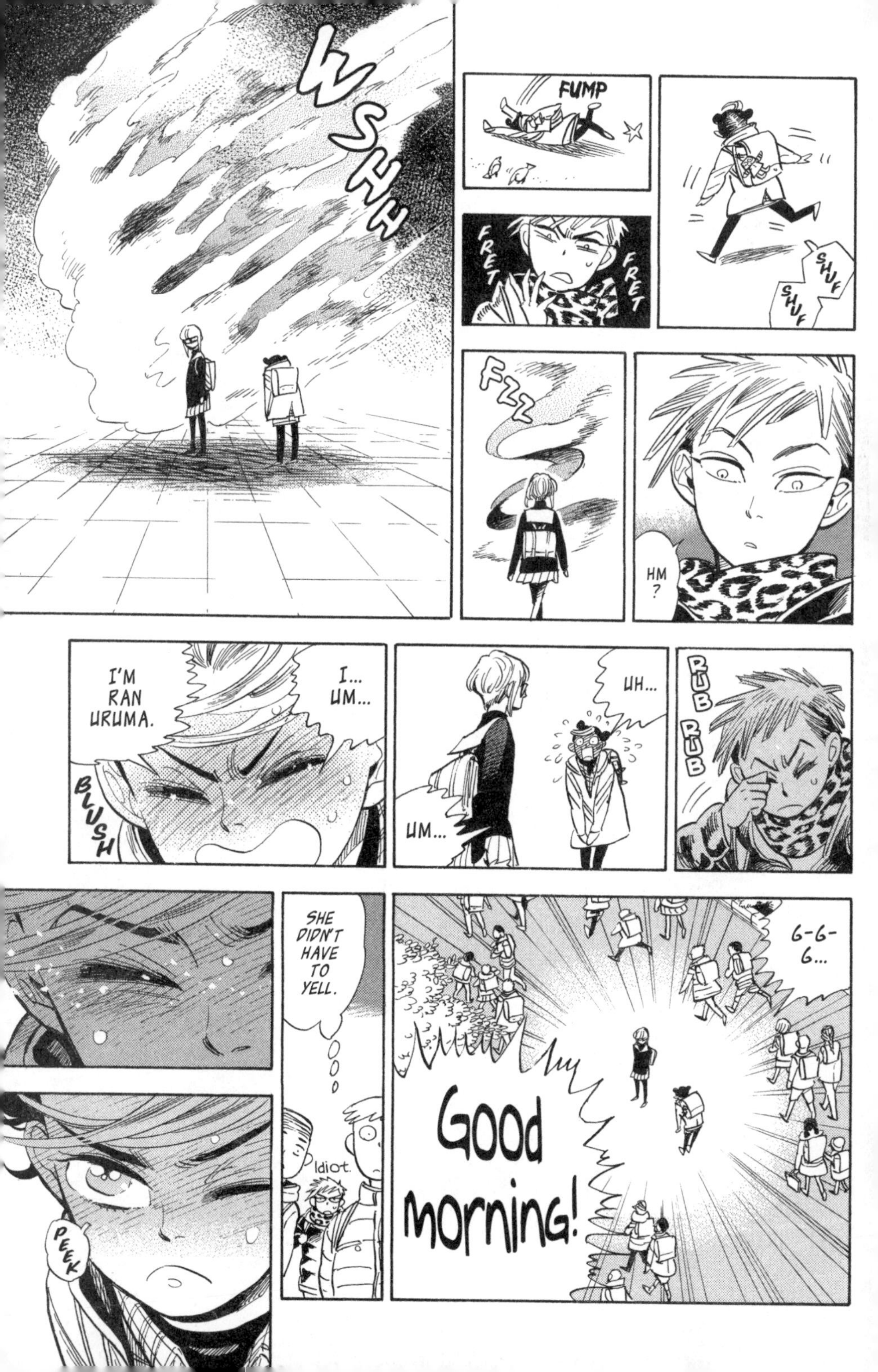
SHUF
SHUF
FUMP
FRET
FRET
HM?
FZZ
WSHH
RUB RUB
UH...
UM...
I... UM...
I'M RAN URUMA.
BLUSH
G-G-G...
Good morning!
SHE DIDN'T HAVE TO YELL.
Idiot.
PEEK

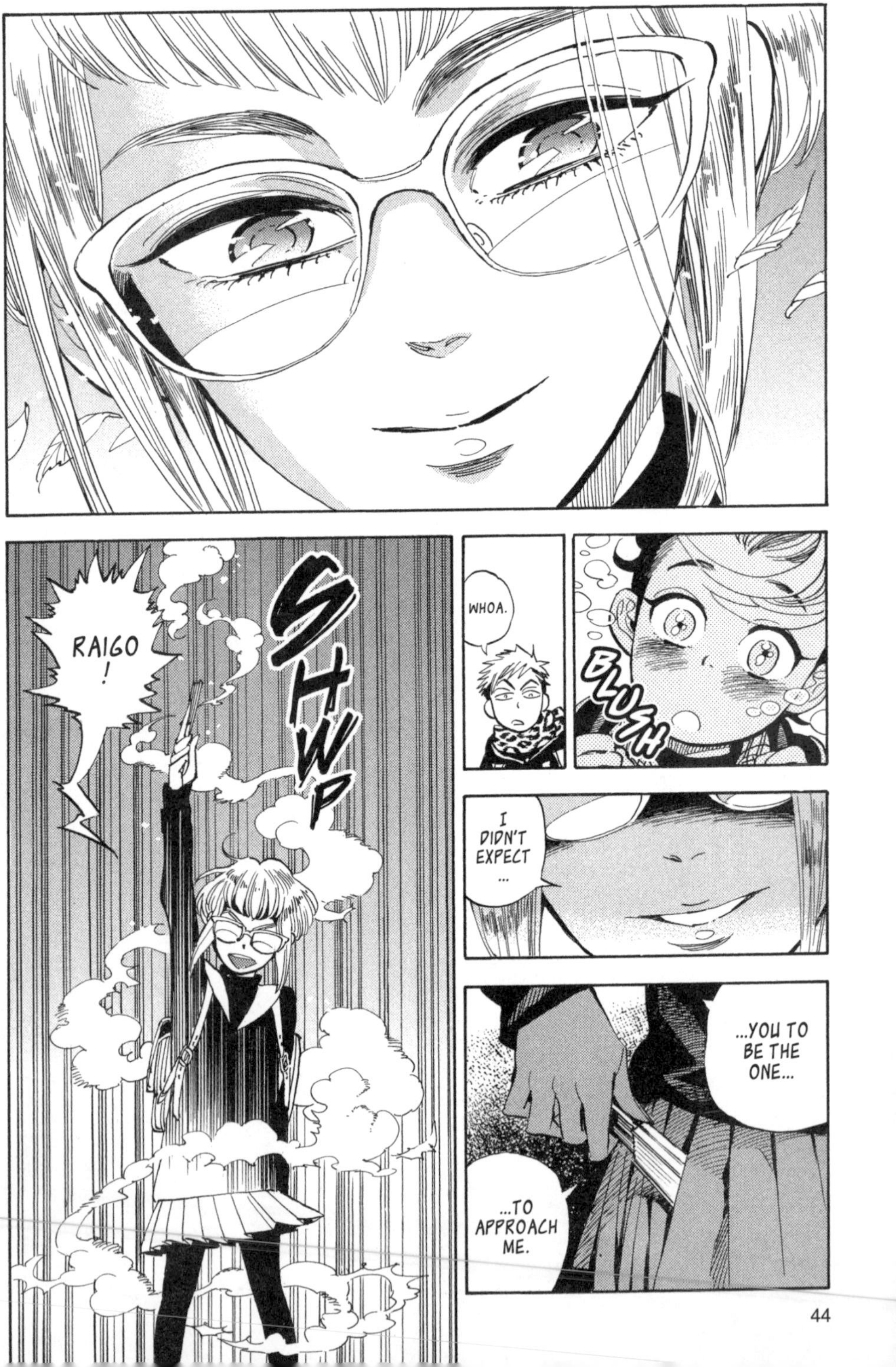
BLUSH
WHOA.
I DIDN'T EXPECT ...
...YOU TO BE THE ONE...
...TO APPROACH ME.
SHWP
RAIGO!

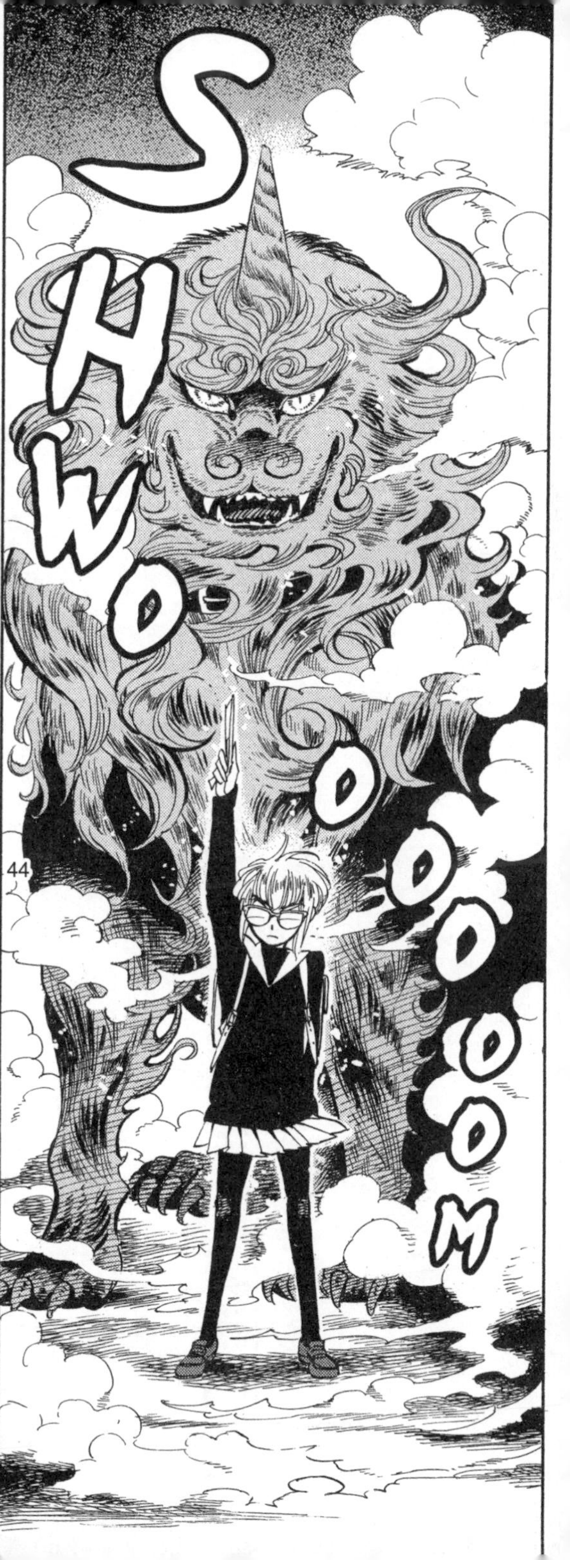
SHWOOOOOOOM

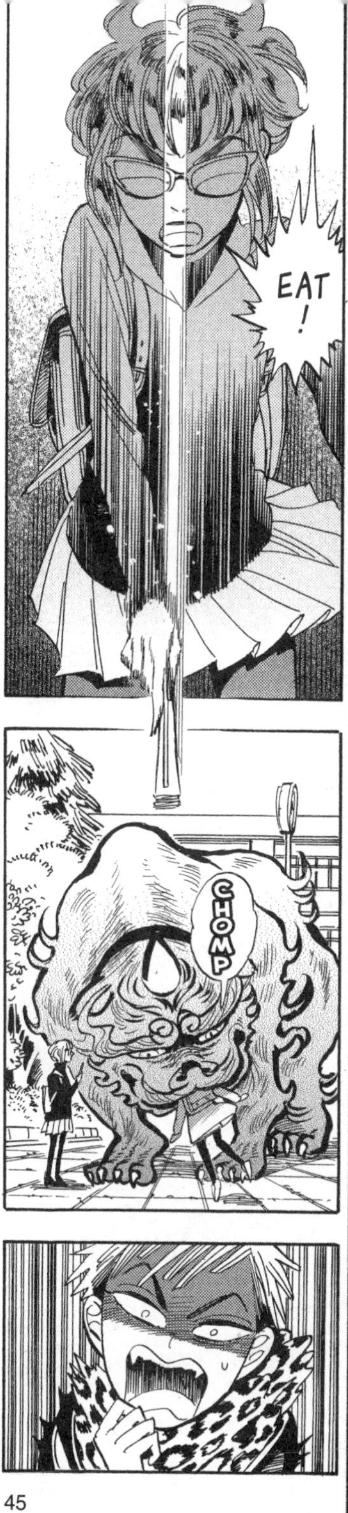
EAT!
CHOMP

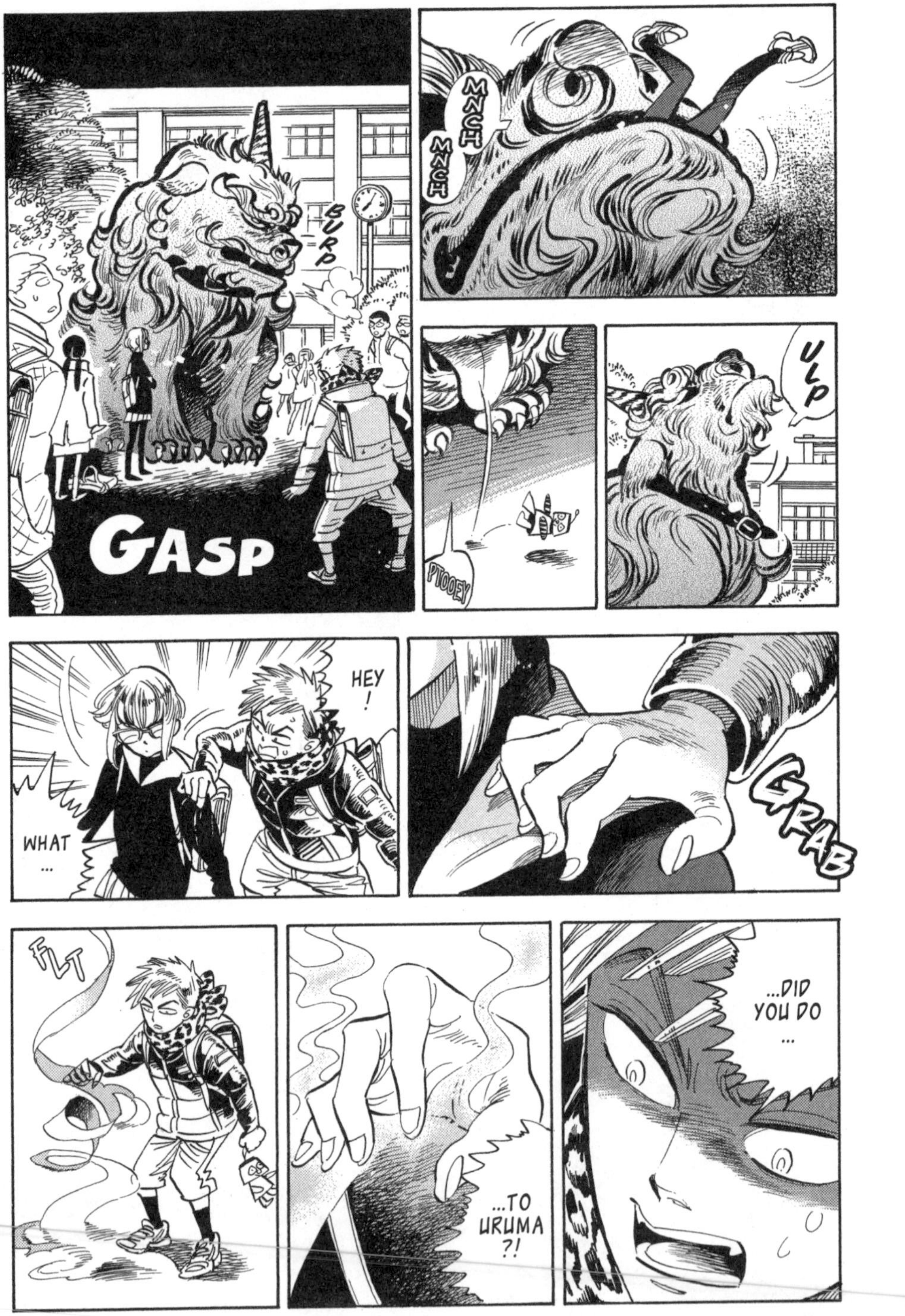
MNCH
MNCH
ULP
PTOOEY
BURP
GASP
GRAB
HEY!
WHAT...
...DID YOU DO...
...TO URUMA?!
FLT

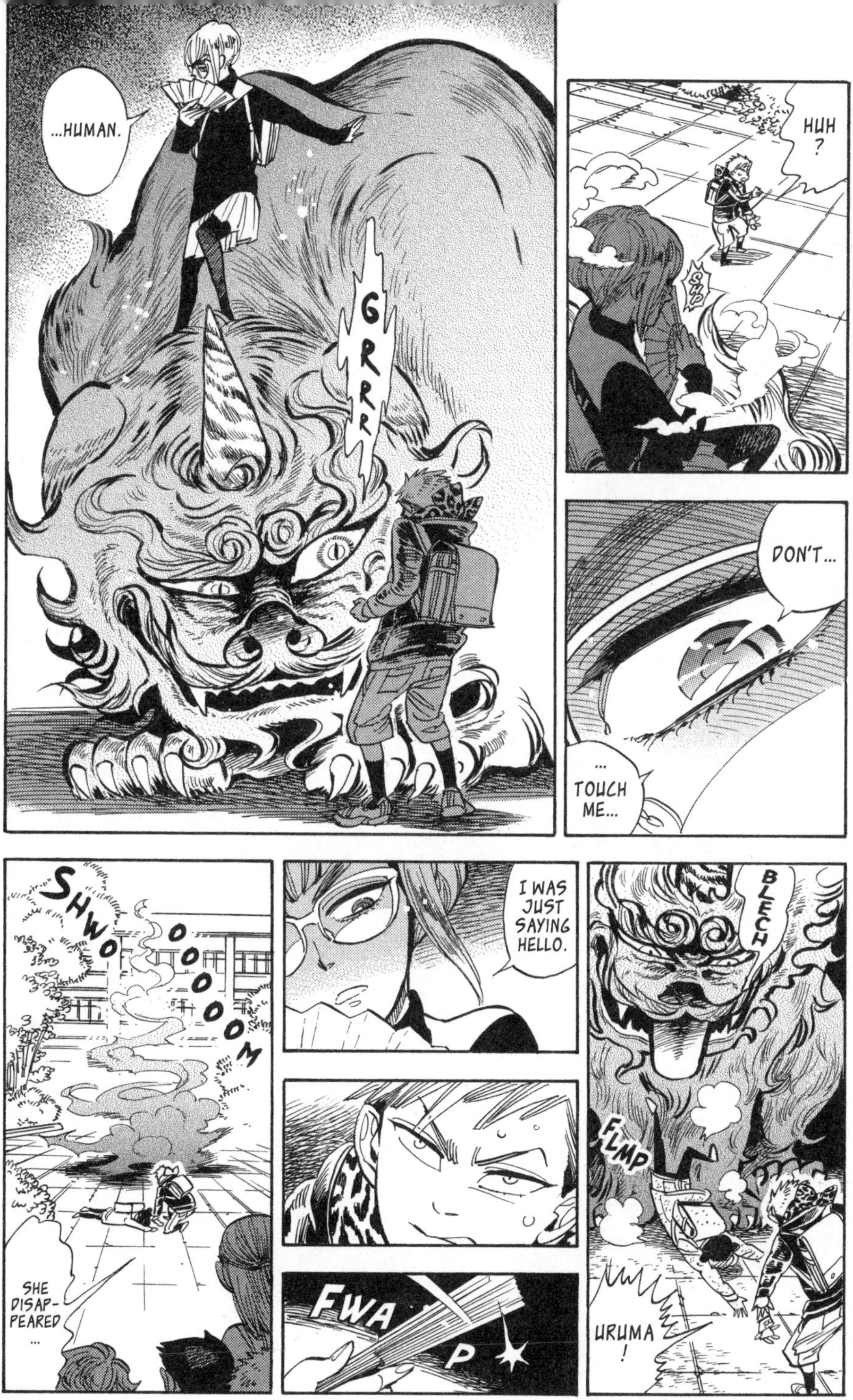
HUH ?
SHO
DON'T...
... TOUCH ME...
...HUMAN.
GRRRR
BLECH
FLMP
URUMA !
I WAS JUST SAYING HELLO.
FWAP
SHWOOOOOOOOM
SHE DISAP-PEARED ...

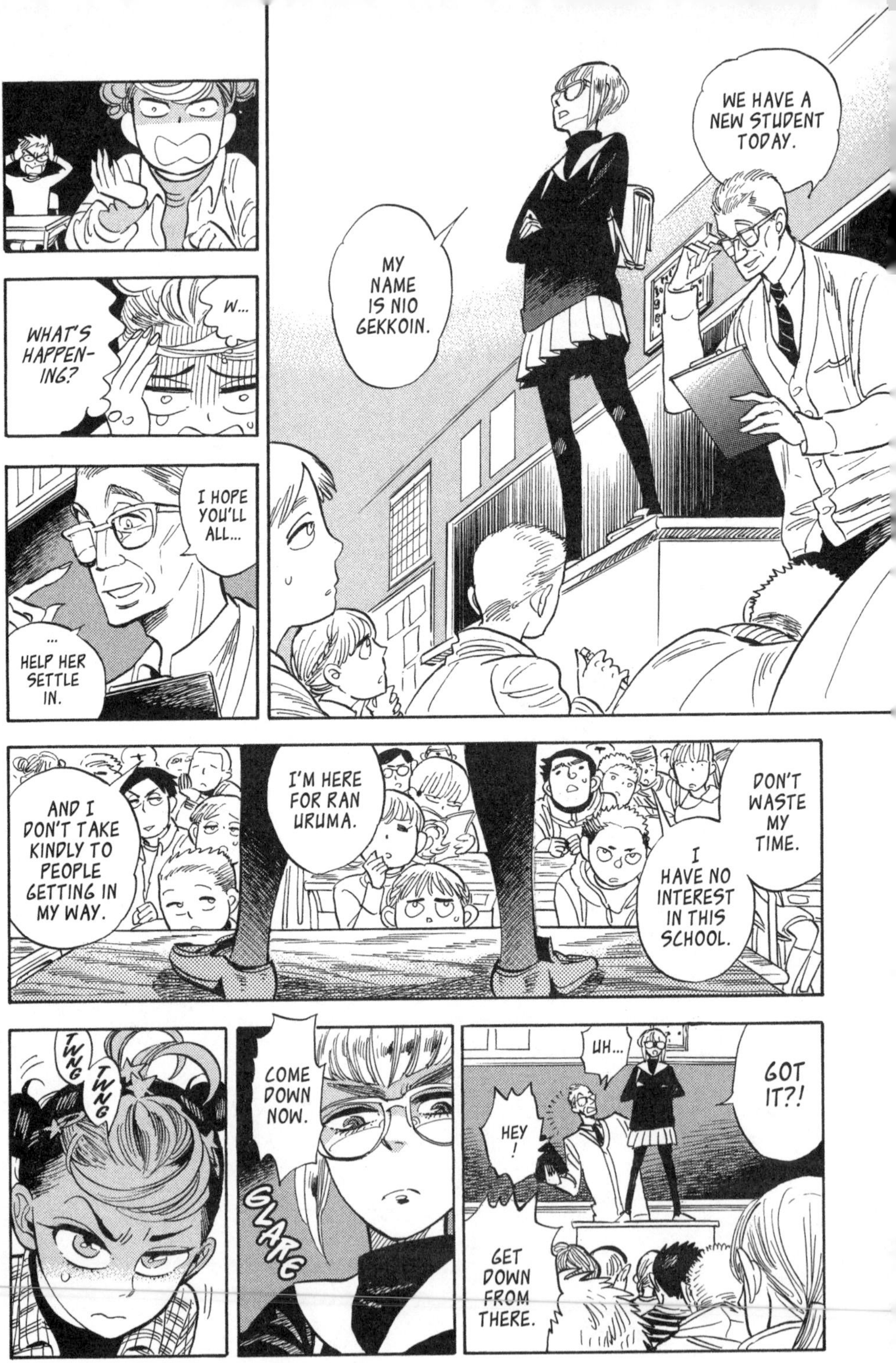
WE HAVE A NEW STUDENT TODAY.
MY NAME IS NIO GEKKOIN.
W...
WHAT'S HAPPEN-ING?
I HOPE YOU'LL ALL...
... HELP HER SETTLE IN.
DON'T WASTE MY TIME.
I HAVE NO INTEREST IN THIS SCHOOL.
I'M HERE FOR RAN URUMA.
AND I DON'T TAKE KINDLY TO PEOPLE GETTING IN MY WAY.
GOT IT?!
UH...
HEY!
GET DOWN FROM THERE.
COME DOWN NOW.
GLARE
TWNG
TWNG

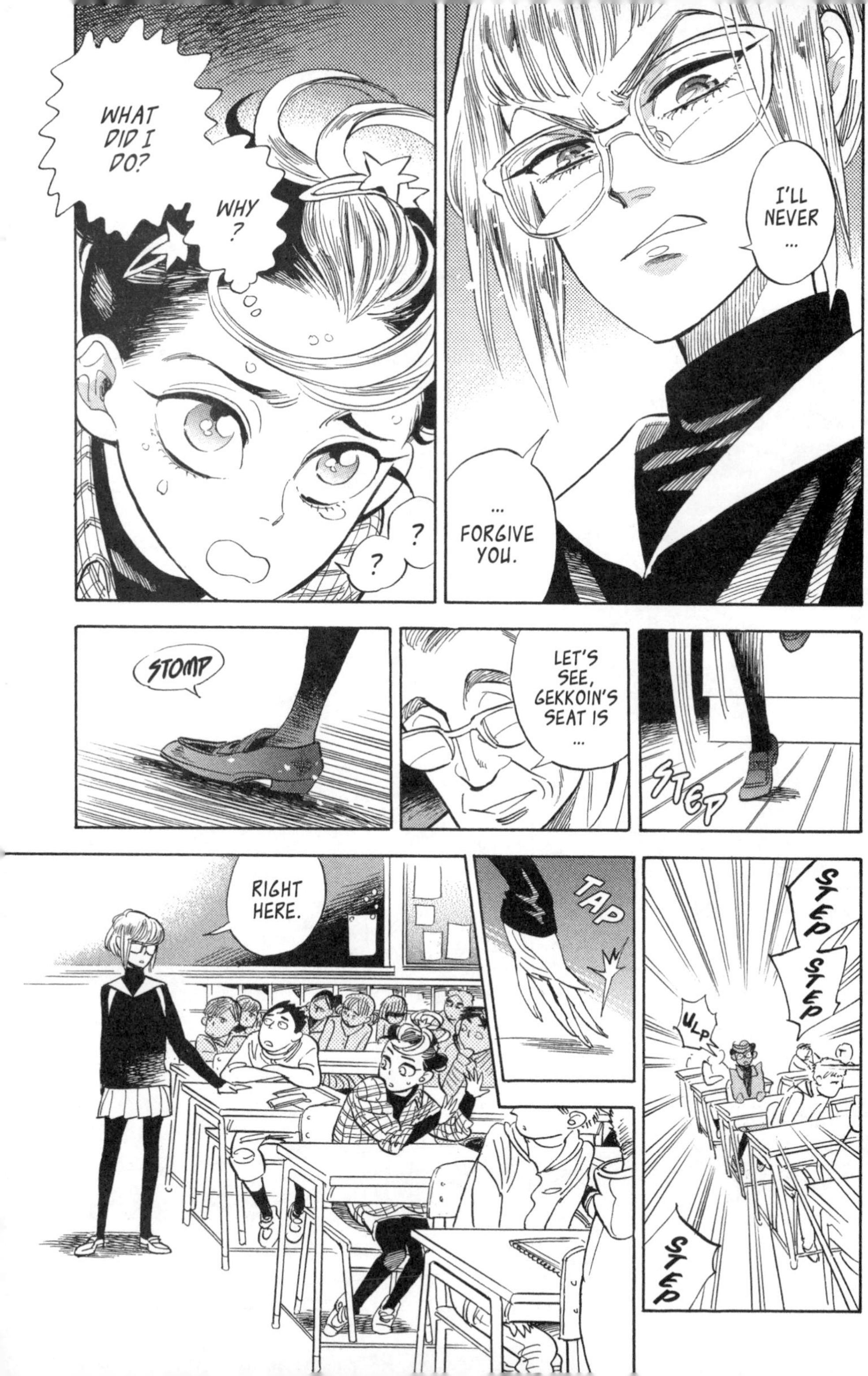
I'LL NEVER ...
... FORGIVE YOU.
WHAT DID I DO?
WHY?
?
?
STEP
LET'S SEE, GEKKOIN'S SEAT IS ...
STOMP
STEP STEP
ULP
STEP
TAP
RIGHT HERE.

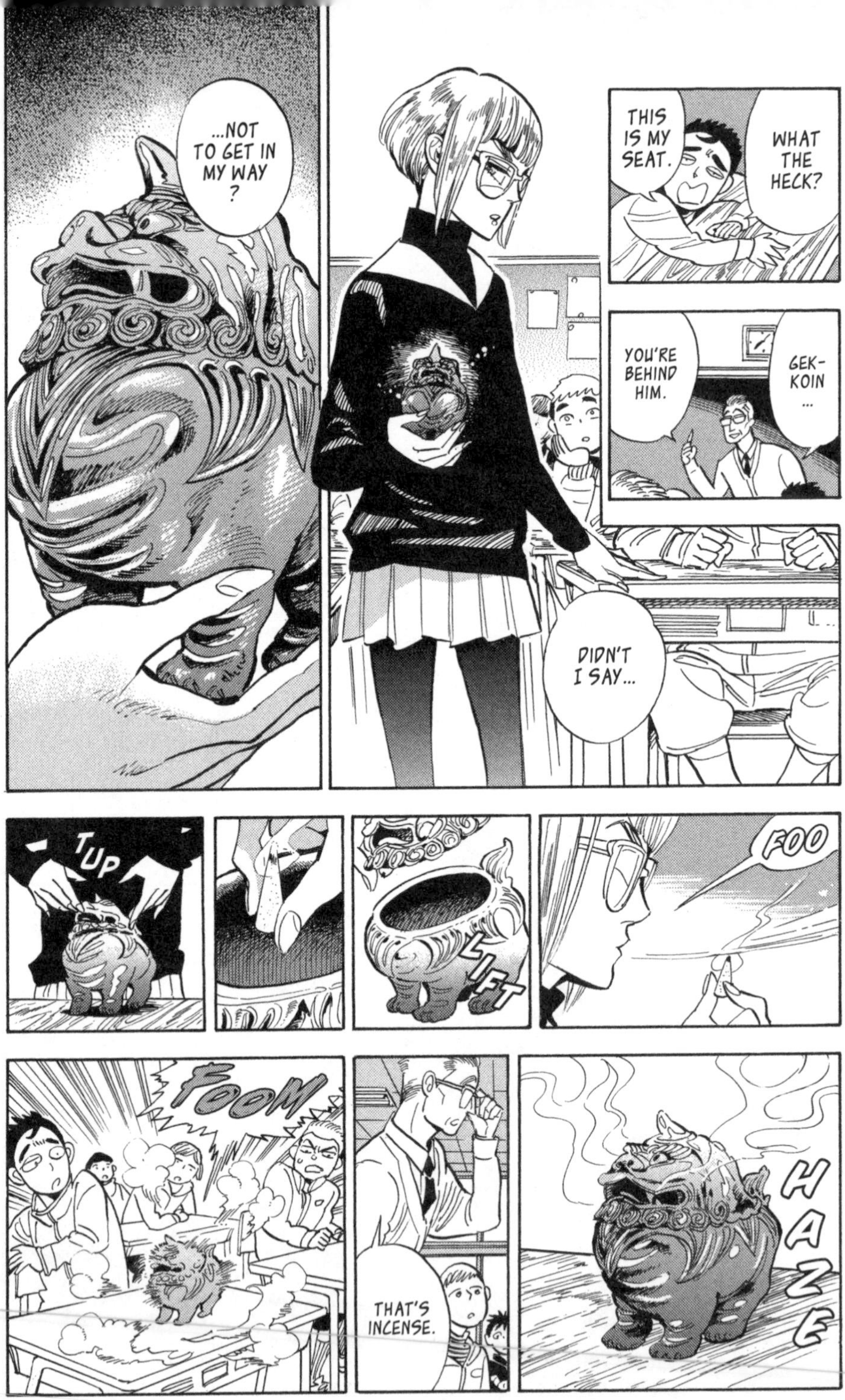
WHAT THE HECK?
THIS IS MY SEAT.
GEK-KOIN...
YOU'RE BEHIND HIM.
DIDN'T I SAY...
...NOT TO GET IN MY WAY?
FOO
LIFT
TUP
HAZE
THAT'S INCENSE.
FOOM

OOH

ミ ミ ミ

WHOA!

RAIGO!

THAT LION...

UH...

...OH.

CHOMP

WHA?

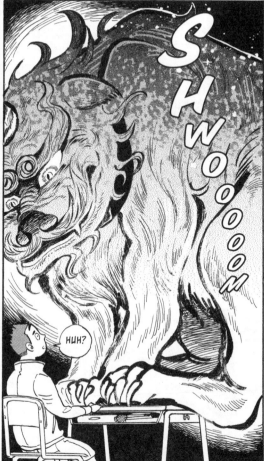
SHWOOOOON

HUH?

ULP ULP

GYAAH

KRAK

51

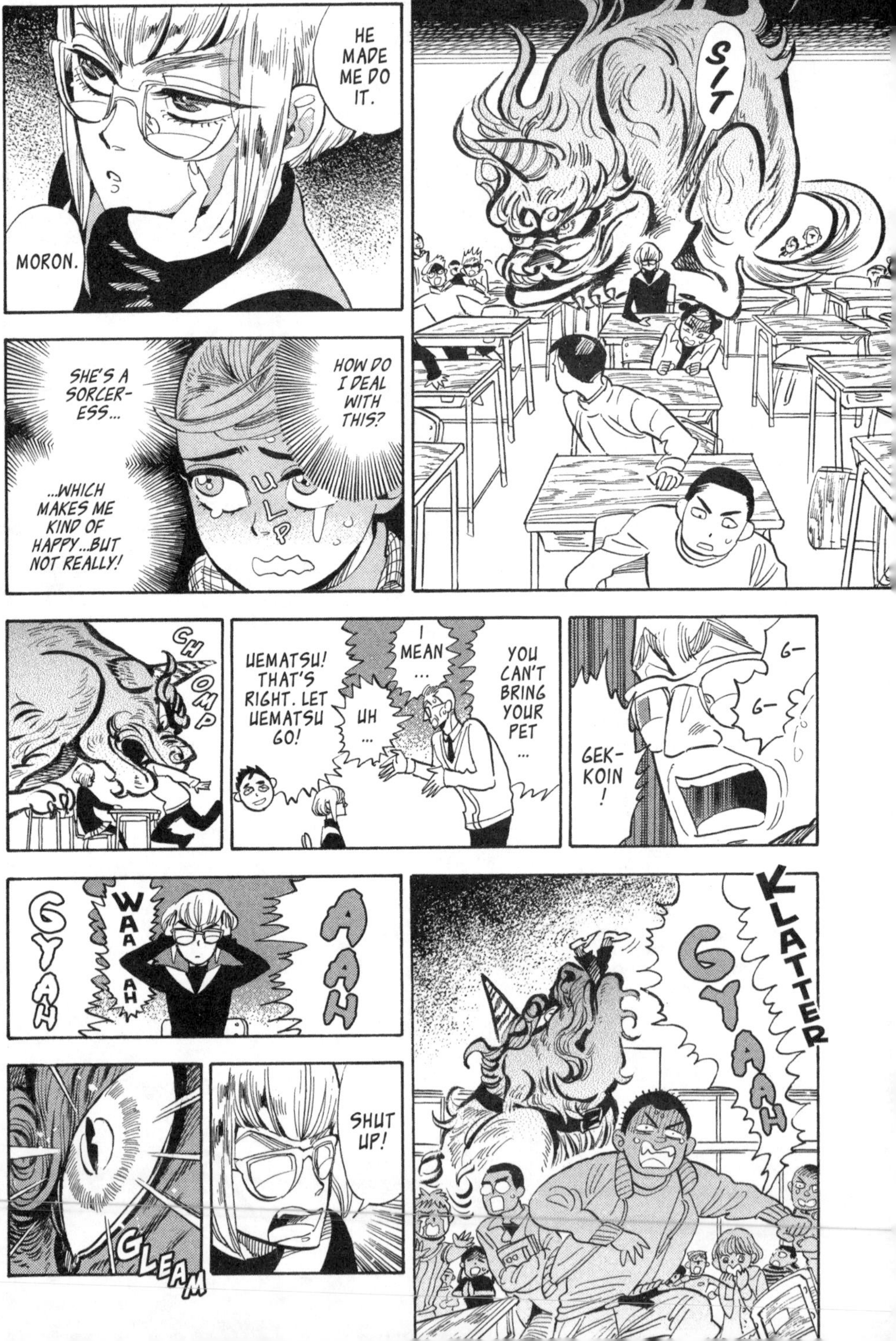
SIT
HE MADE ME DO IT.
MORON.
HOW DO I DEAL WITH THIS?
SHE'S A SORCER-ESS...
ULP
...WHICH MAKES ME KIND OF HAPPY...BUT NOT REALLY!
G—
G—
GEK-KOIN!
YOU CAN'T BRING YOUR PET...
I MEAN...
UH...
UEMATSU! THAT'S RIGHT. LET UEMATSU GO!
CHOMP
KLATTER
GYAAAH
AAAH
WAAAH
GYAAH
SHUT UP!
GLEAM

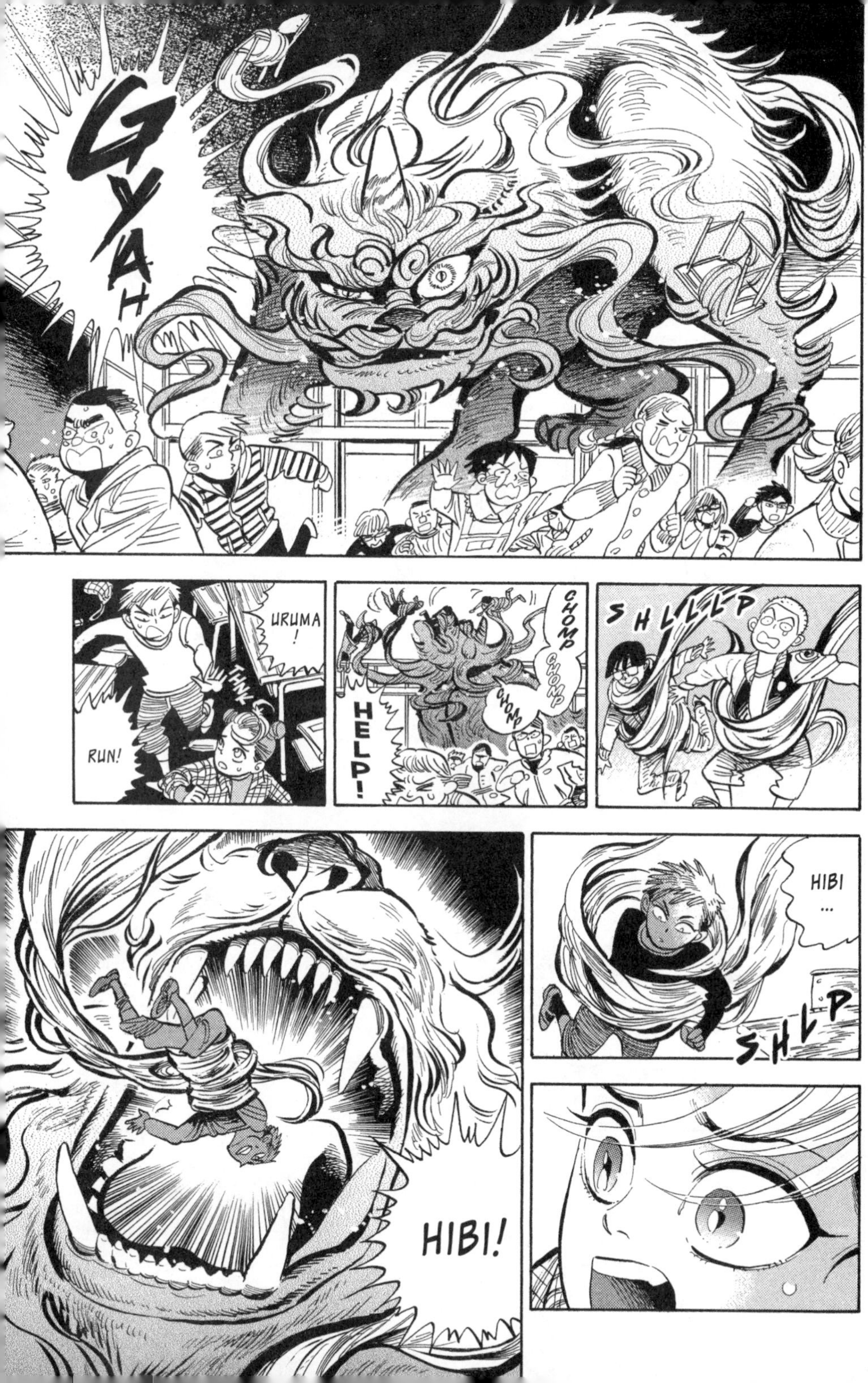
GYAH
SHLLLP
CHOMP
CHOMP
CHOMP
HELP!
URUMA!
THNK
RUN!
HIBI...
SHLP
HIBI!

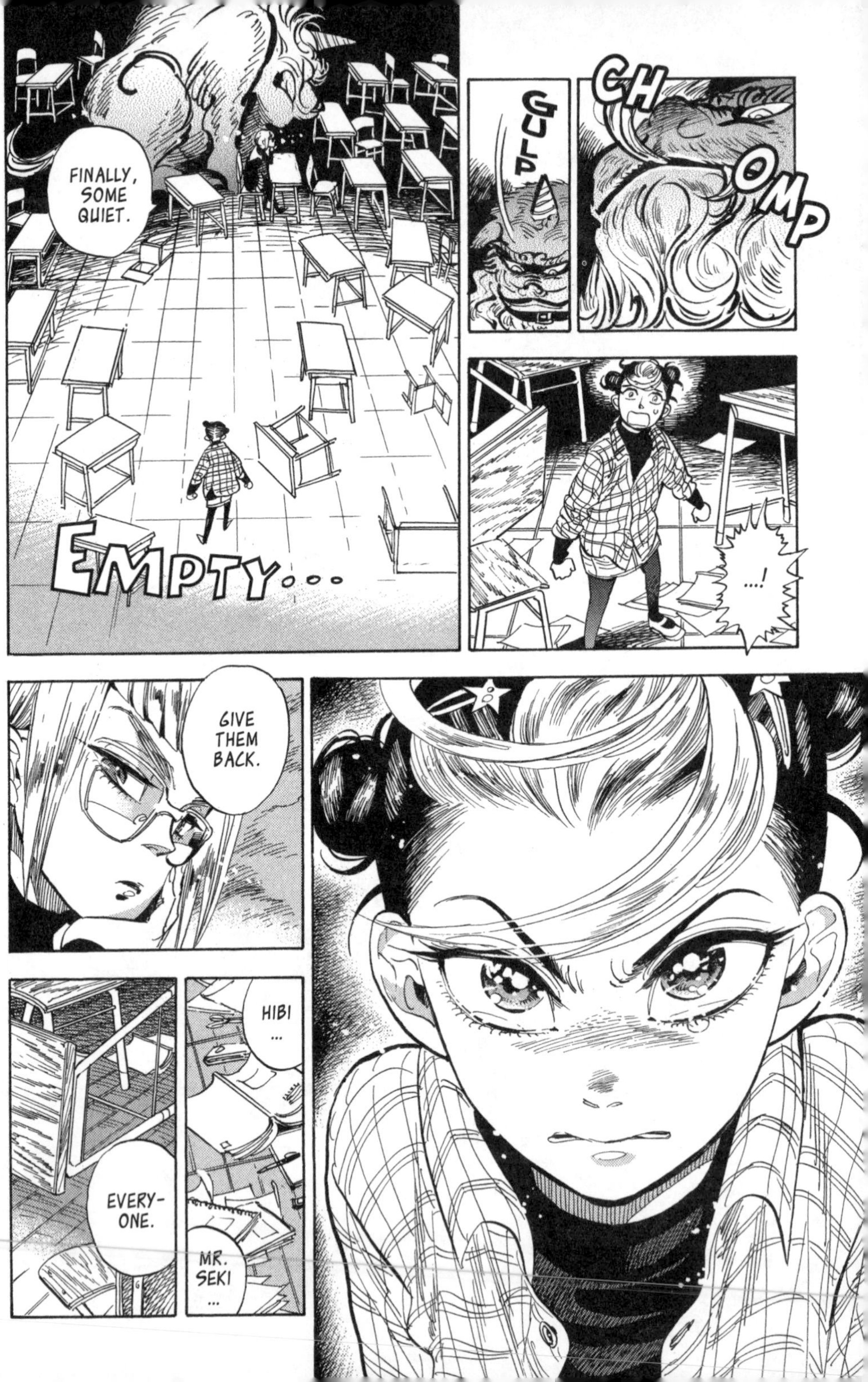
CH
OMP
GULP
...!
FINALLY, SOME QUIET.
EMPTY...
GIVE THEM BACK.
HIBI ...
MR. SEKI ...
EVERY-ONE.

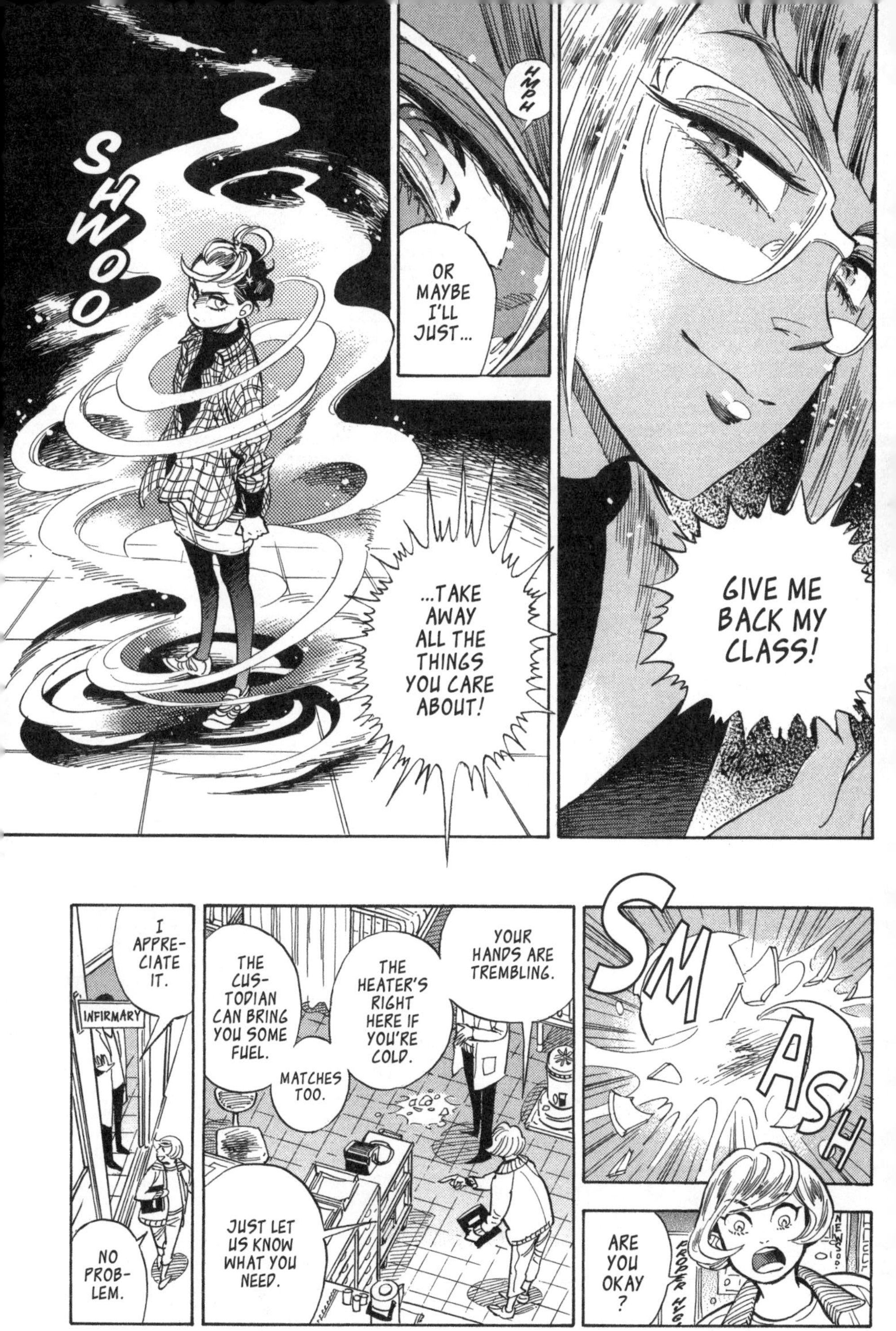
GIVE ME BACK MY CLASS!
HMPH
OR MAYBE I'LL JUST...
SHWOOO
...TAKE AWAY ALL THE THINGS YOU CARE ABOUT!
SMASH
ARE YOU OKAY?
YOUR HANDS ARE TREMBLING.
THE HEATER'S RIGHT HERE IF YOU'RE COLD.
THE CUSTODIAN CAN BRING YOU SOME FUEL.
MATCHES TOO.
JUST LET US KNOW WHAT YOU NEED.
I APPRECIATE IT.
INFIRMARY
NO PROBLEM.

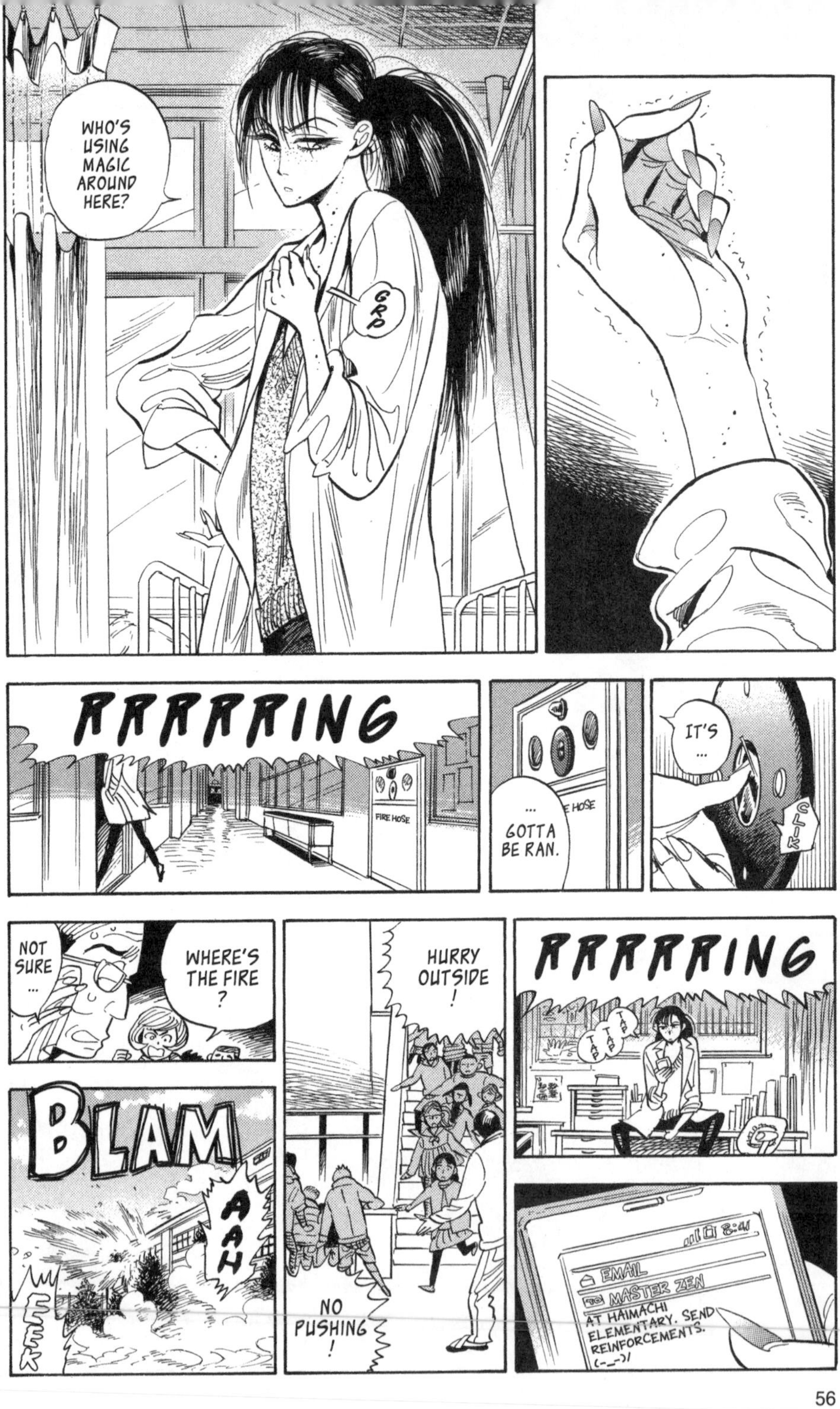
WHO'S USING MAGIC AROUND HERE?
GRP
IT'S ...
CLIK
... GOTTA BE RAN.
RRRRRING
RRRRRING
TAP TAP TAP
EMAIL
TO MASTER ZEN
AT HAIMACHI ELEMENTARY. SEND REINFORCEMENTS.
HURRY OUTSIDE!
NO PUSHING!
WHERE'S THE FIRE?
NOT SURE ...
BLAM
AAH
EEK

ULP

WHAT'S HAPPENING?

...

I CAN'T SEE...

...ANY-THING BUT SMOKE.

HEY! STAY BACK!

LET'S TAKE ROLL.

WHERE'S THE FIRE DEPART-MENT?

FLOWER PETALS?

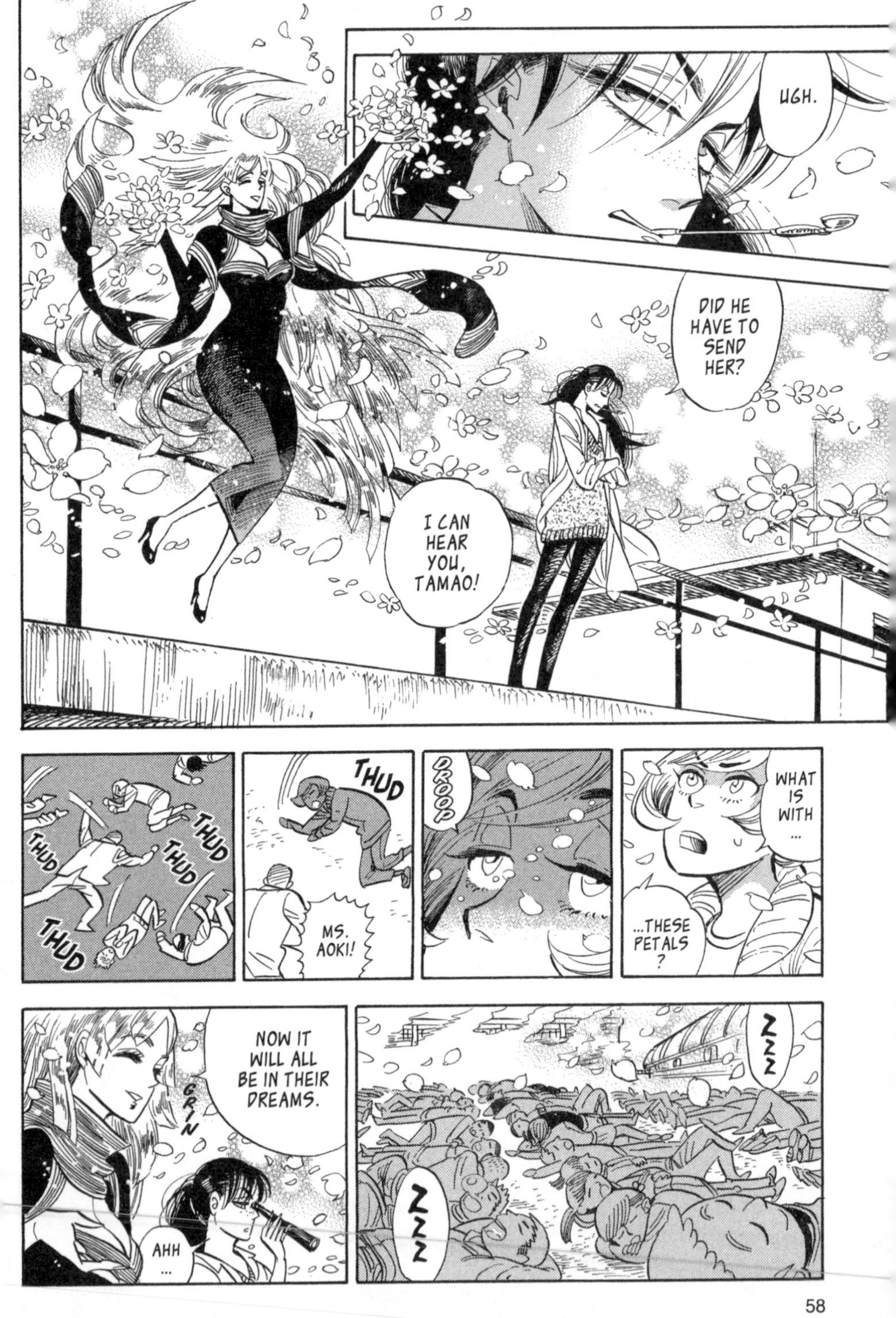
UGH.
DID HE HAVE TO SEND HER?
I CAN HEAR YOU, TAMAO!
WHAT IS WITH ...
...THESE PETALS ?
DROOP
THUD
MS. AOKI!
THUD
THUD
THUD
THUD
ZZZ
ZZZ
NOW IT WILL ALL BE IN THEIR DREAMS.
GRIN
AHH ...

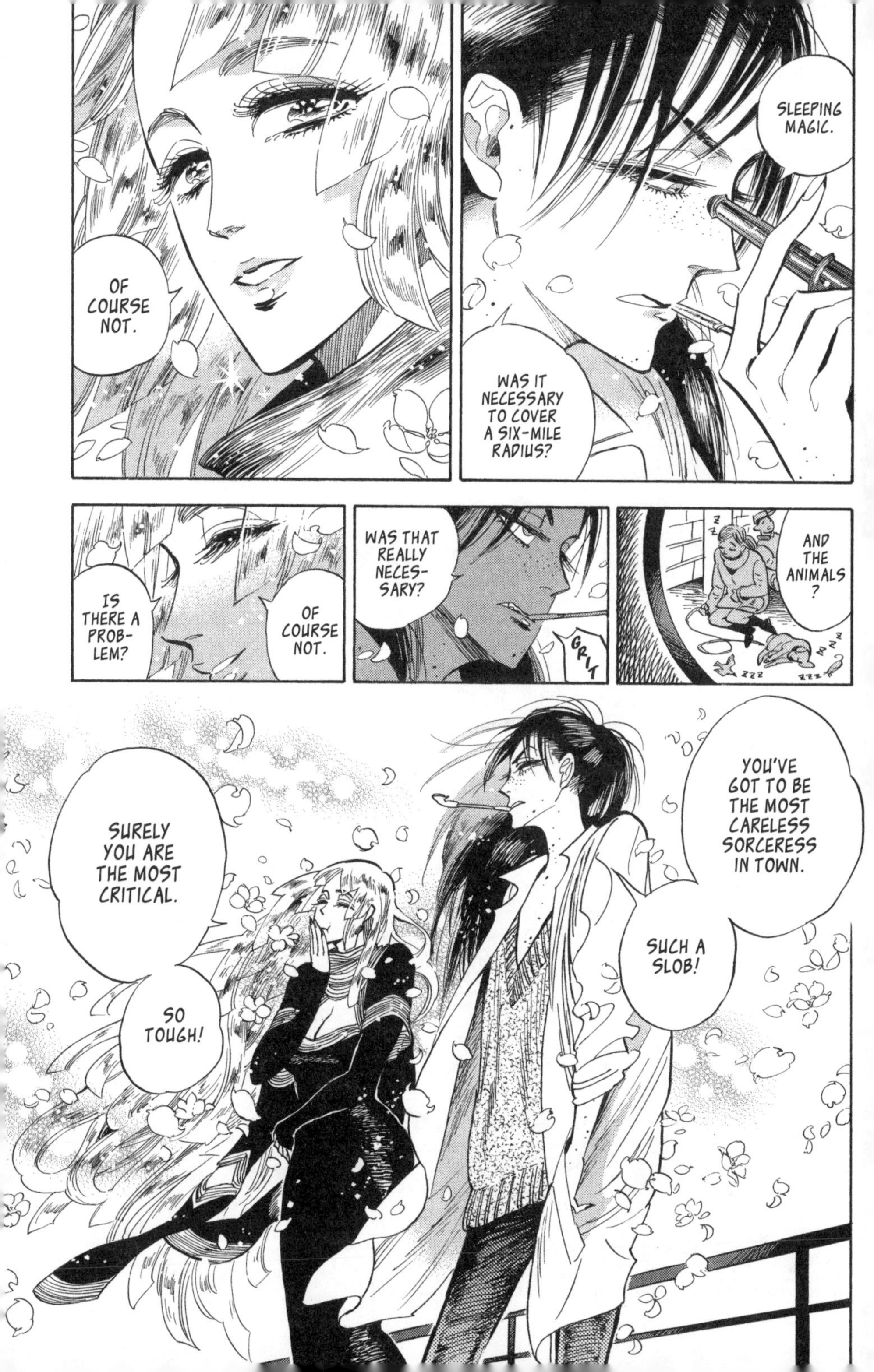
SLEEPING MAGIC.
WAS IT NECESSARY TO COVER A SIX-MILE RADIUS?
OF COURSE NOT.
AND THE ANIMALS?
WAS THAT REALLY NECES-SARY?
GRIT
OF COURSE NOT.
IS THERE A PROB-LEM?
YOU'VE GOT TO BE THE MOST CARELESS SORCERESS IN TOWN.
SUCH A SLOB!
SURELY YOU ARE THE MOST CRITICAL.
SO TOUGH!

FLAP
FLAP
FLAP

FLT FLT

FLT

FWOO
JUST KEEP GOING!

COME ON...

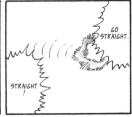
GO STRAIGHT.
STRAIGHT

OH NO!
HEY...
HEY...
FLT FLT

FWOO

FWOO
FWOO

SWSH

SORRY, MR. SEKI!
BOOM
AAH

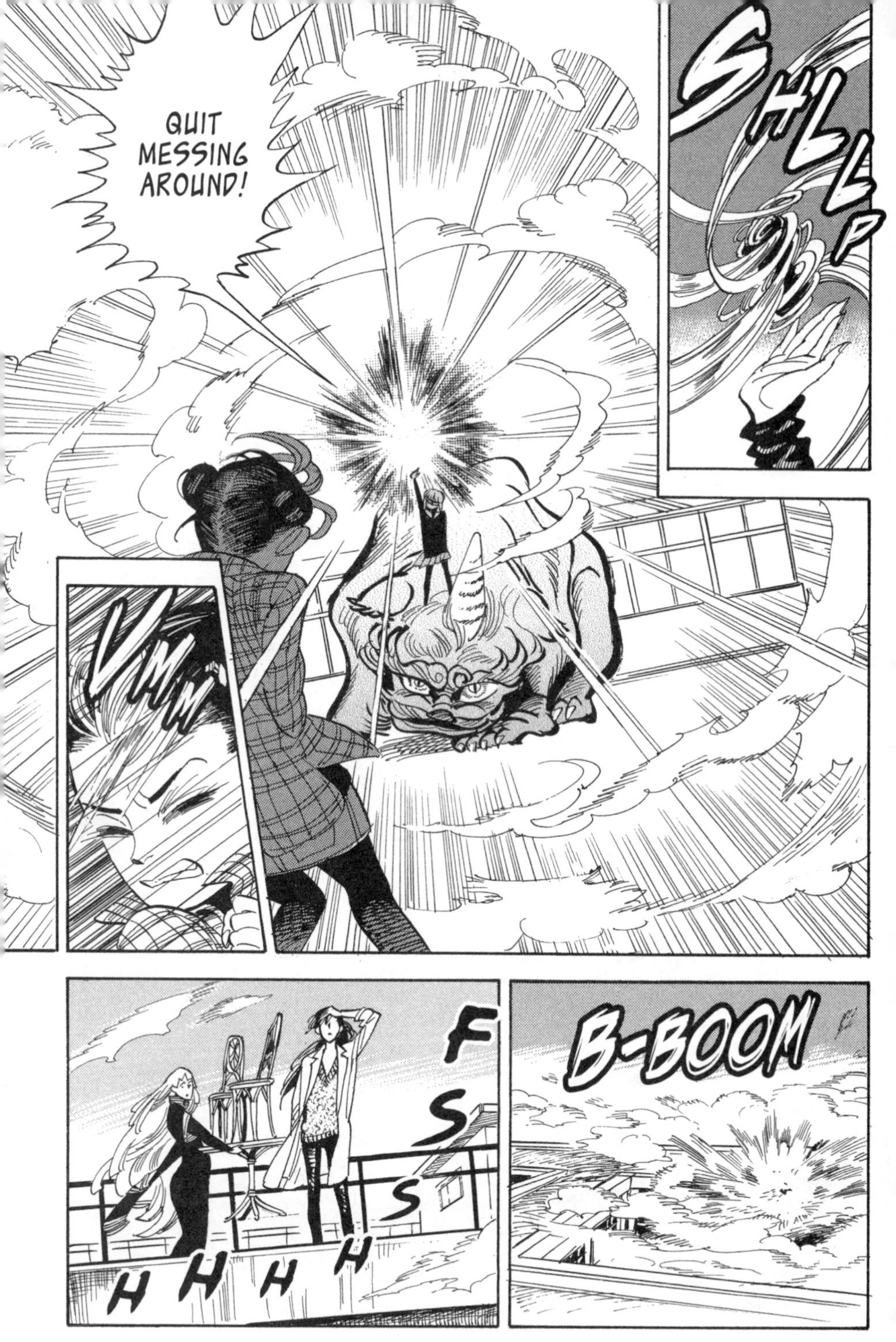
SHLLP
QUIT MESSING AROUND!
VMMM
B-BOOM
FSSHHHH

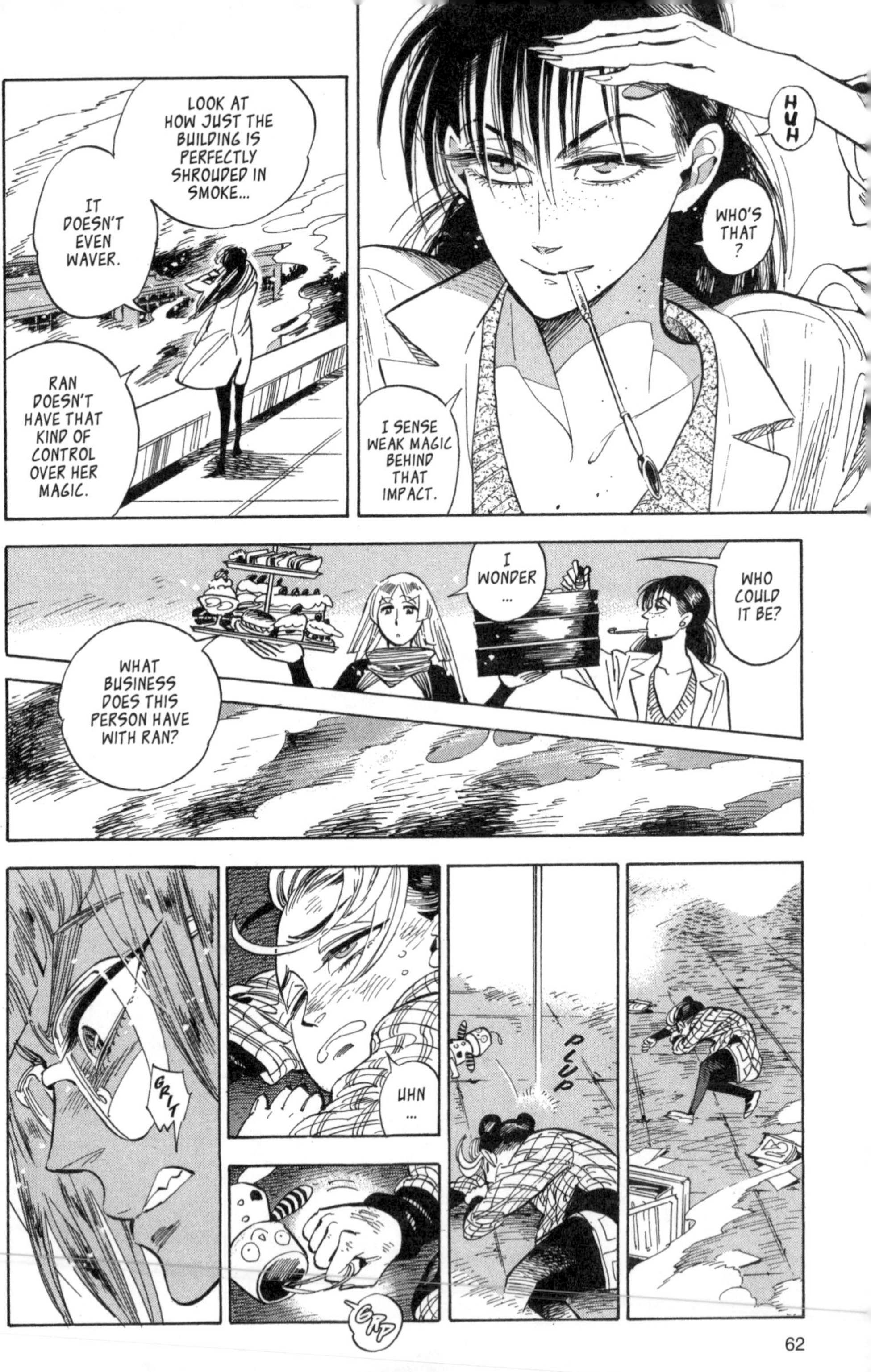
HUH
WHO'S THAT?
I SENSE WEAK MAGIC BEHIND THAT IMPACT.
LOOK AT HOW JUST THE BUILDING IS PERFECTLY SHROUDED IN SMOKE...
IT DOESN'T EVEN WAVER.
RAN DOESN'T HAVE THAT KIND OF CONTROL OVER HER MAGIC.
WHO COULD IT BE?
I WONDER...
WHAT BUSINESS DOES THIS PERSON HAVE WITH RAN?
PLUP
UHN...
GRIP
GRIT

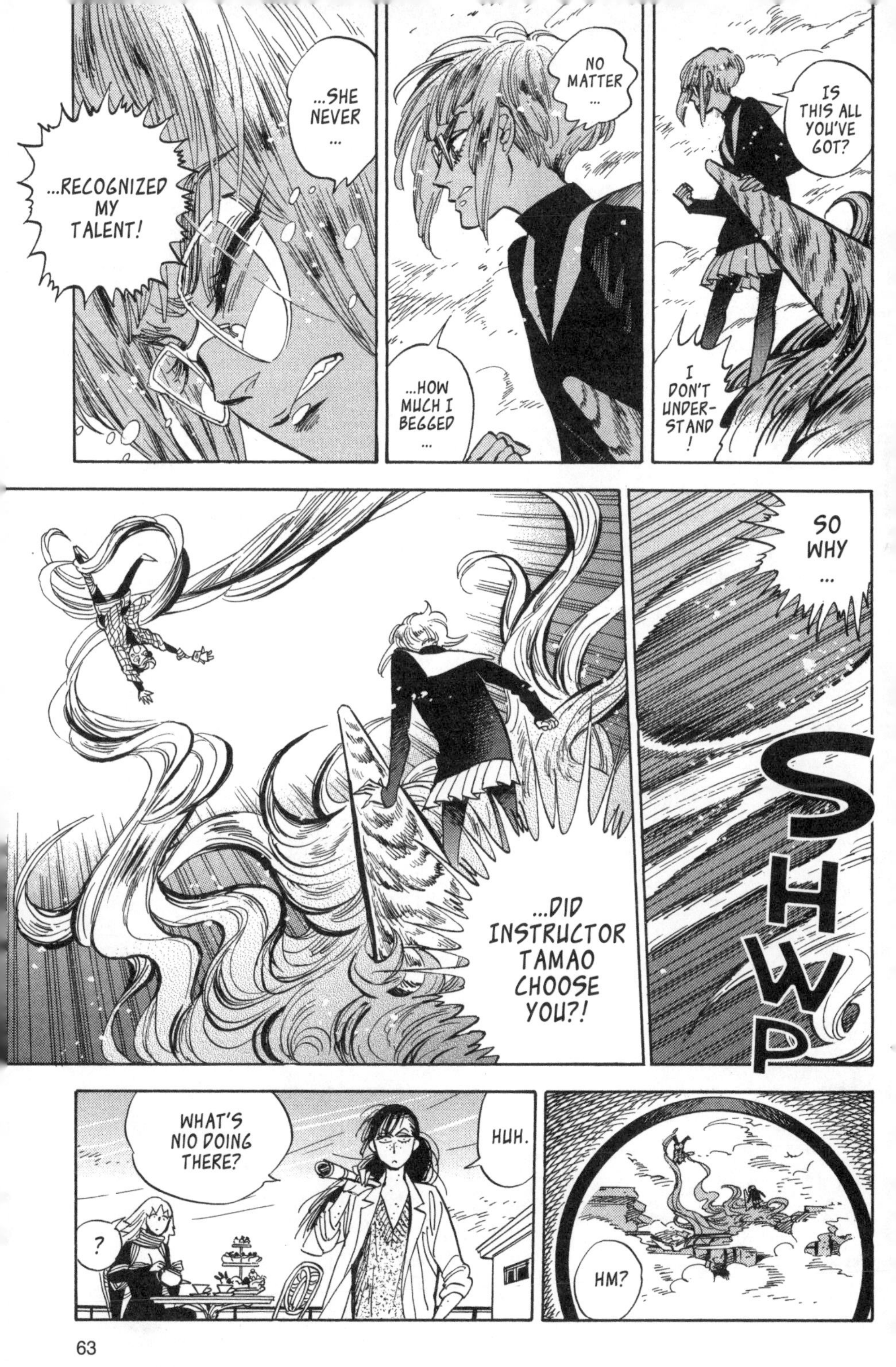

IS THIS ALL YOU'VE GOT?
I DON'T UNDER-STAND!
NO MATTER...
...HOW MUCH I BEGGED...
...SHE NEVER...
...RECOGNIZED MY TALENT!
SO WHY...
SHWP
...DID INSTRUCTOR TAMAO CHOOSE YOU?!
HM?
HUH.
WHAT'S NIO DOING THERE?
?

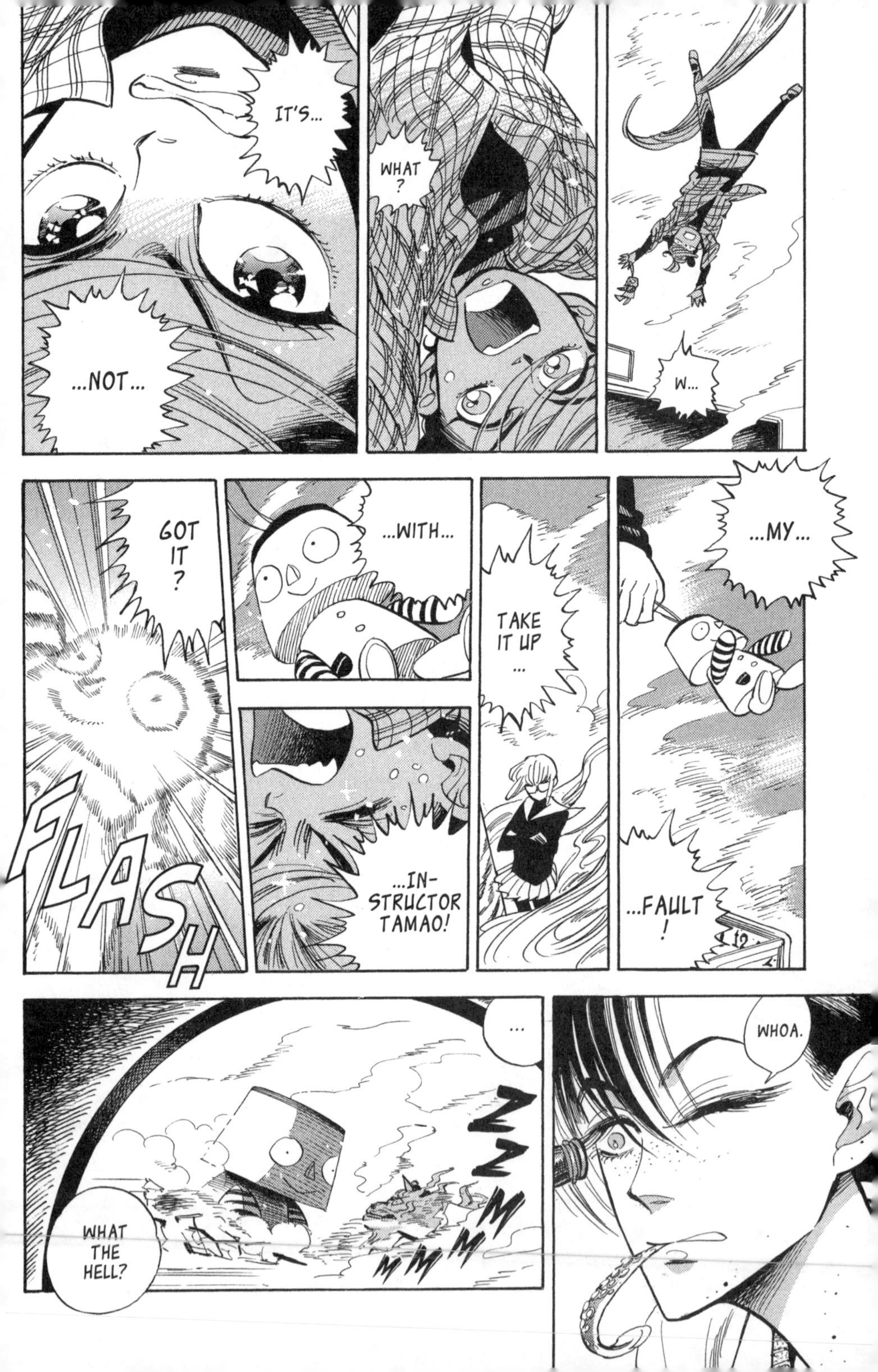
W...
WHAT?
IT'S...
...NOT...
...MY...
...FAULT!
TAKE IT UP...
...WITH...
...IN-STRUCTOR TAMAO!
GOT IT?
FLASH
WHOA.
...
ZZMMMMM
WHAT THE HELL?

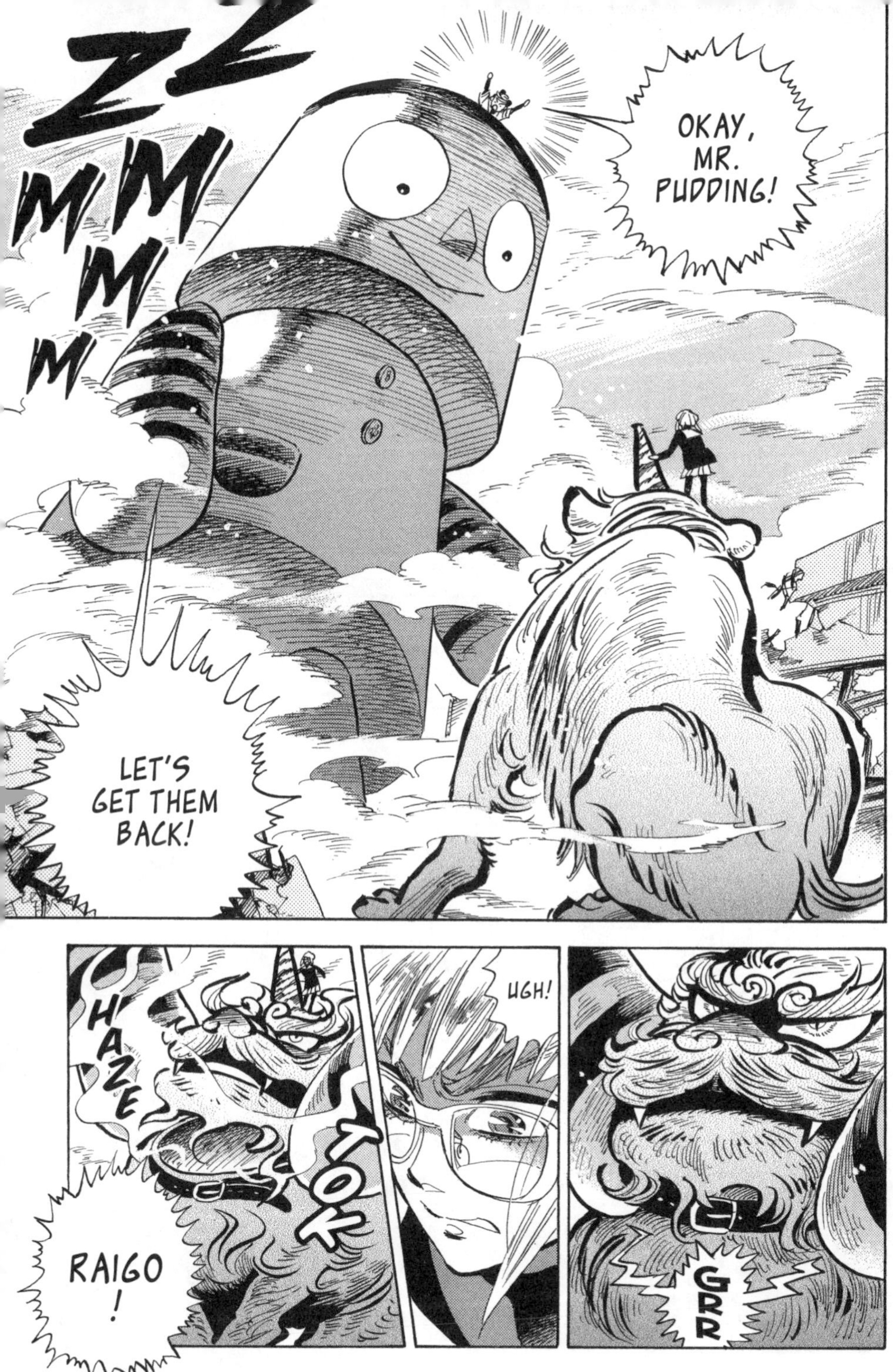
OKAY, MR. PUDDING!
ZZMMMM
LET'S GET THEM BACK!
GRR
UGH!
TOK
HAZE
RAIGO!

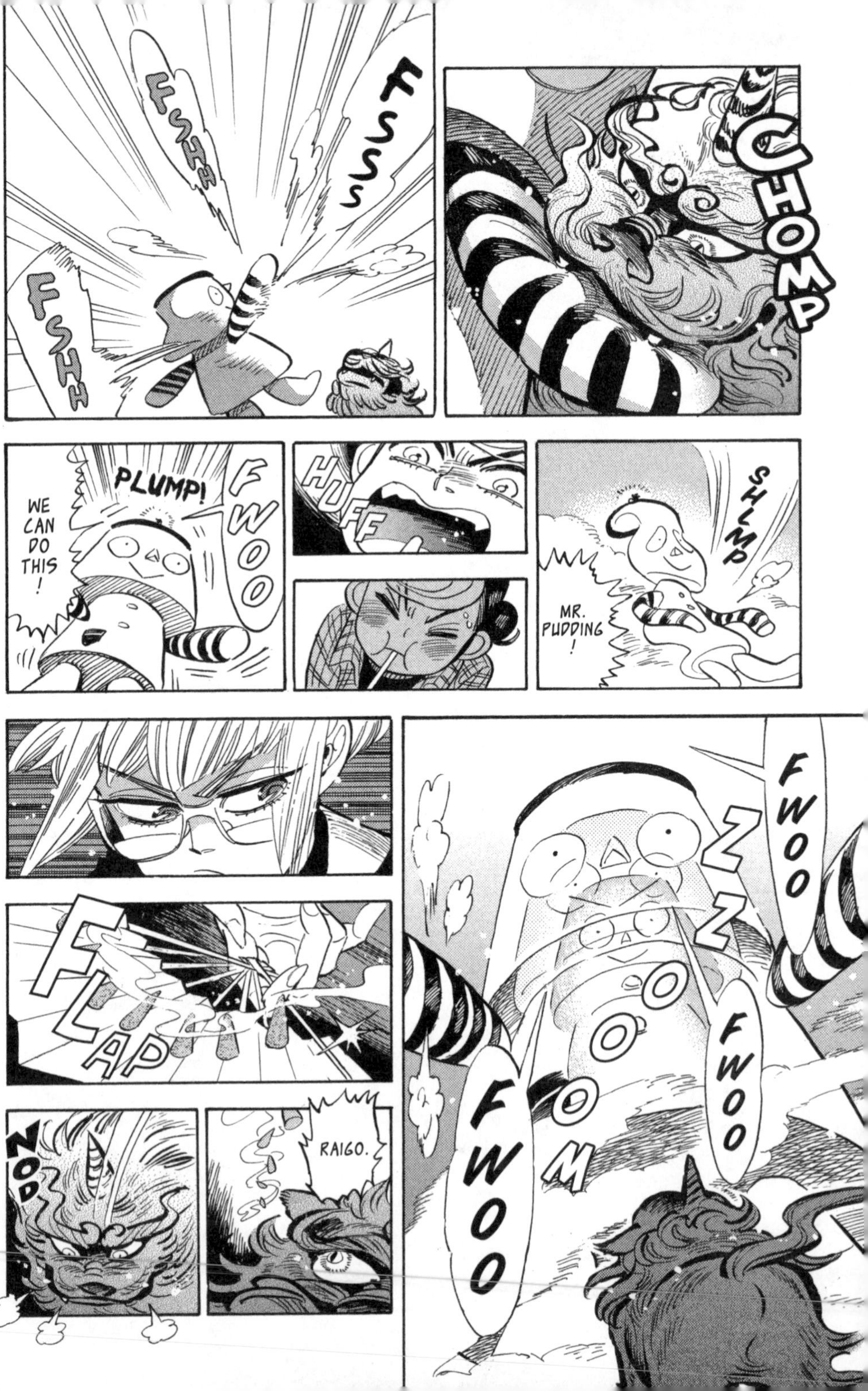
CHOMP
FSSSS
FSHH
FSHH
SHLMP
MR. PUDDING!
HUFF
FWOO
PLUMP!
WE CAN DO THIS!
FWOO
ZZOOOM
FWOO
FWOO
FLAP
RAIGO.
NOD

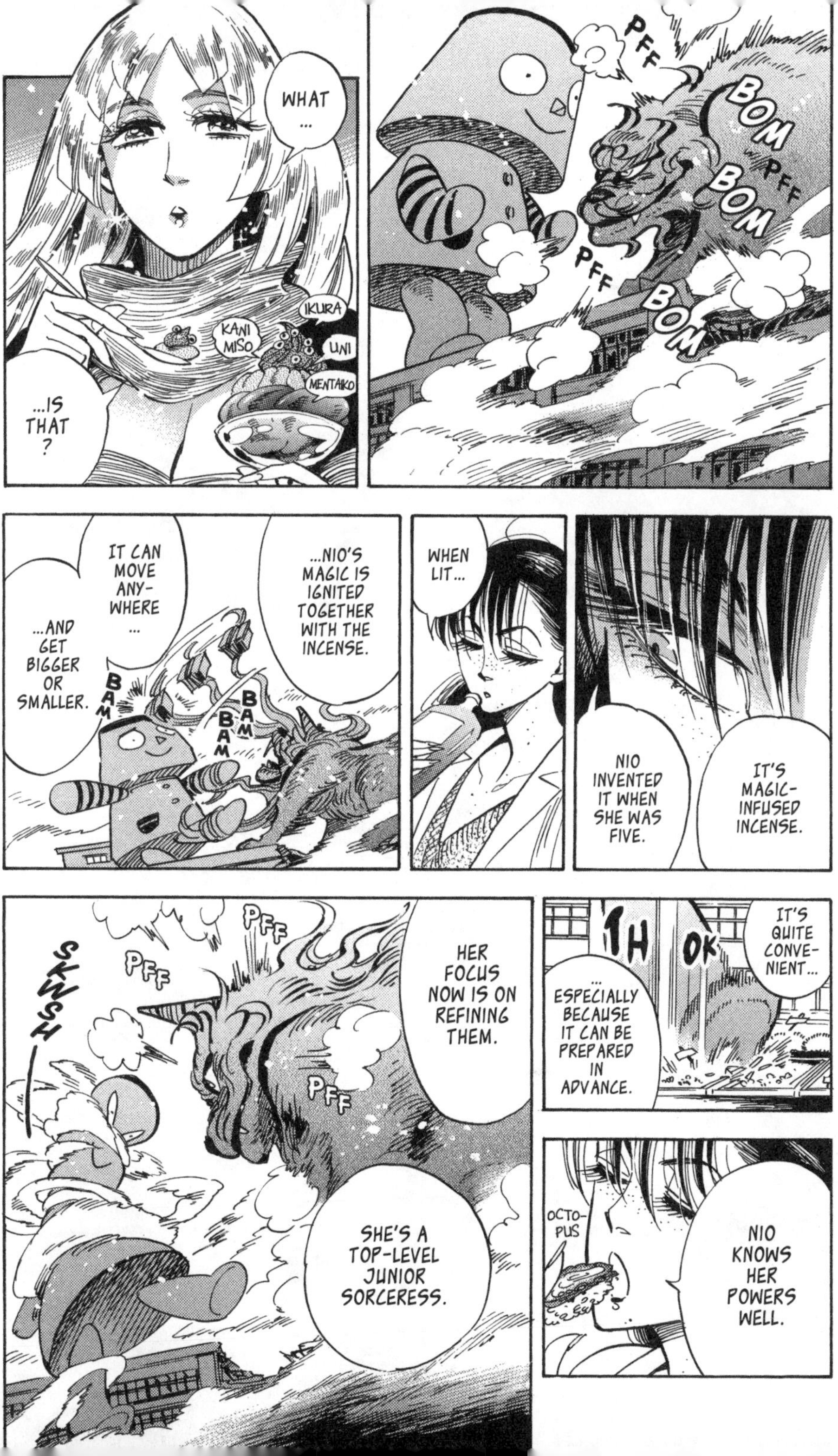

PFF
BOM
PFF
BOM
PFF
BOM
WHAT ...
IKURA
KANI MISO
UNI
MENTAIKO
...IS THAT?
IT'S MAGIC-INFUSED INCENSE.
NIO INVENTED IT WHEN SHE WAS FIVE.
WHEN LIT...
...NIO'S MAGIC IS IGNITED TOGETHER WITH THE INCENSE.
IT CAN MOVE ANY-WHERE ...
...AND GET BIGGER OR SMALLER.
BAM
BAM
BAM
THOK
IT'S QUITE CONVE-NIENT...
... ESPECIALLY BECAUSE IT CAN BE PREPARED IN ADVANCE.
NIO KNOWS HER POWERS WELL.
OCTO-PUS
HER FOCUS NOW IS ON REFINING THEM.
PFF
PFF
PFF
SKWSH
SHE'S A TOP-LEVEL JUNIOR SORCERESS.

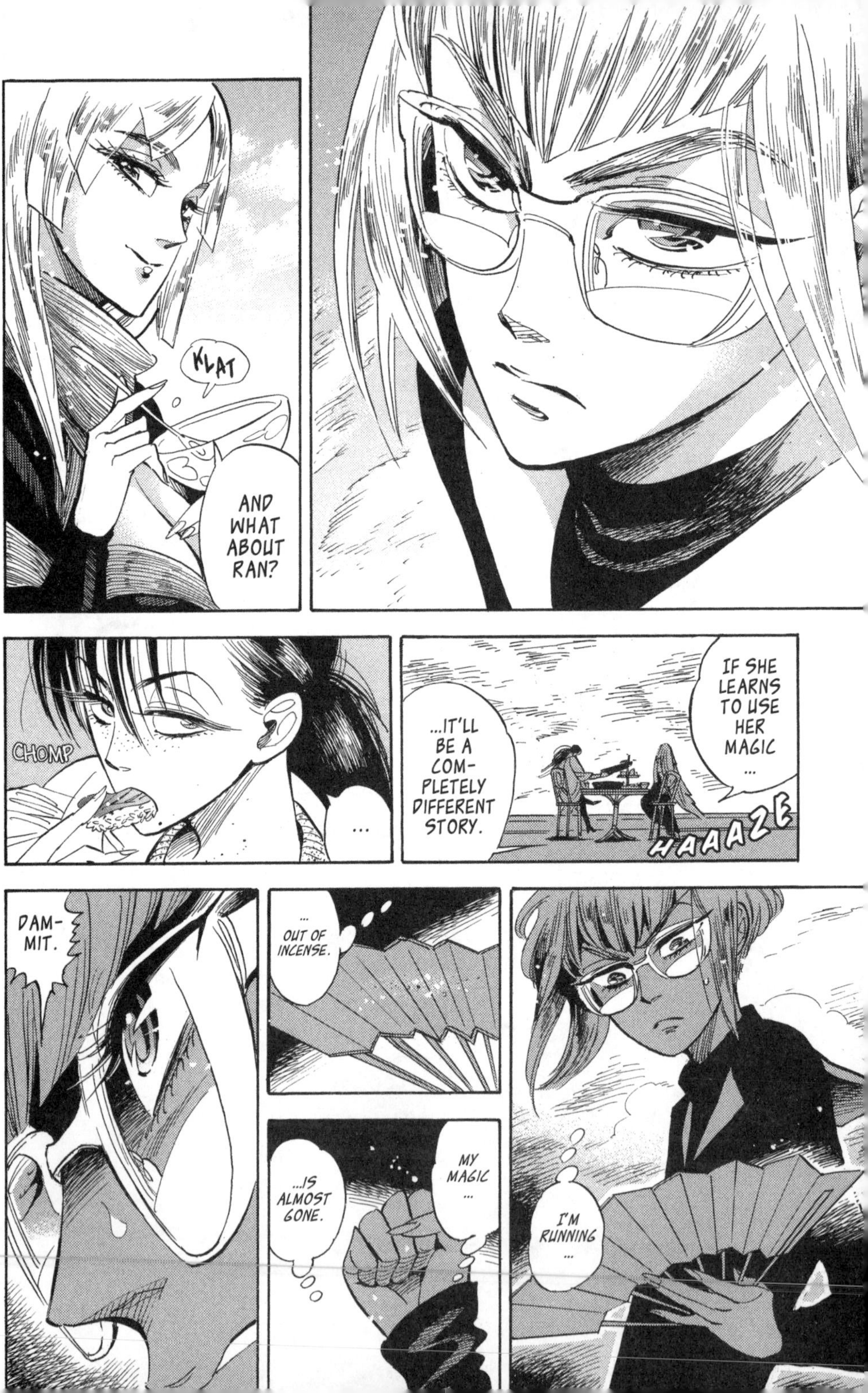
KLAT
AND WHAT ABOUT RAN?
IF SHE LEARNS TO USE HER MAGIC ...
...IT'LL BE A COM-PLETELY DIFFERENT STORY.
HAAAZE
CHOMP
...
I'M RUNNING ...
... OUT OF INCENSE.
MY MAGIC ...
...IS ALMOST GONE.
DAM-MIT.

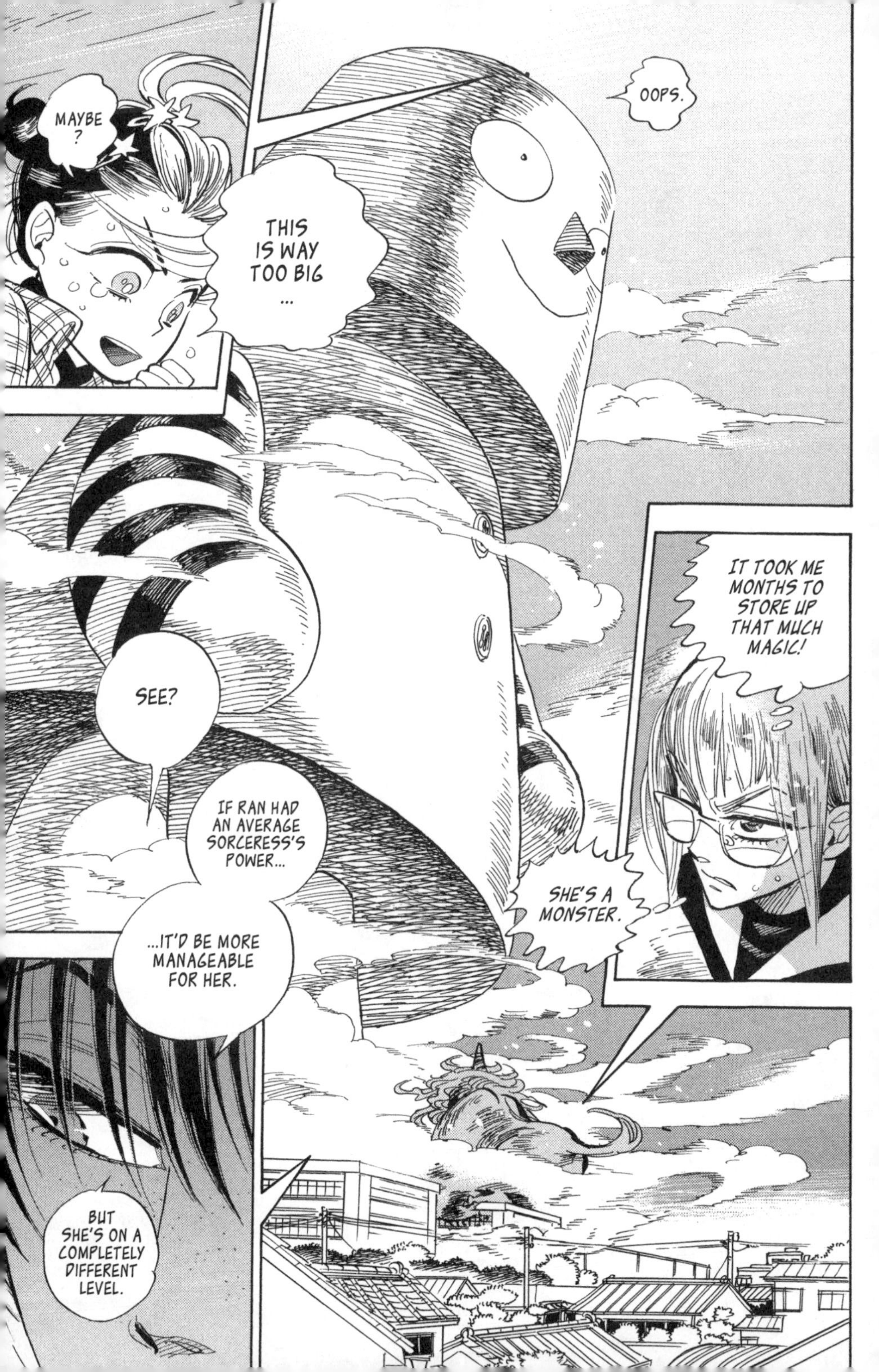
OOPS.
THIS IS WAY TOO BIG ...
MAYBE ?
IT TOOK ME MONTHS TO STORE UP THAT MUCH MAGIC!
SHE'S A MONSTER.
SEE?
IF RAN HAD AN AVERAGE SORCERESS'S POWER...
...IT'D BE MORE MANAGEABLE FOR HER.
BUT SHE'S ON A COMPLETELY DIFFERENT LEVEL.

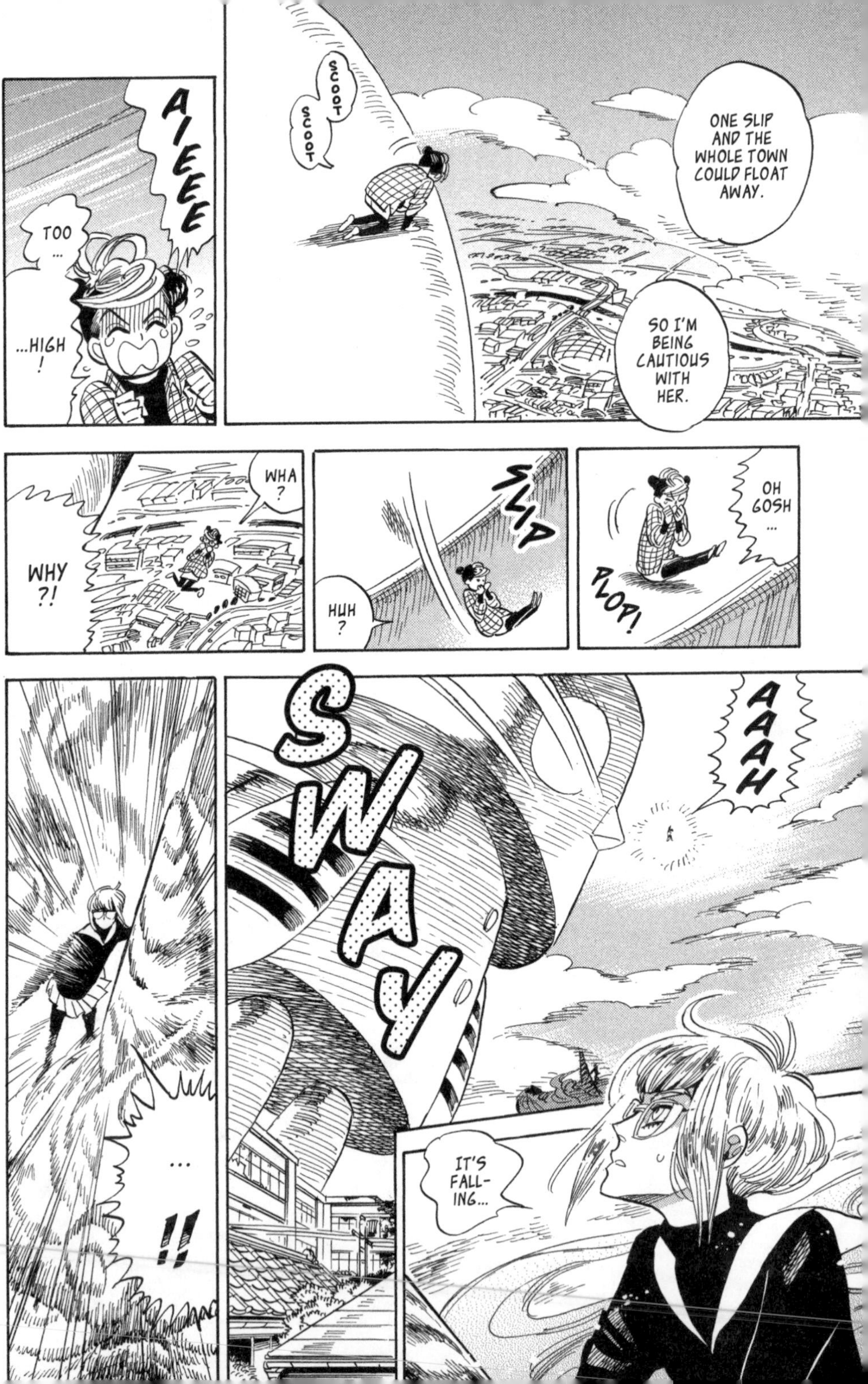

ONE SLIP AND THE WHOLE TOWN COULD FLOAT AWAY.
SCOOT SCOOT
SO I'M BEING CAUTIOUS WITH HER.
AIEEE
TOO...
...HIGH!
OH GOSH...
PLOP!
SLIP
HUH?
WHA?
WHY?!
AAAH
SWAY
IT'S FALLING...
...
!!

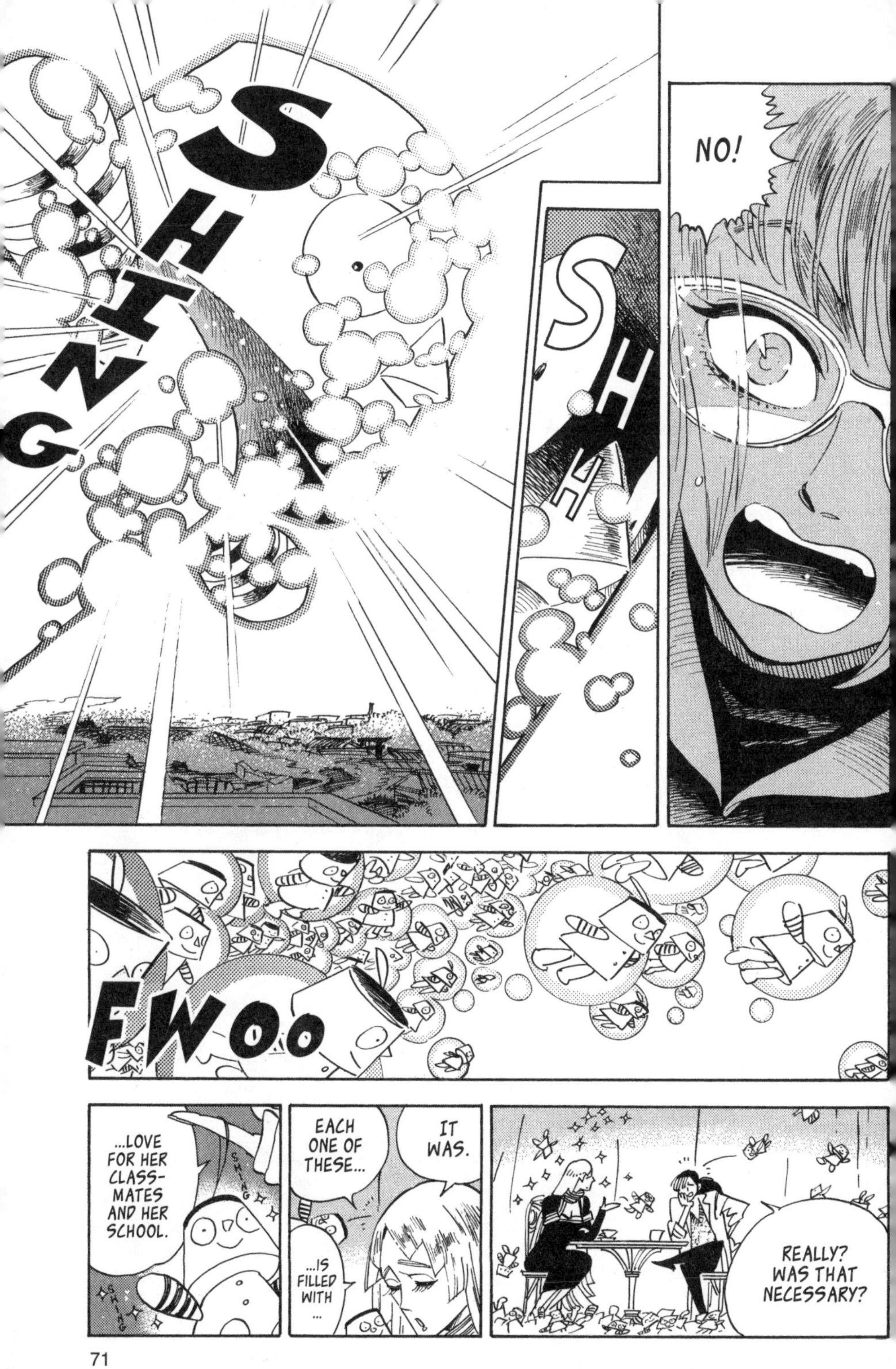
NO!
SHH
SHING
FWOO
REALLY? WAS THAT NECESSARY?
IT WAS.
EACH ONE OF THESE...
...IS FILLED WITH ...
...LOVE FOR HER CLASS-MATES AND HER SCHOOL.
SHING
SHING

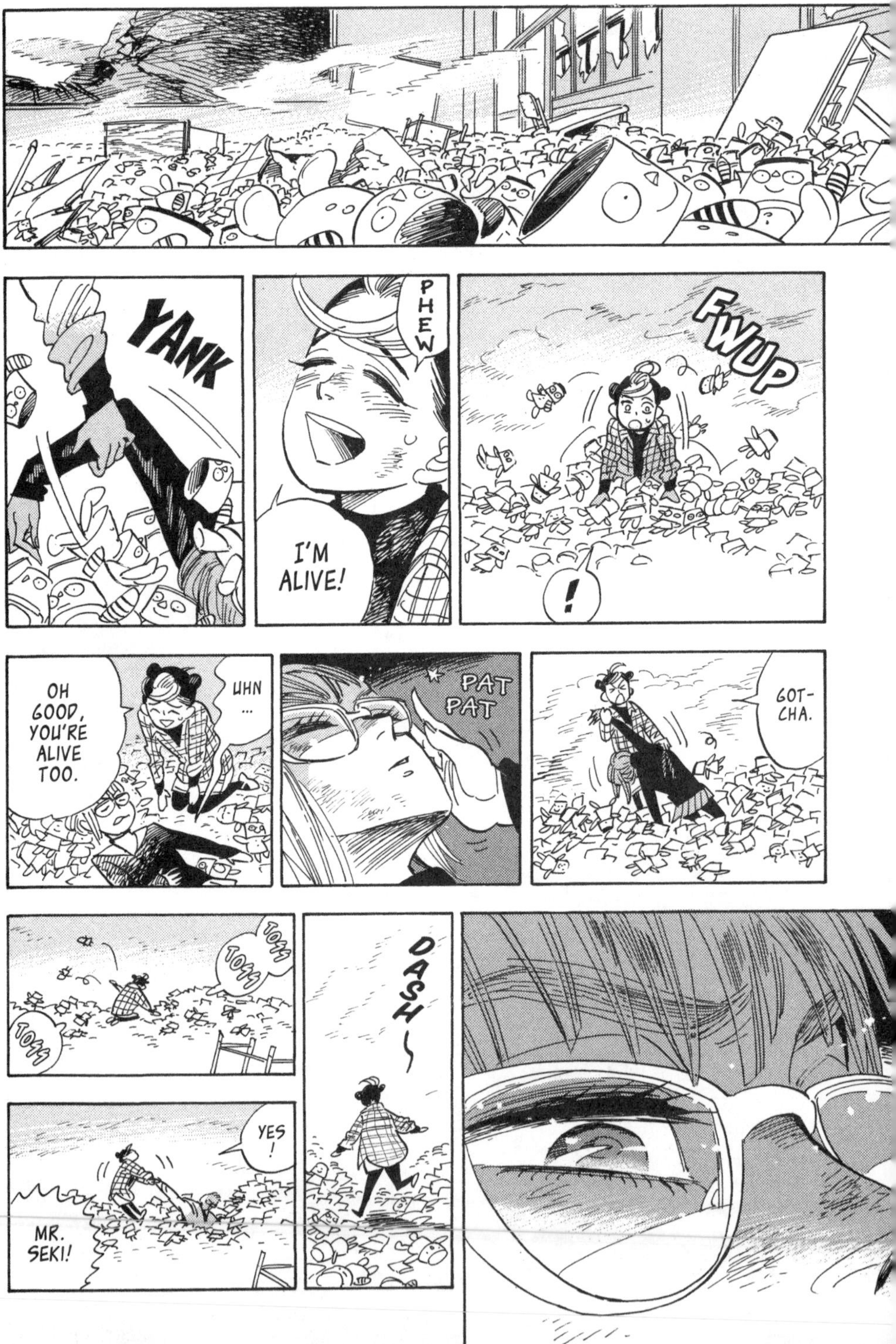
FWUP
!
PHEW
I'M ALIVE!
YANK
GOT-CHA.
PAT PAT
UHN ...
OH GOOD, YOU'RE ALIVE TOO.
DASH
TOSS
TOSS
TOSS
YES!
MR. SEKI!

THAT USED UP ALL OF MY STRENGTH...

I CAN'T EVEN LIFT MY ARMS, AND YET...

WHY IS EVERYONE SO DUSTY?

IS THIS ASH?

SORRY.

I'LL...

...HELP FIX IT.

I...

I BROKE IT.

NO THANKS!

TURN

I DON'T NEED YOUR SYMPATHY.

I'M SORRY.

PLIP

...

BLUSH

GOOD JOB.

HEY, NIO.

I SAW YOU JUST NOW.

LOOKS LIKE YOU HAVE SOME NEW MOVES.

IN...

IN...

BWAA

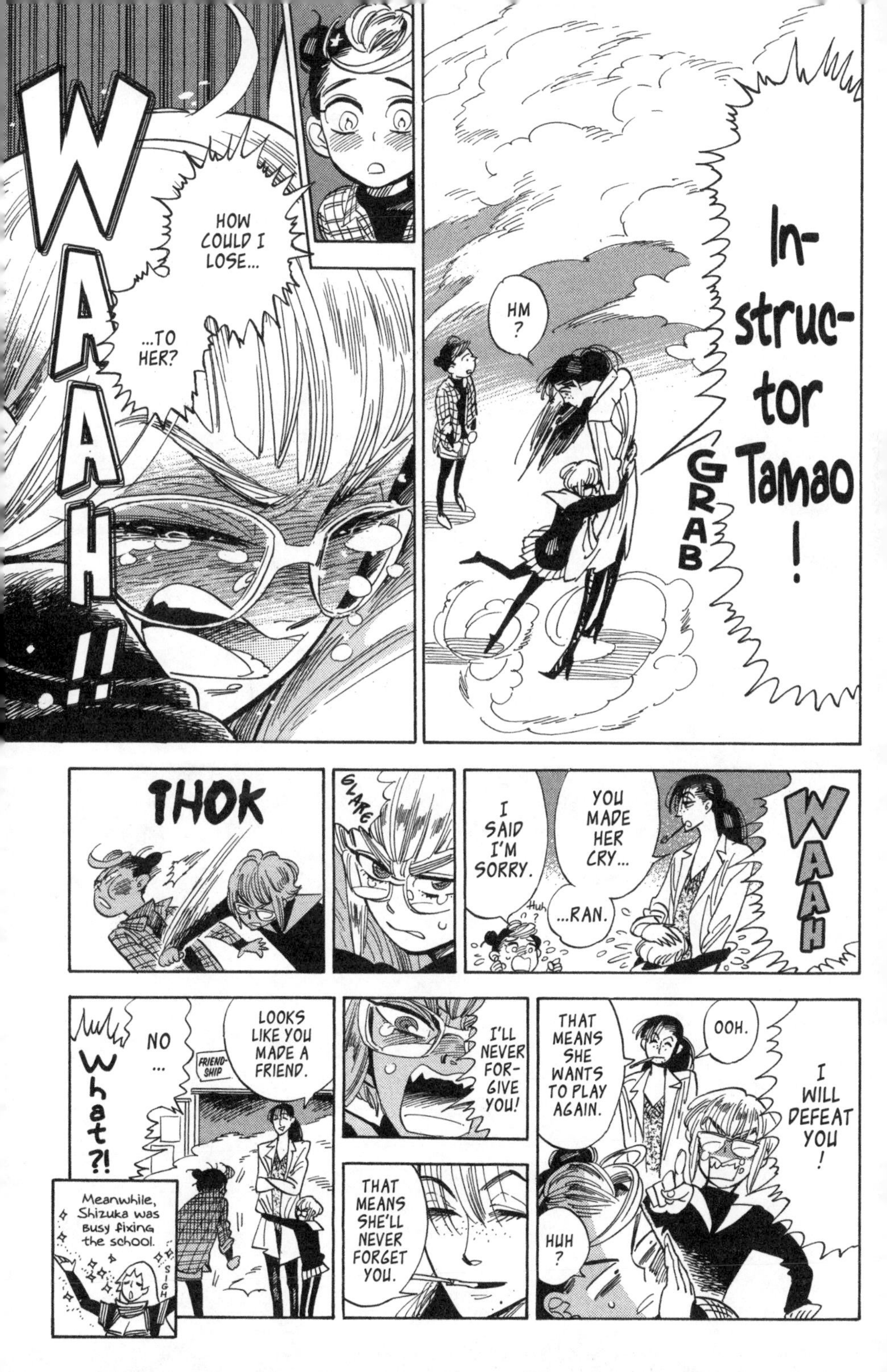

In-structor Tamao!
HM?
GRAB
HOW COULD I LOSE...
...TO HER?
WAAAH!!
WAAH
YOU MADE HER CRY...
...RAN.
I SAID I'M SORRY.
Huh ??
GLARE
THOK
OOH.
THAT MEANS SHE WANTS TO PLAY AGAIN.
I WILL DEFEAT YOU!
HUH?
I'LL NEVER FOR-GIVE YOU!
THAT MEANS SHE'LL NEVER FORGET YOU.
LOOKS LIKE YOU MADE A FRIEND.
NO ...
What?!
FRIEND-SHIP
Meanwhile, Shizuka was busy fixing the school.
SIGH

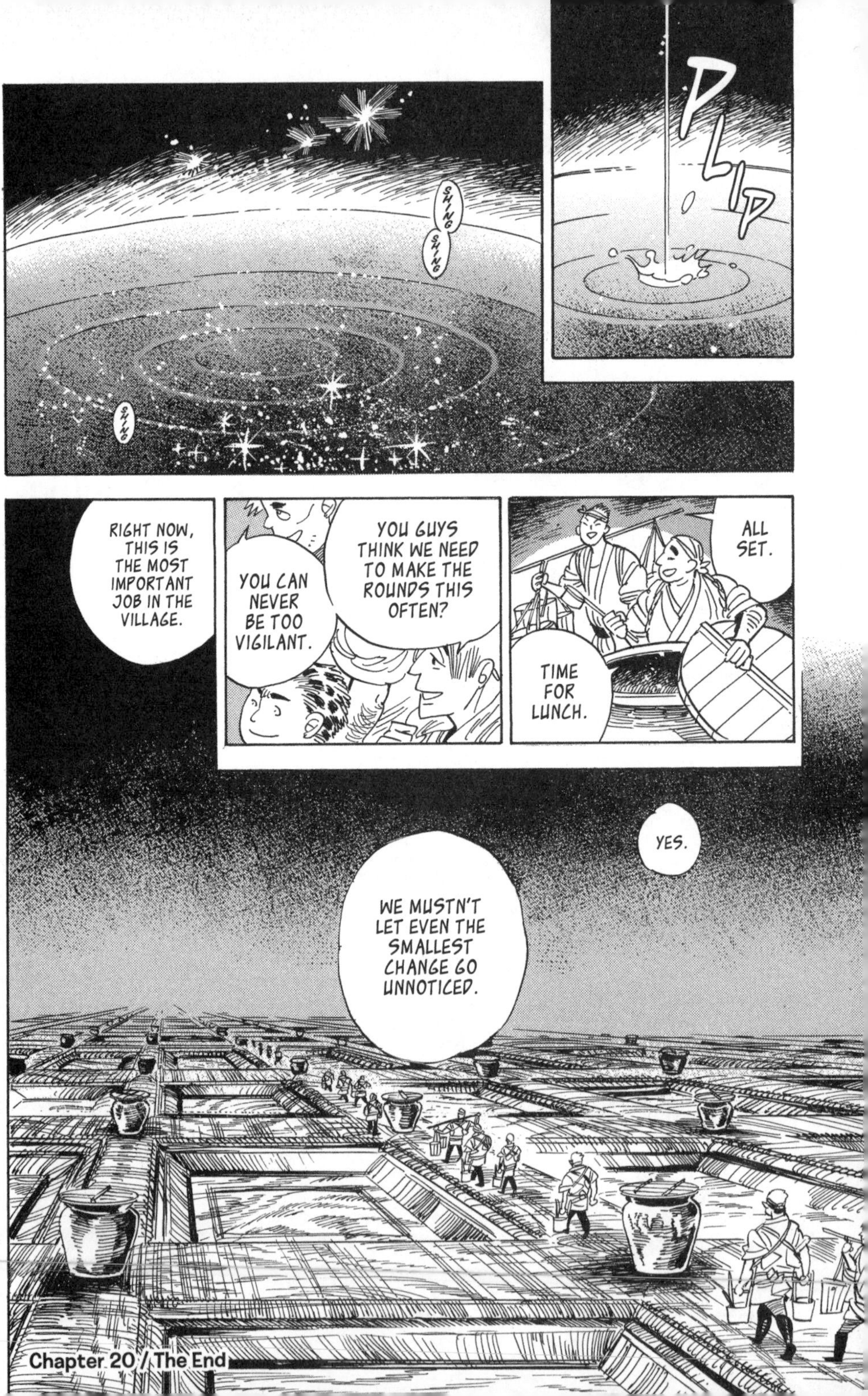
PLIP
SHING SHING
SHING
SHING
ALL SET.
TIME FOR LUNCH.
YOU GUYS THINK WE NEED TO MAKE THE ROUNDS THIS OFTEN?
YOU CAN NEVER BE TOO VIGILANT.
RIGHT NOW, THIS IS THE MOST IMPORTANT JOB IN THE VILLAGE.
YES.
WE MUSTN'T LET EVEN THE SMALLEST CHANGE GO UNNOTICED.

Chapter 20 / The End

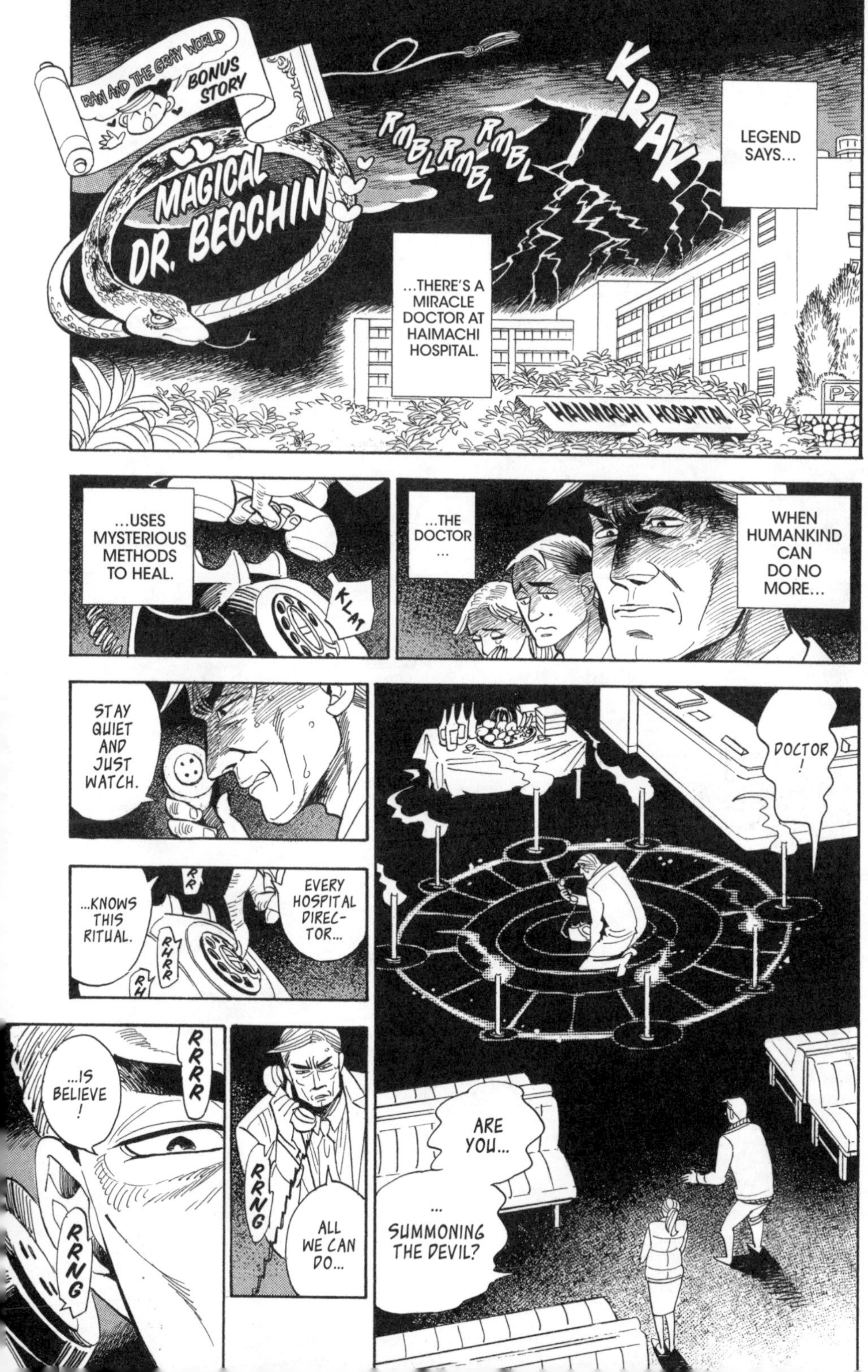
RAN AND THE GRAY WORLD
BONUS STORY
MAGICAL DR. BECCHIN
LEGEND SAYS...
KRAK
RMBL RMBL RMBL
...THERE'S A MIRACLE DOCTOR AT HAIMACHI HOSPITAL.
HAIMACHI HOSPITAL
WHEN HUMANKIND CAN DO NO MORE...
...THE DOCTOR ...
...USES MYSTERIOUS METHODS TO HEAL.
KLAT
DOCTOR!
ARE YOU...
...SUMMONING THE DEVIL?
STAY QUIET AND JUST WATCH.
EVERY HOSPITAL DIRECTOR...
...KNOWS THIS RITUAL.
RR
RHRR
RH
RRNG
ALL WE CAN DO...
RRRR
...IS BELIEVE!
RRNG

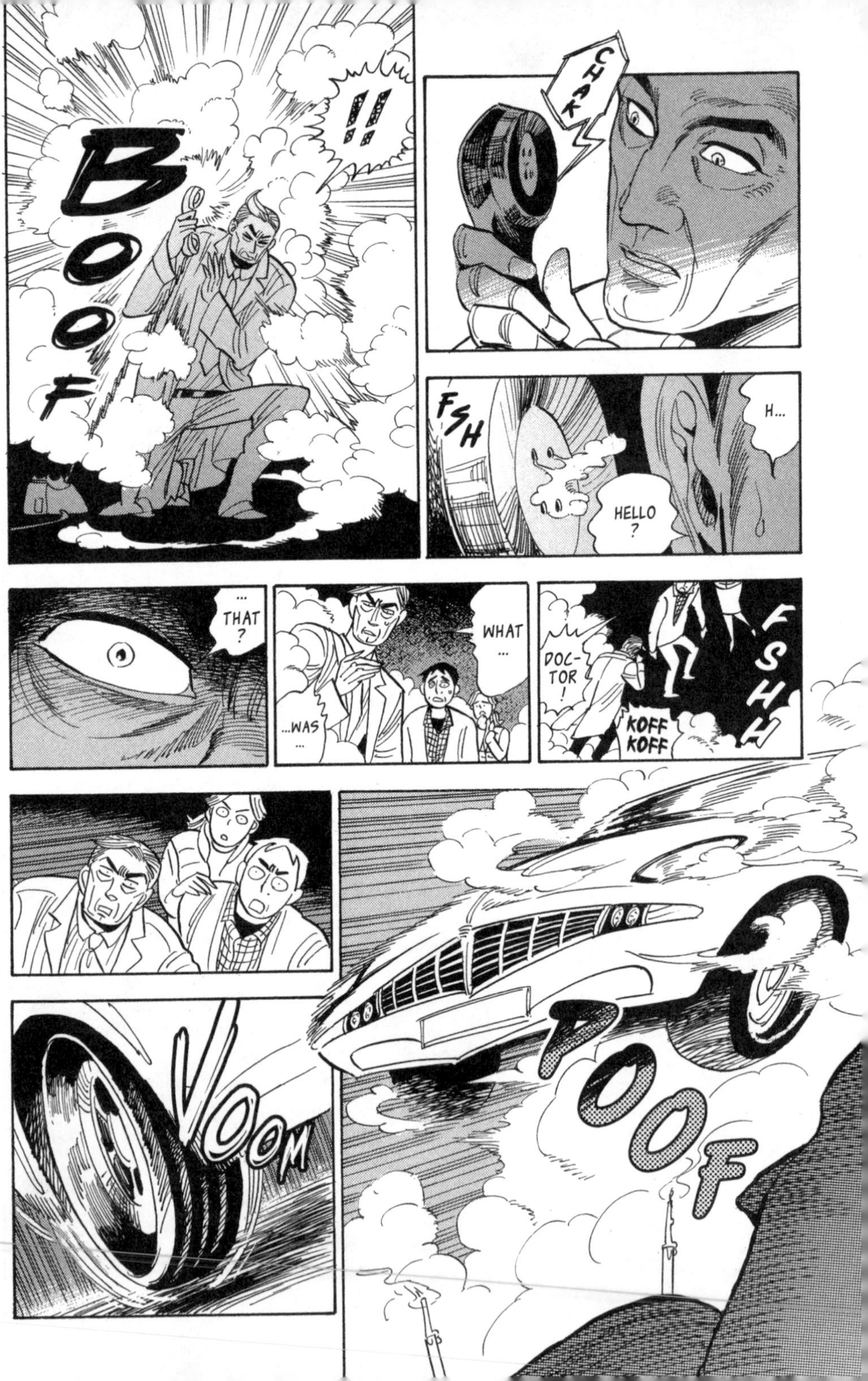
CHAK
FSH
H...
HELLO?
!!
BOOOOF
DOCTOR!
FSHH
KOFF KOFF
WHAT...
...WAS...
...THAT?
POOOF
VOOOM

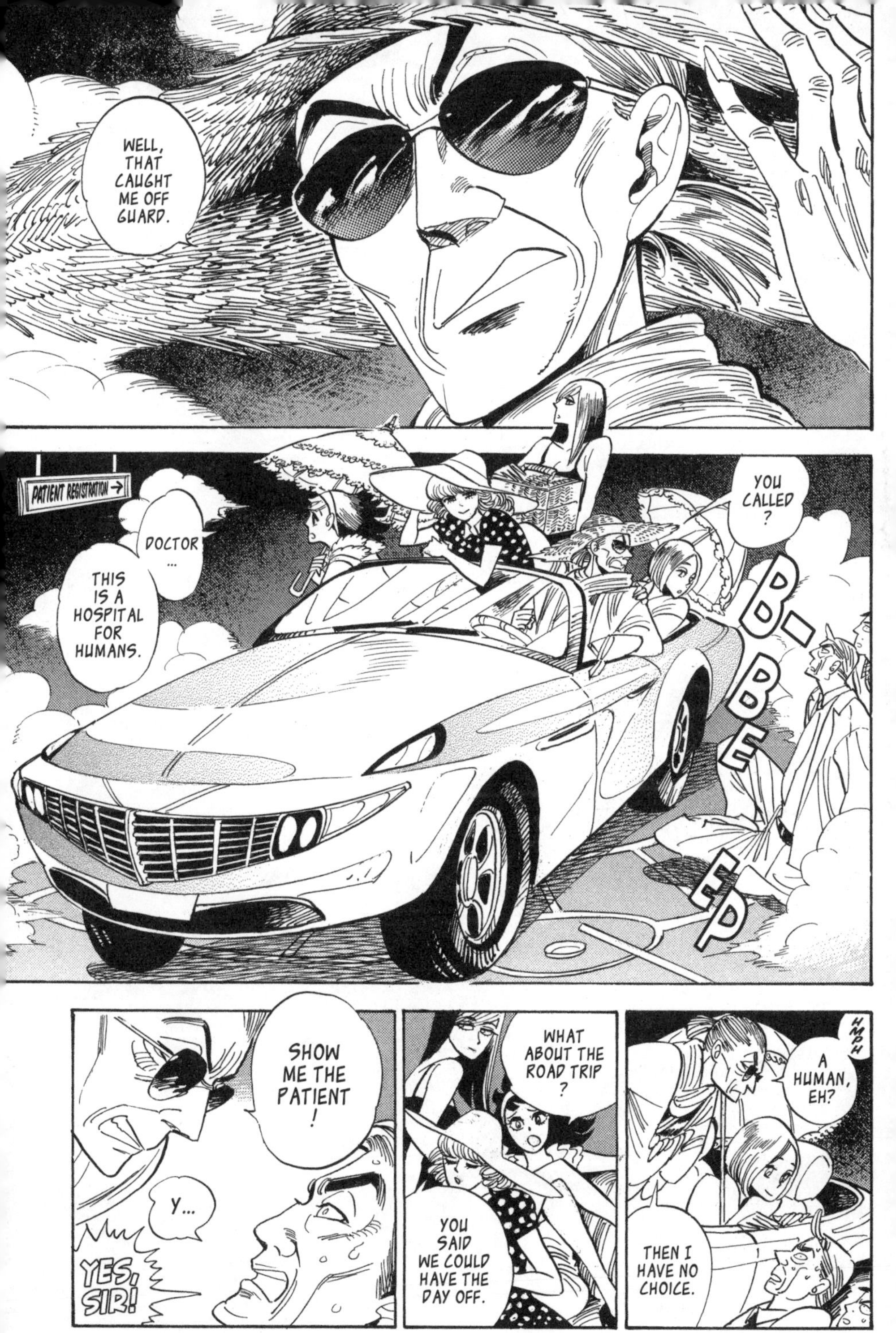
WELL, THAT CAUGHT ME OFF GUARD.
YOU CALLED?
B-BEEP
PATIENT REGISTRATION →
DOCTOR...
THIS IS A HOSPITAL FOR HUMANS.
HMPH
A HUMAN, EH?
THEN I HAVE NO CHOICE.
WHAT ABOUT THE ROAD TRIP?
YOU SAID WE COULD HAVE THE DAY OFF.
SHOW ME THE PATIENT!
Y...
YES, SIR!

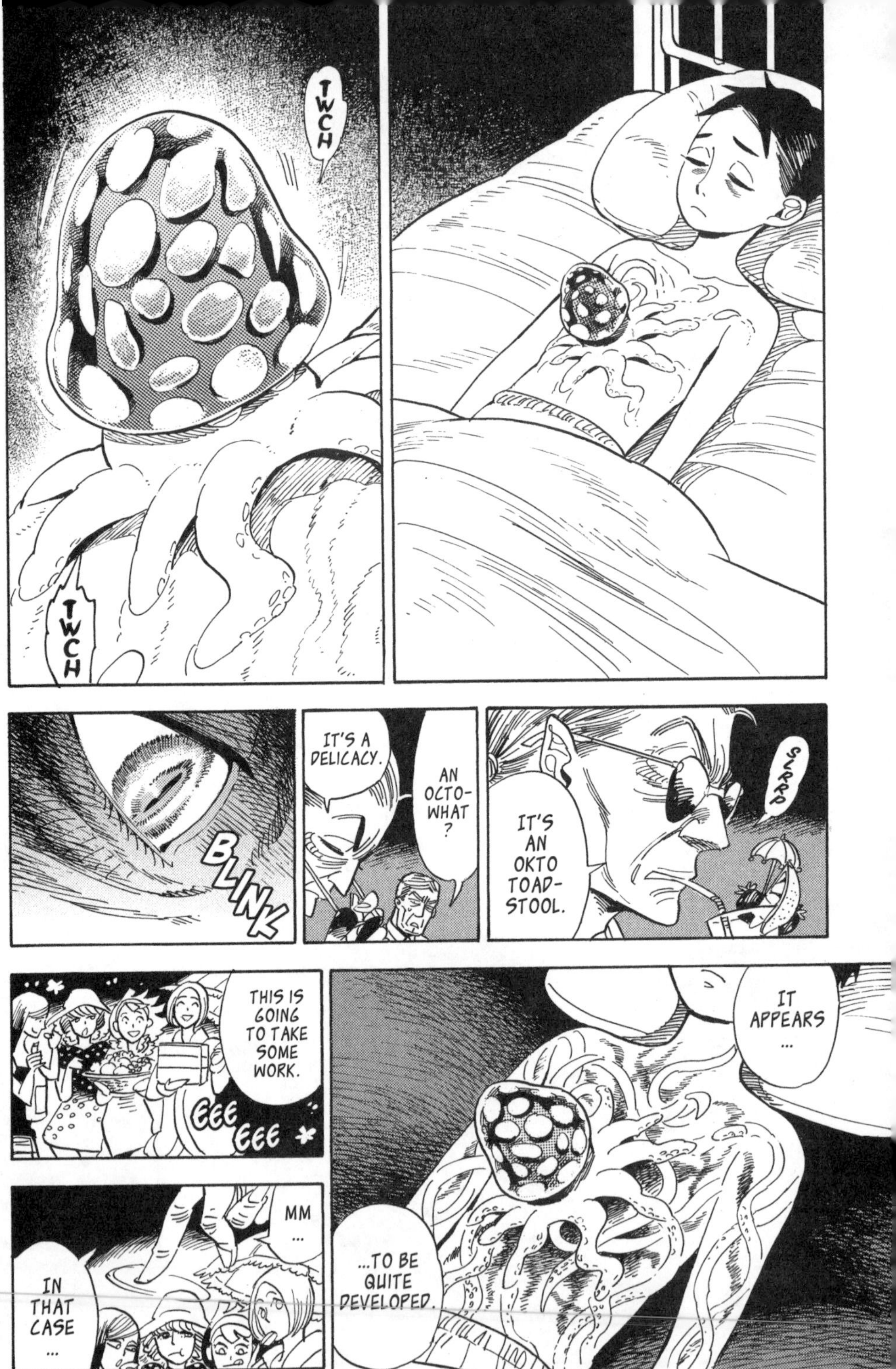
TWCH
TWCH
SLURP
IT'S AN OKTO TOADSTOOL.
AN OCTO-WHAT?
IT'S A DELICACY.
BLINK
IT APPEARS ...
...TO BE QUITE DEVELOPED.
THIS IS GOING TO TAKE SOME WORK.
EEE EEE
MM ...
IN THAT CASE ...

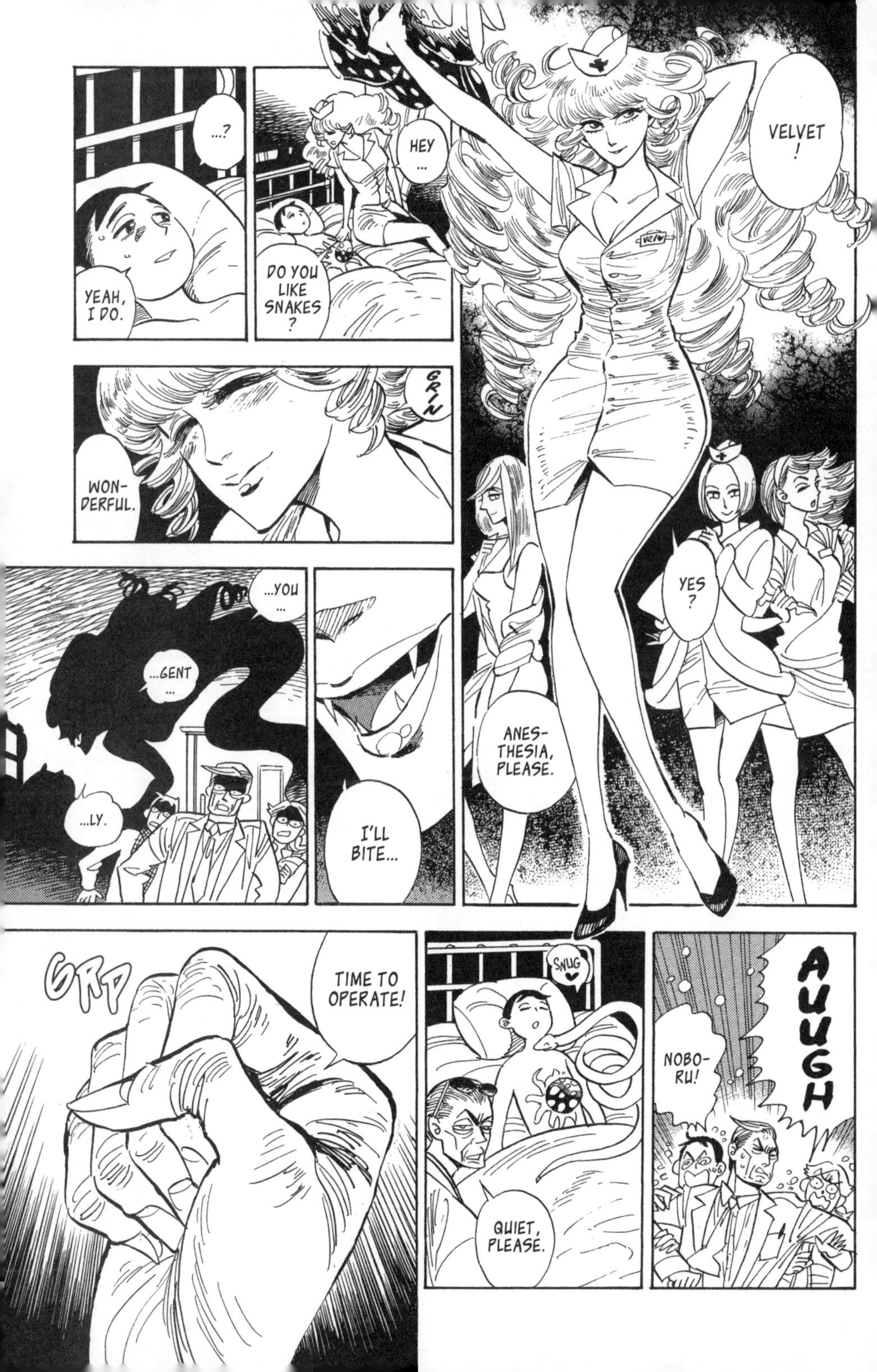
VELVET!
YES?
ANES-THESIA, PLEASE.
HEY ...
DO YOU LIKE SNAKES?
...?
YEAH, I DO.
GRIN
WON-DERFUL.
I'LL BITE...
...YOU ...
...GENT ...
...LY.
AUUGH
NOBO-RU!
SNUG
QUIET, PLEASE.
GRP
TIME TO OPERATE!

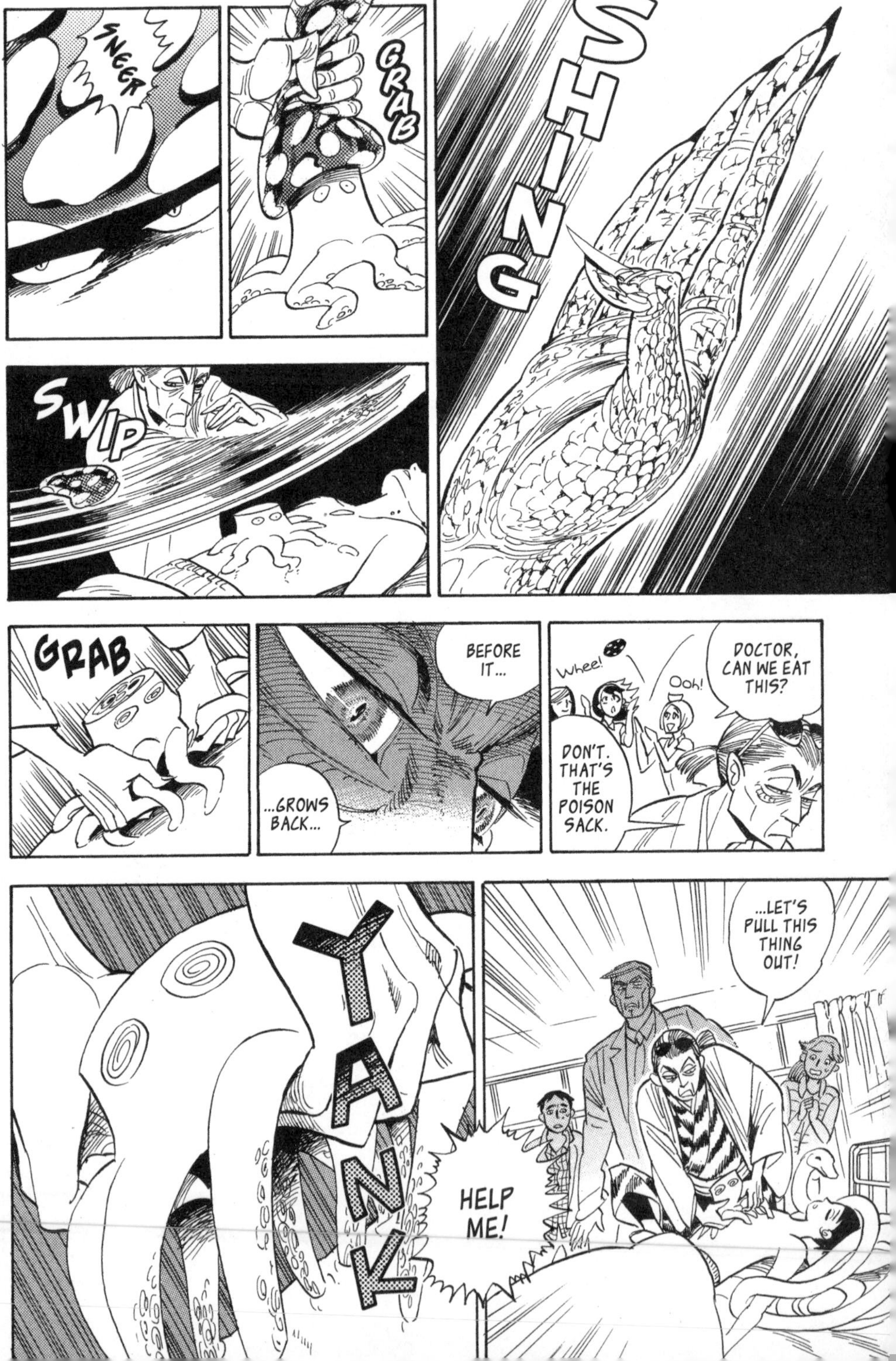
SHING
GRAB
SNEER
SWIP
DOCTOR, CAN WE EAT THIS?
Whee!
Ooh!
DON'T. THAT'S THE POISON SACK.
BEFORE IT...
...GROWS BACK...
GRAB
...LET'S PULL THIS THING OUT!
HELP ME!
YANK

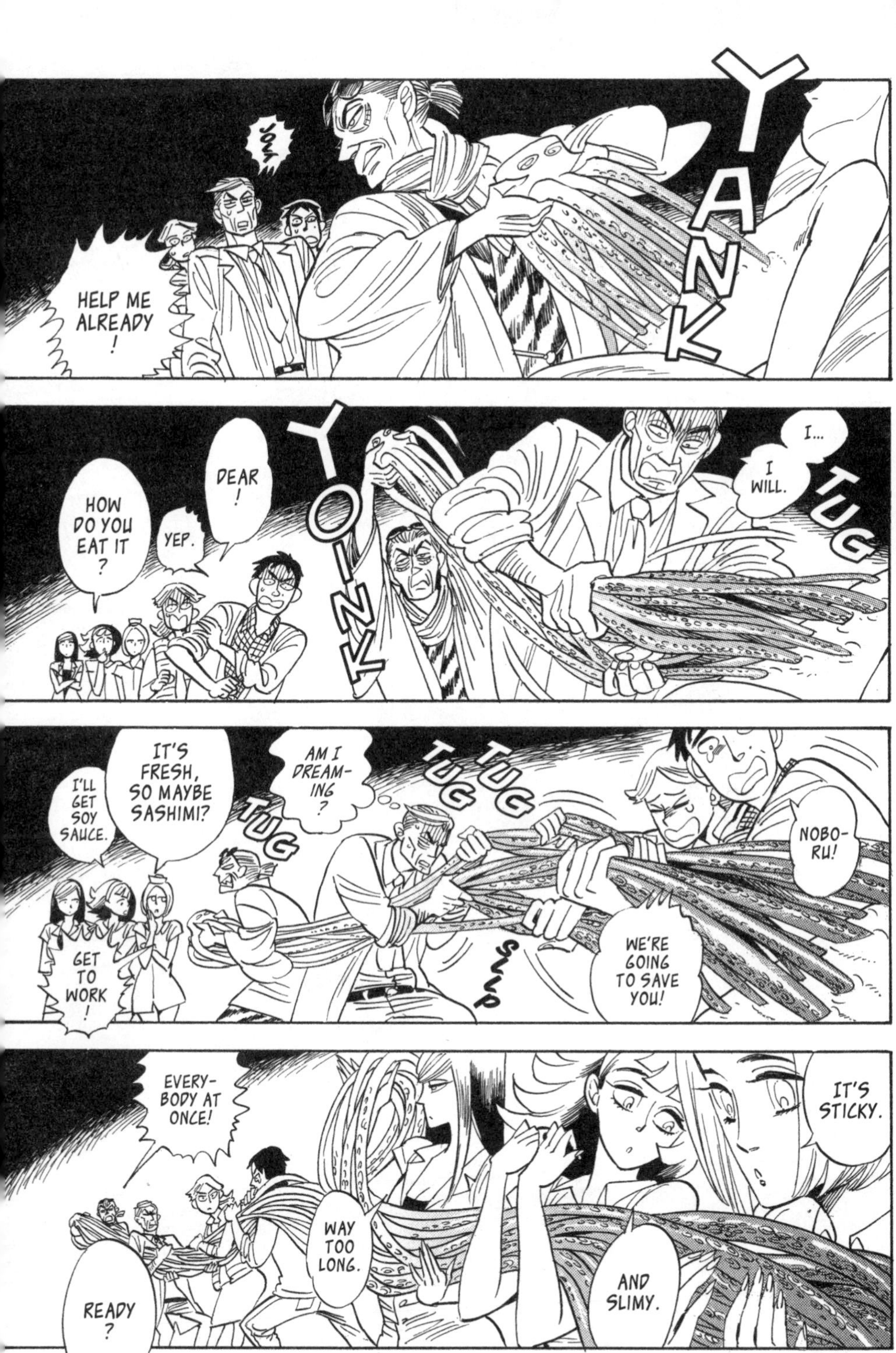
YANK
JOLT
HELP ME ALREADY!
I... I WILL.
TUG
YOINK
DEAR!
YEP.
HOW DO YOU EAT IT?
NOBO-RU!
WE'RE GOING TO SAVE YOU!
TUG TUG
AM I DREAMING?
TUG
IT'S FRESH, SO MAYBE SASHIMI?
I'LL GET SOY SAUCE.
GET TO WORK!
IT'S STICKY.
AND SLIMY.
WAY TOO LONG.
EVERYBODY AT ONCE!
READY?

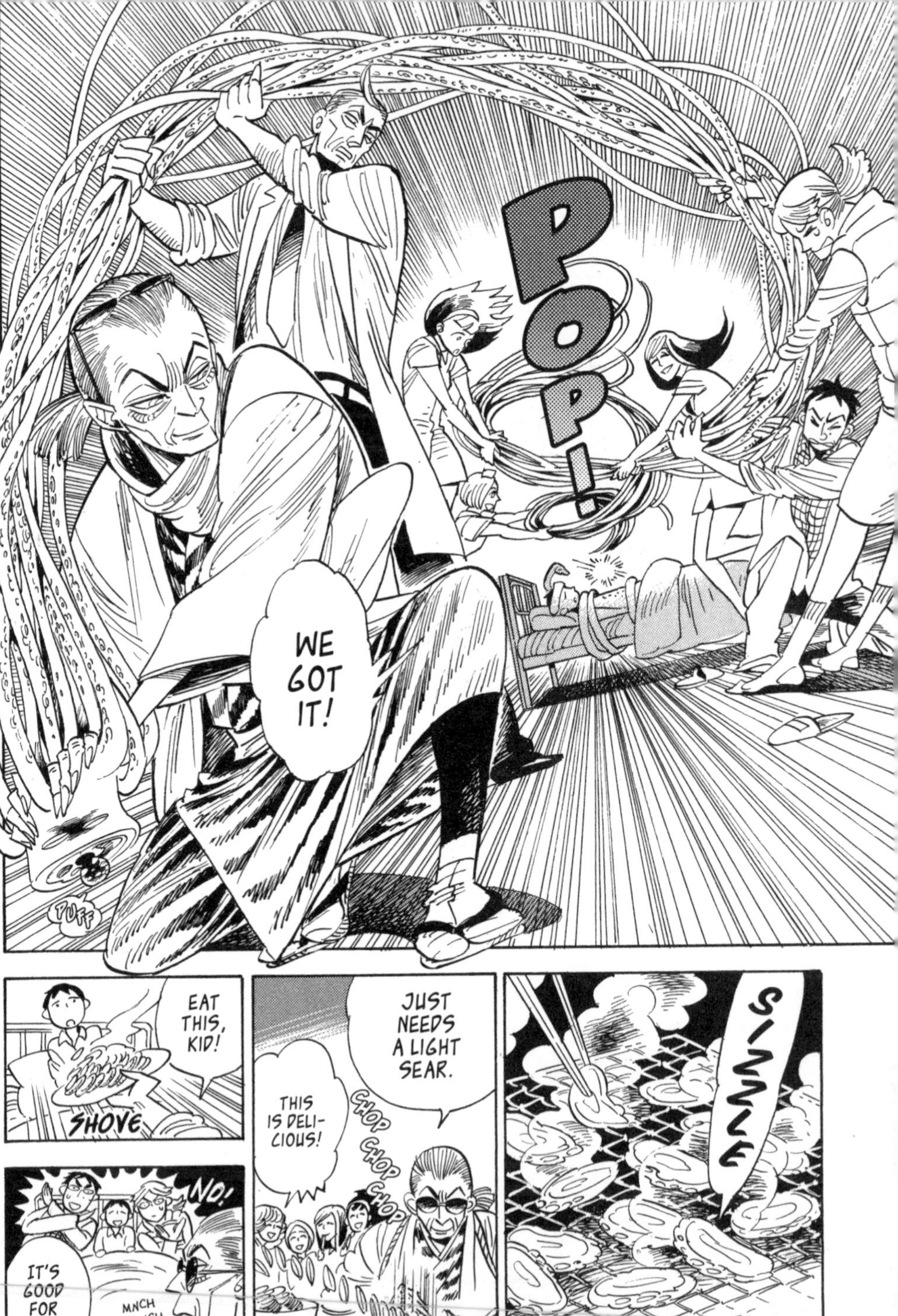
POP!
WE GOT IT!
PUFF
SIZZLE
JUST NEEDS A LIGHT SEAR.
CHOP CHOP CHOP CHOP
THIS IS DELICIOUS!
EAT THIS, KID!
SHOVE
NO!
IT'S GOOD FOR VITALITY.
MNCH MNCH

Bonus Story / The End

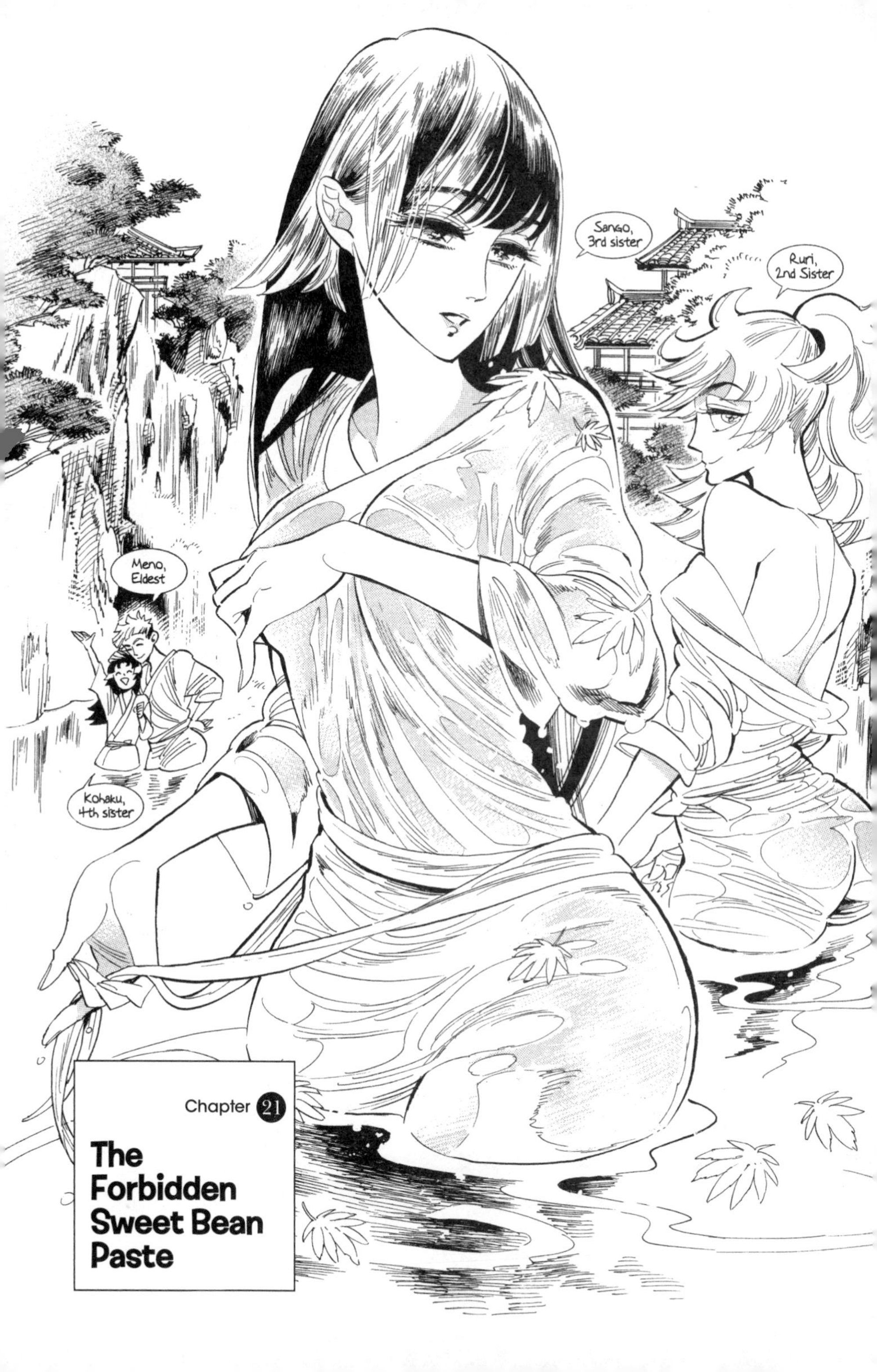
Ruri, 2nd Sister
Sango, 3rd sister
Meno, Eldest
Kohaku, 4th sister

Chapter 21

The Forbidden Sweet Bean Paste

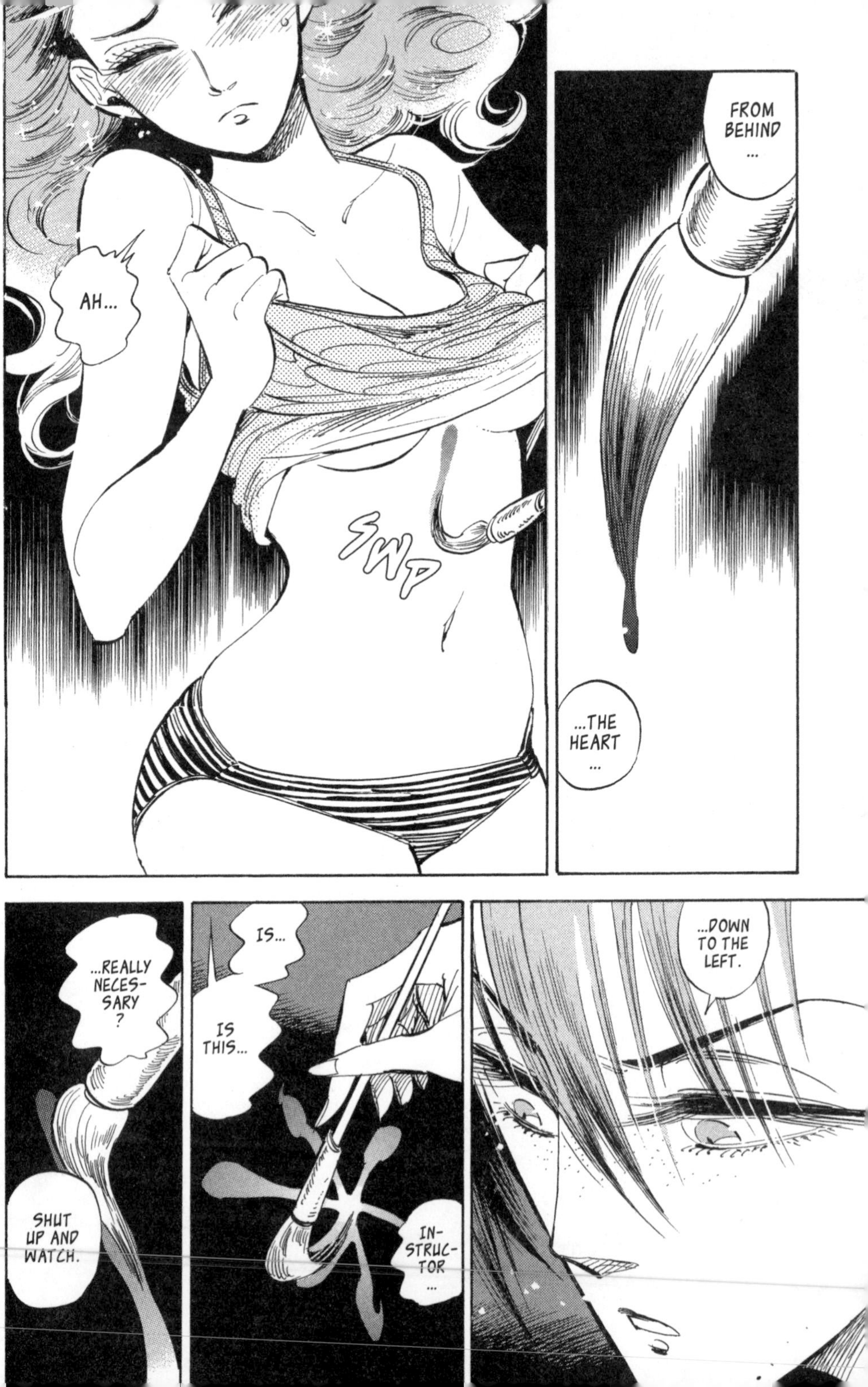
FROM BEHIND ...
...THE HEART ...
AH...
SWP
...DOWN TO THE LEFT.
IS...
IS THIS...
IN-STRUC-TOR ...
...REALLY NECES-SARY ?
SHUT UP AND WATCH.

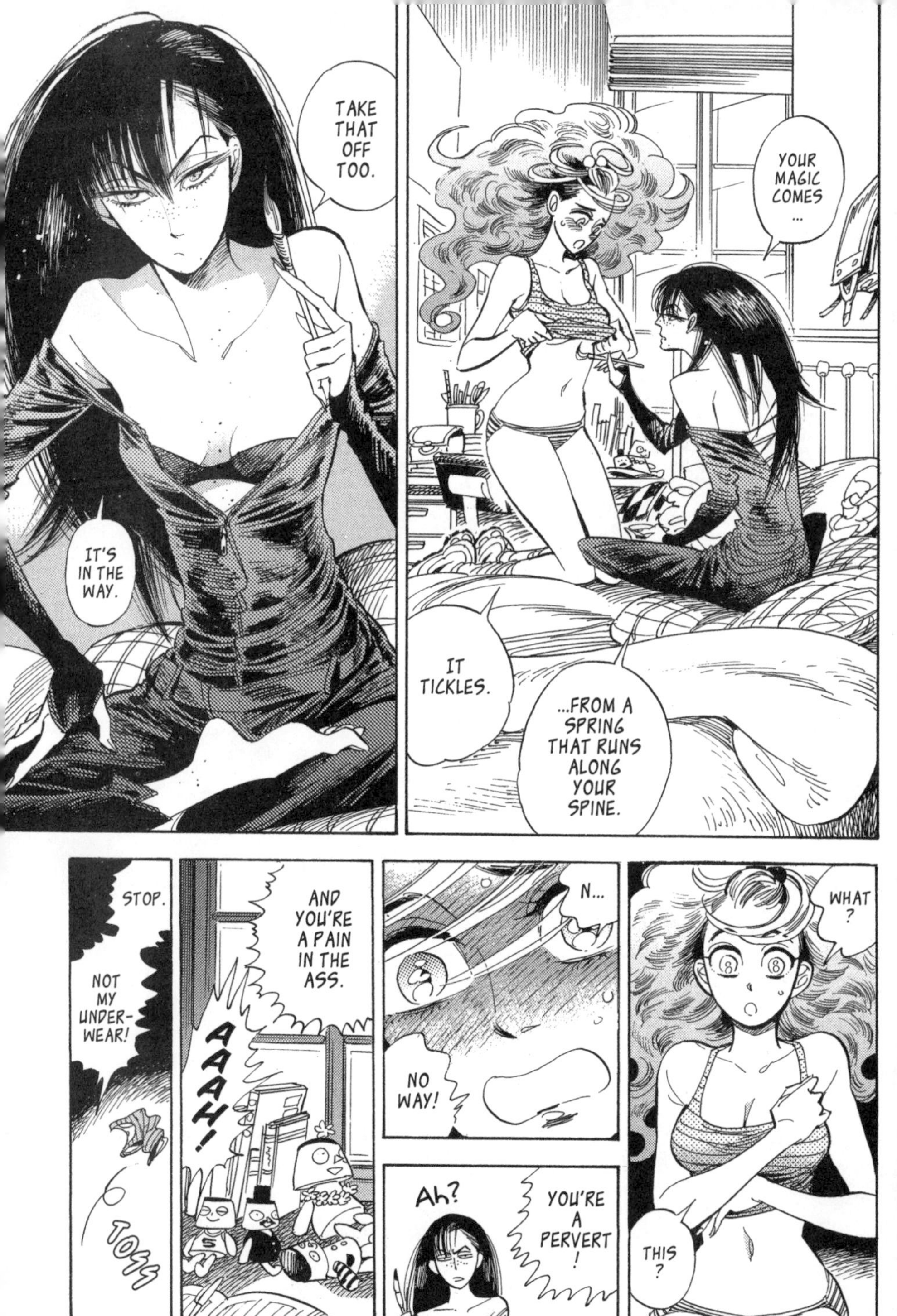
YOUR MAGIC COMES ...
...FROM A SPRING THAT RUNS ALONG YOUR SPINE.
IT TICKLES.
TAKE THAT OFF TOO.
IT'S IN THE WAY.
WHAT?
THIS?
N...
NO WAY!
Ah?
YOU'RE A PERVERT!
AND YOU'RE A PAIN IN THE ASS.
AAAAH!
STOP.
NOT MY UNDER-WEAR!
TOSS

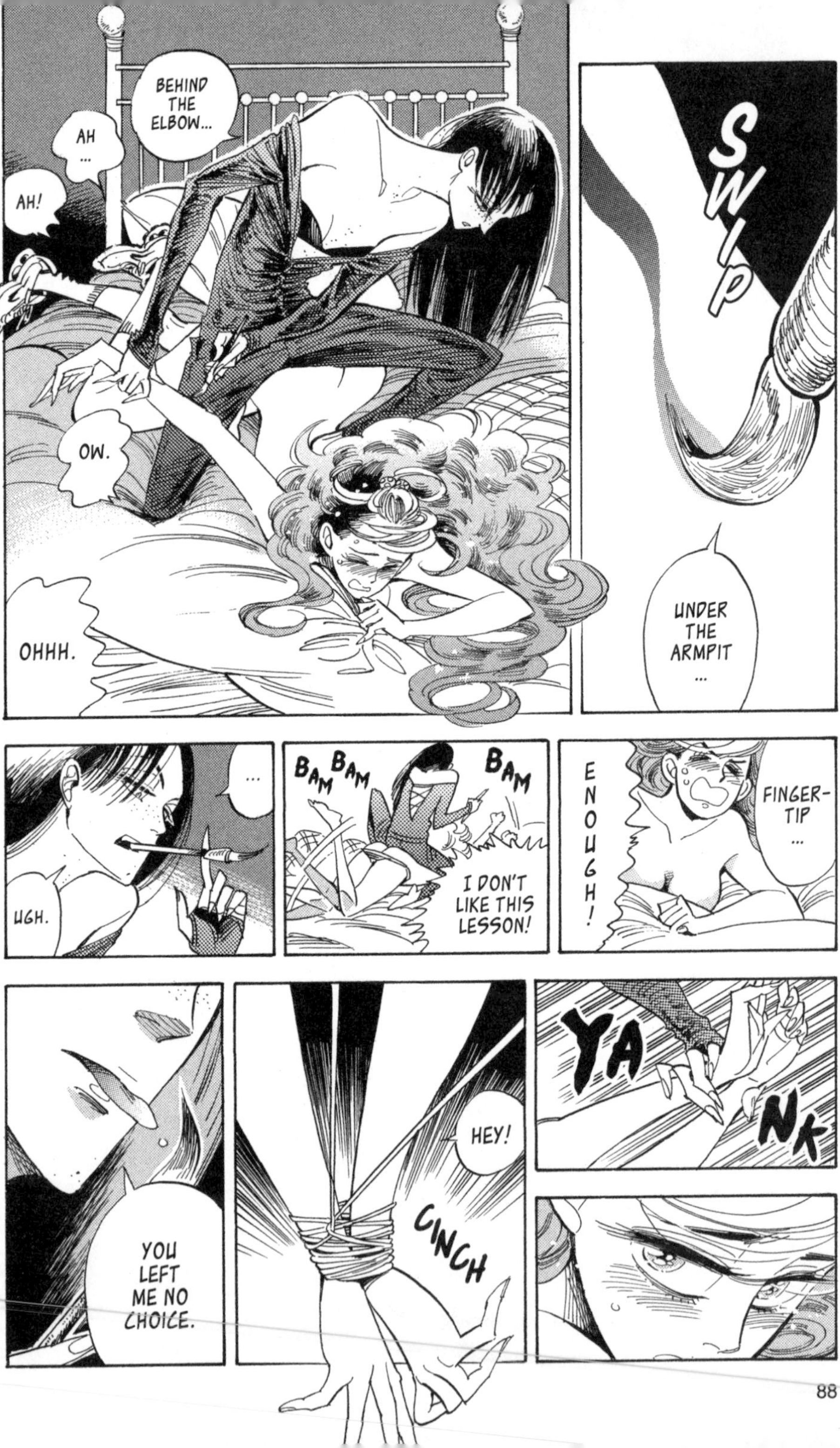
SWIP
UNDER THE ARMPIT ...
BEHIND THE ELBOW...
AH ...
AH!
OW.
OHHH.
FINGER-TIP ...
ENOUGH!
BAM BAM BAM
I DON'T LIKE THIS LESSON!
...
UGH.
YANK
HEY!
CINCH
YOU LEFT ME NO CHOICE.

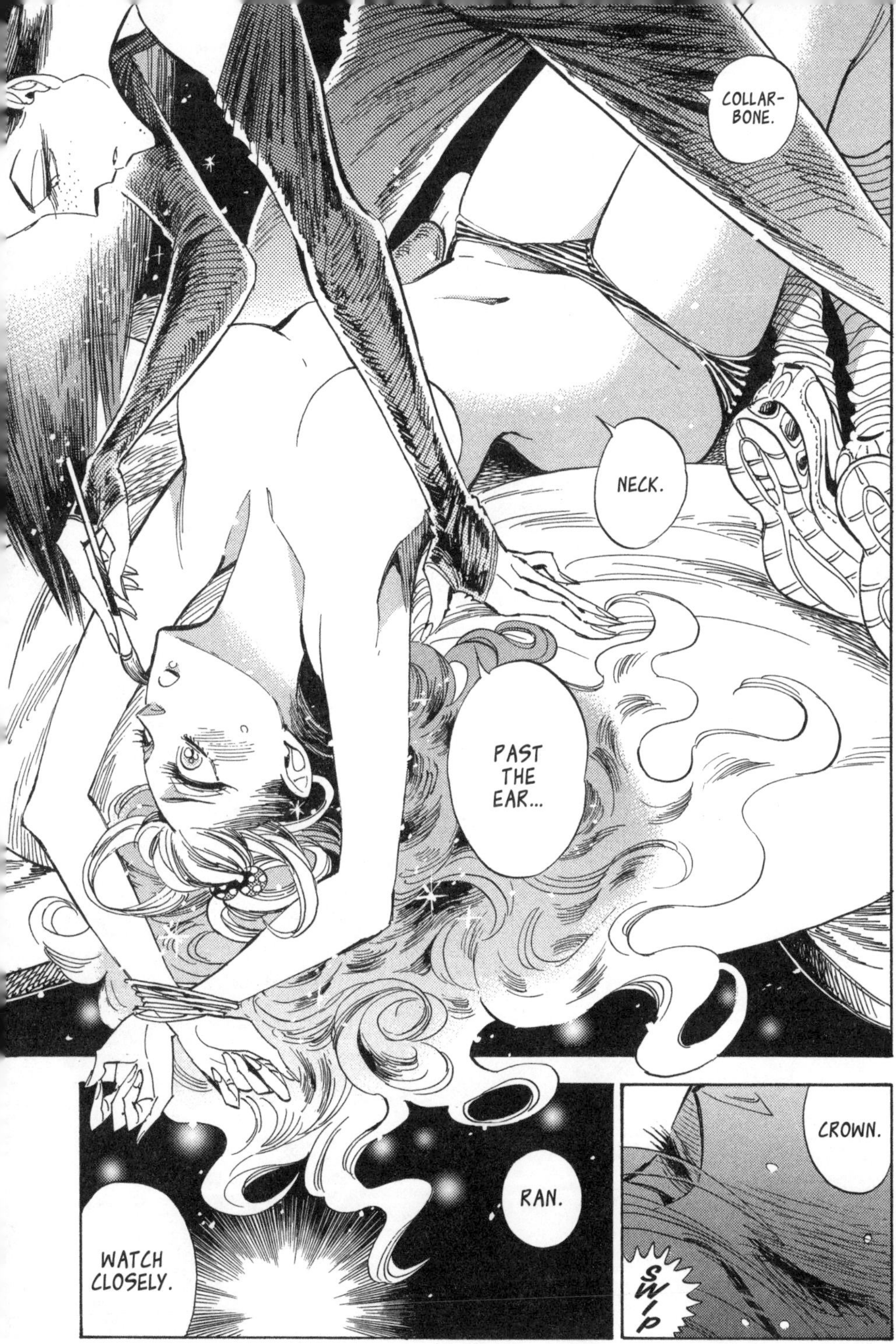
COLLAR-BONE.
NECK.
PAST THE EAR...
CROWN.
SWIP
RAN.
WATCH CLOSELY.

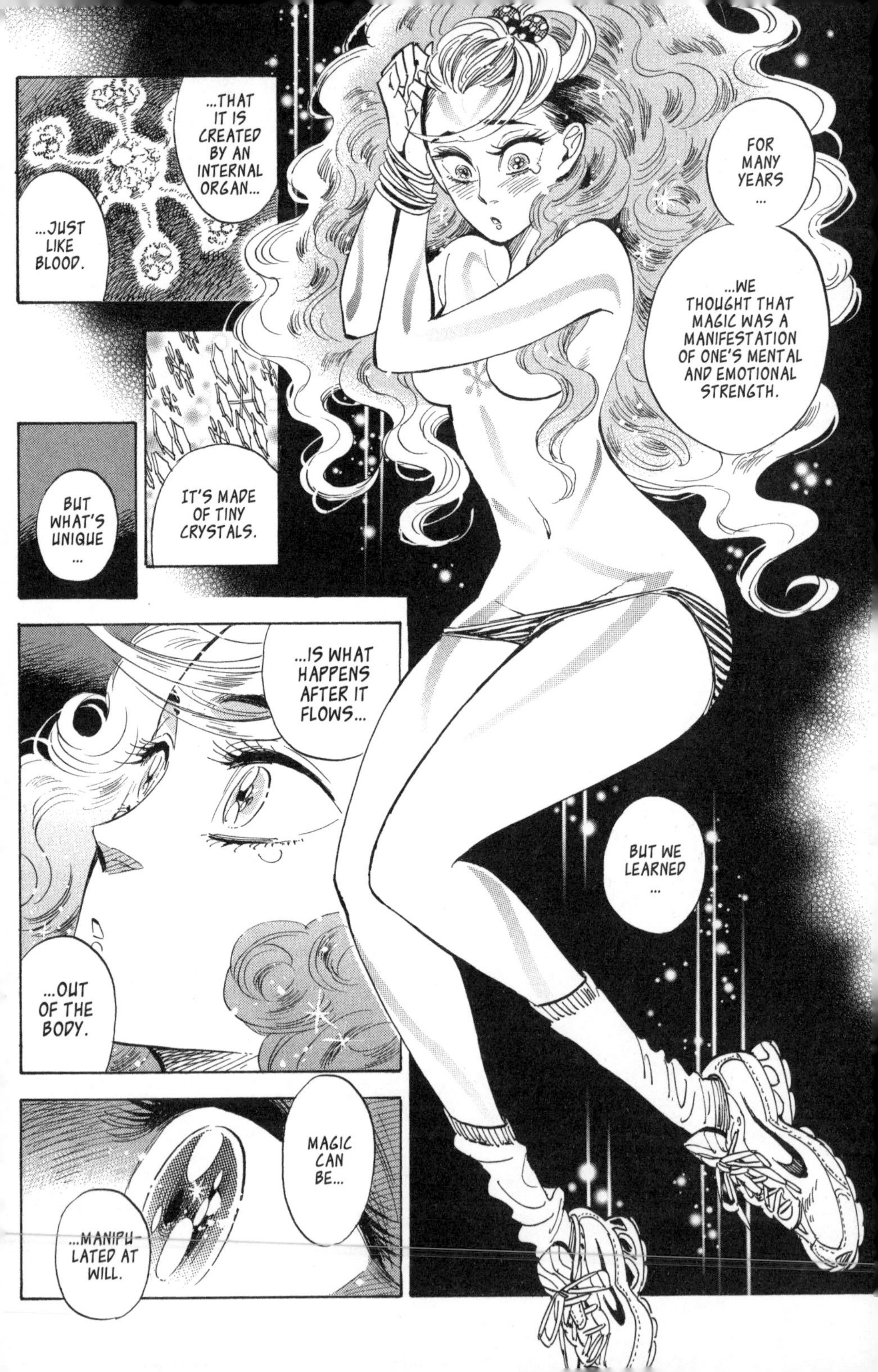
FOR MANY YEARS...
...WE THOUGHT THAT MAGIC WAS A MANIFESTATION OF ONE'S MENTAL AND EMOTIONAL STRENGTH.
BUT WE LEARNED...
...THAT IT IS CREATED BY AN INTERNAL ORGAN...
...JUST LIKE BLOOD.
IT'S MADE OF TINY CRYSTALS.
BUT WHAT'S UNIQUE...
...IS WHAT HAPPENS AFTER IT FLOWS...
...OUT OF THE BODY.
MAGIC CAN BE...
...MANIPULATED AT WILL.

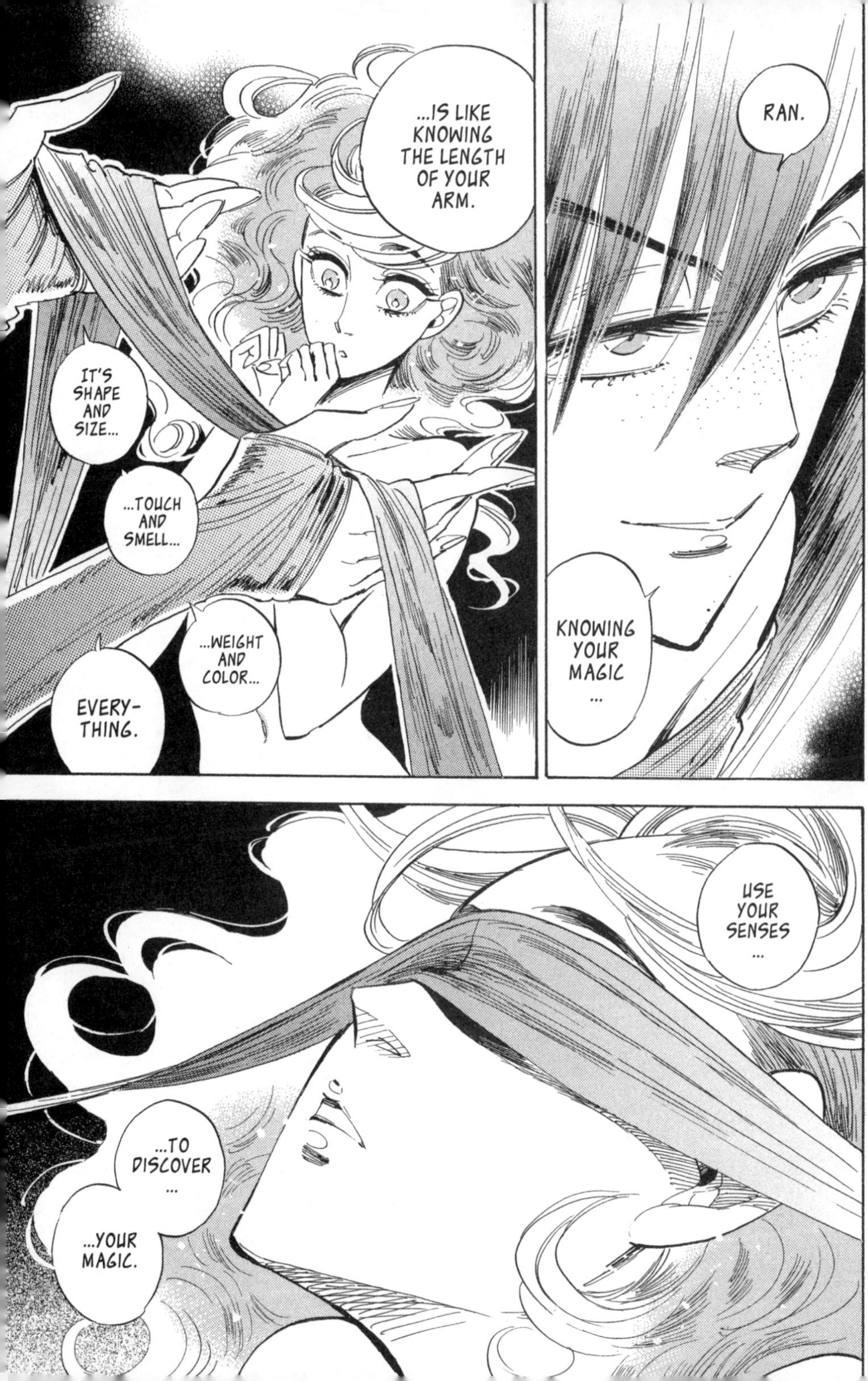
RAN.
KNOWING YOUR MAGIC...
...IS LIKE KNOWING THE LENGTH OF YOUR ARM.
IT'S SHAPE AND SIZE...
...TOUCH AND SMELL...
...WEIGHT AND COLOR...
EVERY-THING.
USE YOUR SENSES...
...TO DISCOVER...
...YOUR MAGIC.

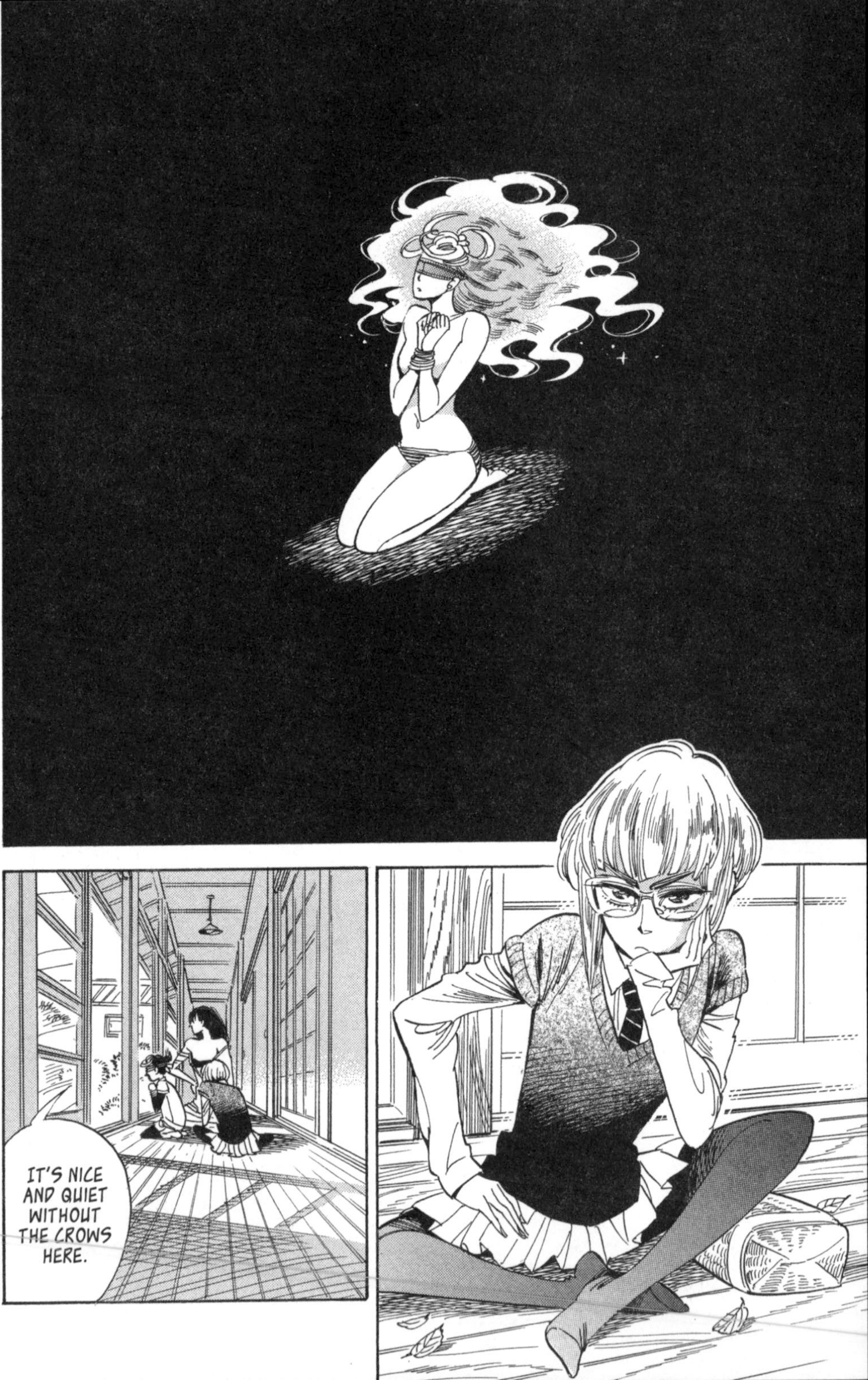
IT'S NICE AND QUIET WITHOUT THE CROWS HERE.

...SHIZUKA SAID HER MAGIC...

YEARS AGO...

...WAS LIKE THE OCEAN.

...OF AIR.

FWT

THE MOVE-MENT...

RUSTLE

AIR.

...

WHAT'S YOURS LIKE, NIO?

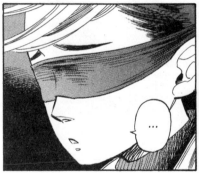

...

RAN?

...WIND.

LIKE...

FWOO

93

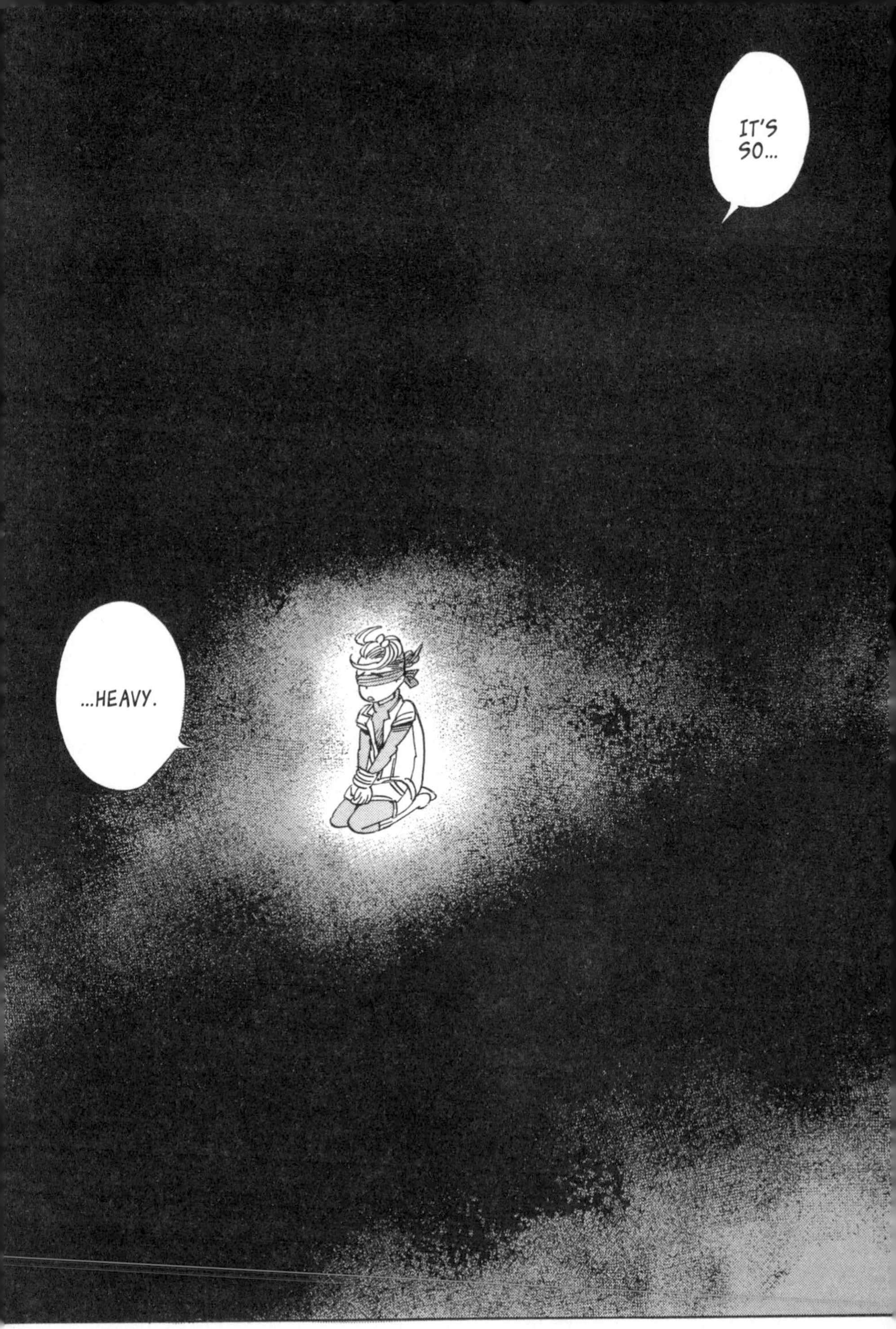
IT'S SO...
...HEAVY.

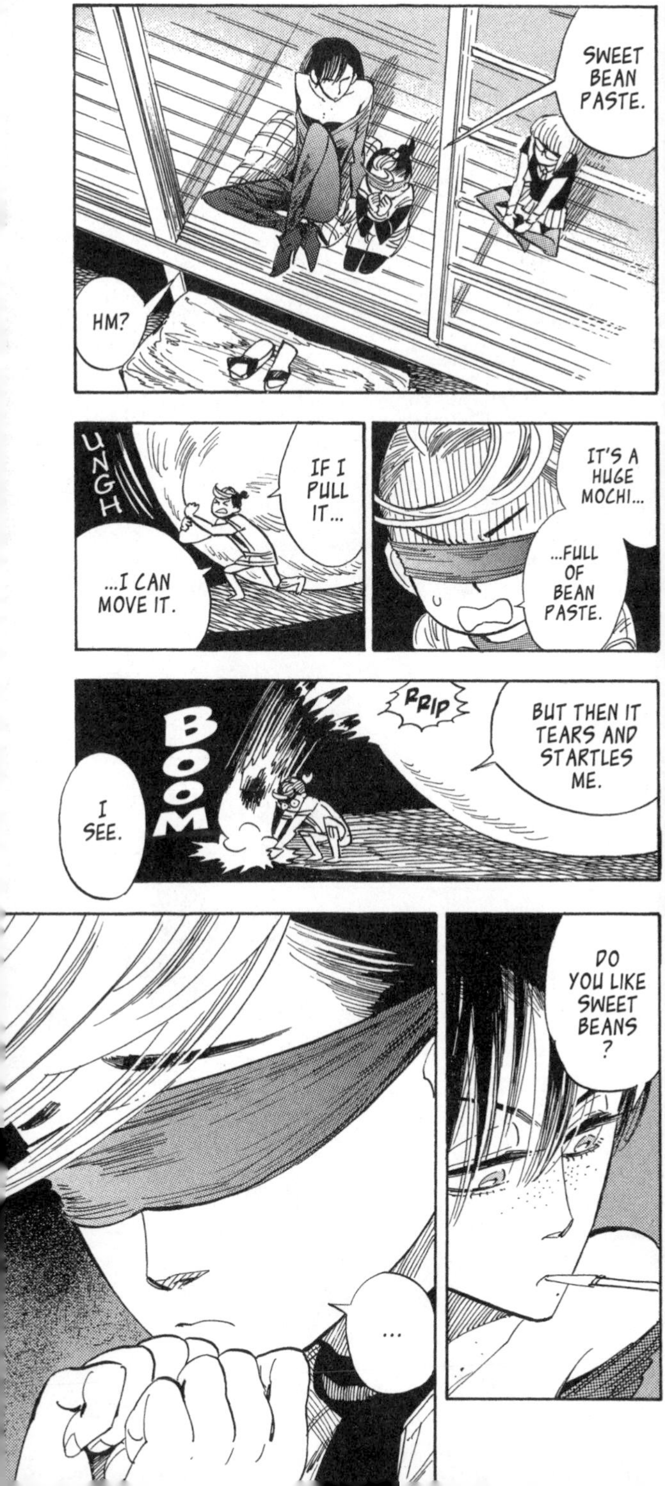
SWEET BEAN PASTE.
HM?
IT'S A HUGE MOCHI...
...FULL OF BEAN PASTE.
IF I PULL IT...
UNGH
...I CAN MOVE IT.
RRIP
BUT THEN IT TEARS AND STARTLES ME.
BOOM
I SEE.
DO YOU LIKE SWEET BEANS?
...

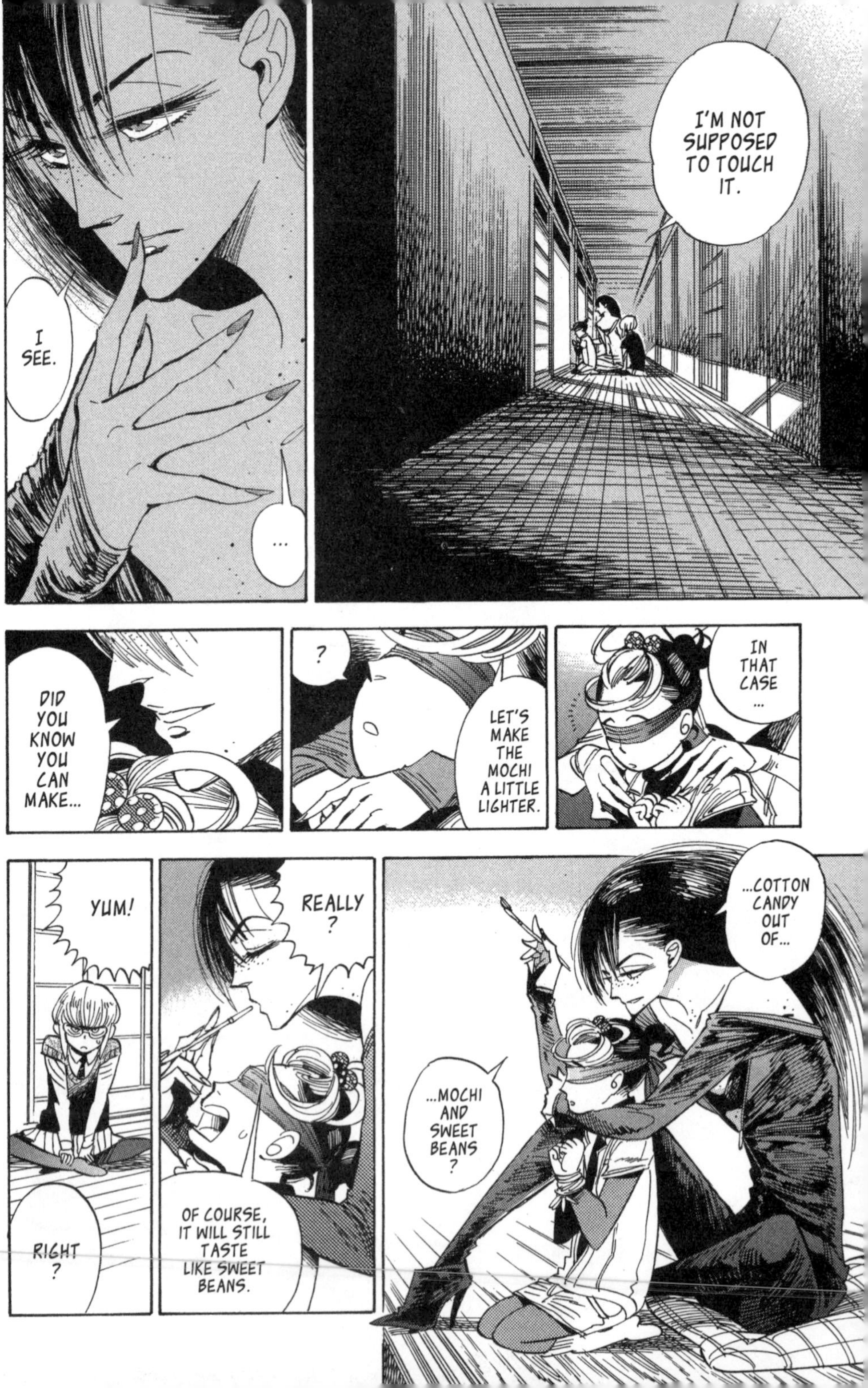
I'M NOT SUPPOSED TO TOUCH IT.
I SEE.
...
IN THAT CASE ...
LET'S MAKE THE MOCHI A LITTLE LIGHTER.
?
DID YOU KNOW YOU CAN MAKE...
...COTTON CANDY OUT OF...
...MOCHI AND SWEET BEANS ?
REALLY ?
OF COURSE, IT WILL STILL TASTE LIKE SWEET BEANS.
YUM!
RIGHT ?

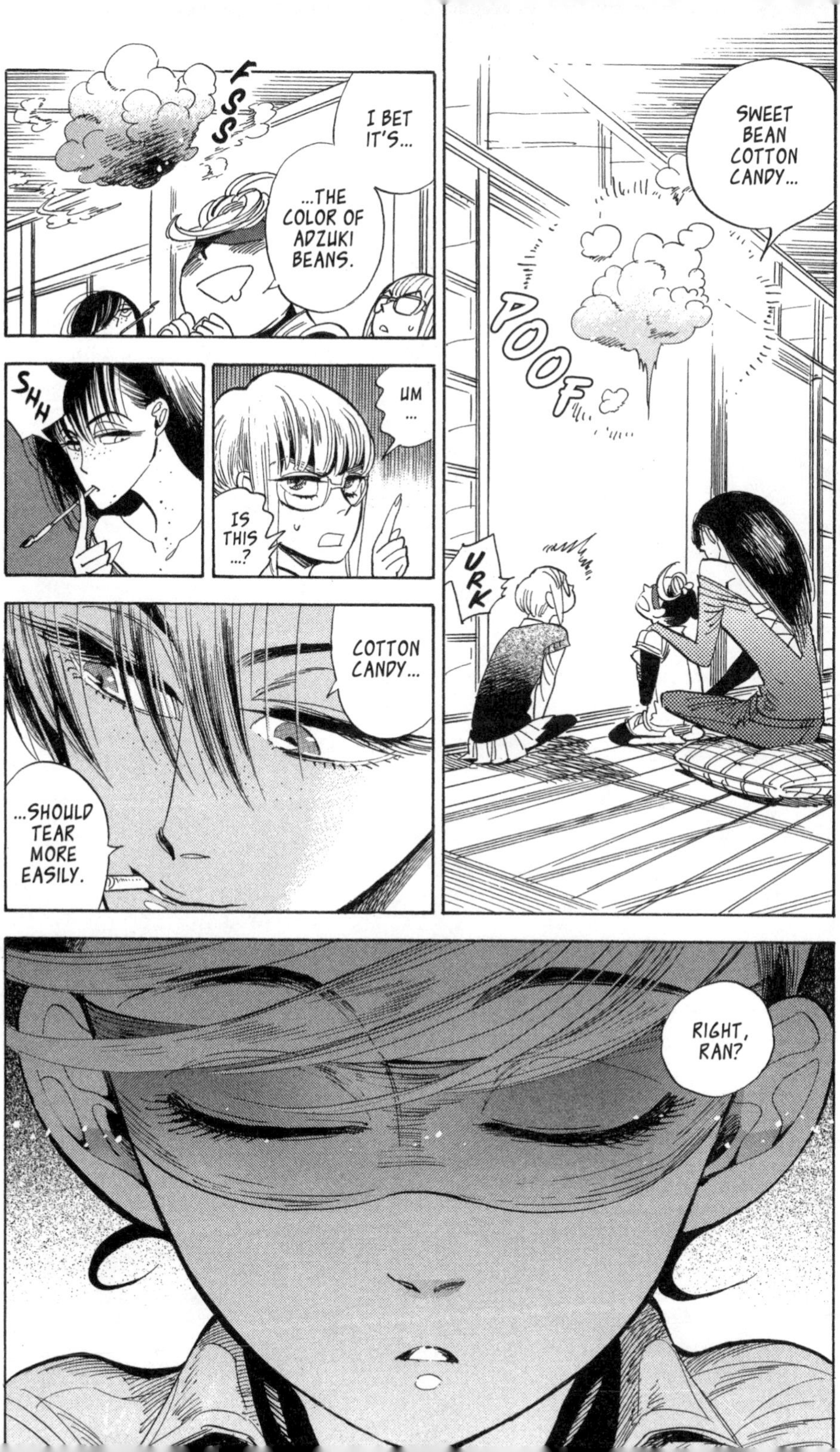
SWEET BEAN COTTON CANDY...
POOF
URK
I BET IT'S...
...THE COLOR OF ADZUKI BEANS.
FSS
UM ...
IS THIS ...?
SHH
COTTON CANDY...
...SHOULD TEAR MORE EASILY.
RIGHT, RAN?

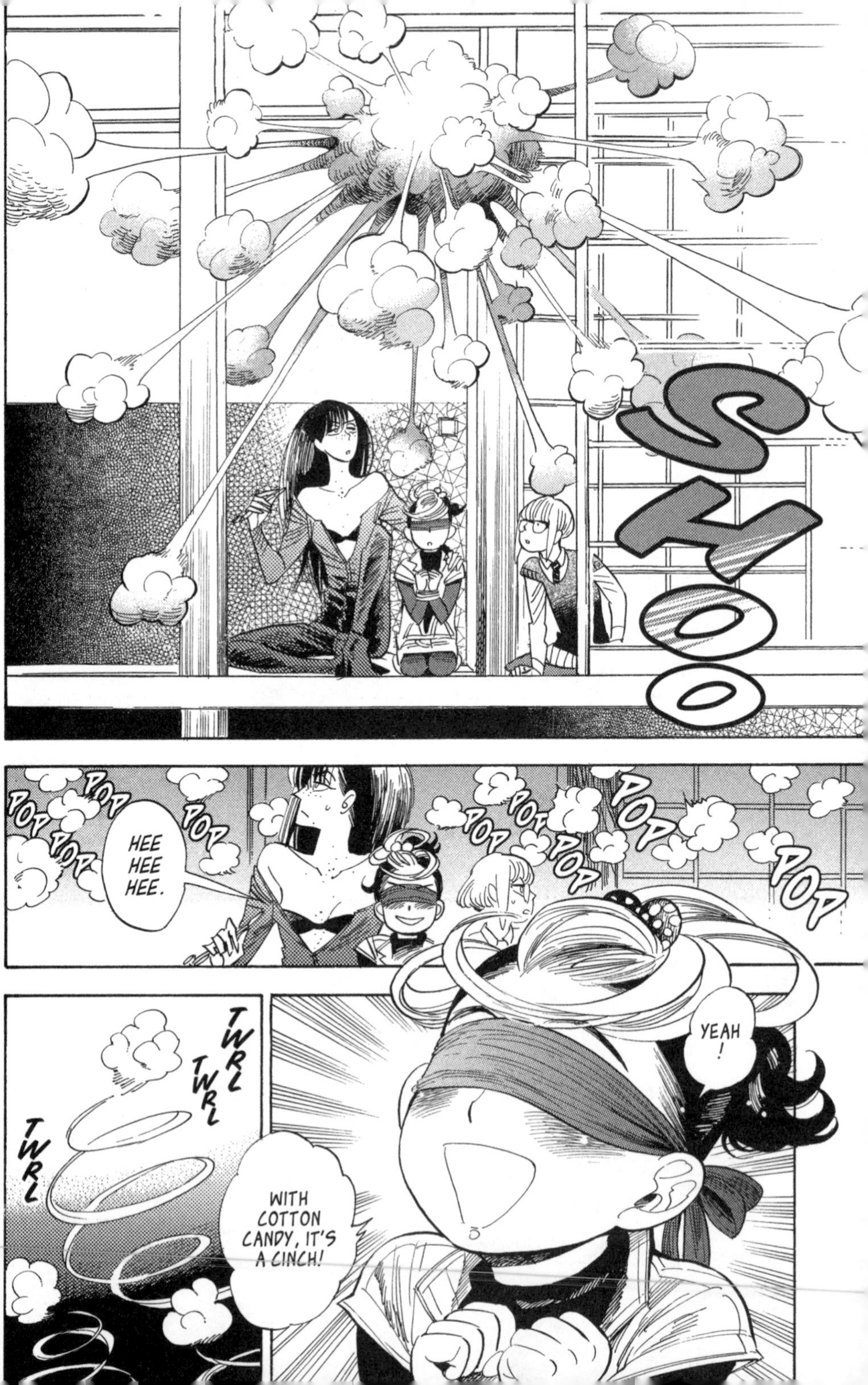
SHOOO
POP POP POP POP
POP
HEE HEE HEE.
POP POP POP POP
POP
POP
YEAH!
TWRL TWRL
TWRL
WITH COTTON CANDY, IT'S A CINCH!

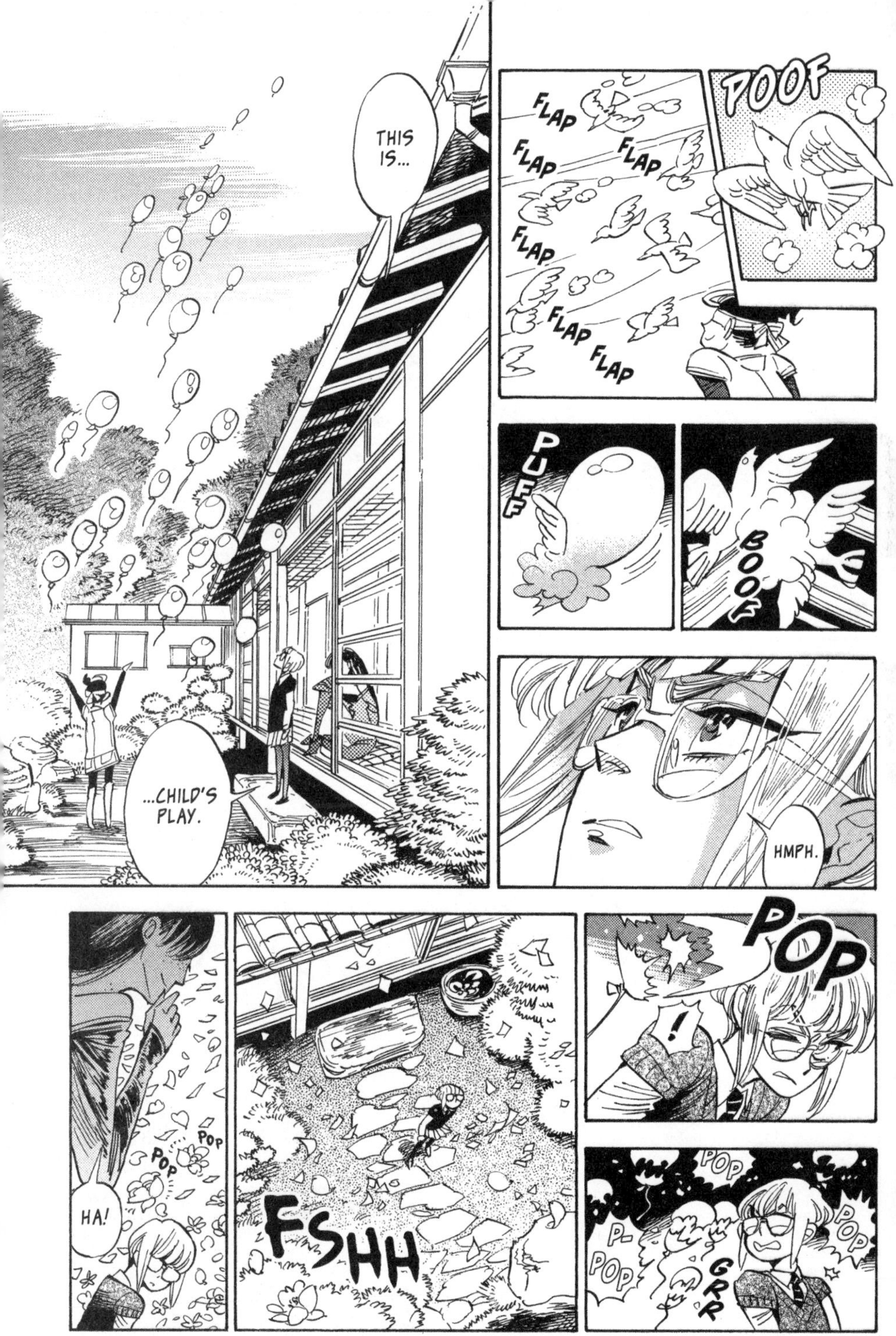
POOF
FLAP
FLAP
FLAP
FLAP
FLAP
FLAP
FLAP
THIS IS...
...CHILD'S PLAY.
BOOF
PUFF
HMPH.
POP
!
POP
P-
POP
GRR
POP
FSHH
POP
POP
HA!

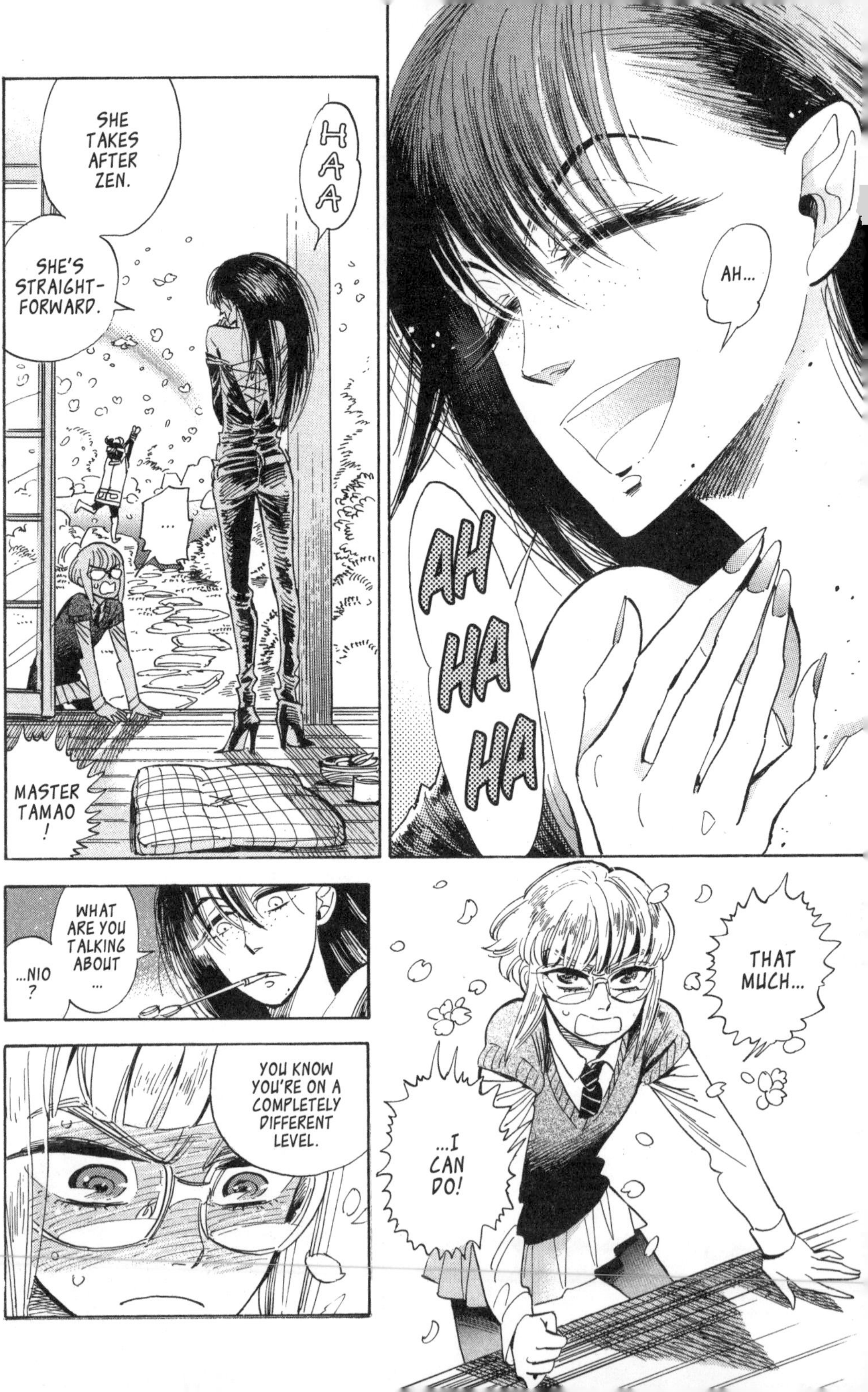
AH...
AH HA HA HA
HAA
SHE TAKES AFTER ZEN.
SHE'S STRAIGHT-FORWARD.
...
MASTER TAMAO!
WHAT ARE YOU TALKING ABOUT ... ...NIO?
YOU KNOW YOU'RE ON A COMPLETELY DIFFERENT LEVEL.
THAT MUCH...
...I CAN DO!

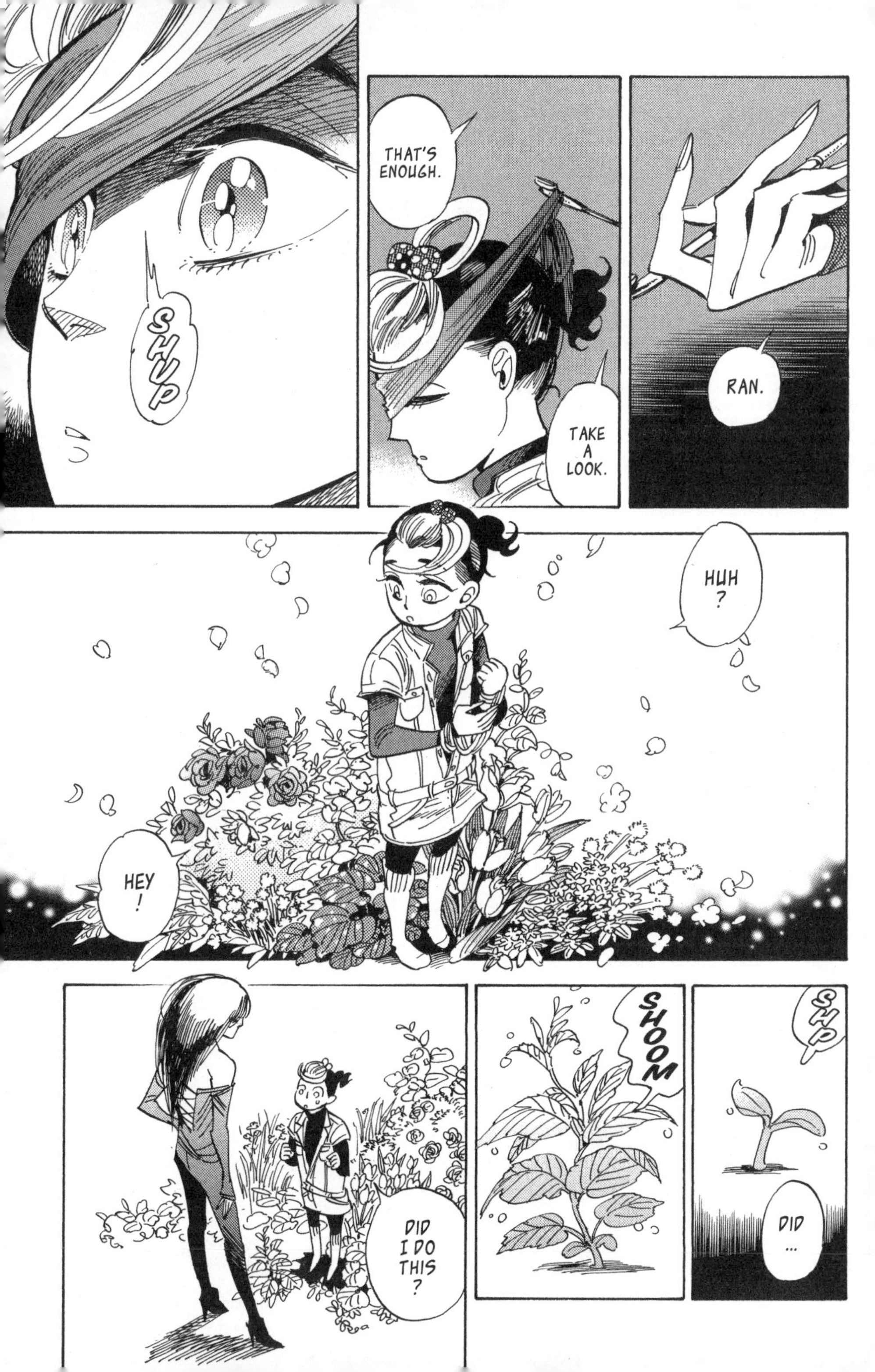

RAN.
THAT'S ENOUGH.
TAKE A LOOK.
SHUP
HUH?
HEY!
SHP
DID...
SHOOM
DID I DO THIS?

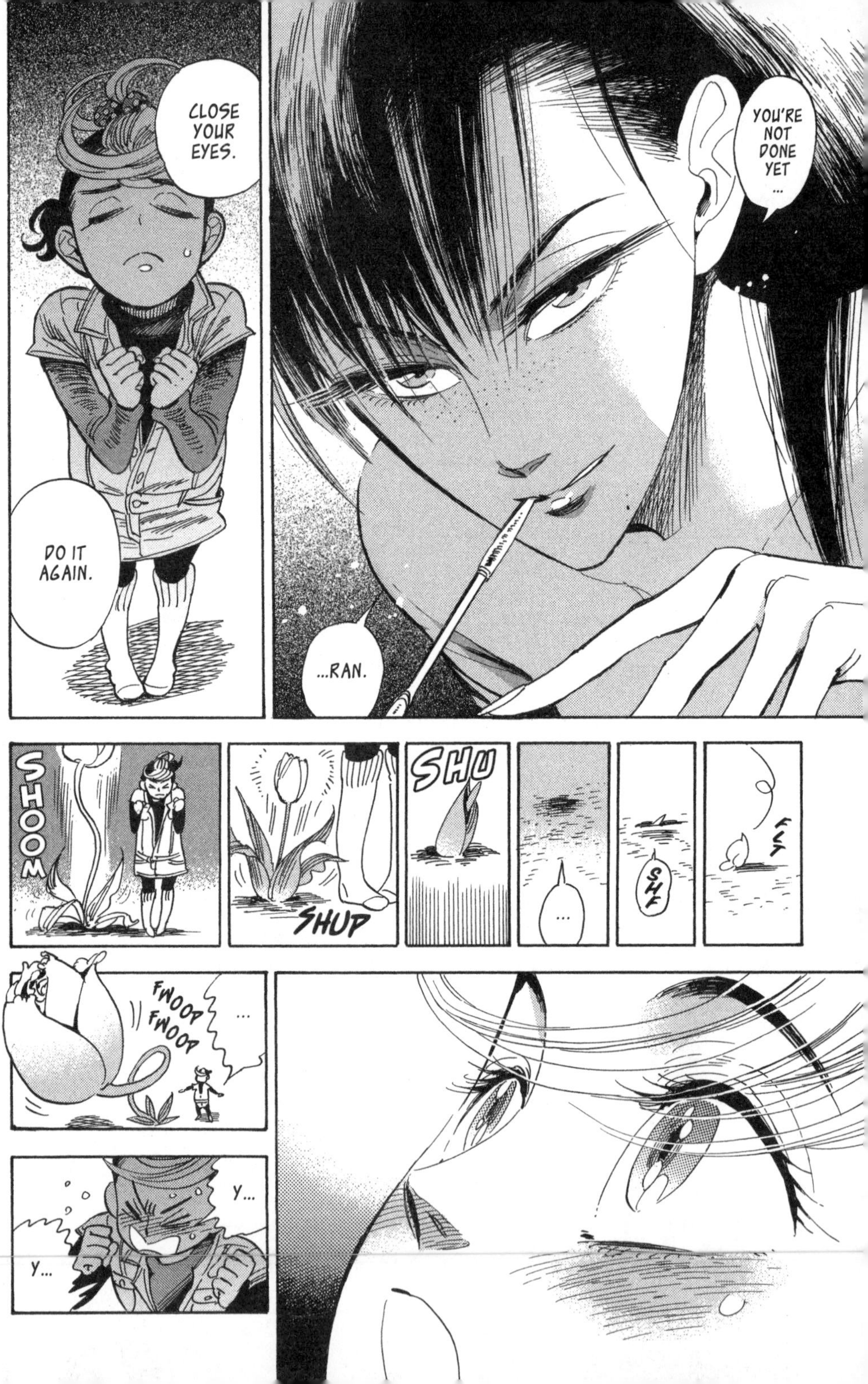
YOU'RE NOT DONE YET ...
...RAN.
CLOSE YOUR EYES.
DO IT AGAIN.
FLT
SHF
...
SHU
SHUP
SHOOM
FWOOP FWOOP
...
Y...
Y...

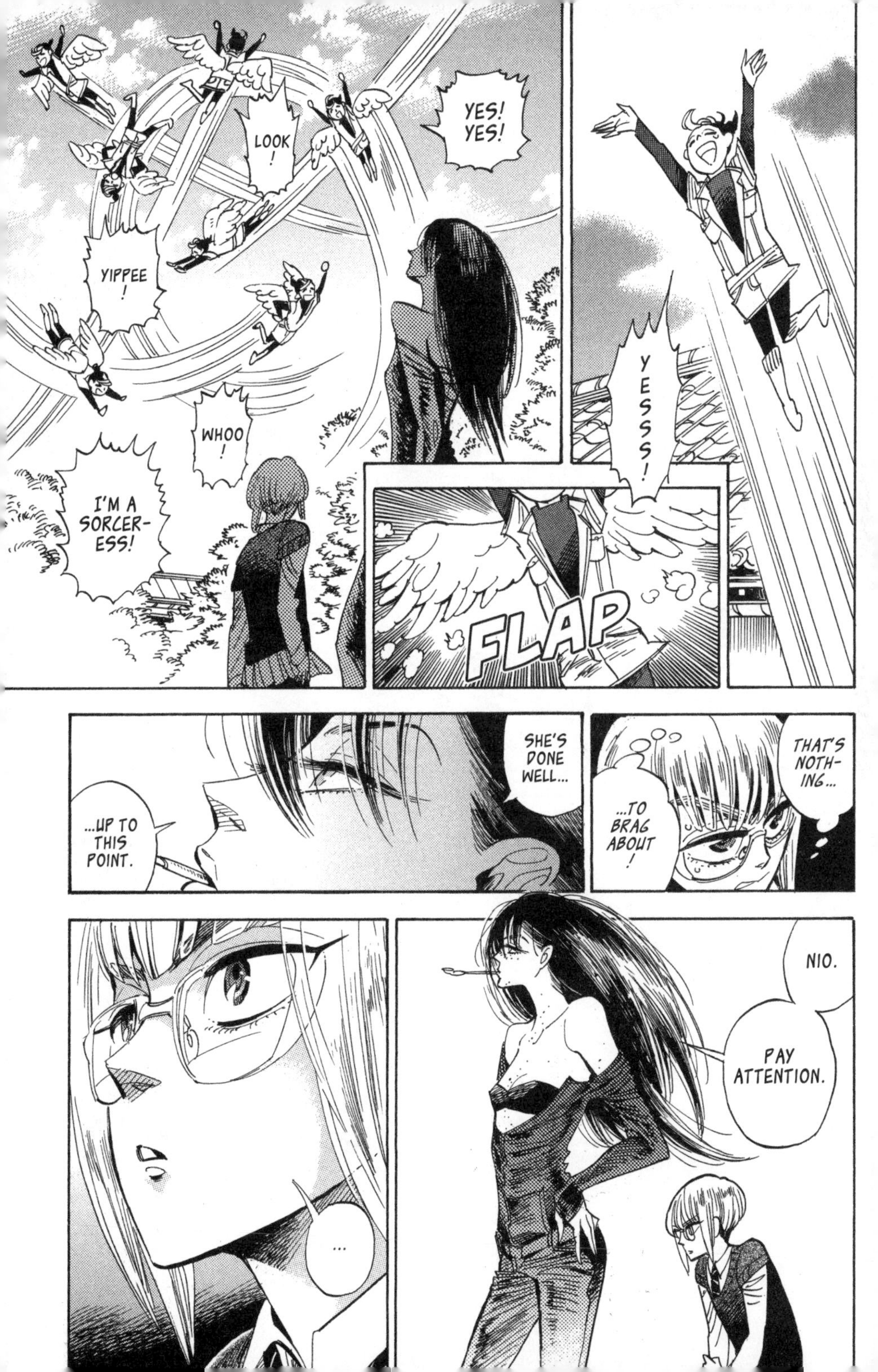
YESSS!
FLAP
YES! YES!
LOOK!
YIPPEE!
WHOO!
I'M A SORCERESS!
THAT'S NOTHING...
...TO BRAG ABOUT!
SHE'S DONE WELL...
...UP TO THIS POINT.
NIO.
PAY ATTENTION.
...

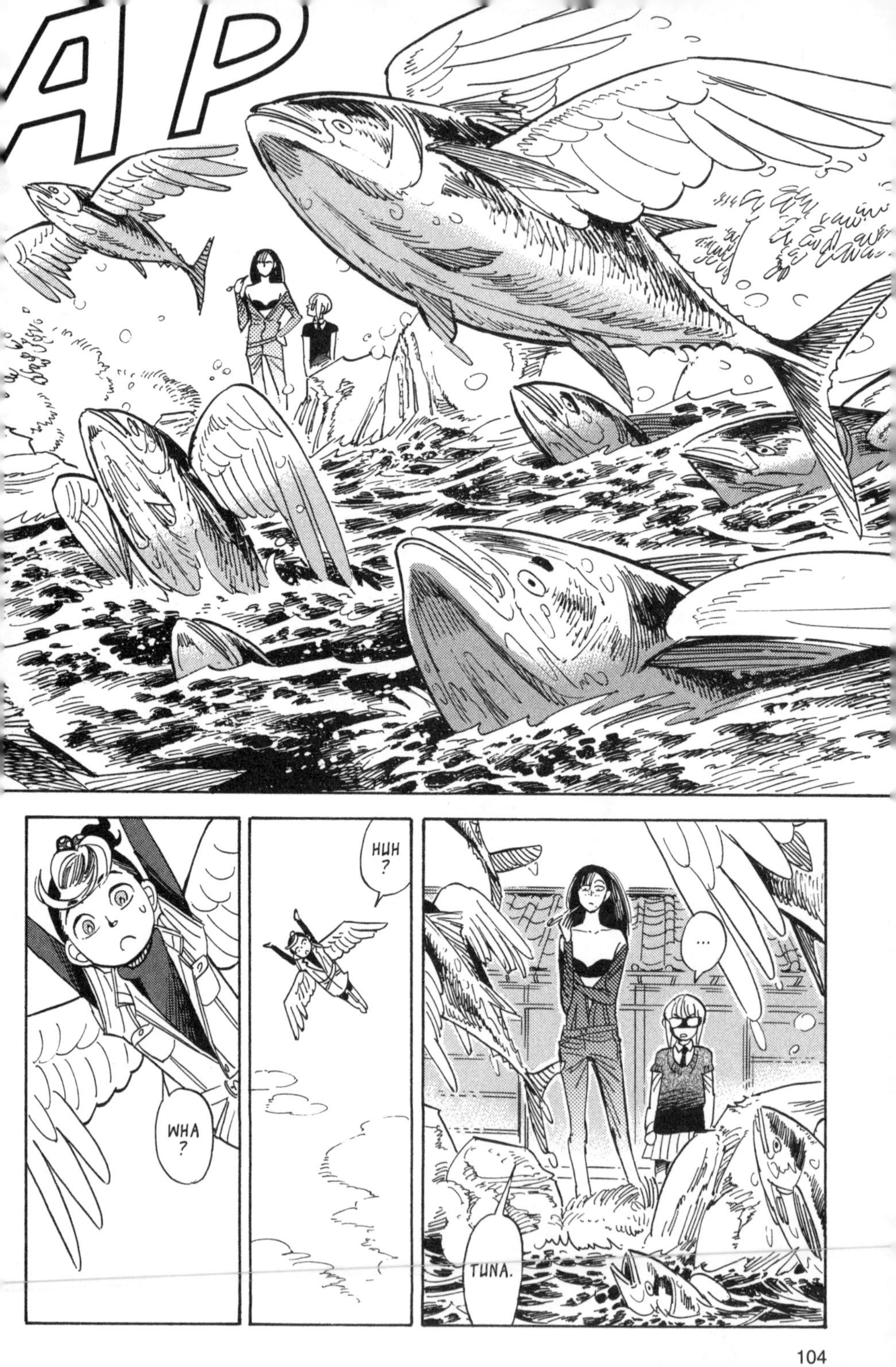
AP
WHA ?
HUH ?
...
TUNA.

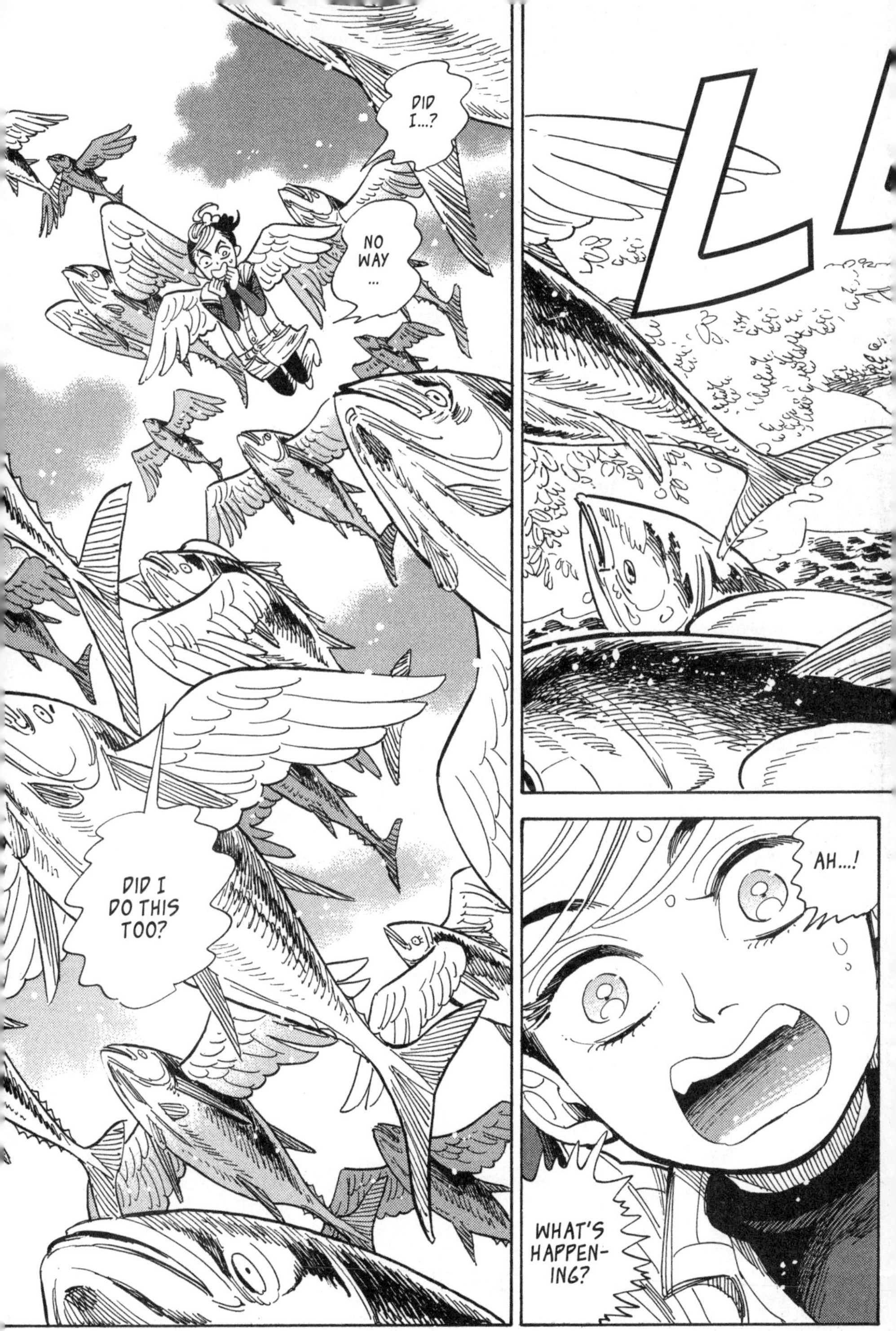
AH...!
WHAT'S HAPPENING?
DID I...?
NO WAY...
DID I DO THIS TOO?

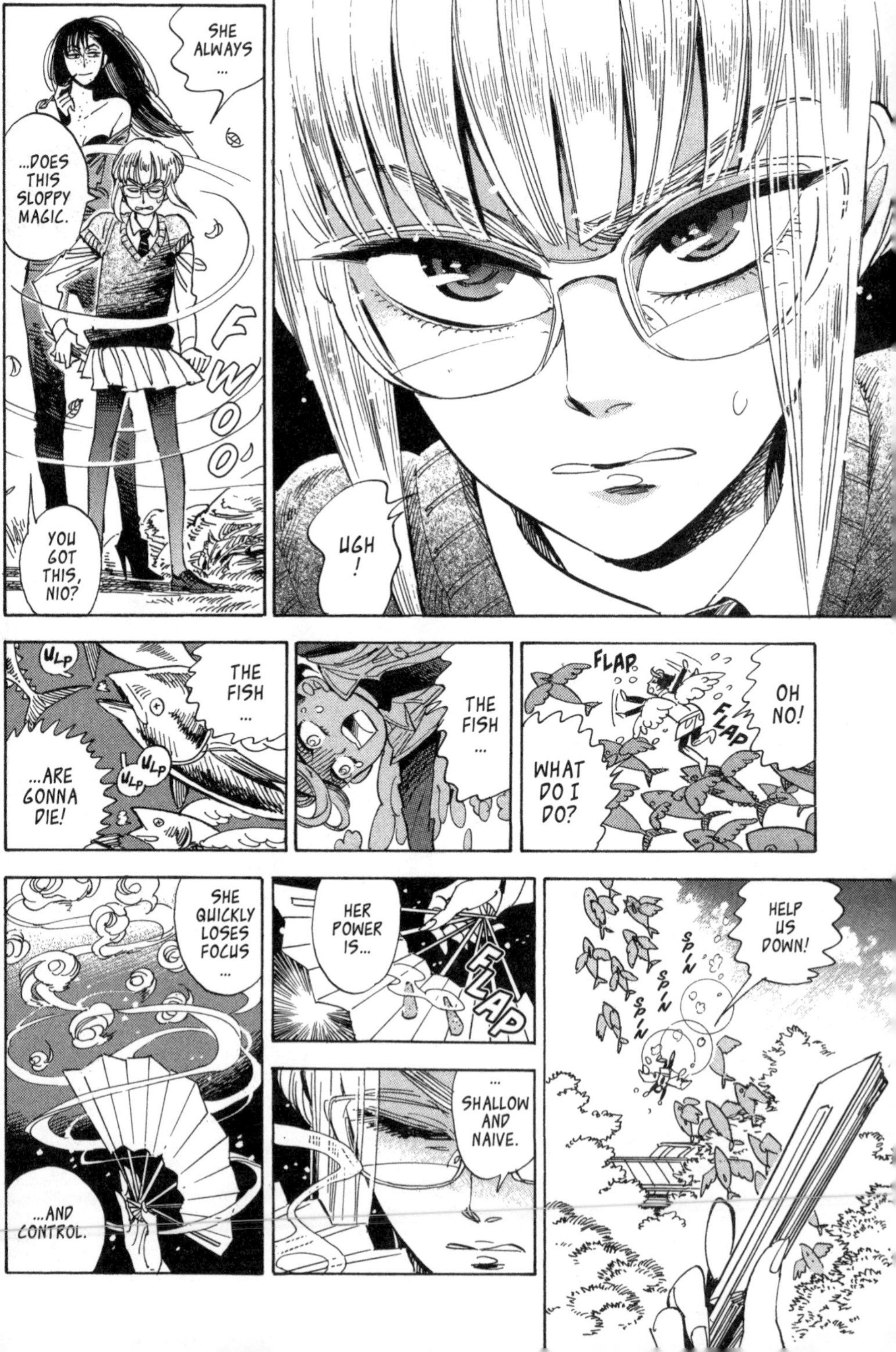
UGH!
SHE ALWAYS...
...DOES THIS SLOPPY MAGIC.
FWOOO
YOU GOT THIS, NIO?
OH NO!
WHAT DO I DO?
FLAP
FLAP
THE FISH...
THE FISH...
ULP
ULP
ULP
...ARE GONNA DIE!
HELP US DOWN!
SPIN SPIN SPIN
HER POWER IS...
FLAP
...SHALLOW AND NAIVE.
SHE QUICKLY LOSES FOCUS...
...AND CONTROL.

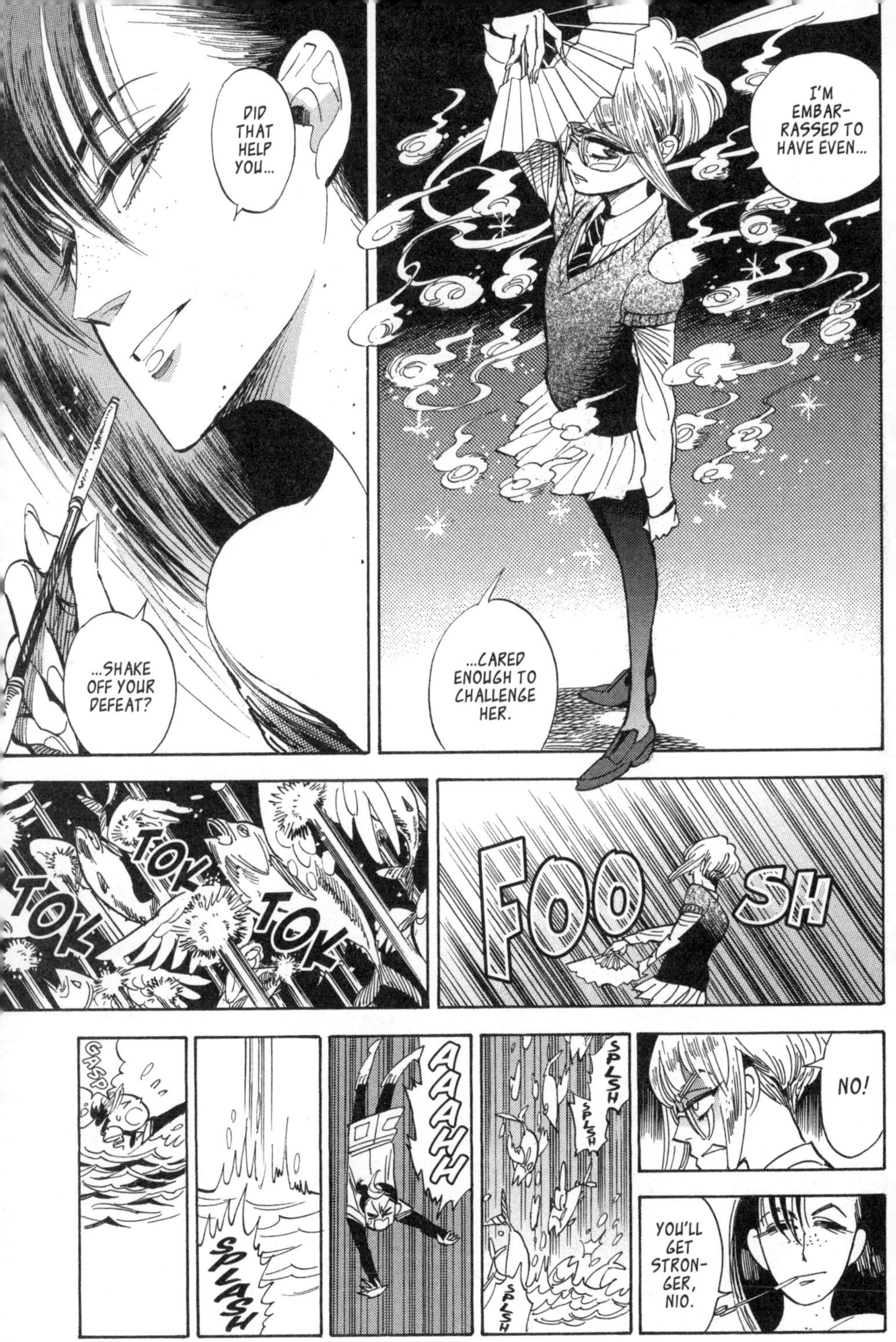
I'M EMBAR-RASSED TO HAVE EVEN...
...CARED ENOUGH TO CHALLENGE HER.
DID THAT HELP YOU...
...SHAKE OFF YOUR DEFEAT?
FOOSH
TOK
TOK
TOK
TOK
NO!
YOU'LL GET STRON-GER, NIO.
SPLSH
SPLSH
SPLSH
AAAAHH
SPLASH
GASP

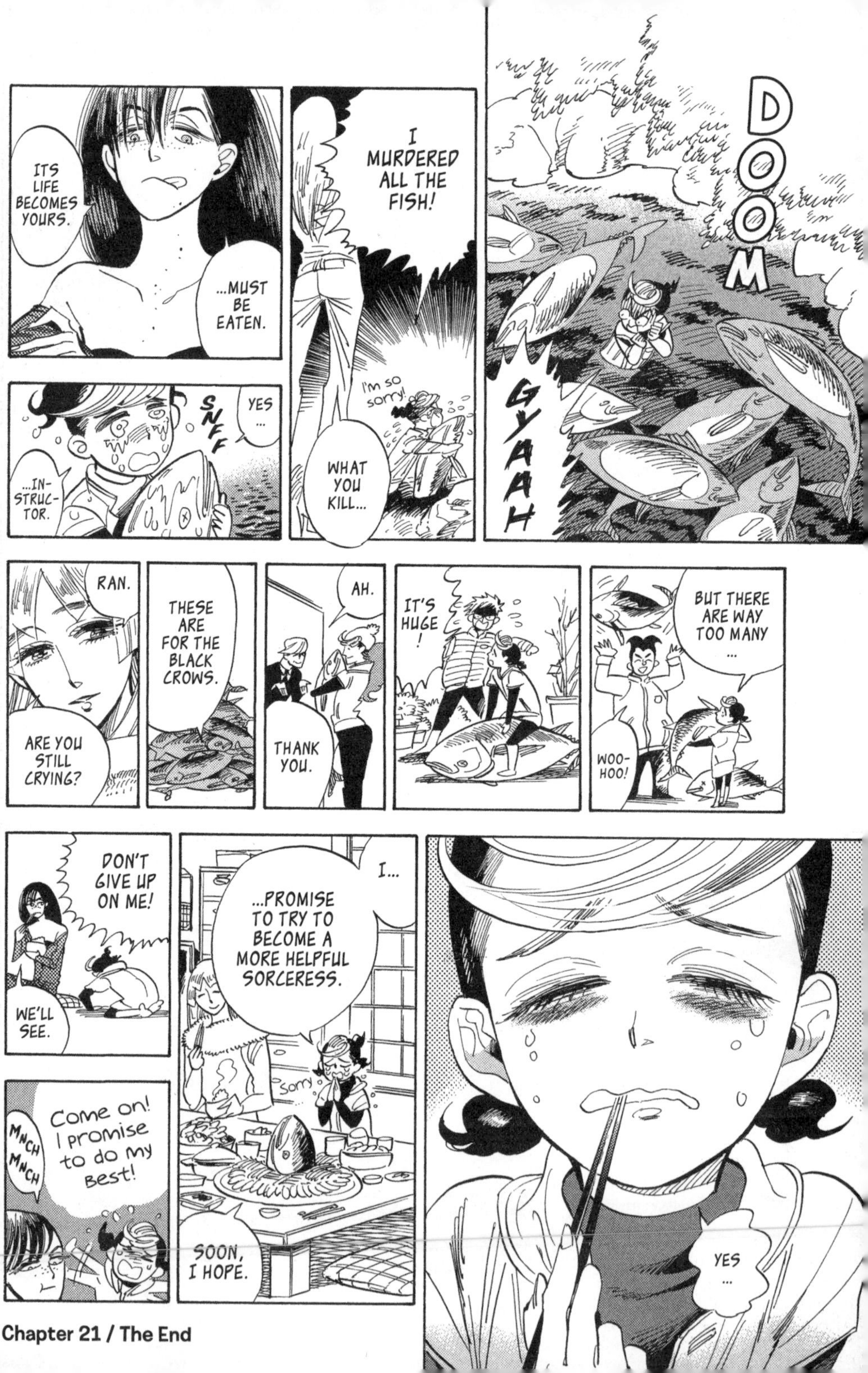
DOOM
GYAAH
I MURDERED ALL THE FISH!
I'm so sorry!
WHAT YOU KILL...
ITS LIFE BECOMES YOURS.
...MUST BE EATEN.
YES...
SNFF
...INSTRUCTOR.
BUT THERE ARE WAY TOO MANY...
WOO-HOO!
IT'S HUGE!
AH.
THANK YOU.
THESE ARE FOR THE BLACK CROWS.
RAN.
ARE YOU STILL CRYING?
YES...
I...
...PROMISE TO TRY TO BECOME A MORE HELPFUL SORCERESS.
Sorry
SOON, I HOPE.
DON'T GIVE UP ON ME!
WE'LL SEE.
Come on! I promise to do my best!
MNCH MNCH

Chapter 21 / The End

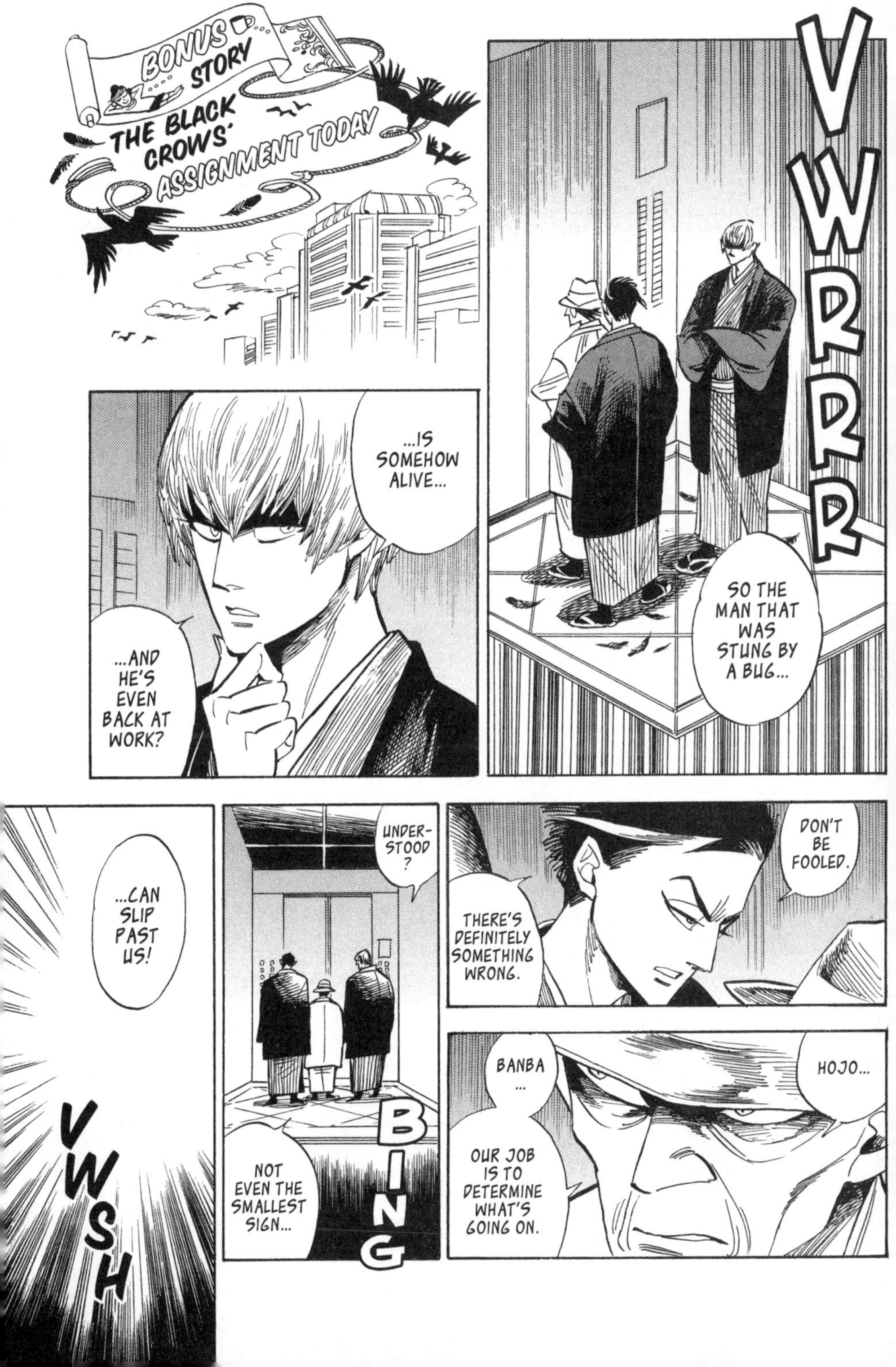
BONUS STORY
THE BLACK CROWS' ASSIGNMENT TODAY
VWRRR
SO THE MAN THAT WAS STUNG BY A BUG...
...IS SOMEHOW ALIVE...
...AND HE'S EVEN BACK AT WORK?
DON'T BE FOOLED.
THERE'S DEFINITELY SOMETHING WRONG.
HOJO...
BANBA...
OUR JOB IS TO DETERMINE WHAT'S GOING ON.
UNDER-STOOD?
NOT EVEN THE SMALLEST SIGN...
BING
...CAN SLIP PAST US!
VWSH

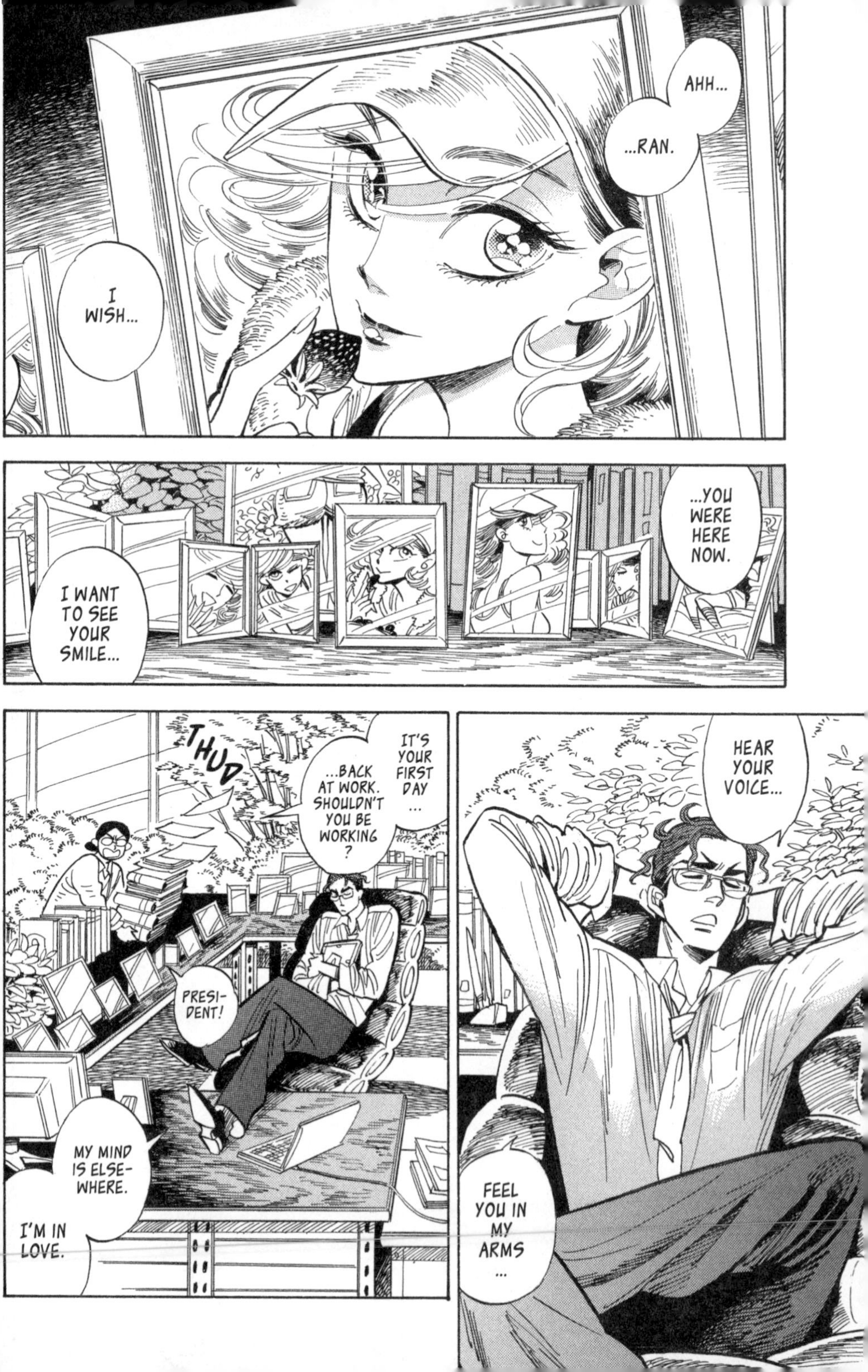
AHH...
...RAN.
I WISH...
...YOU WERE HERE NOW.
I WANT TO SEE YOUR SMILE...
HEAR YOUR VOICE...
FEEL YOU IN MY ARMS...
THUD
PRESIDENT!
IT'S YOUR FIRST DAY...
...BACK AT WORK. SHOULDN'T YOU BE WORKING?
MY MIND IS ELSEWHERE.
I'M IN LOVE.

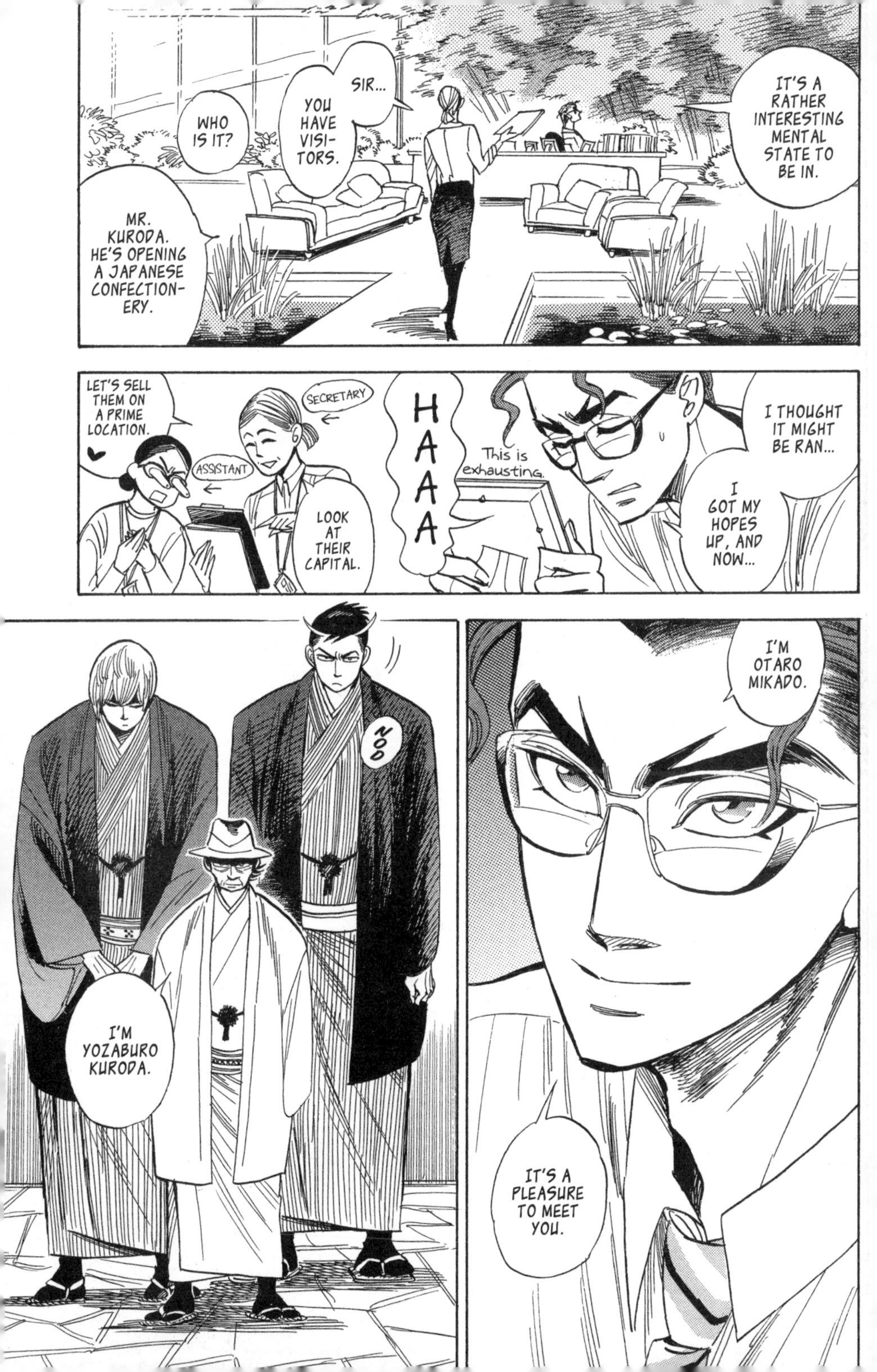
IT'S A RATHER INTERESTING MENTAL STATE TO BE IN.
SIR... YOU HAVE VISITORS.
WHO IS IT?
MR. KURODA. HE'S OPENING A JAPANESE CONFECTIONERY.
I THOUGHT IT MIGHT BE RAN...
I GOT MY HOPES UP, AND NOW...
This is exhausting.
HAAAA
SECRETARY
LOOK AT THEIR CAPITAL.
LET'S SELL THEM ON A PRIME LOCATION.
ASSISTANT
I'M OTARO MIKADO.
IT'S A PLEASURE TO MEET YOU.
NOD
I'M YOZABURO KURODA.

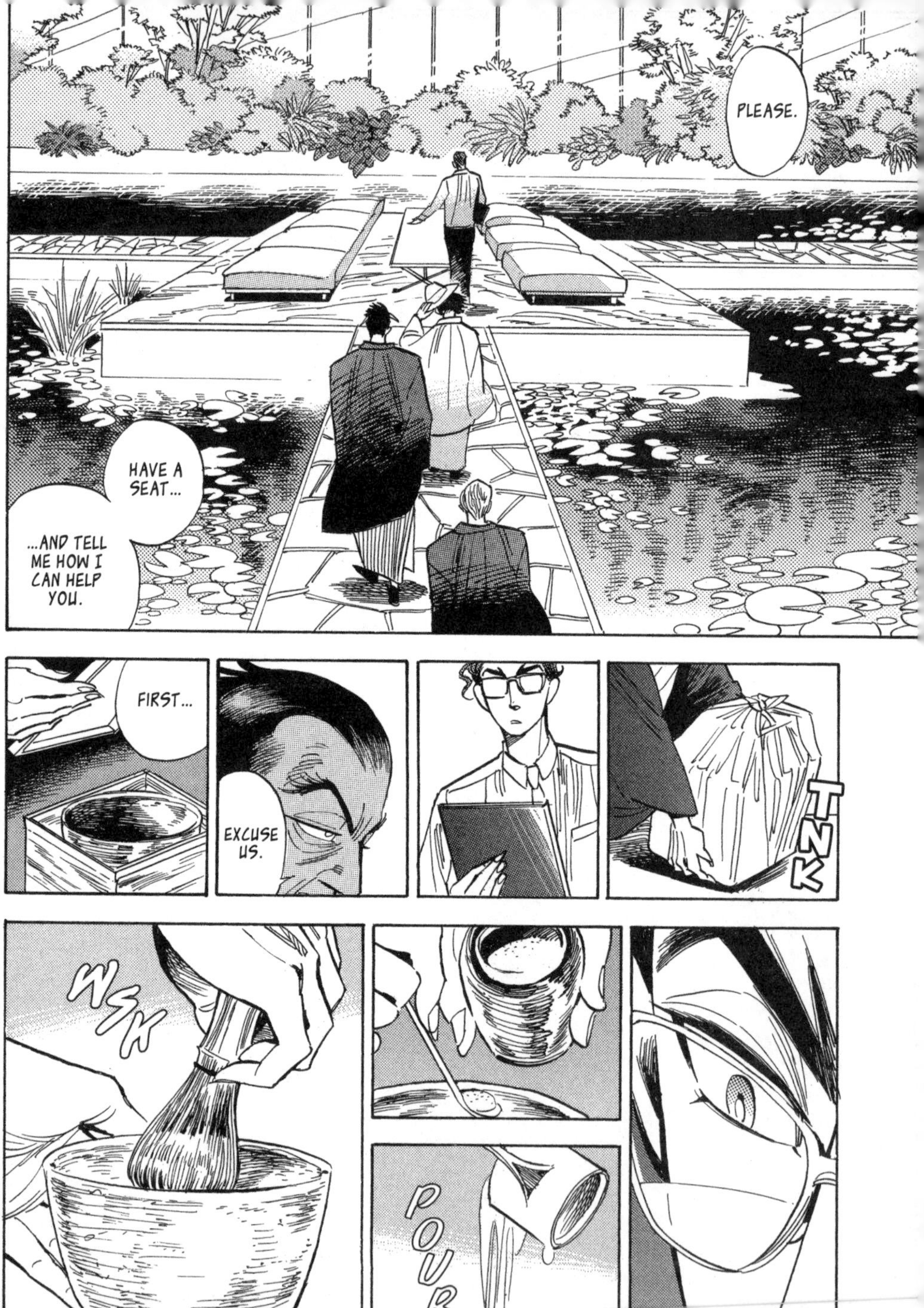
PLEASE.
HAVE A SEAT...
...AND TELL ME HOW I CAN HELP YOU.
TNK
EXCUSE US.
FIRST...
WSK
POUR

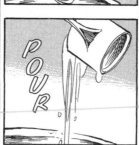

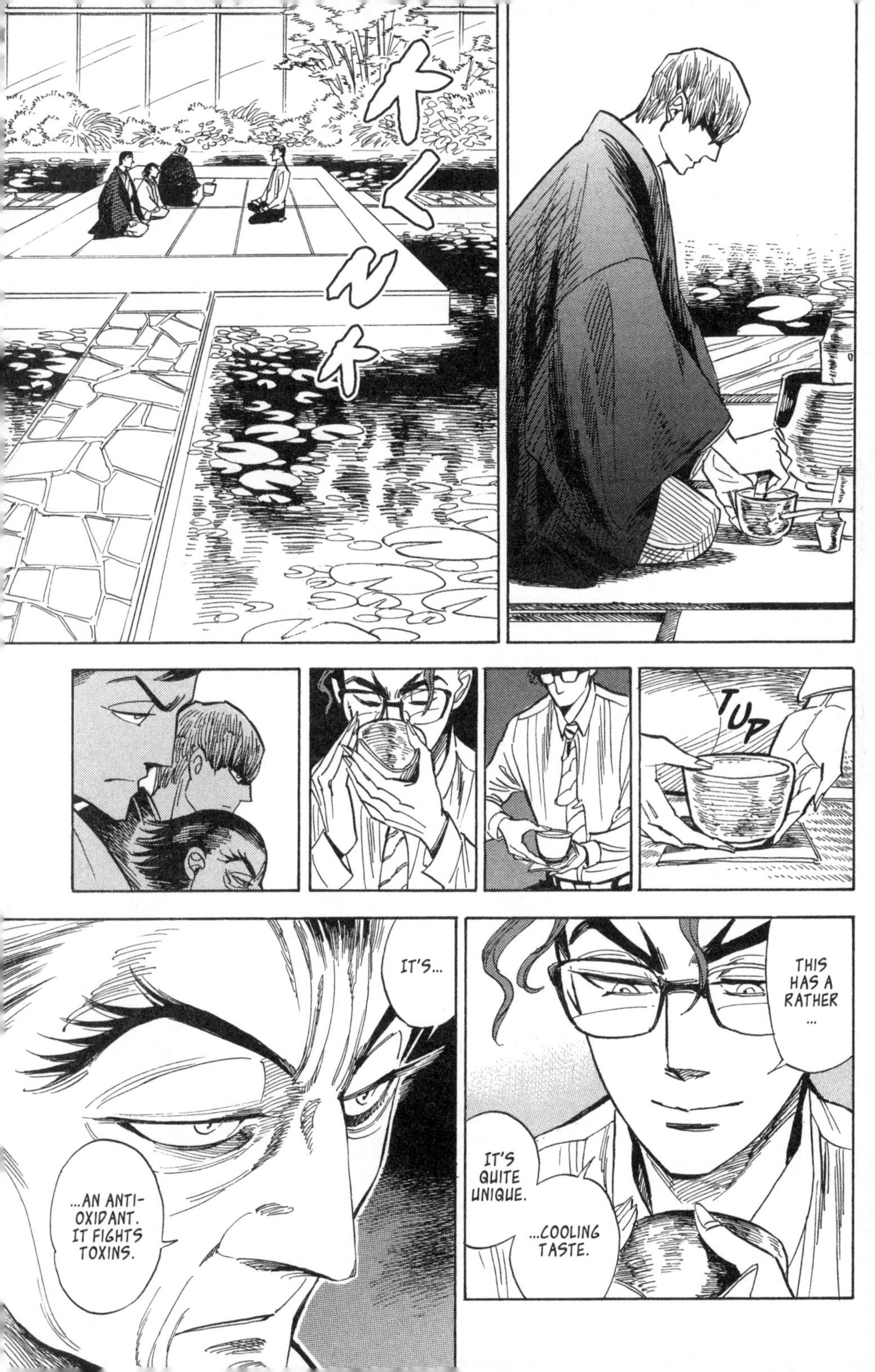
KLNK
TUP
THIS HAS A RATHER ...
...COOLING TASTE.
IT'S QUITE UNIQUE.
IT'S...
...AN ANTI-OXIDANT. IT FIGHTS TOXINS.

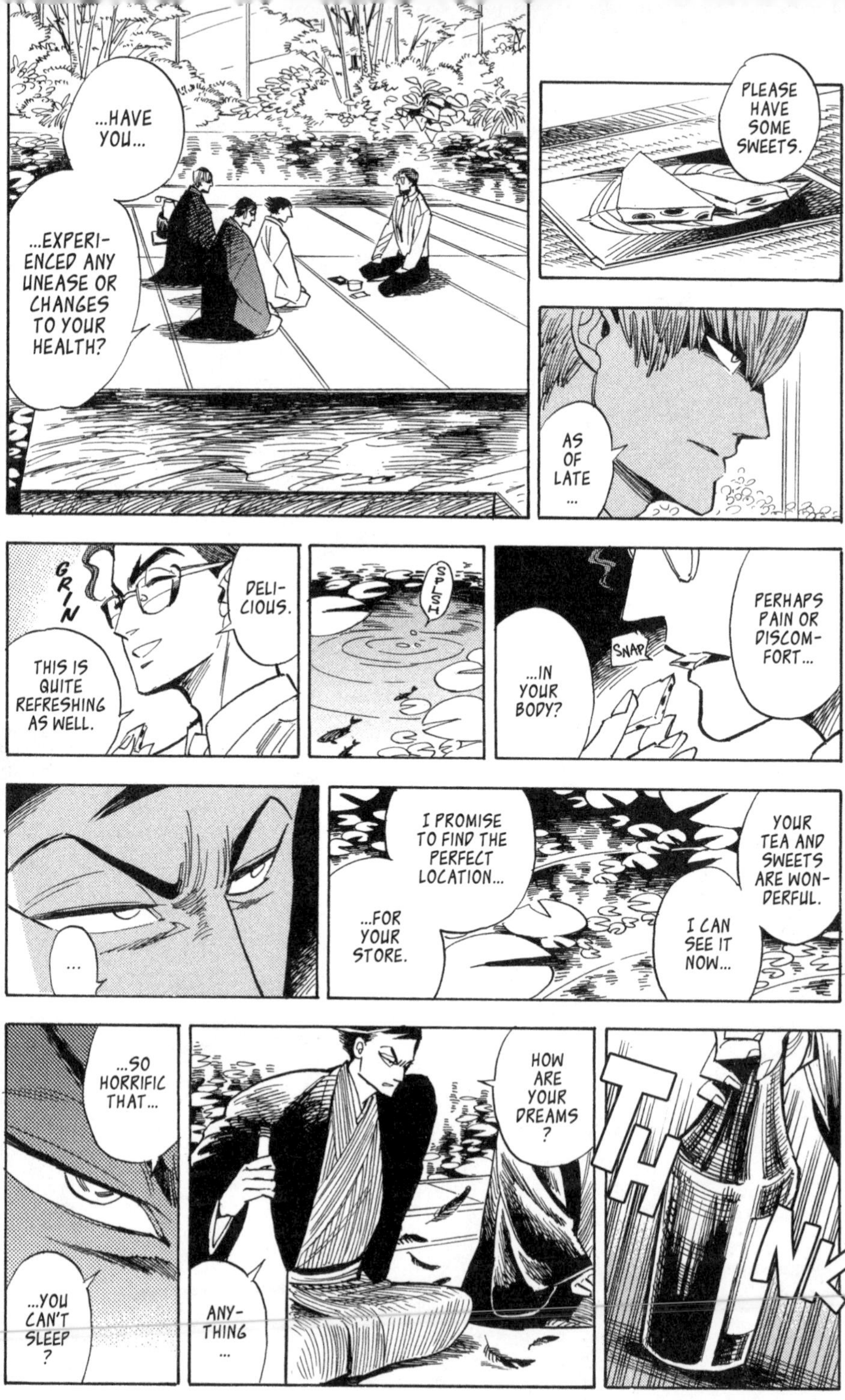

PLEASE HAVE SOME SWEETS.
AS OF LATE ...
...HAVE YOU...
...EXPERIENCED ANY UNEASE OR CHANGES TO YOUR HEALTH?
PERHAPS PAIN OR DISCOMFORT...
SNAP
...IN YOUR BODY?
SPLSH
DELICIOUS.
GRIN
THIS IS QUITE REFRESHING AS WELL.
YOUR TEA AND SWEETS ARE WONDERFUL.
I CAN SEE IT NOW...
I PROMISE TO FIND THE PERFECT LOCATION...
...FOR YOUR STORE.
...
TH
NK
HOW ARE YOUR DREAMS?
ANYTHING...
...SO HORRIFIC THAT...
...YOU CAN'T SLEEP?

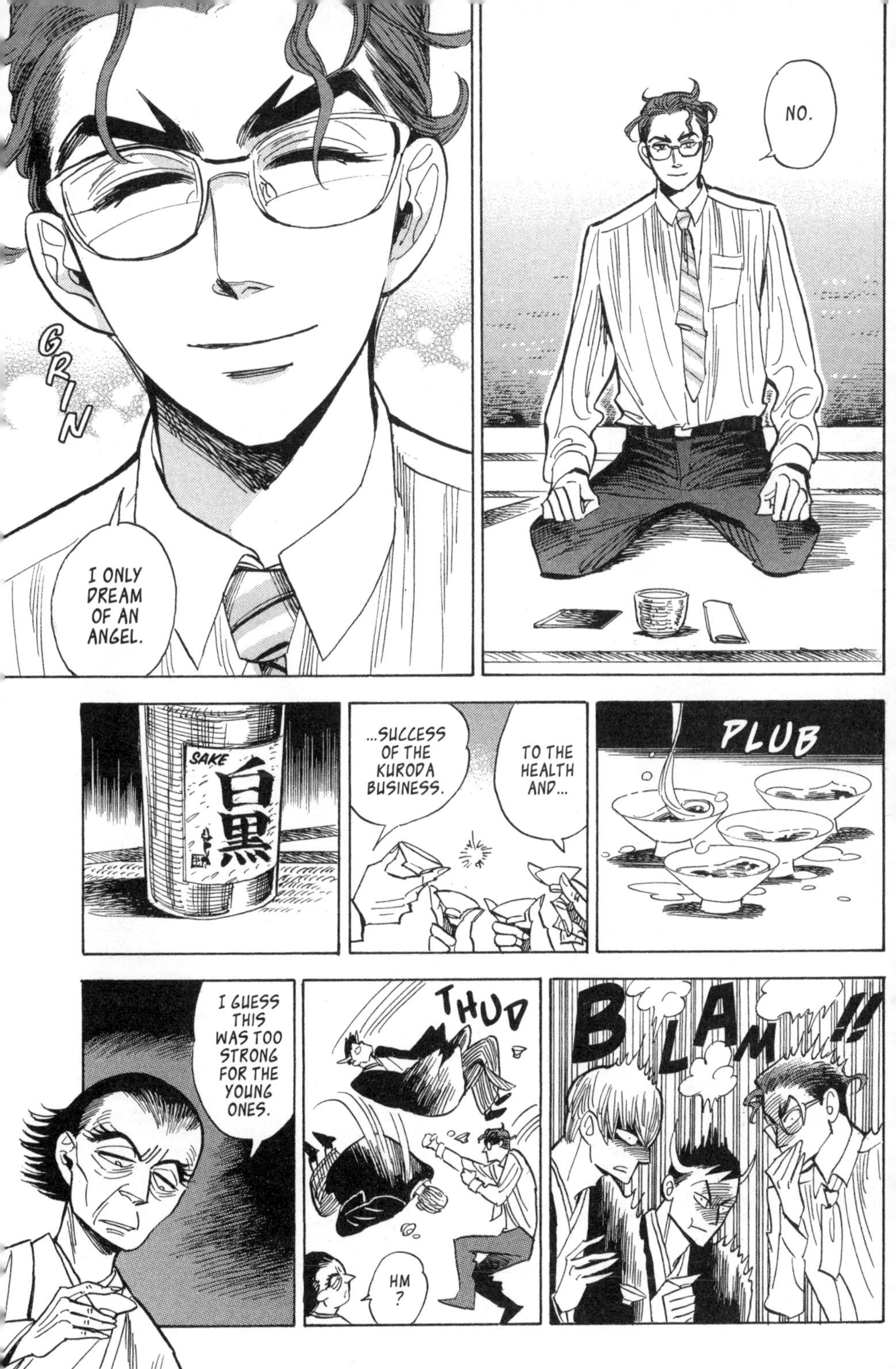
NO.
GRIN
I ONLY DREAM OF AN ANGEL.
PLUB
TO THE HEALTH AND...
...SUCCESS OF THE KURODA BUSINESS.
SAKE
白黒
BLAM!!
THUD
HM?
I GUESS THIS WAS TOO STRONG FOR THE YOUNG ONES.

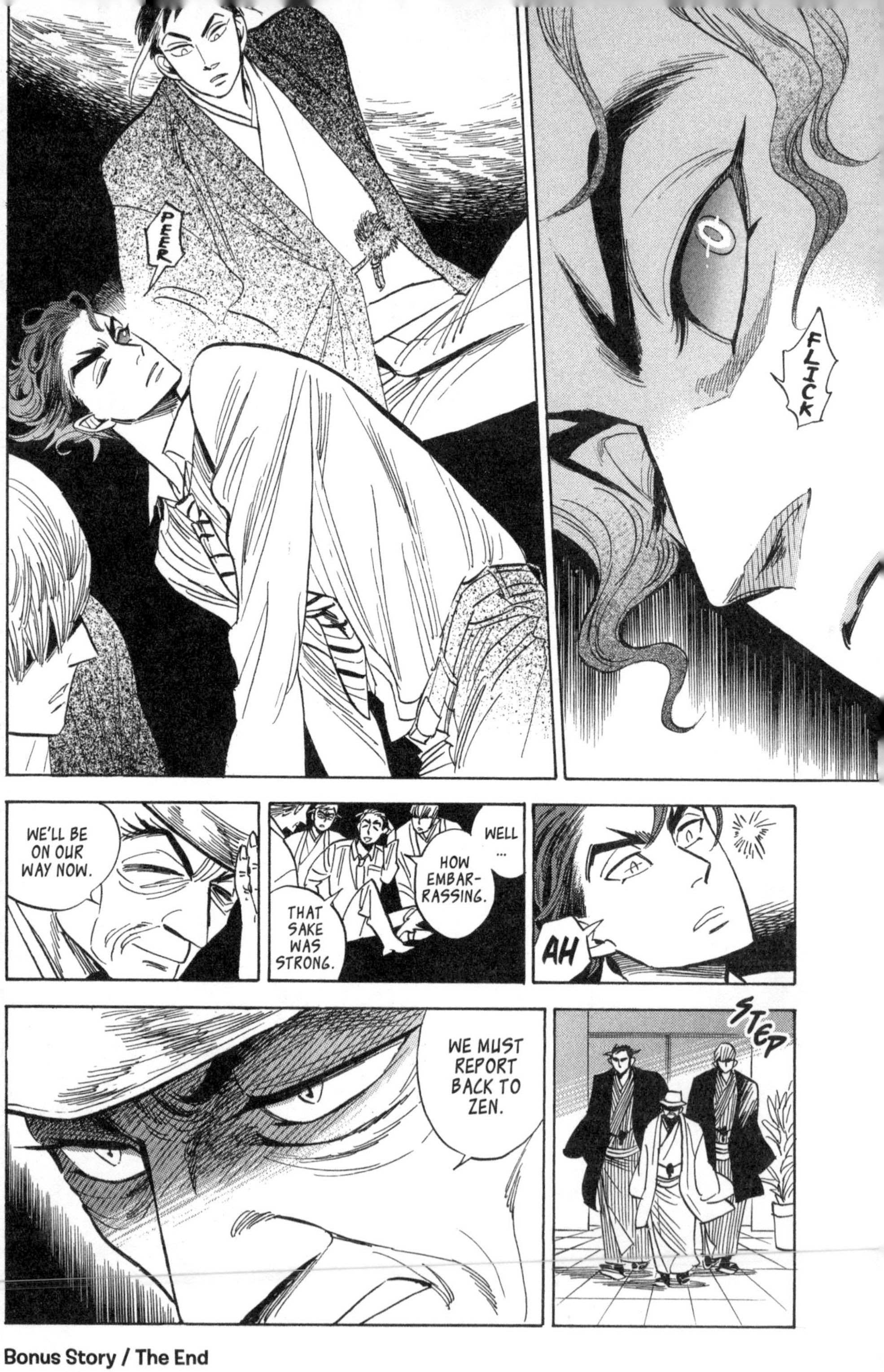
FLICK
PEER
AH
WELL ...
HOW EMBARRASSING.
THAT SAKE WAS STRONG.
WE'LL BE ON OUR WAY NOW.
STEP
WE MUST REPORT BACK TO ZEN.

Bonus Story / The End

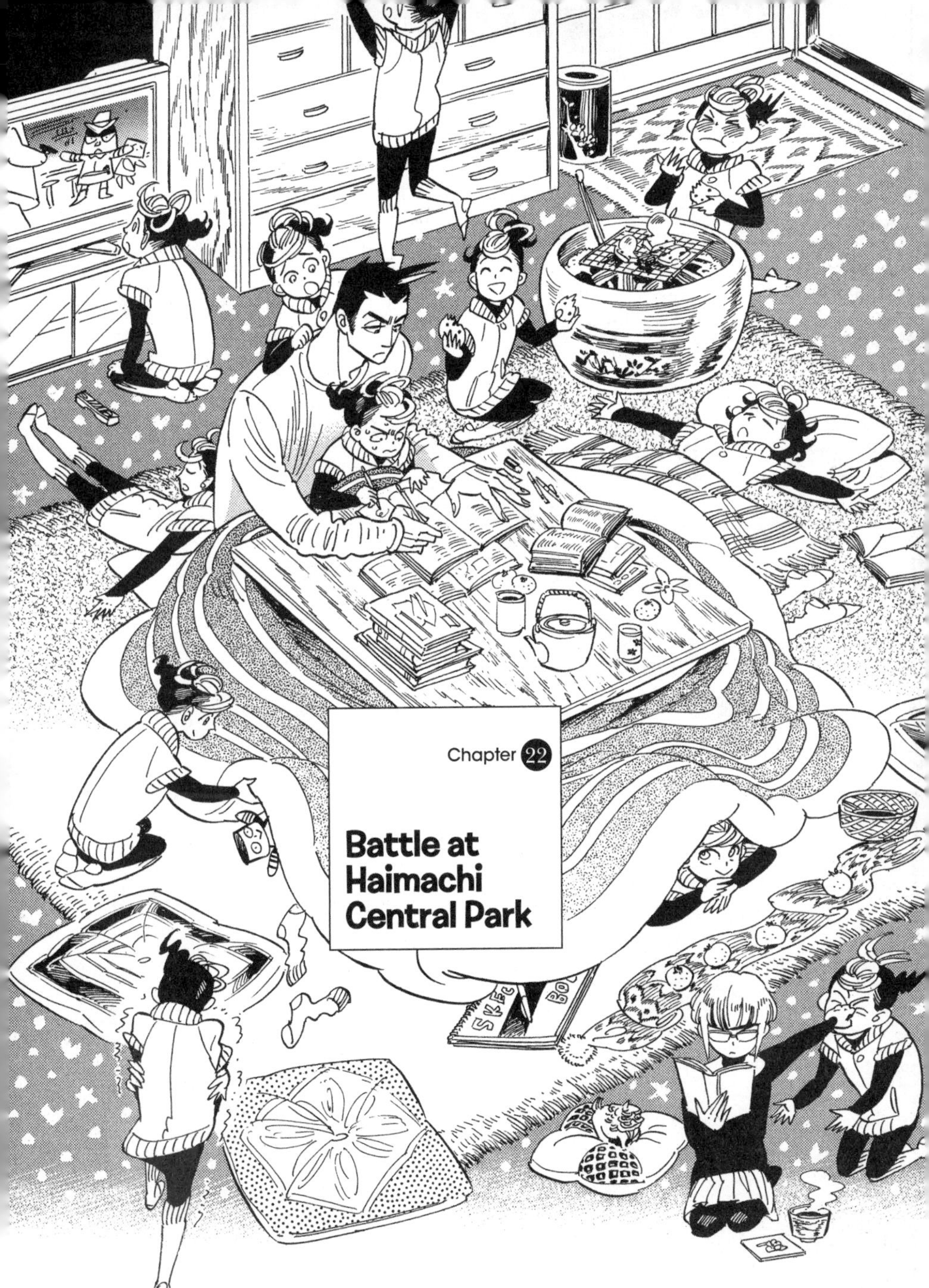

Chapter 22

Battle at Haimachi Central Park

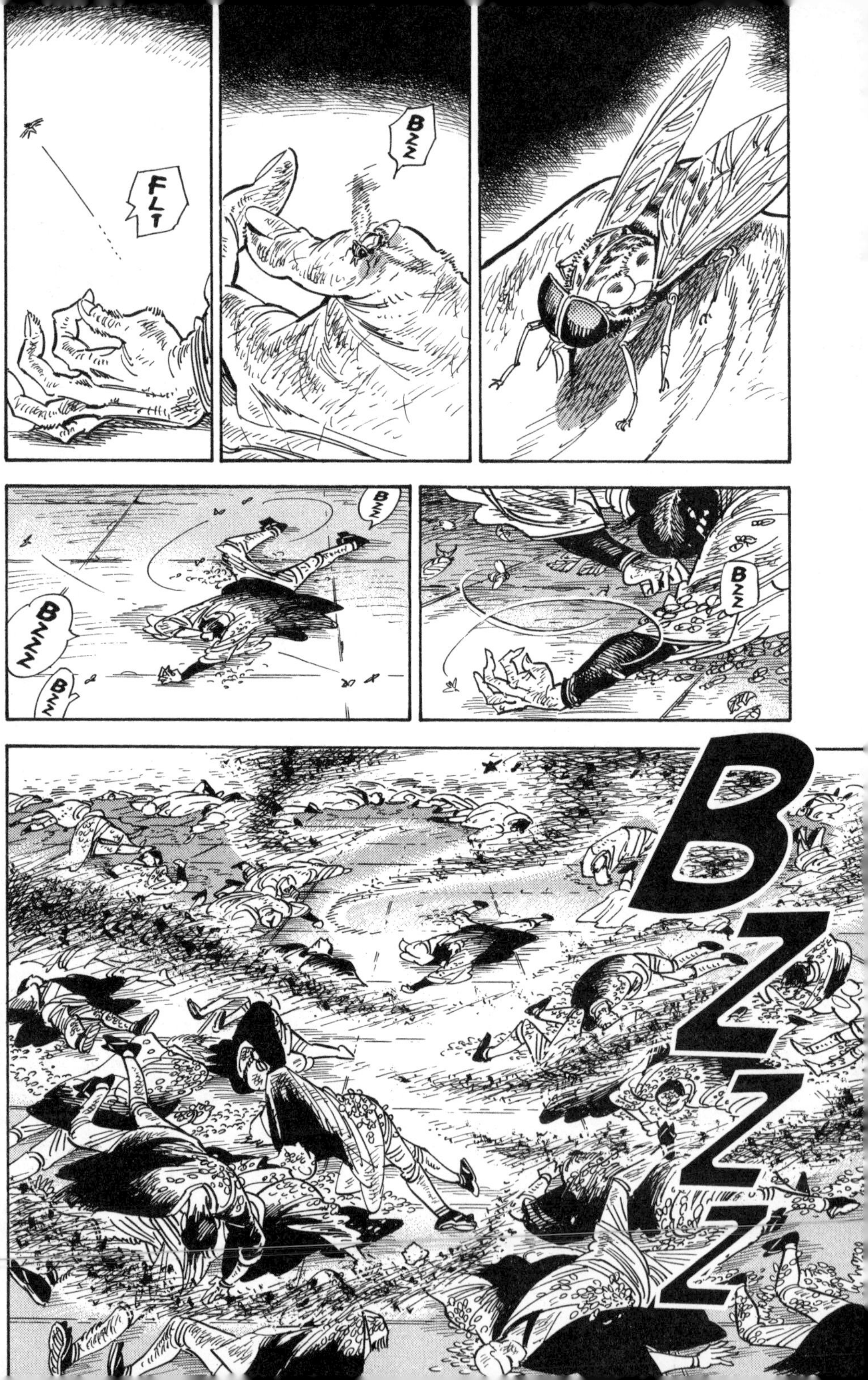
BZZ
FLT
BZZ
BZZ
BNNNN
BZZ
BZZ

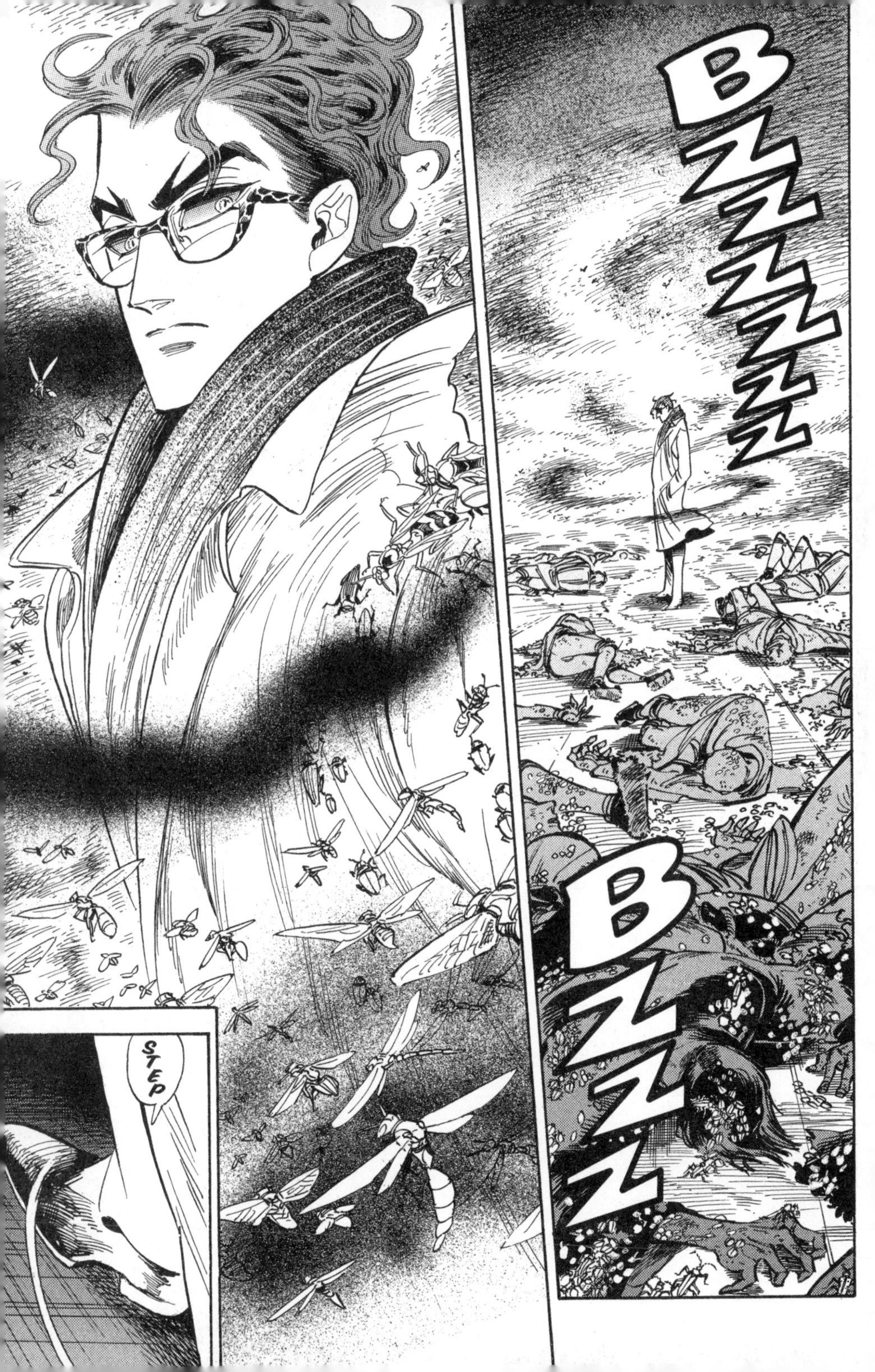
BZZZZZZ
BZZZ
STEP

THERE'S STILL...

WAIT.

...ONE STANDING.

...MY BLADES.

SHWP

...TO FEEL...

RSTL

TIME...

FWSH

VWMM

FWP

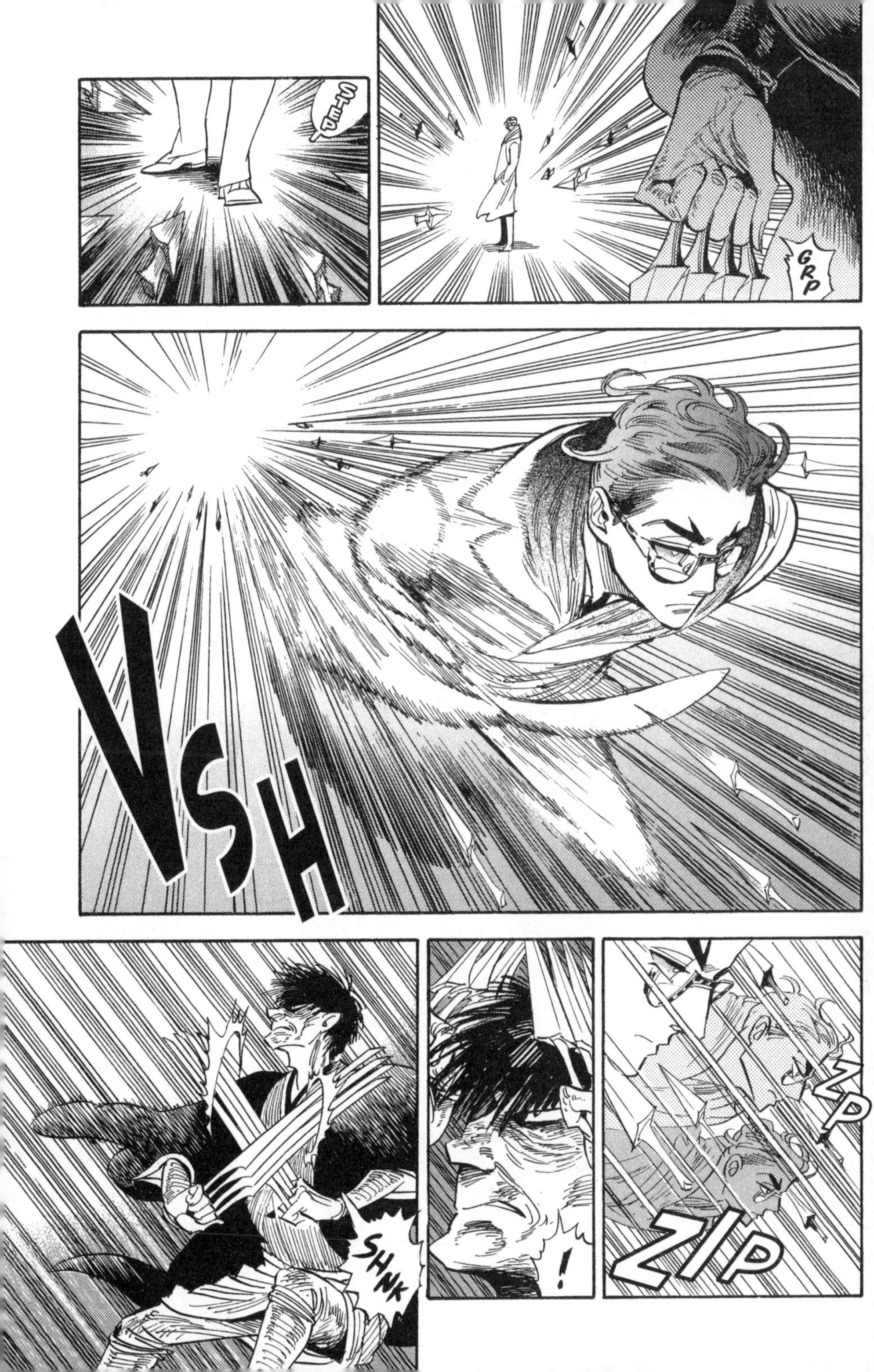
GRP
STEP
VSH
ZP
ZIP
!
SHNK

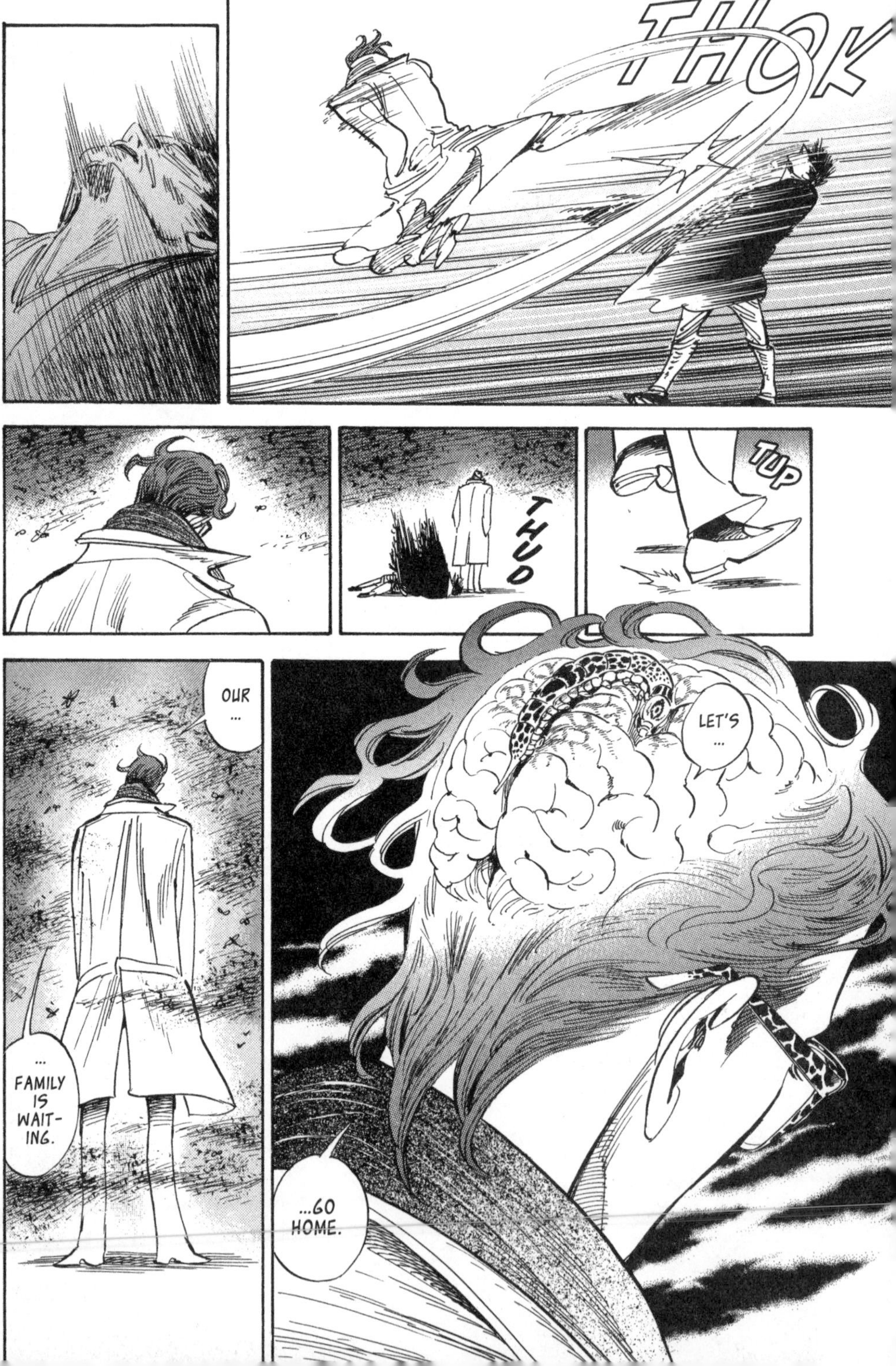
THOK
TUP
THUD
LET'S ...
...GO HOME.
OUR ...
... FAMILY IS WAIT-ING.

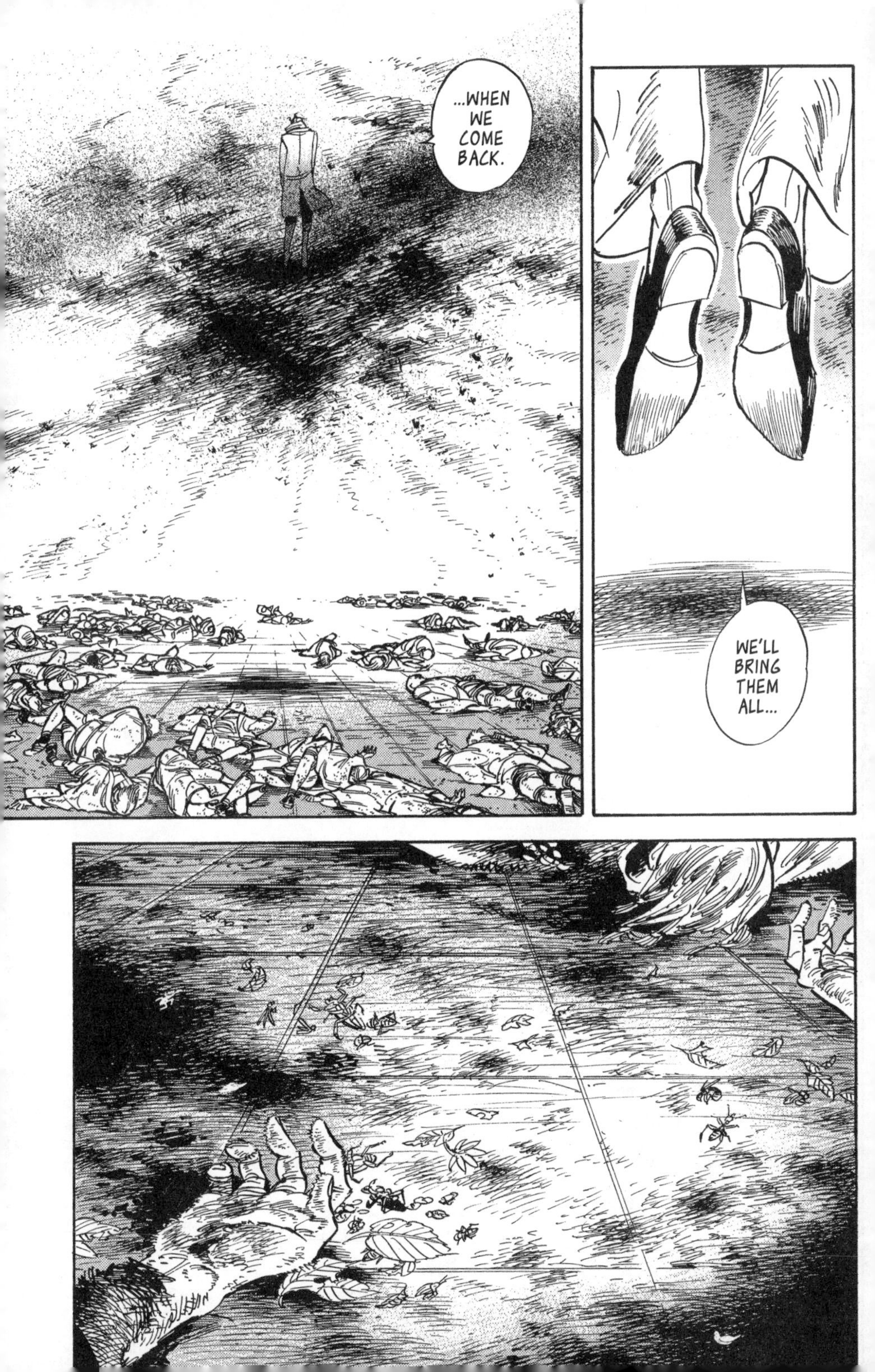
WE'LL BRING THEM ALL...
...WHEN WE COME BACK.

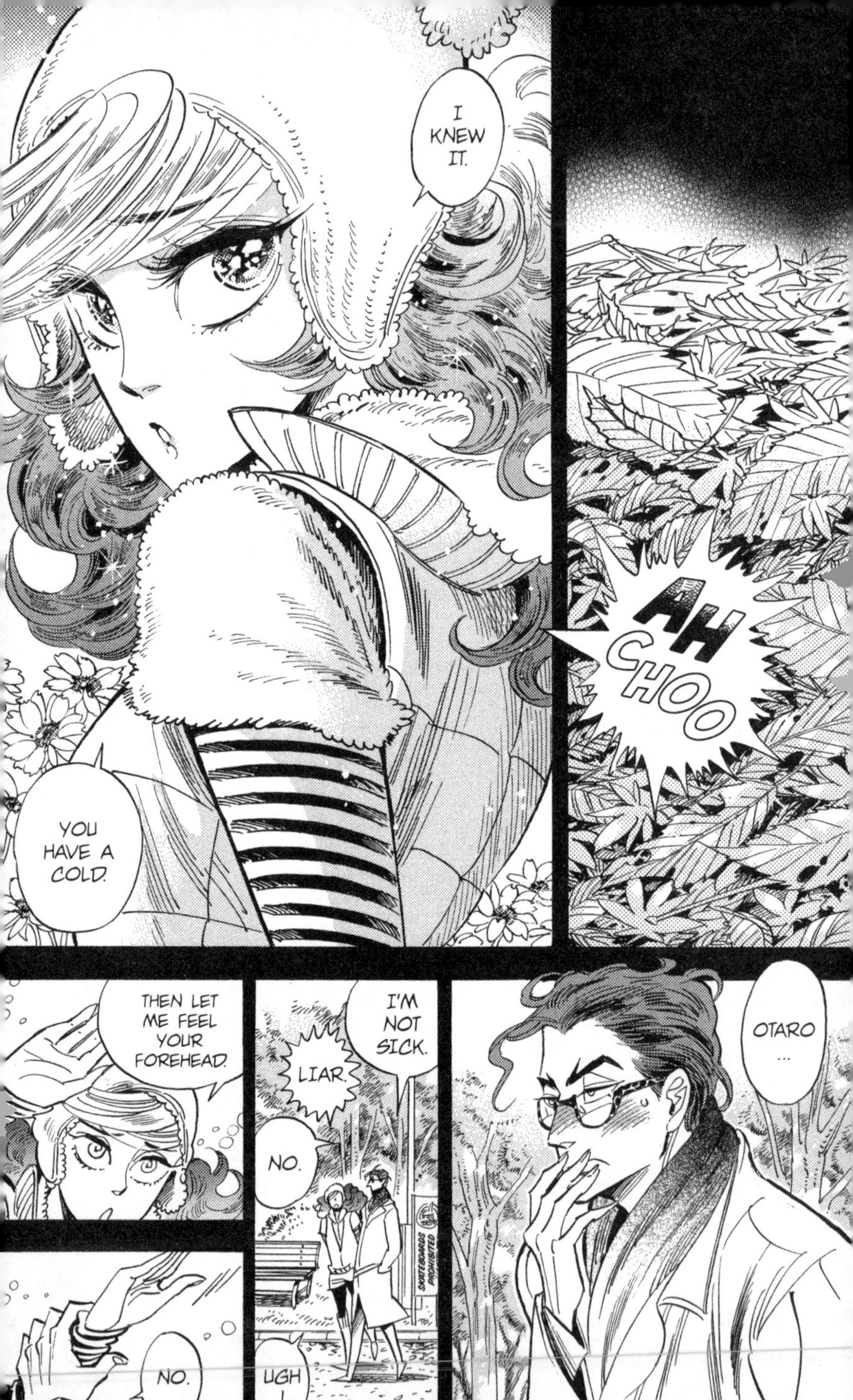
AH CHOO
I KNEW IT.
YOU HAVE A COLD.
OTARO ...
I'M NOT SICK.
LIAR.
NO.
SKATEBOARDS PROHIBITED
UGH!
THEN LET ME FEEL YOUR FOREHEAD.
NO.

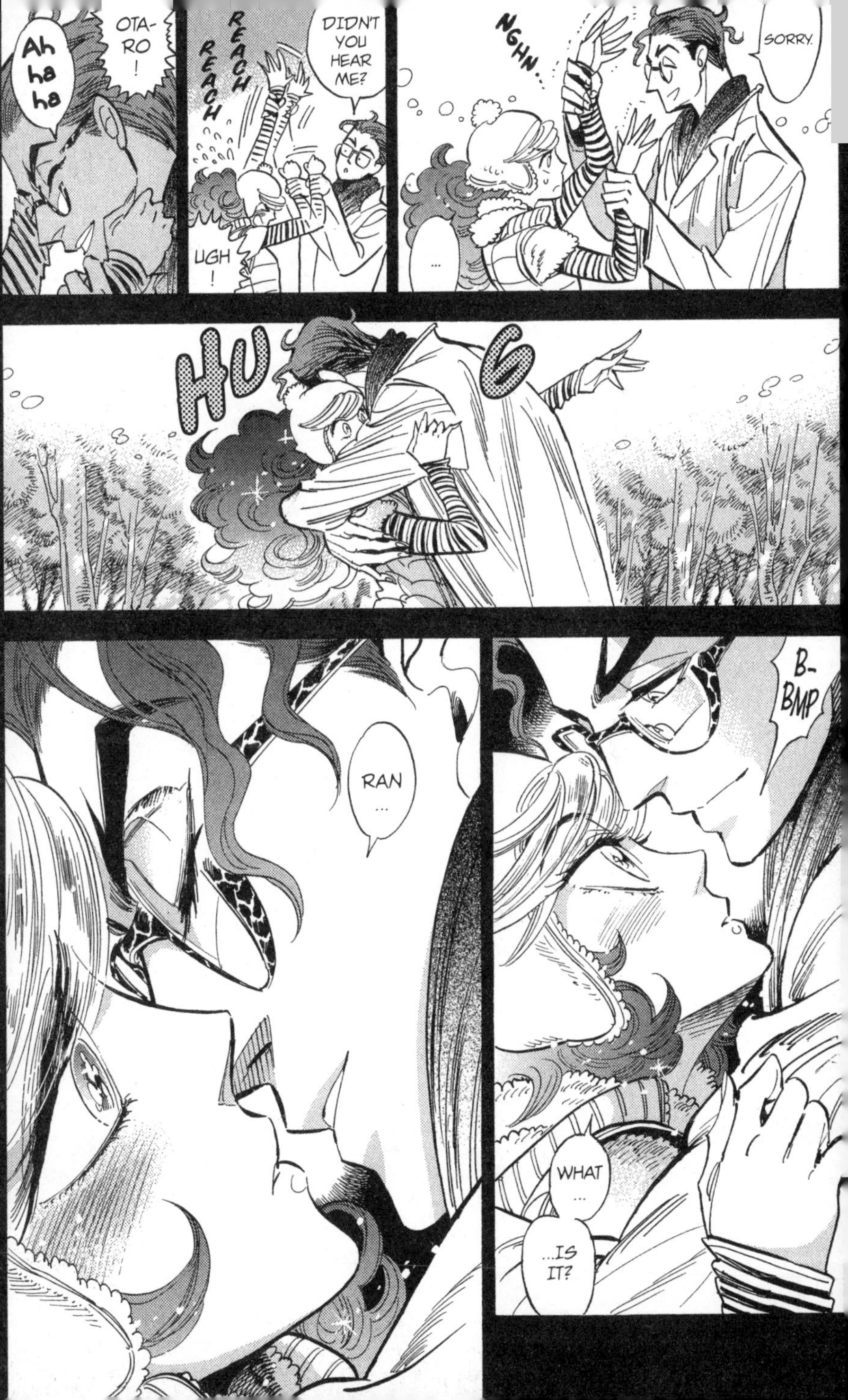
SORRY.
NGHN...
...
DIDN'T YOU HEAR ME?
REACH REACH REACH
UGH!
OTA-RO!
Ah ha ha
HUG
B-BMP
WHAT...
...IS IT?
RAN...

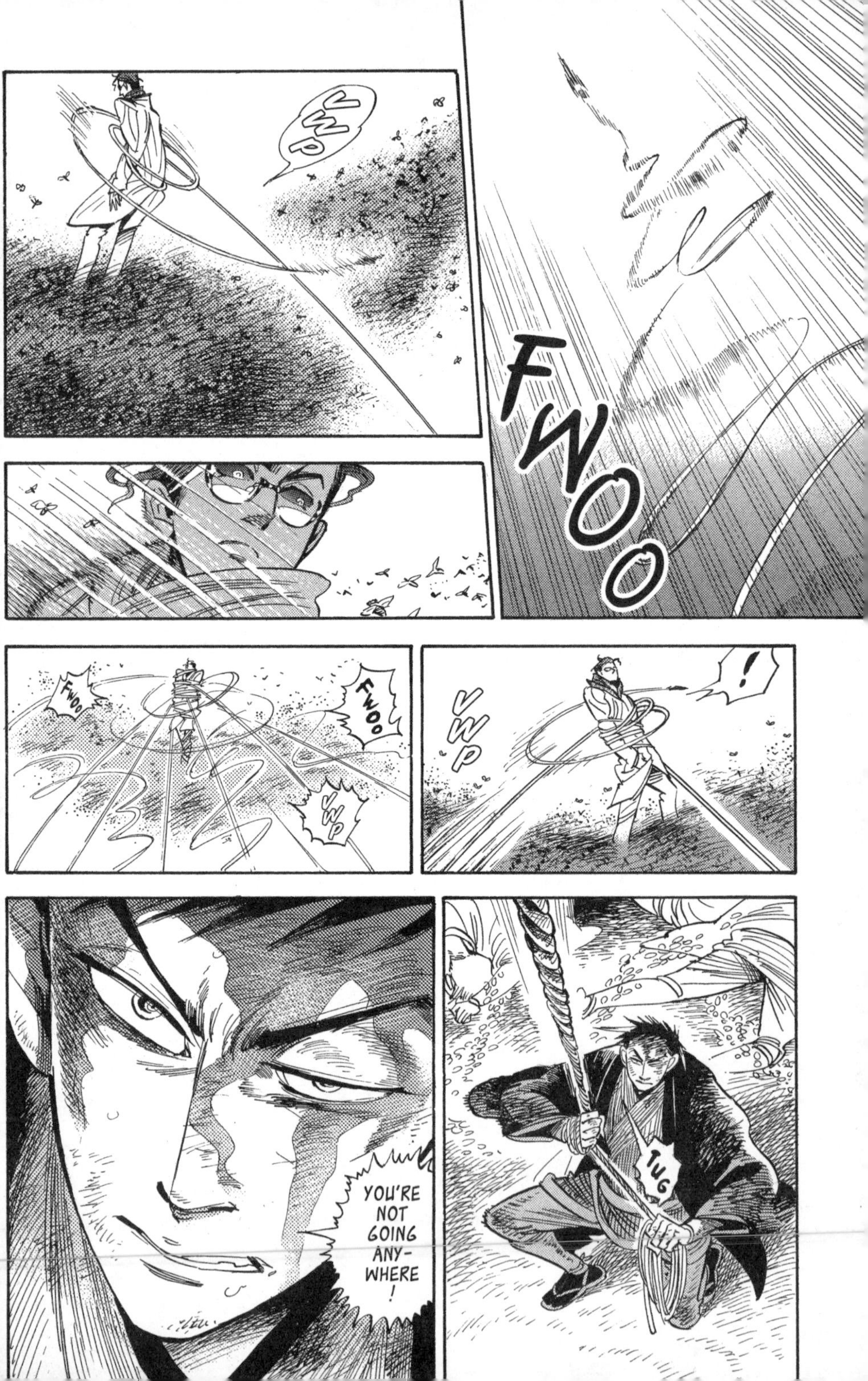
FWOOO
VWP
!
VWP
FWOO
FWOO
VWP
TUG
YOU'RE NOT GOING ANYWHERE!

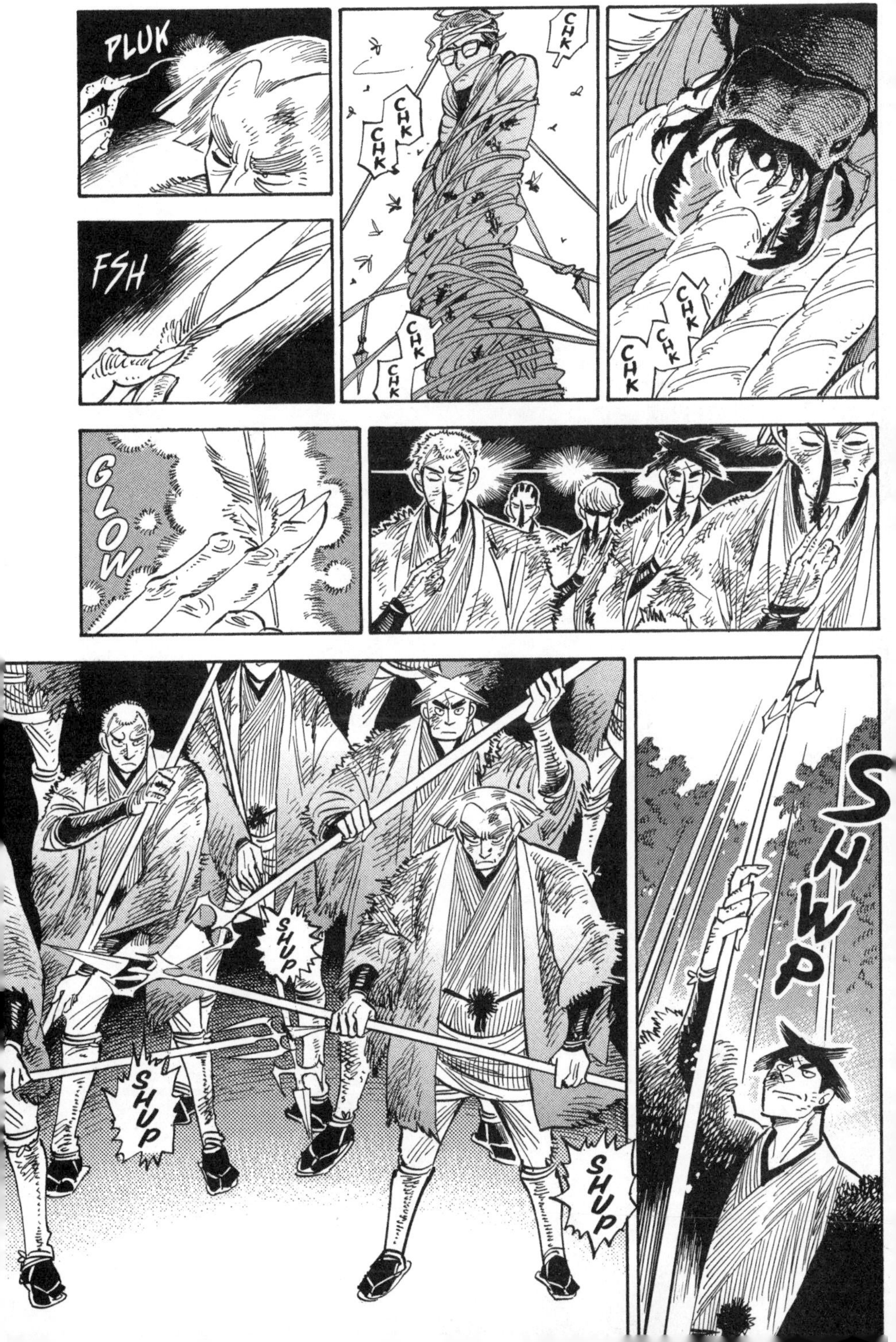
CHK
CHK
CHK
CHK
CHK
CHK
CHK
CHK
PLUK
FSH
GLOW
SHWP
SHUP
SHUP
SHUP

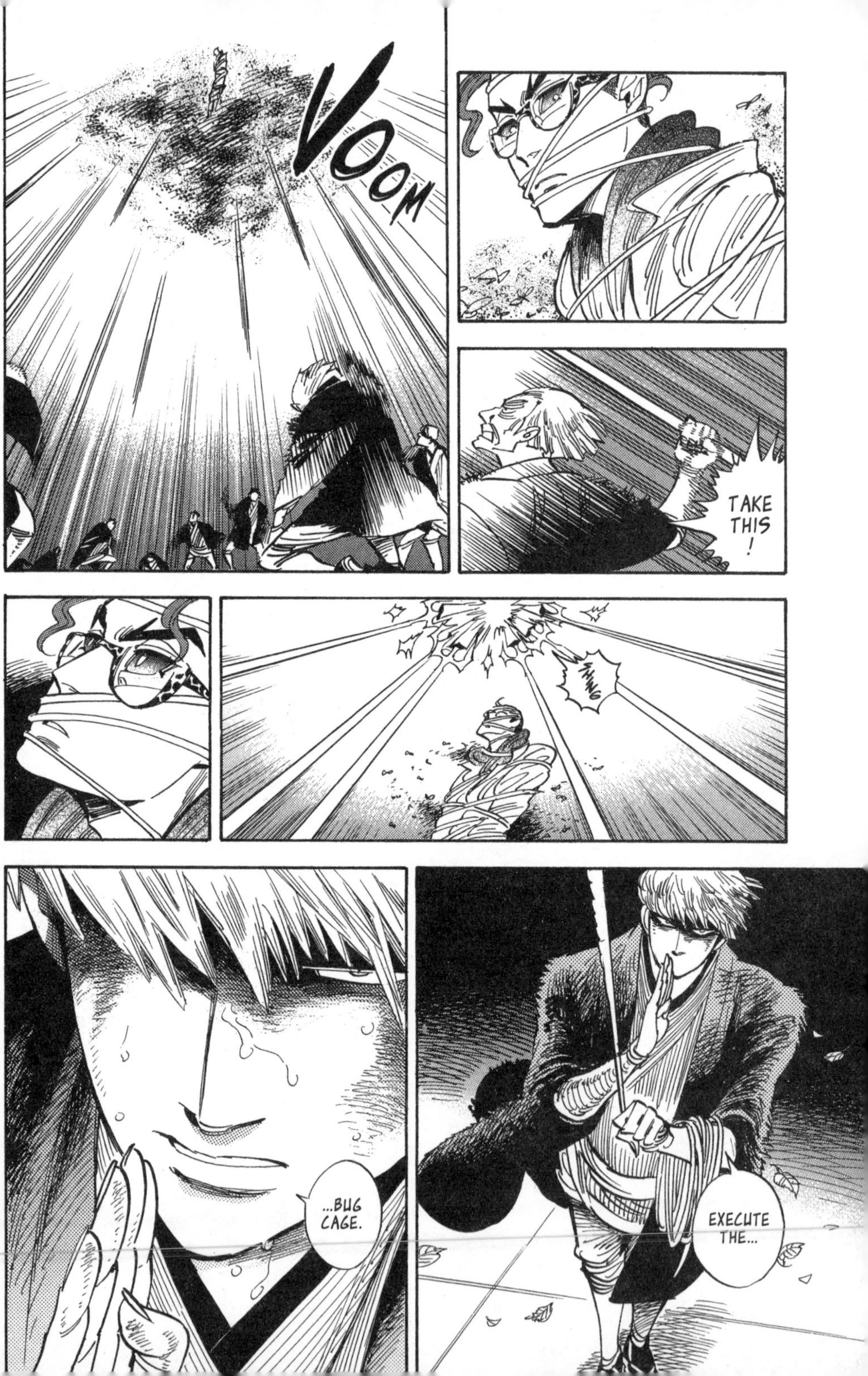
TAKE THIS!
VOOM
THING
EXECUTE THE...
...BUG CAGE.

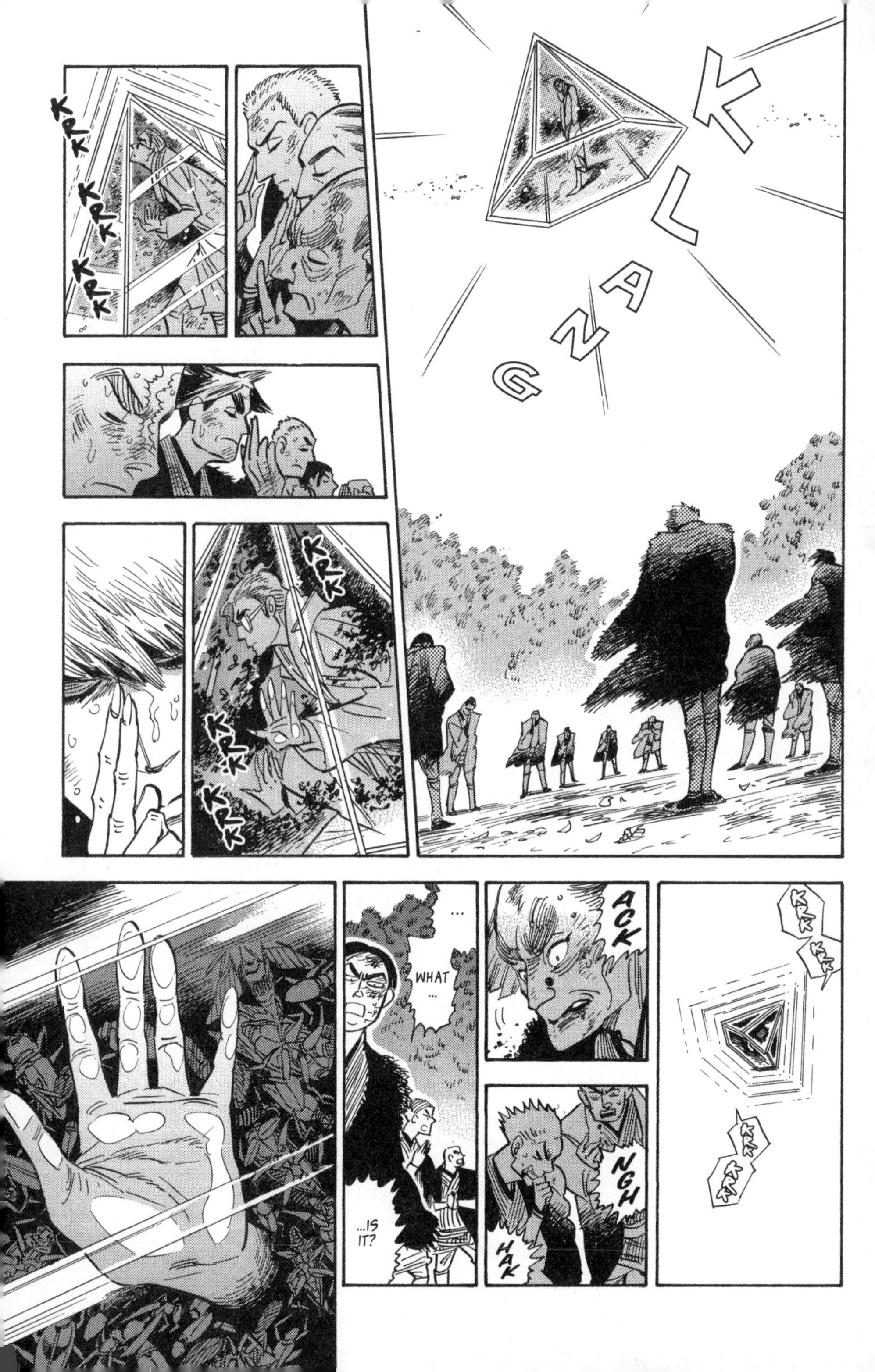
KLANG
KRK
KRK
KRK
KRK
KRK
KRK
KRK
KRK
KRK
KRK
ACK
NGH
HAK
...
WHAT ...
...IS IT?

KRAK

EVEN
...

...THIS
CAN'T...

...

W...

WHAT
...

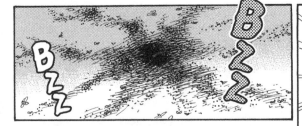

BZZ

BZZ

POW

BZZ

BZZ

BZZ

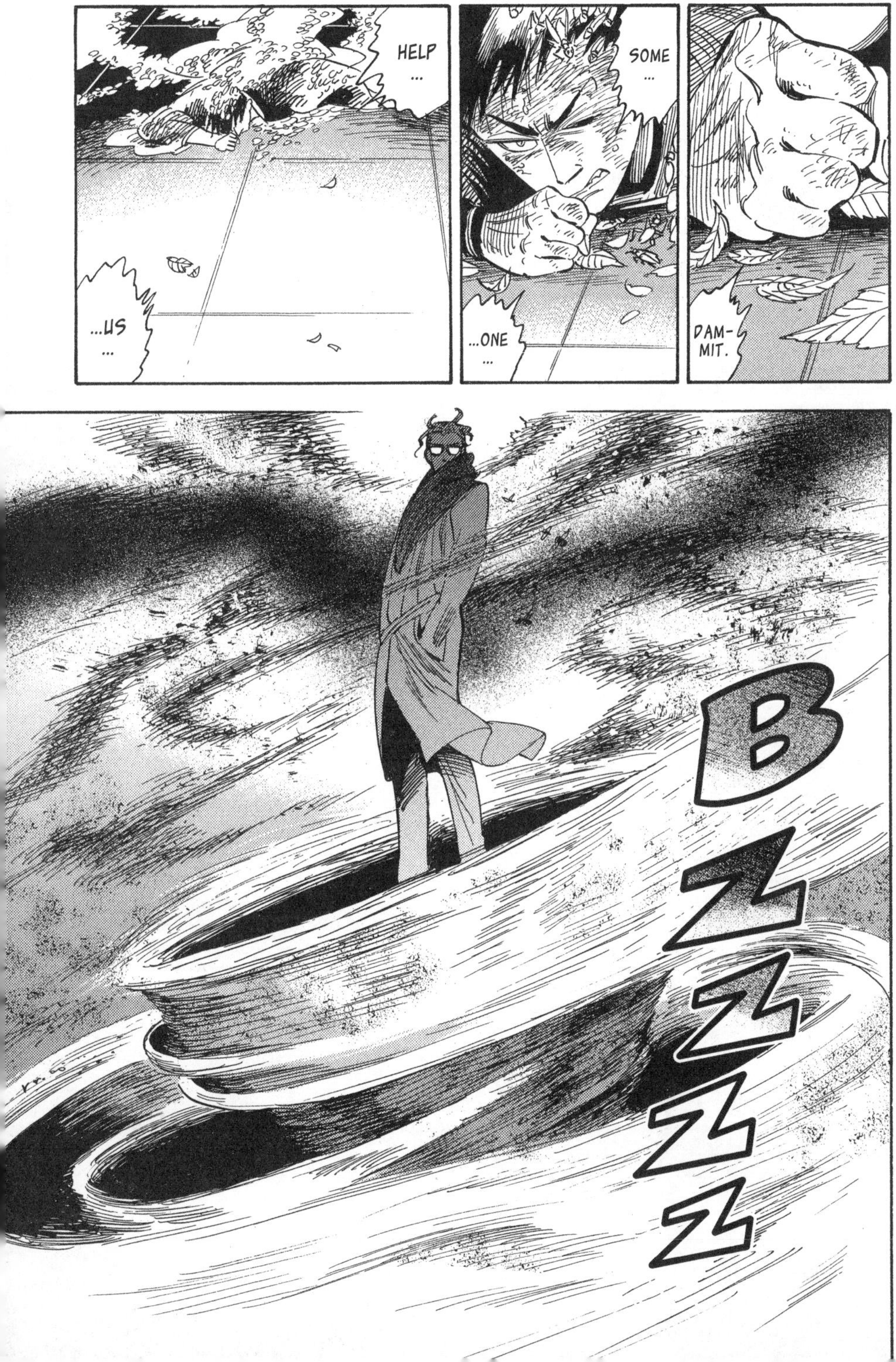
HELP ...
...US ...
SOME ...
...ONE ...
DAM-MIT.
BZZZZ

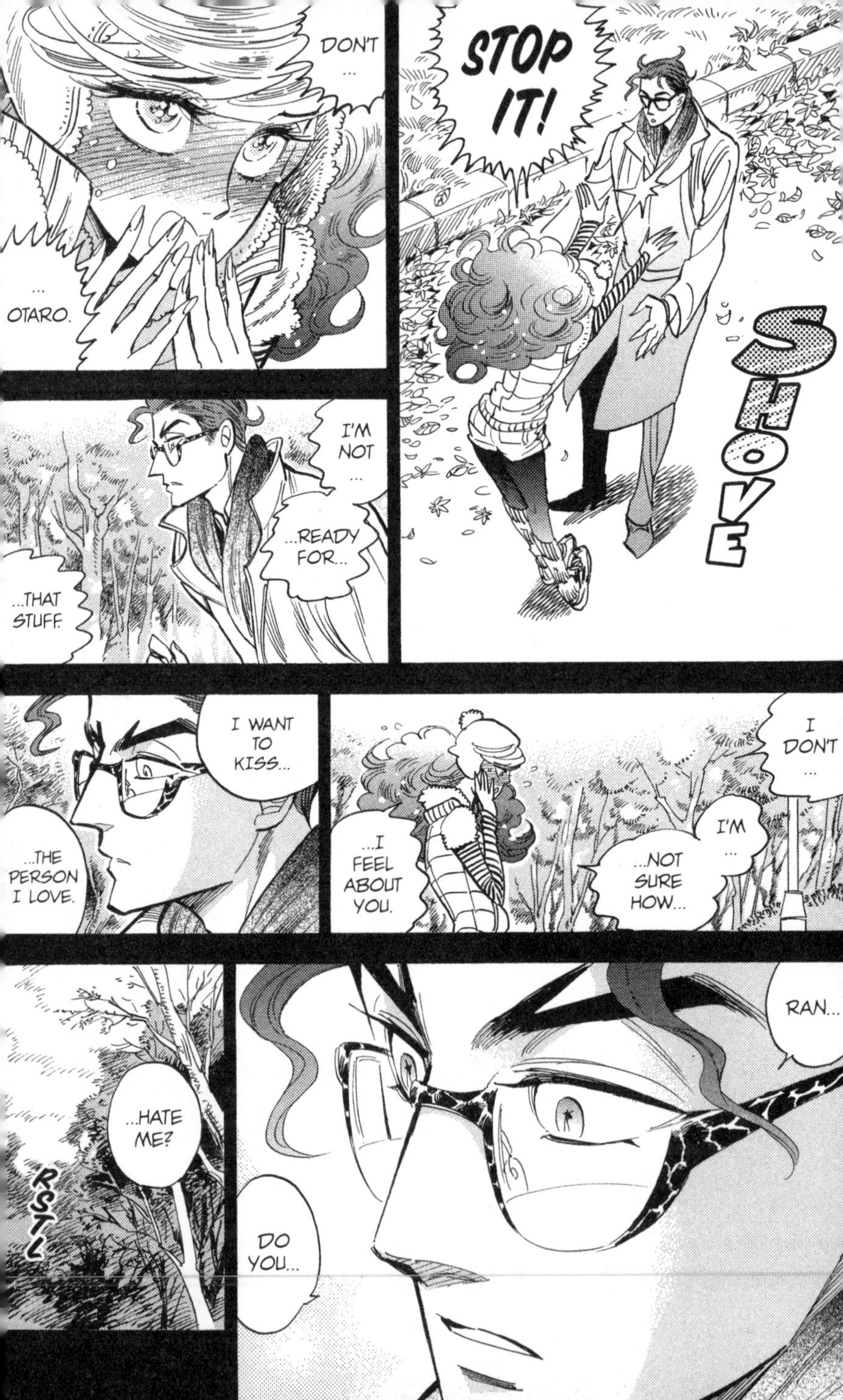
STOP IT!
SHOVE
DON'T ...
... OTARO.
I'M NOT ...
...READY FOR...
...THAT STUFF.
I DON'T ...
I'M ...
...NOT SURE HOW...
...I FEEL ABOUT YOU.
I WANT TO KISS...
...THE PERSON I LOVE.
RAN...
DO YOU...
...HATE ME?
RSTL

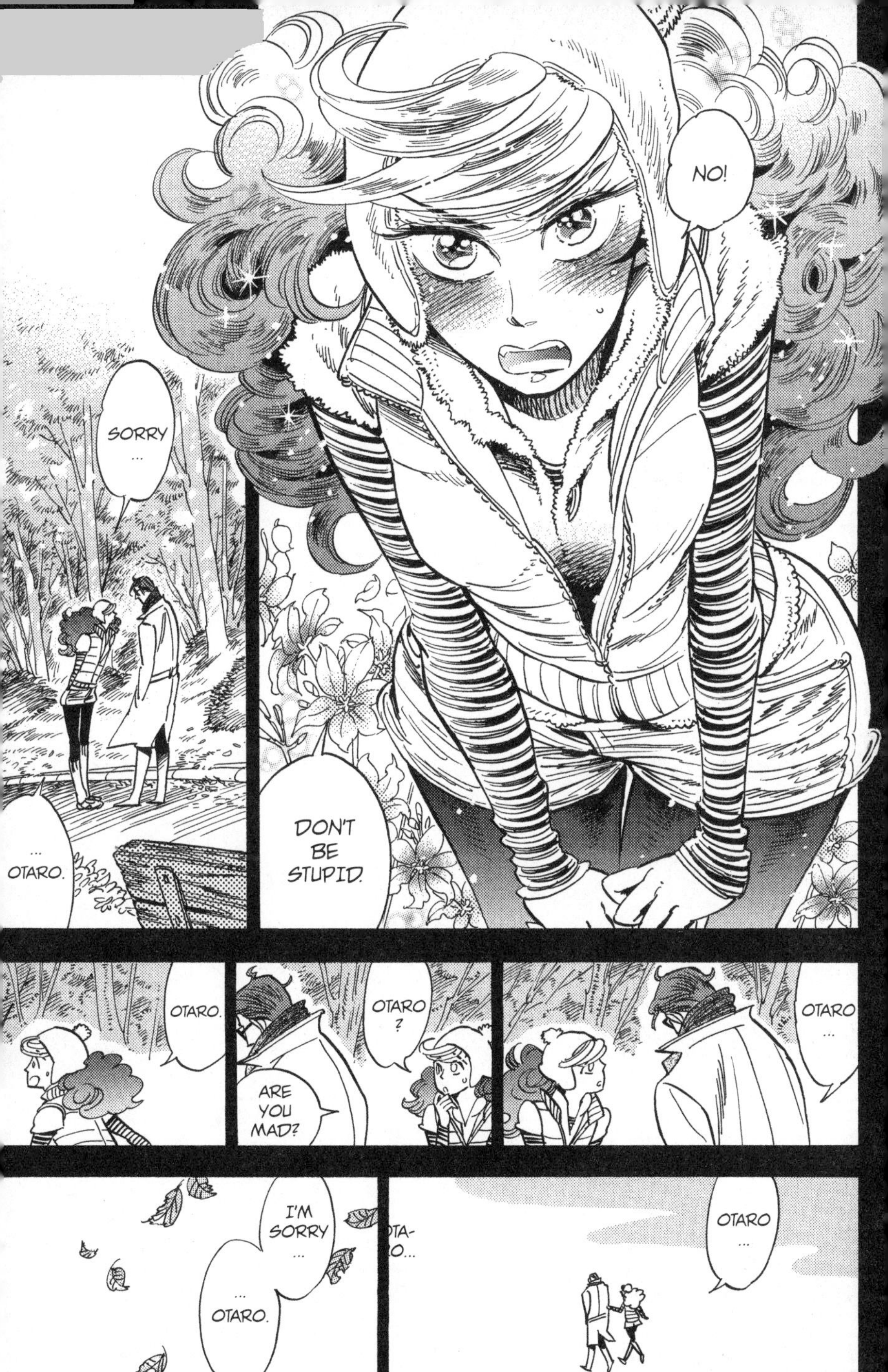
NO!
DON'T BE STUPID.
SORRY ...
... OTARO.
OTARO ...
OTARO ?
ARE YOU MAD?
OTARO.
OTARO ...
OTA-
I'M SORRY ...
... OTARO.

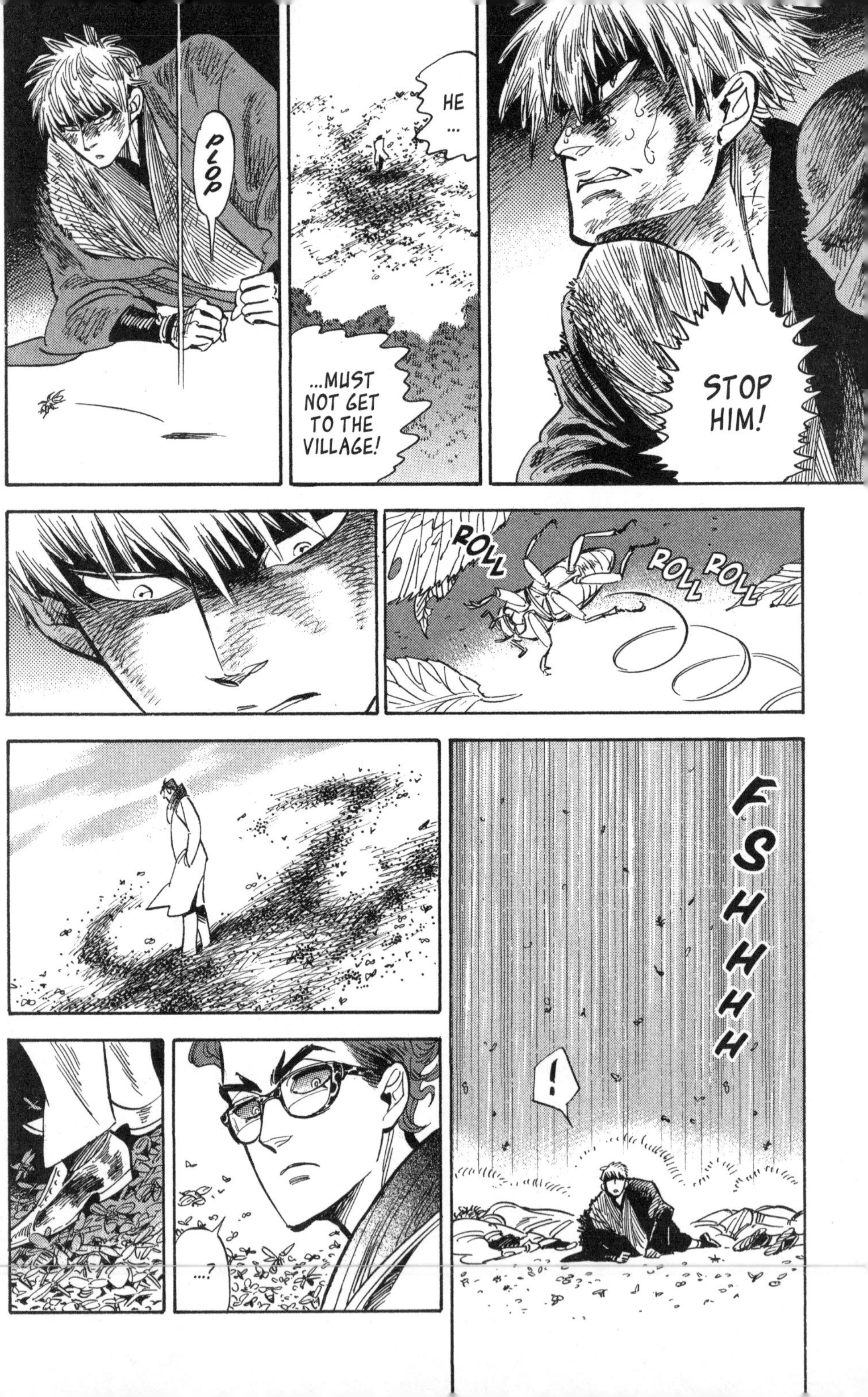
STOP HIM!
HE ...
...MUST NOT GET TO THE VILLAGE!
PLOP
ROLL ROLL ROLL
FSHHHH
!
...?

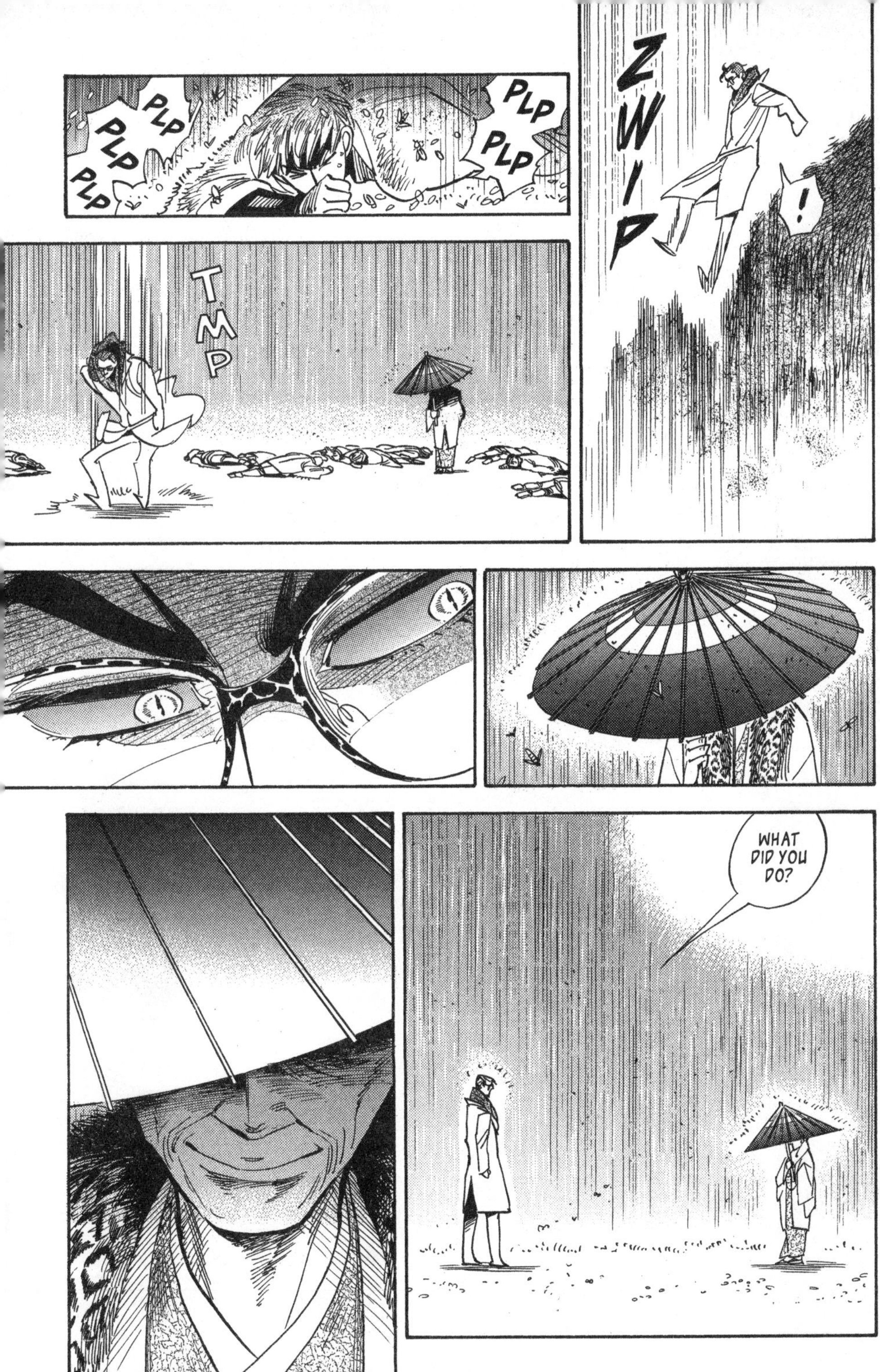
ZWIP
!
PLP
PLP
PLP
PLP
PLP
TMP
WHAT DID YOU DO?

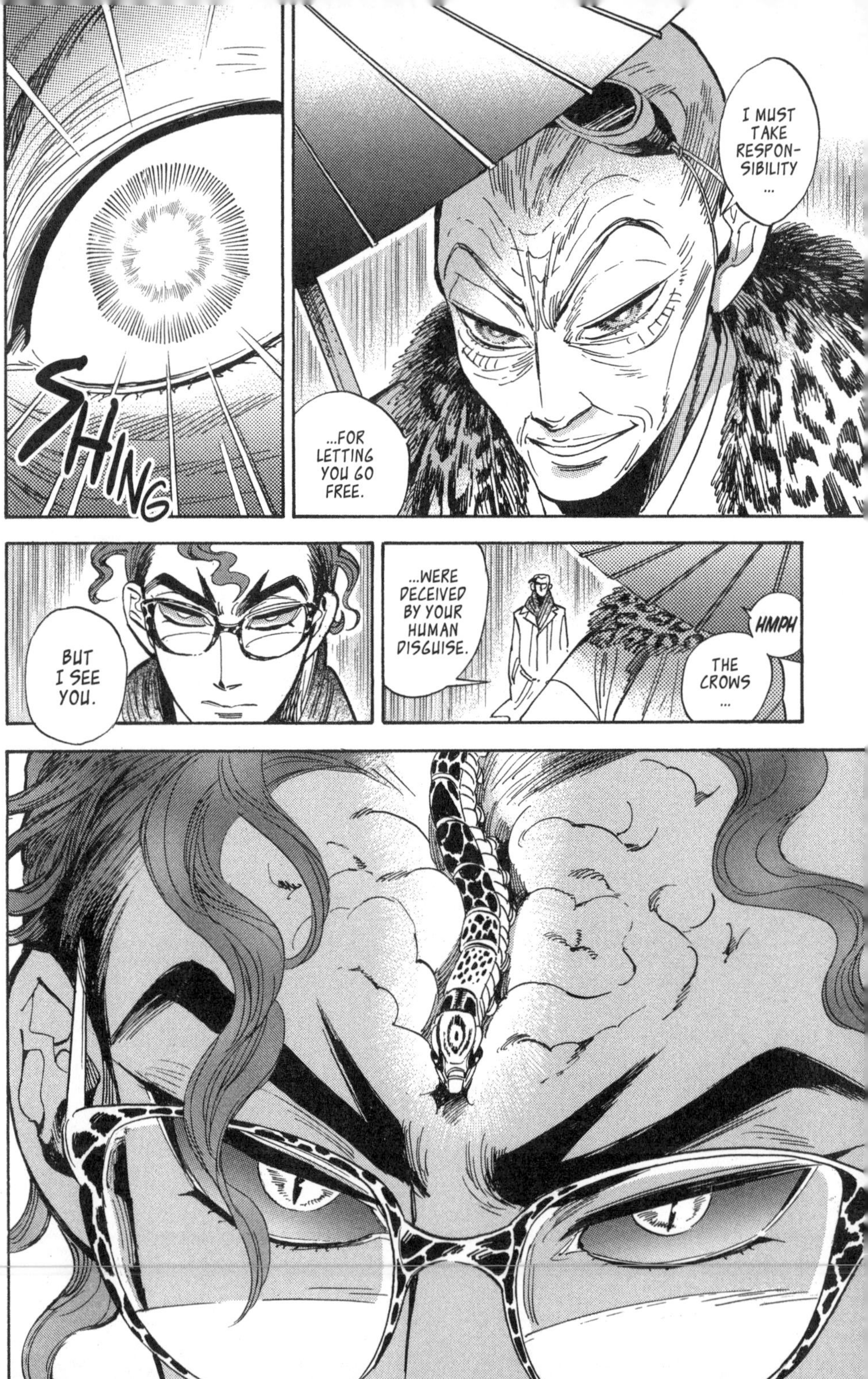
I MUST TAKE RESPON-SIBILITY ...
...FOR LETTING YOU GO FREE.
SHING
HMPH
THE CROWS ...
...WERE DECEIVED BY YOUR HUMAN DISGUISE.
BUT I SEE YOU.

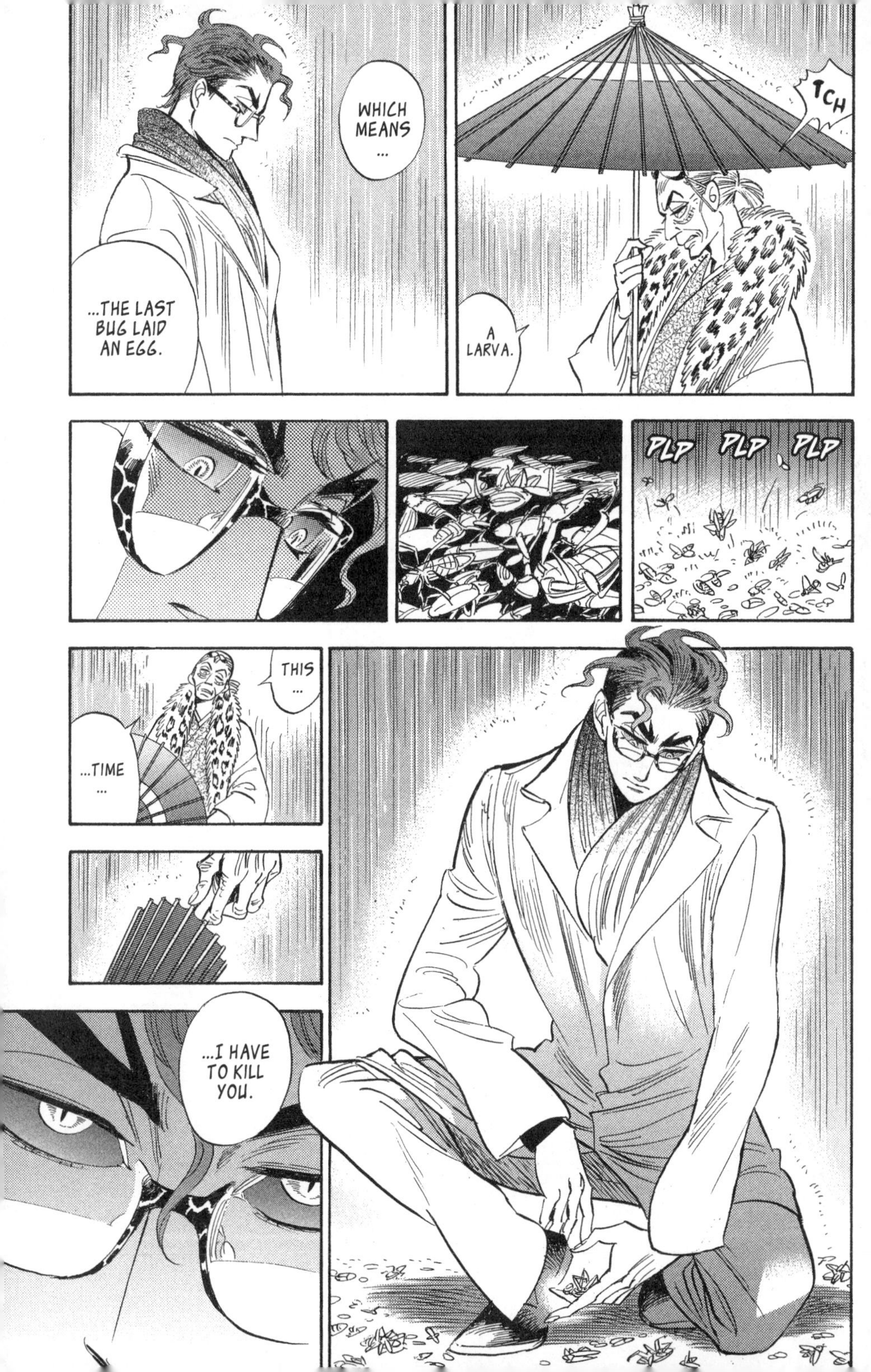
TCH
A LARVA.
WHICH MEANS ...
...THE LAST BUG LAID AN EGG.
PLP PLP PLP
THIS ...
...TIME ...
...I HAVE TO KILL YOU.

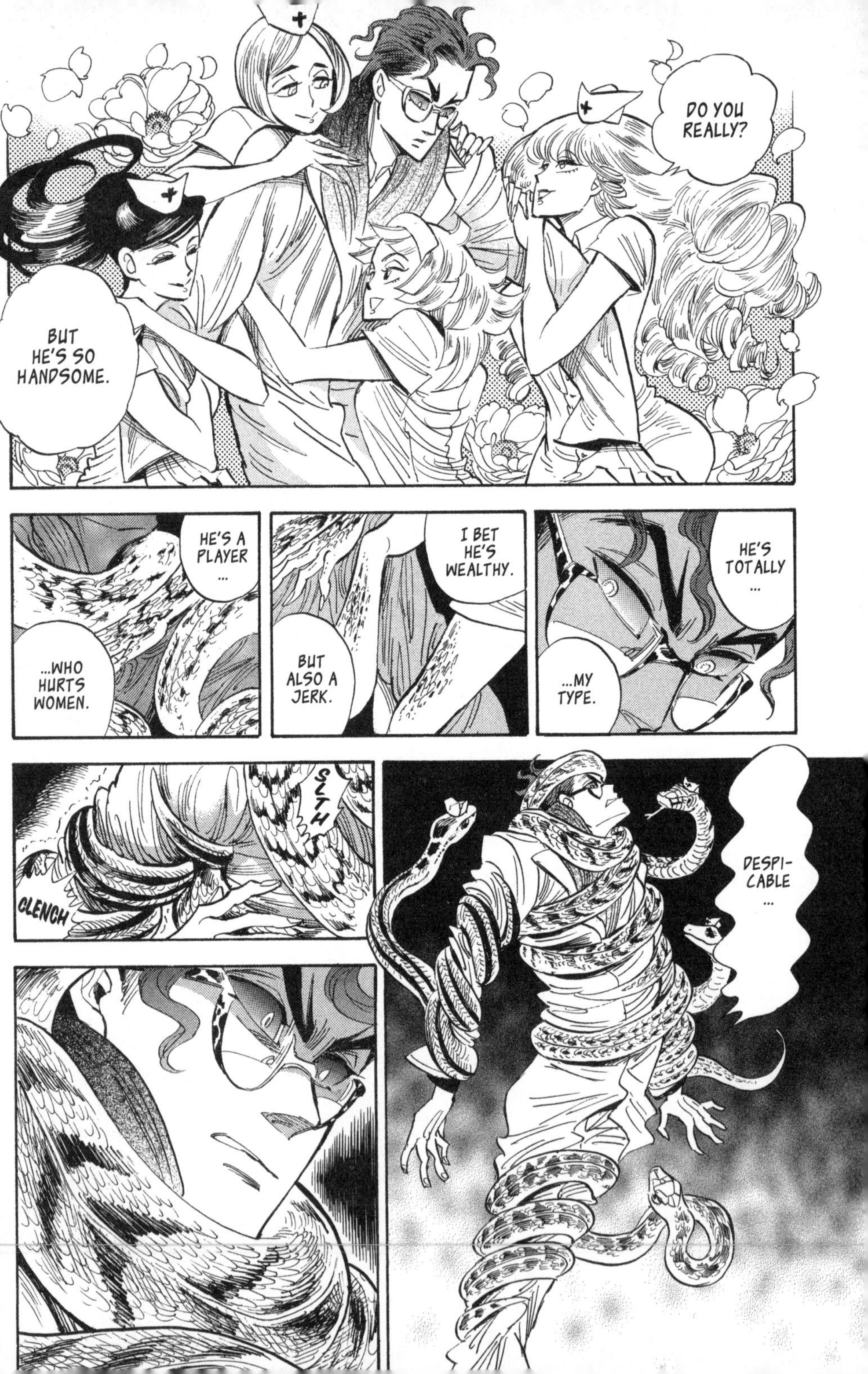
DO YOU REALLY?
BUT HE'S SO HANDSOME.
HE'S TOTALLY ...
...MY TYPE.
I BET HE'S WEALTHY.
BUT ALSO A JERK.
HE'S A PLAYER ...
...WHO HURTS WOMEN.
DESPI-CABLE ...
SLTH
CLENCH

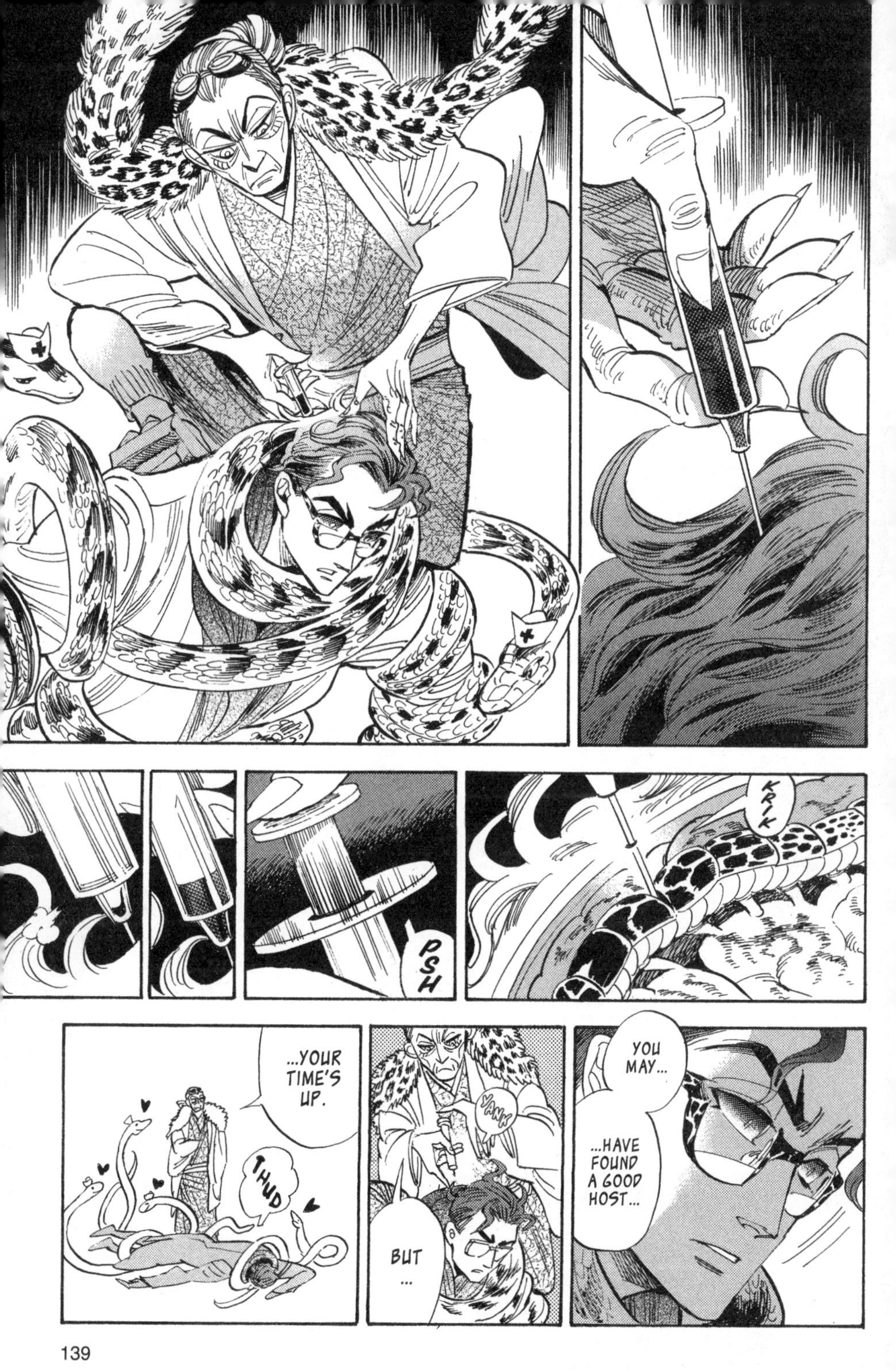
KRIK
PSH
YOU MAY...
...HAVE FOUND A GOOD HOST...
YANK
BUT ...
...YOUR TIME'S UP.
THUD

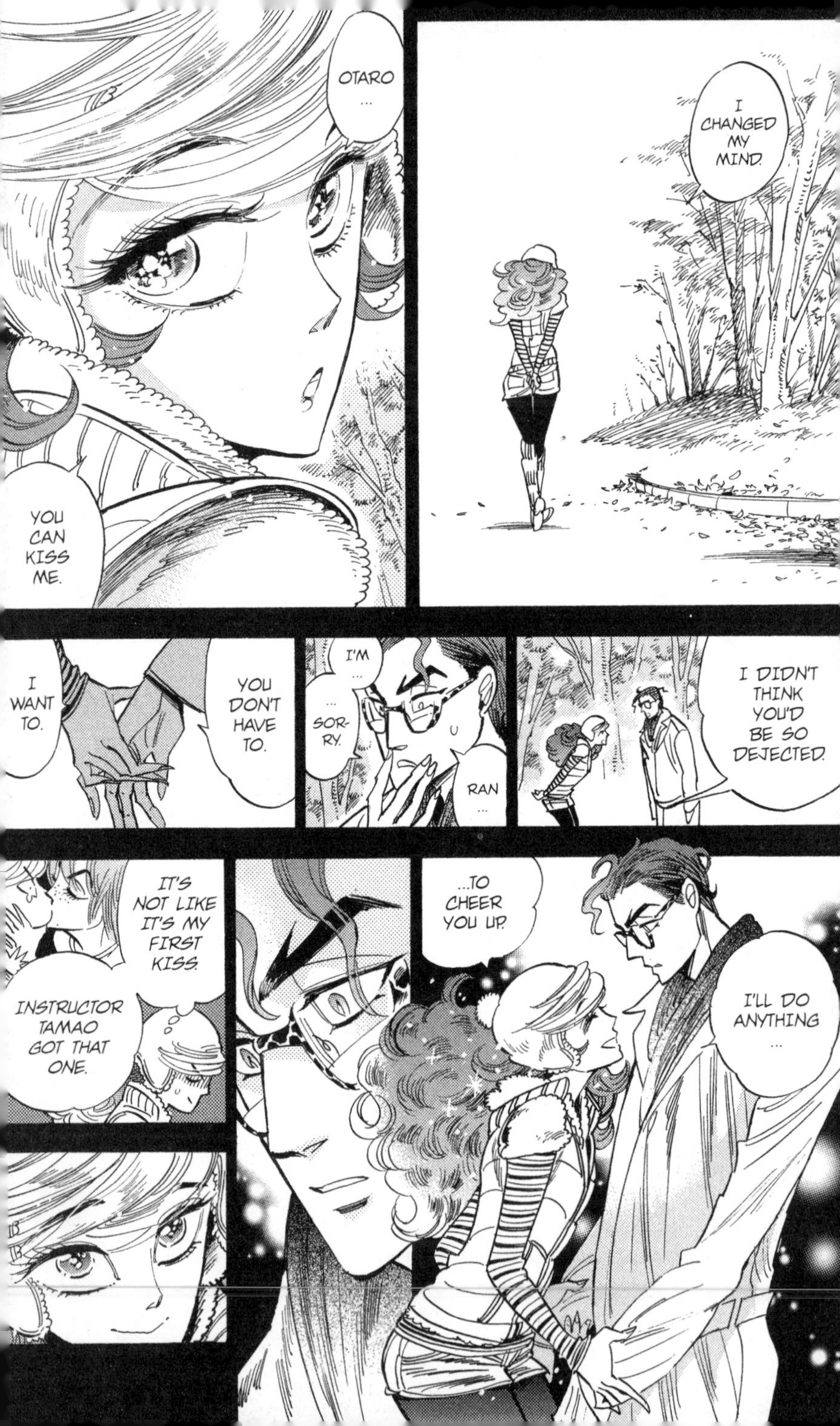
I CHANGED MY MIND.
OTARO ...
YOU CAN KISS ME.
I DIDN'T THINK YOU'D BE SO DEJECTED.
I'M ... ... SOR-RY.
RAN ...
YOU DON'T HAVE TO.
I WANT TO.
I'LL DO ANYTHING ...
...TO CHEER YOU UP.
IT'S NOT LIKE IT'S MY FIRST KISS.
INSTRUCTOR TAMAO GOT THAT ONE.

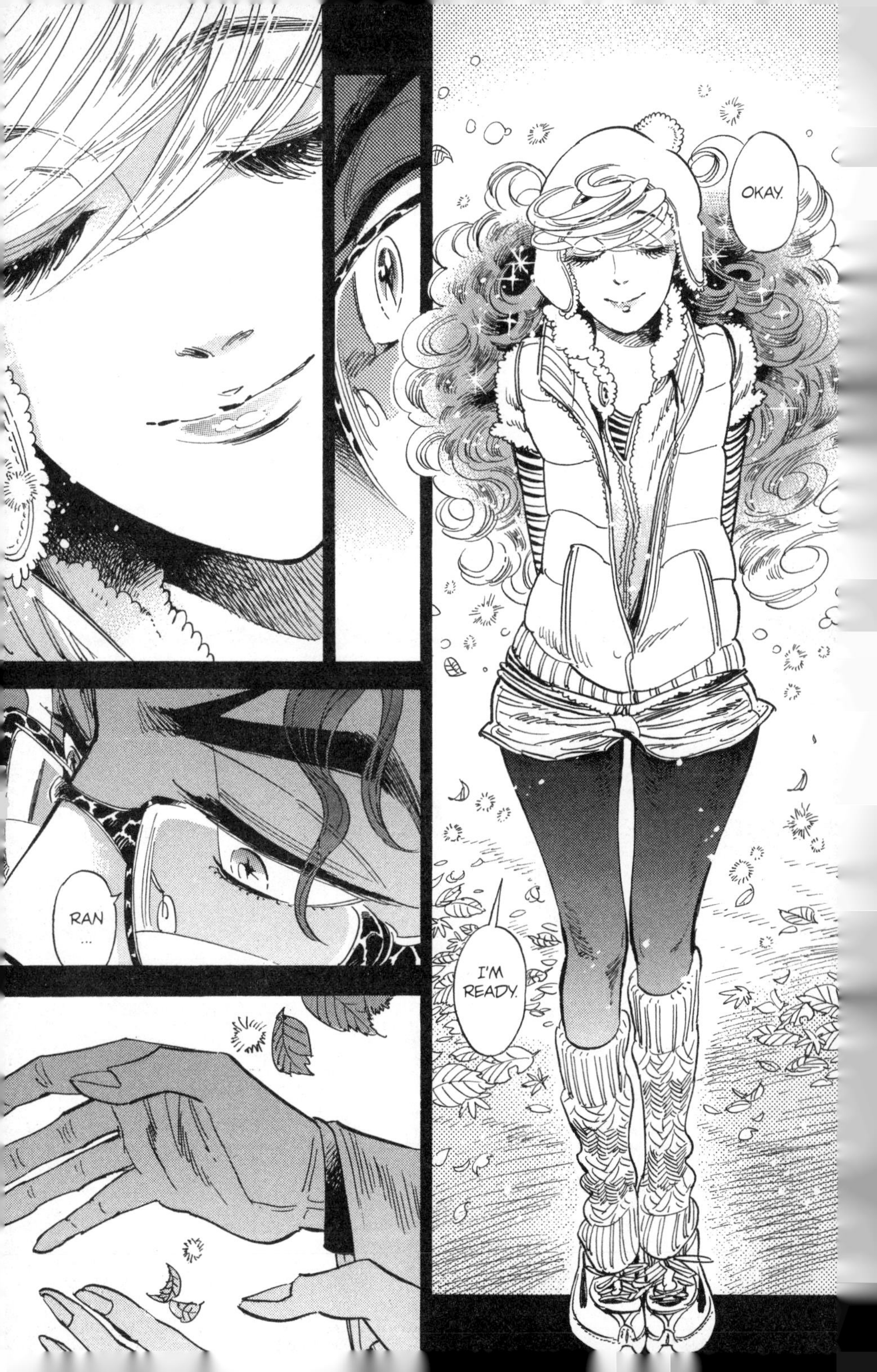
OKAY.
I'M READY.
RAN ...

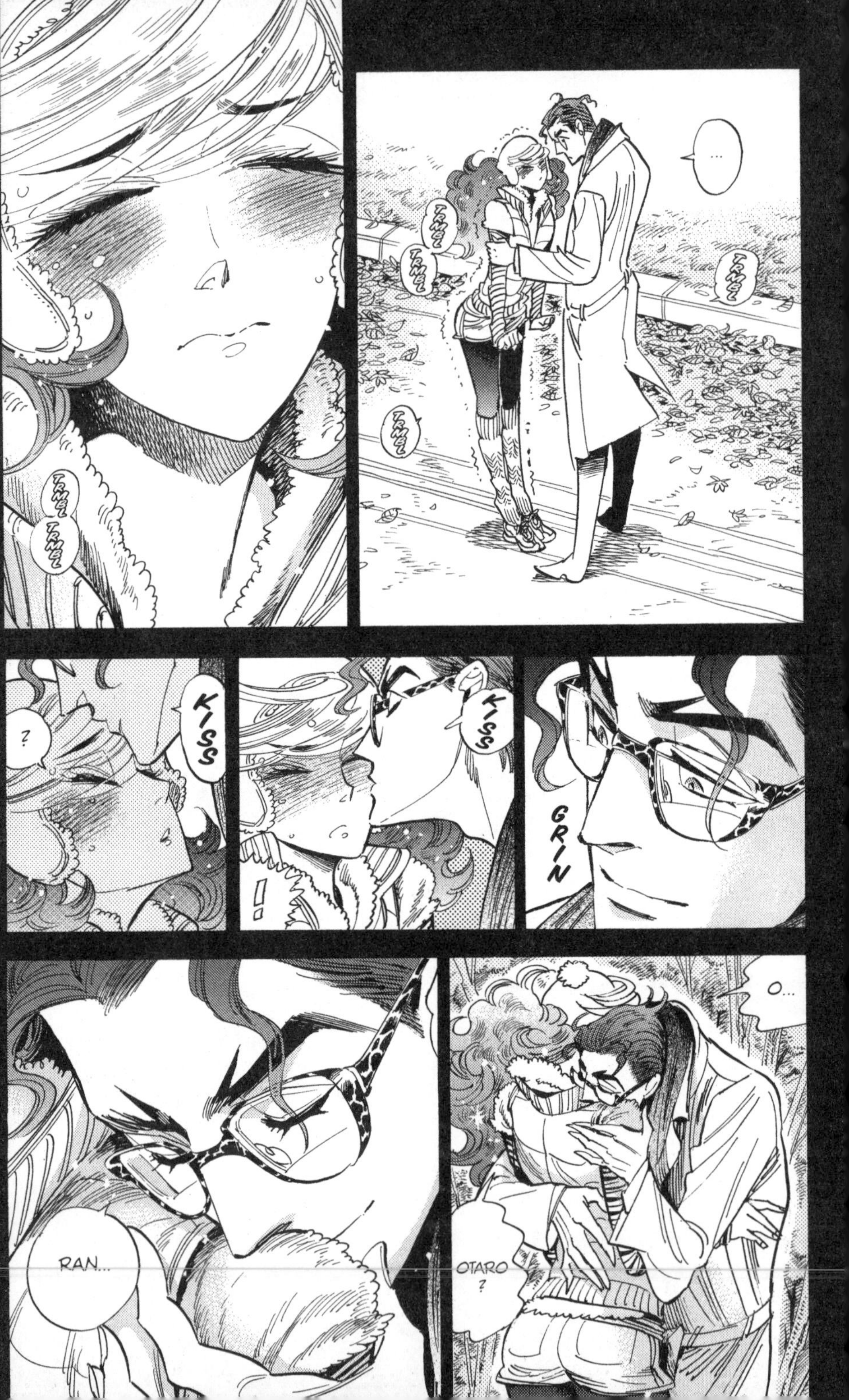
...
TRMBL
TRMBL
TRMBL
TRMBL
TRMBL
TRMBL
GRIN
KISS
!
KISS
?
O...
OTARO ?
RAN...

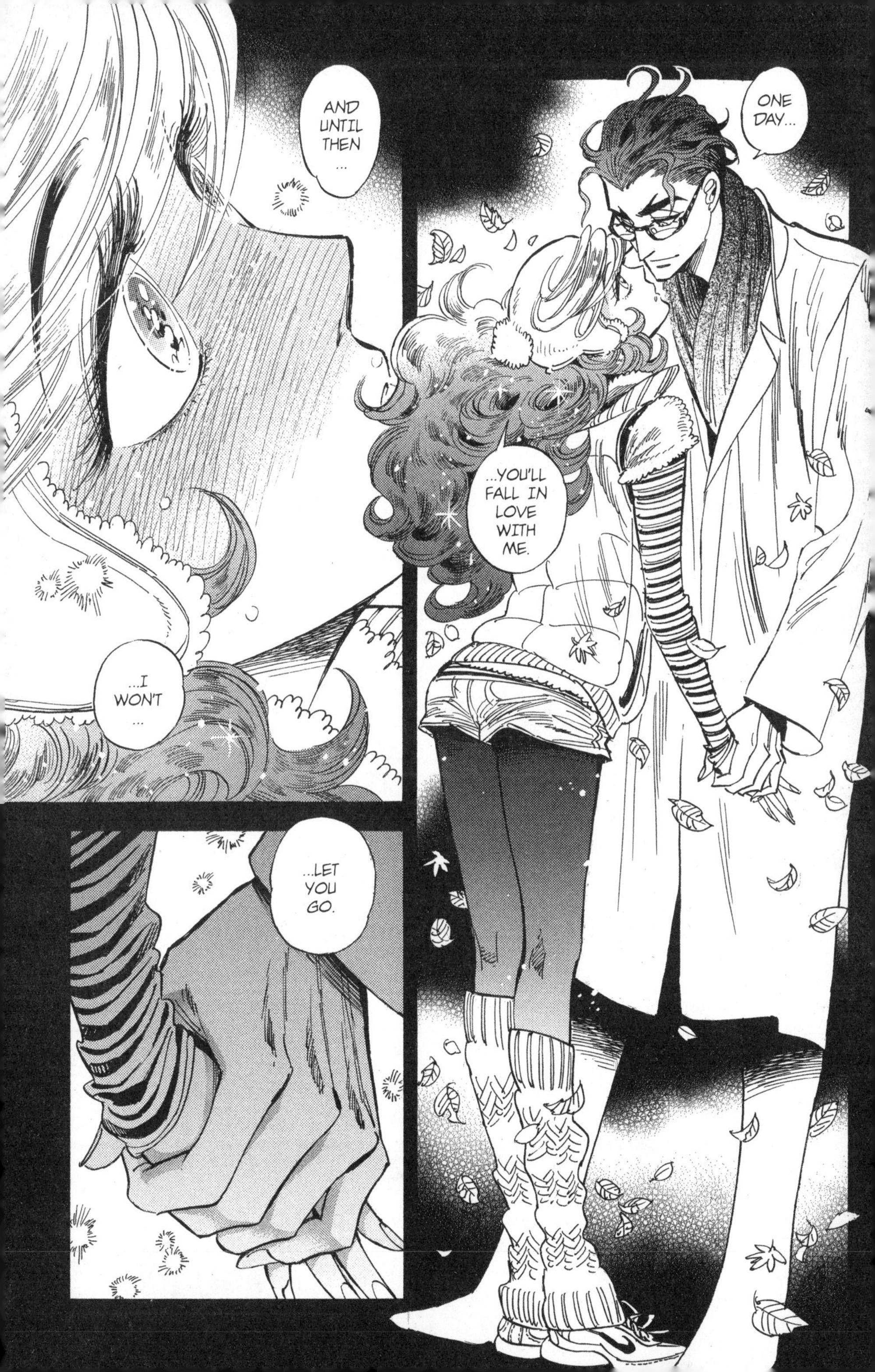
ONE DAY...
...YOU'LL FALL IN LOVE WITH ME.
AND UNTIL THEN ...
...I WON'T ...
...LET YOU GO.

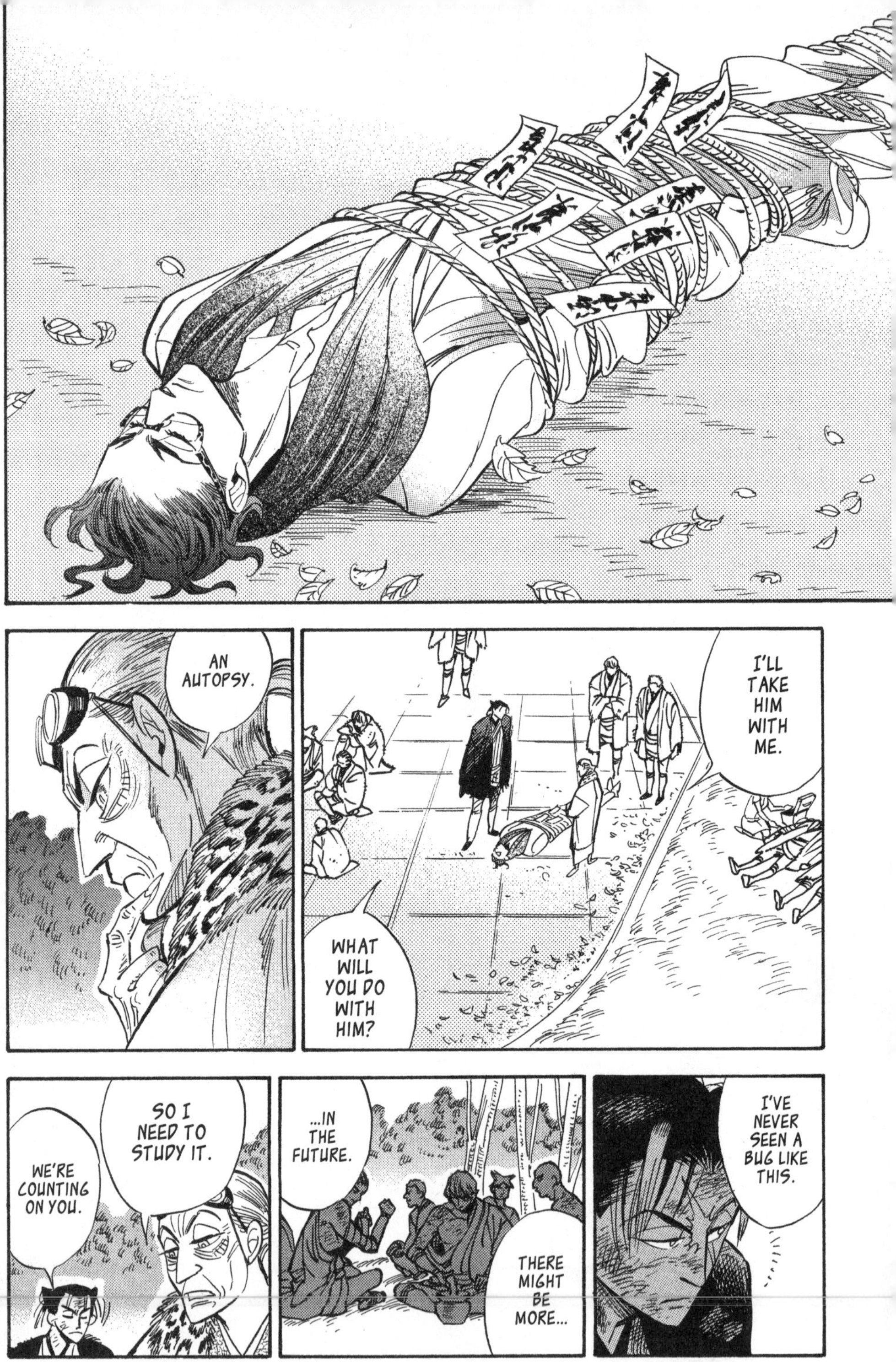
I'LL TAKE HIM WITH ME.
WHAT WILL YOU DO WITH HIM?
AN AUTOPSY.
I'VE NEVER SEEN A BUG LIKE THIS.
THERE MIGHT BE MORE...
...IN THE FUTURE.
SO I NEED TO STUDY IT.
WE'RE COUNTING ON YOU.

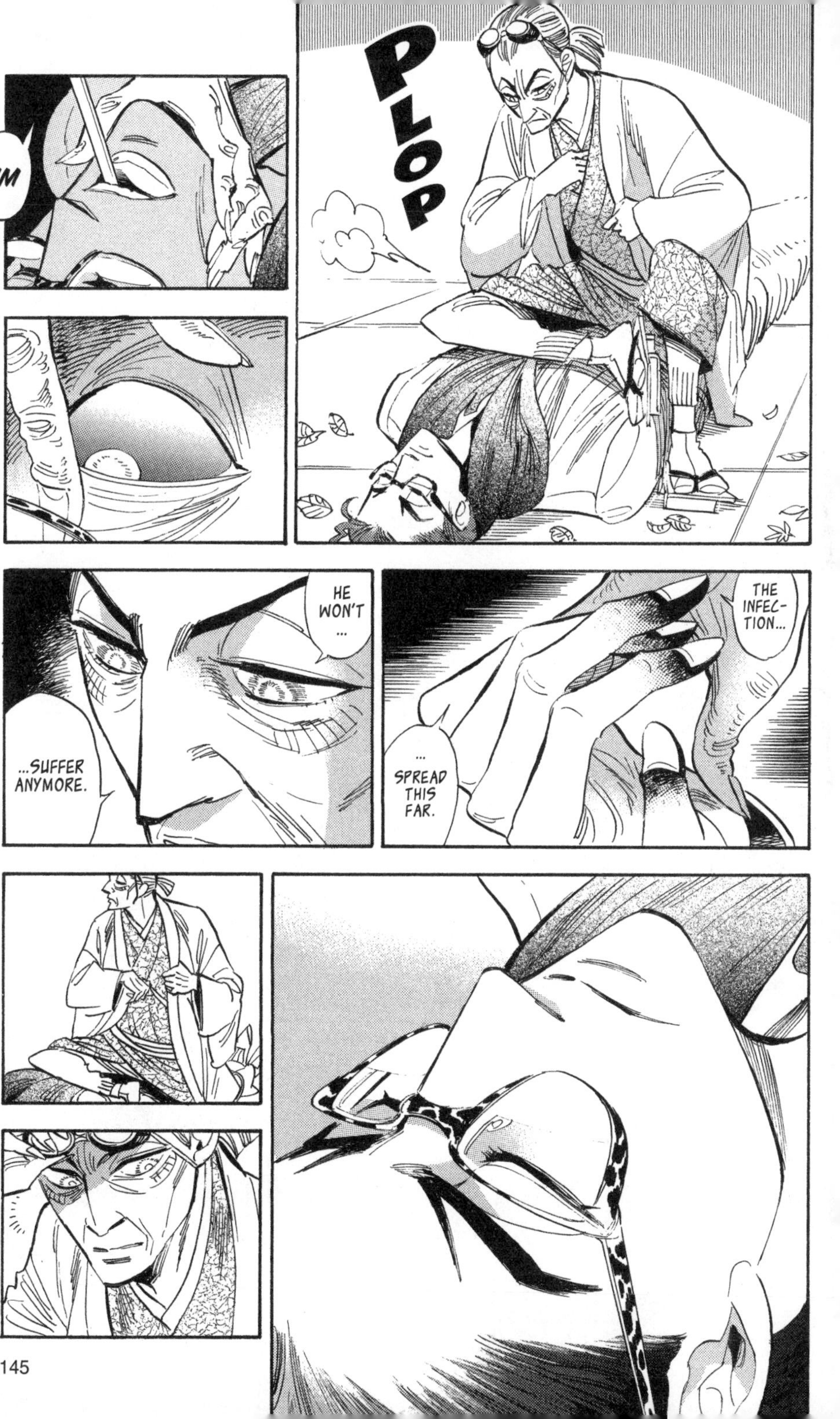
PLOP
HM
THE INFECTION...
... SPREAD THIS FAR.
HE WON'T ...
...SUFFER ANYMORE.

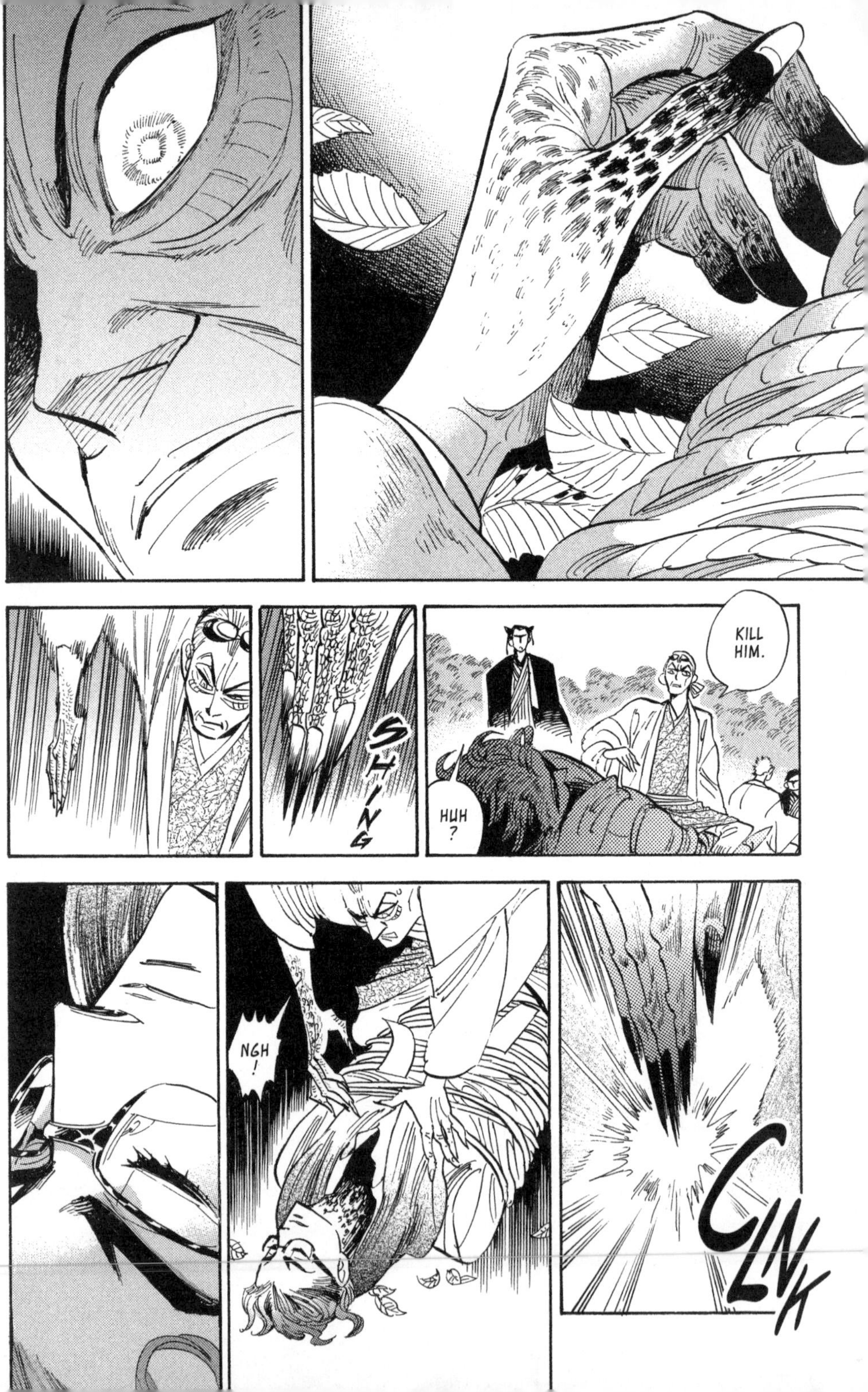
KILL HIM.
HUH?
SHING
CLNK
NGH!

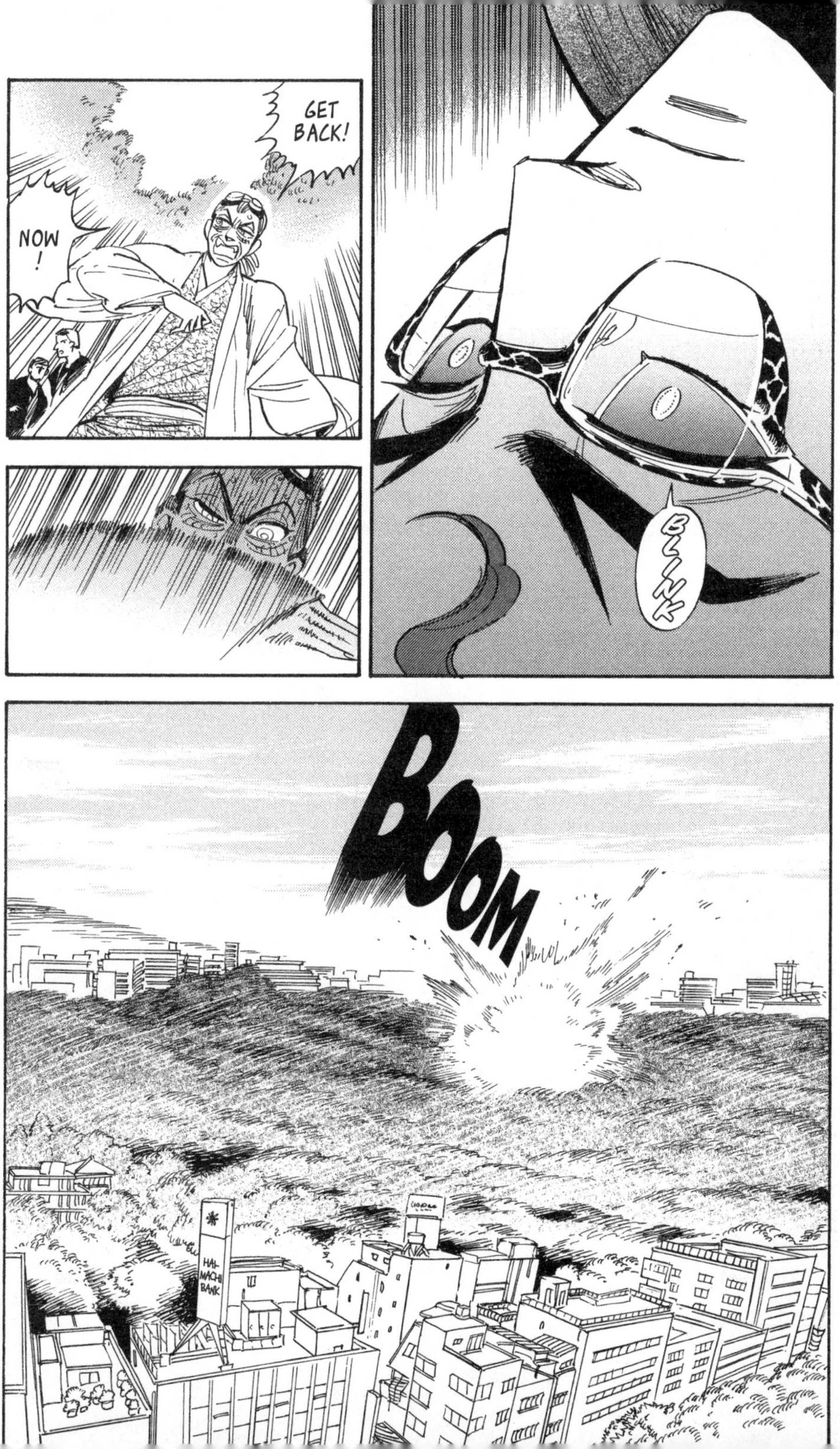
BLINK
GET BACK!
NOW!
BOOM
HAI-MACHI BANK

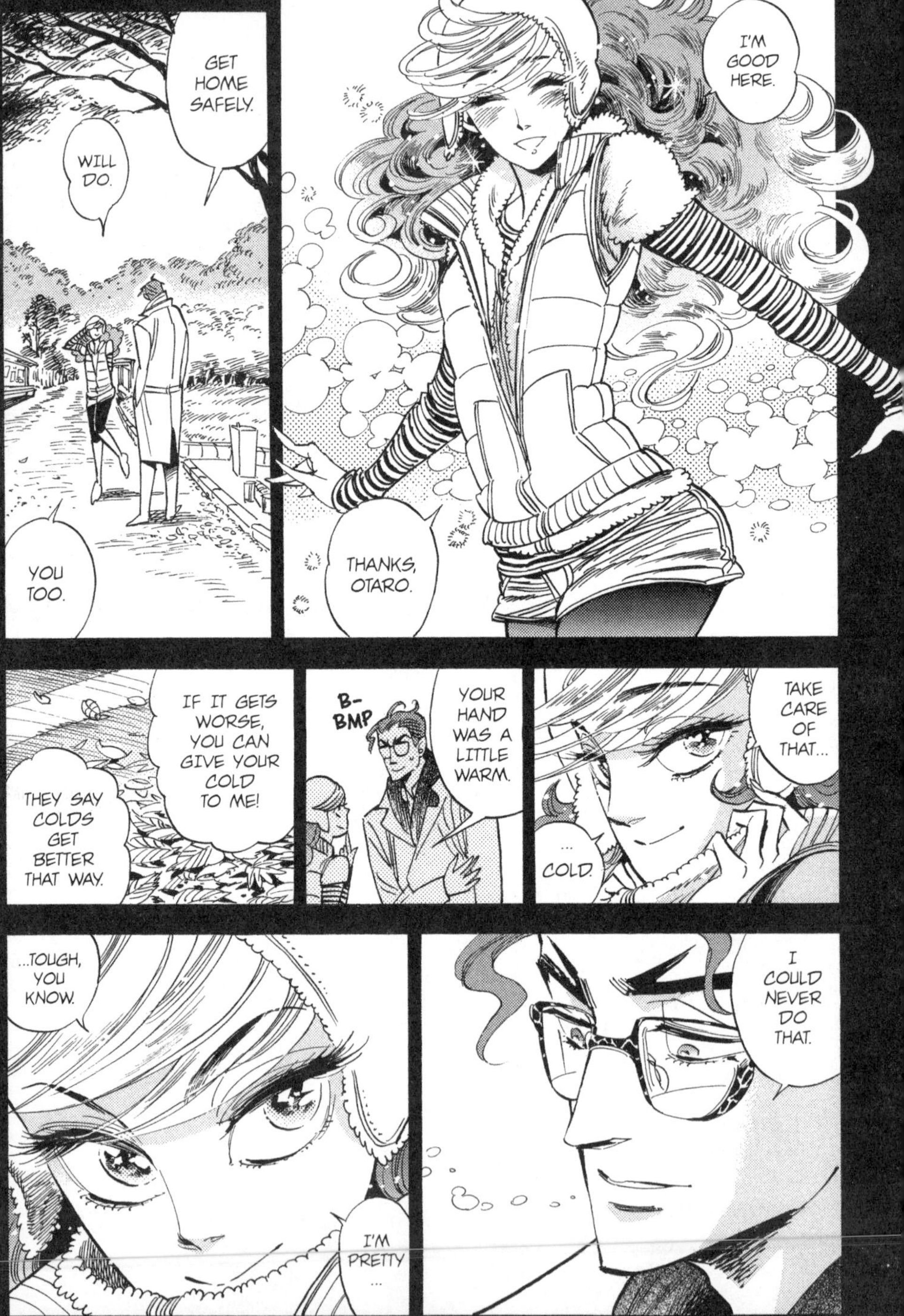

I'M GOOD HERE.
THANKS, OTARO.
GET HOME SAFELY.
WILL DO.
YOU TOO.
TAKE CARE OF THAT...
...COLD.
B-BMP
YOUR HAND WAS A LITTLE WARM.
IF IT GETS WORSE, YOU CAN GIVE YOUR COLD TO ME!
THEY SAY COLDS GET BETTER THAT WAY.
I COULD NEVER DO THAT.
I'M PRETTY ...
...TOUGH, YOU KNOW.

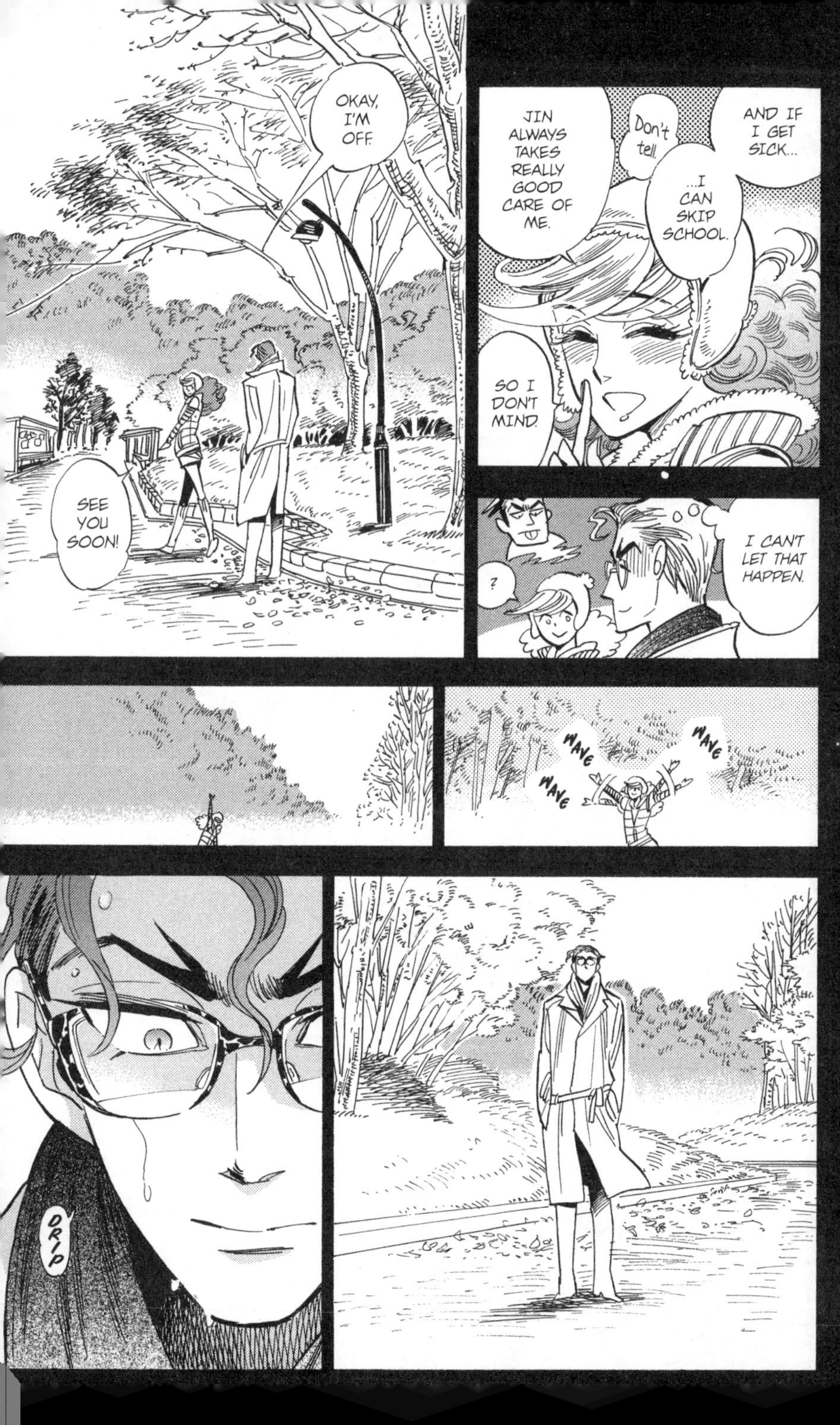
AND IF I GET SICK...
...I CAN SKIP SCHOOL.
Don't tell.
JIN ALWAYS TAKES REALLY GOOD CARE OF ME.
SO I DON'T MIND.
I CAN'T LET THAT HAPPEN.
?
OKAY, I'M OFF.
SEE YOU SOON!
WAVE
WAVE
WAVE
DRIP

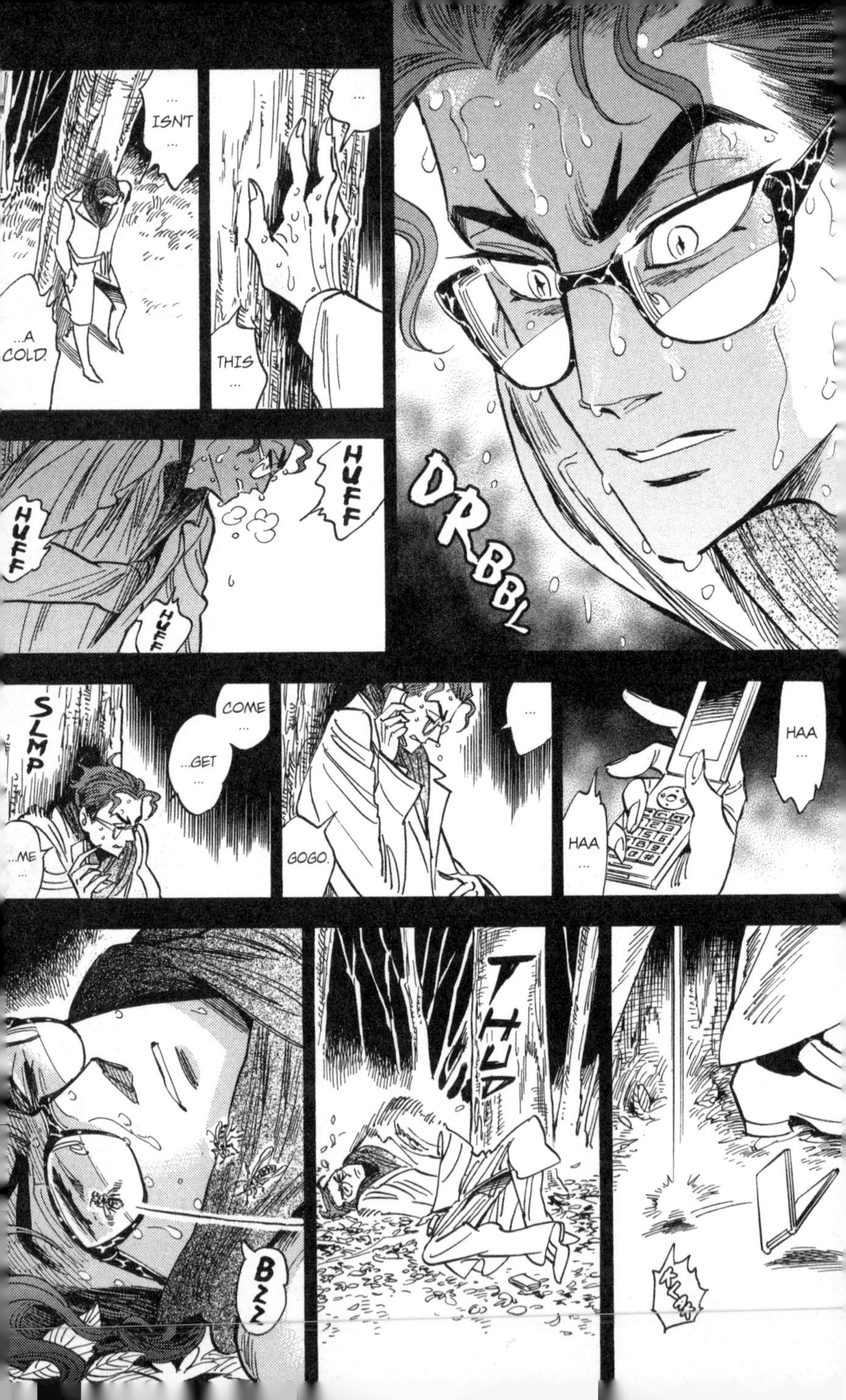
DRBBL
...
THIS ...
... ISN'T ...
...A COLD.
HUFF
HUFF
HUFF
HUFF
HAA ...
HAA ...
...
GOGO.
COME ...
...GET ...
...ME ...
SLMP
KLAK
THUD
BZZ

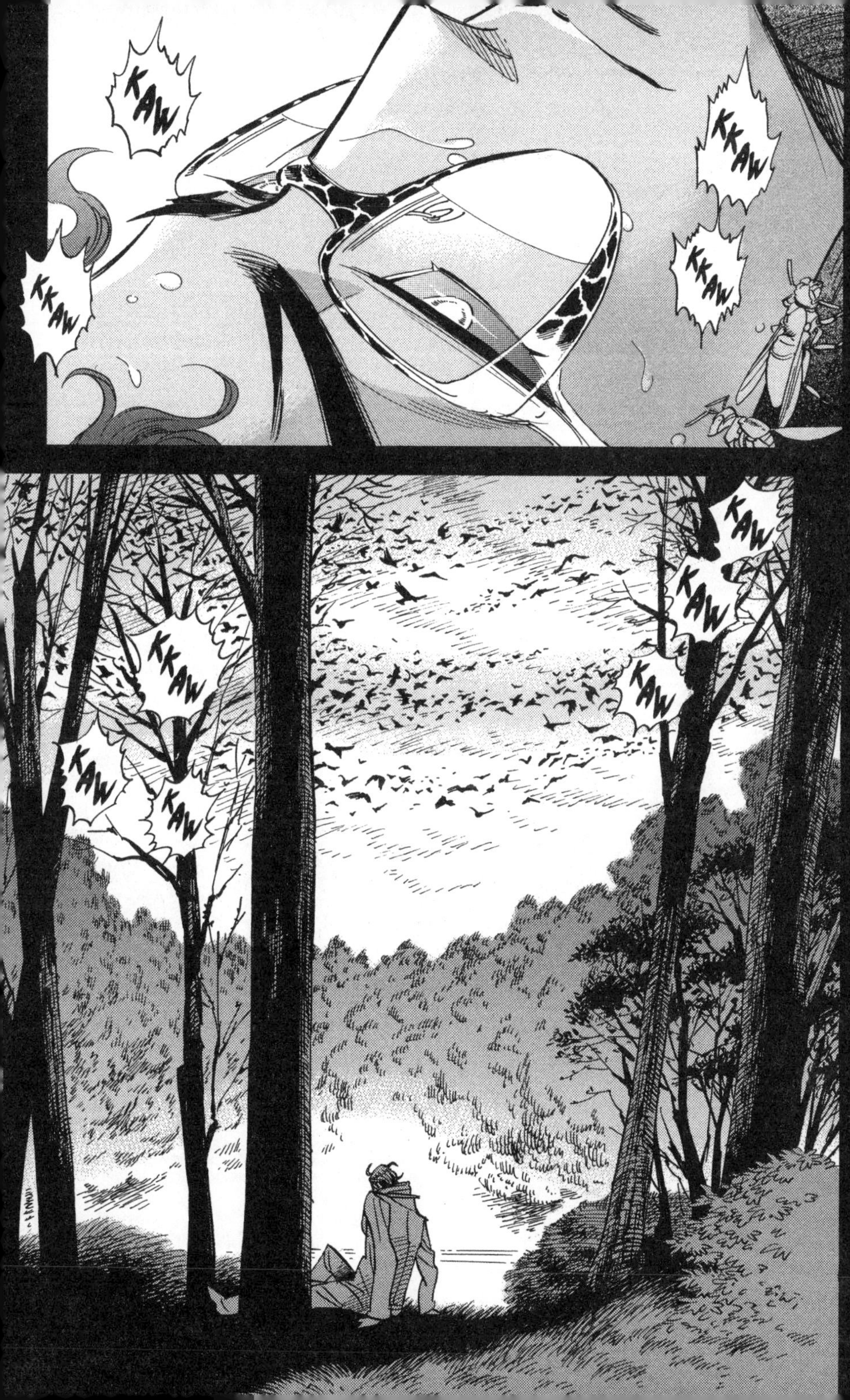
KKAW
KKAW
KAW
KKAW
KAW
KAW
KAW
KKAW
KAW
KAW

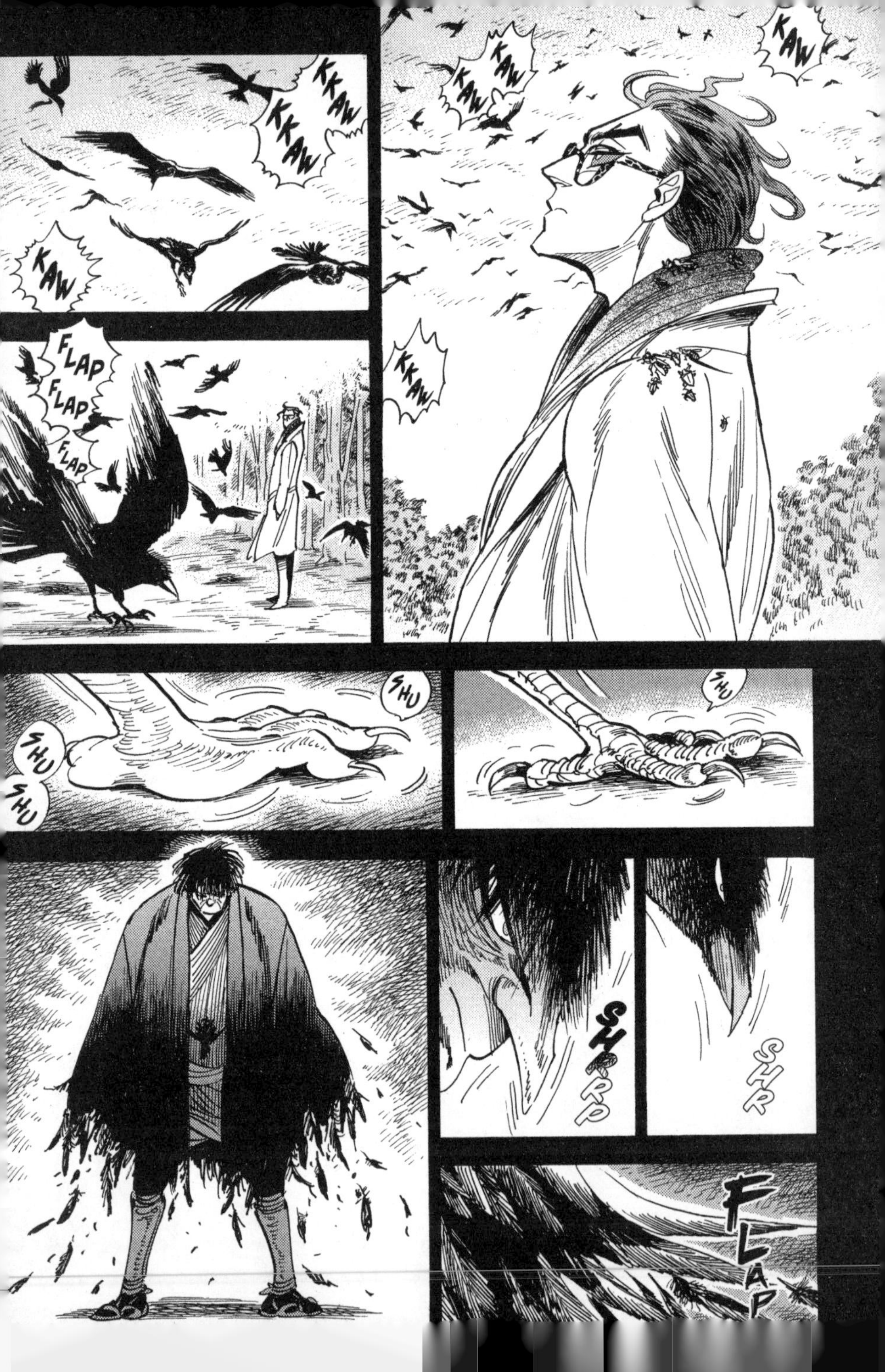
KAW
KKAW KKAW
KKAW
KKAW
KKAW
KAW
FLAP
FLAP
FLAP
SHU
SHU
SHU
SHU
SHR
SHRP
FLAP

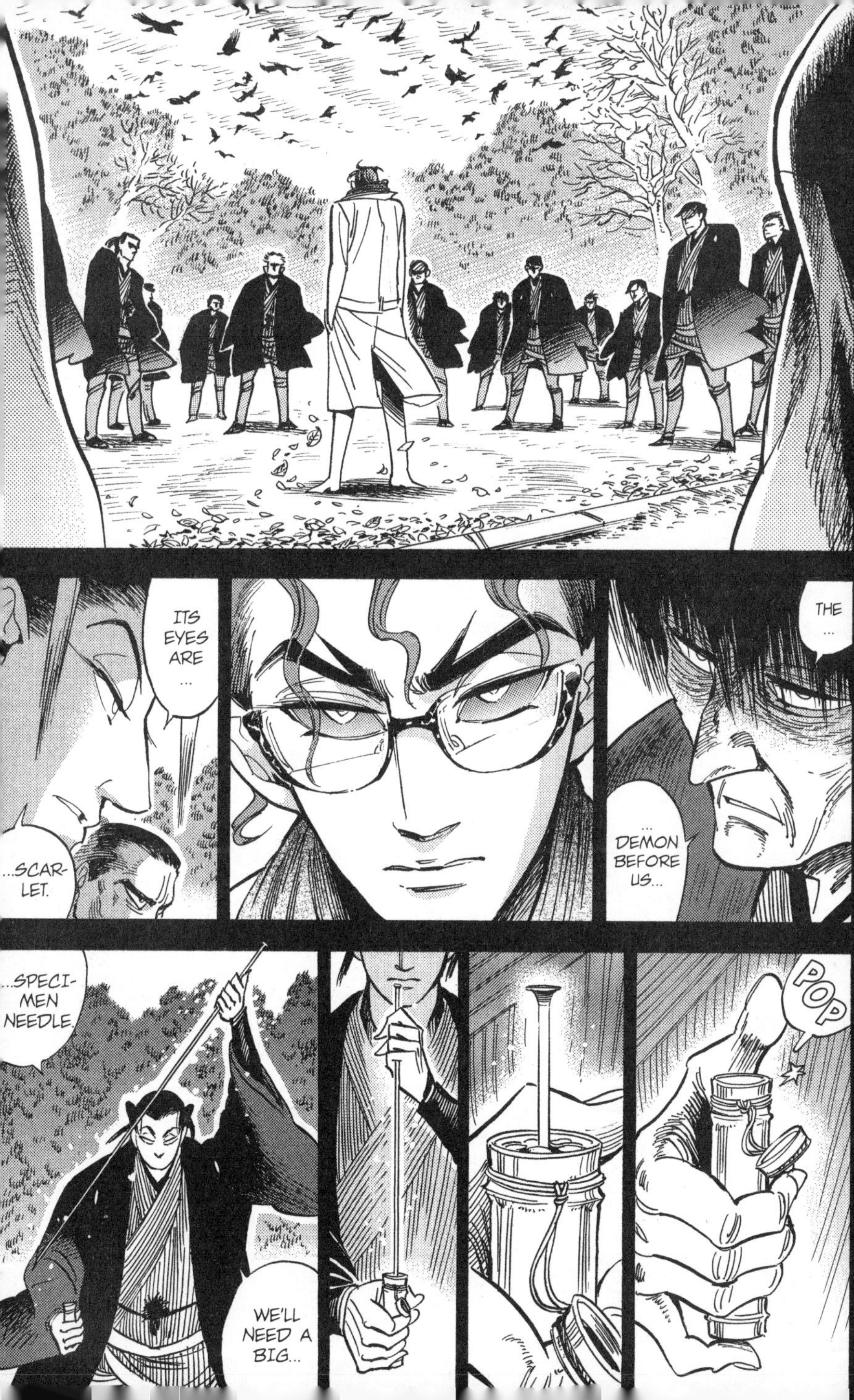
THE ...
... DEMON BEFORE US...
ITS EYES ARE ...
...SCAR-LET.
POP
WE'LL NEED A BIG...
...SPECI-MEN NEEDLE.

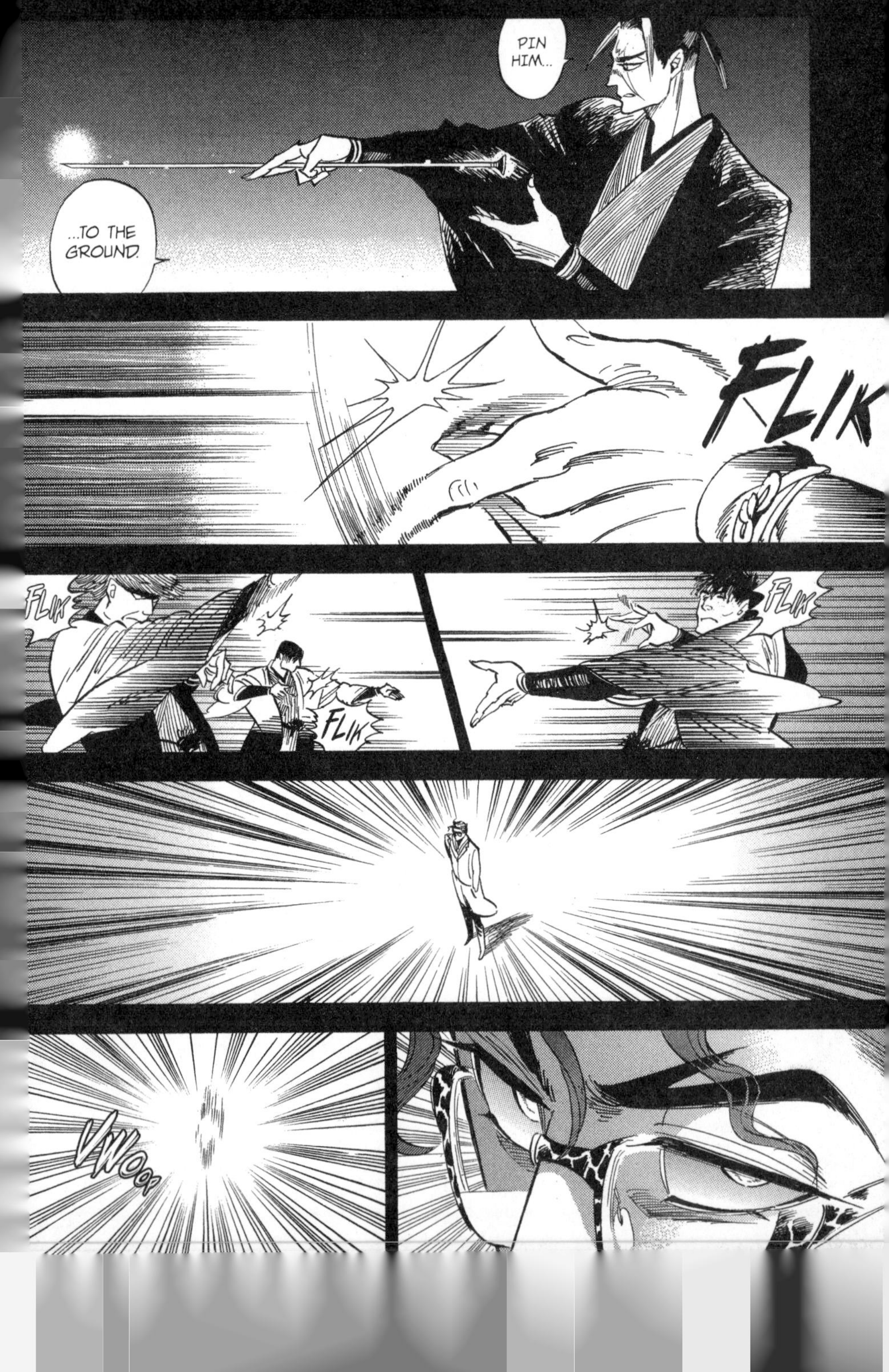
PIN HIM...
...TO THE GROUND.
FLIK
FLIK
FLIK
FLIK
VWOOP

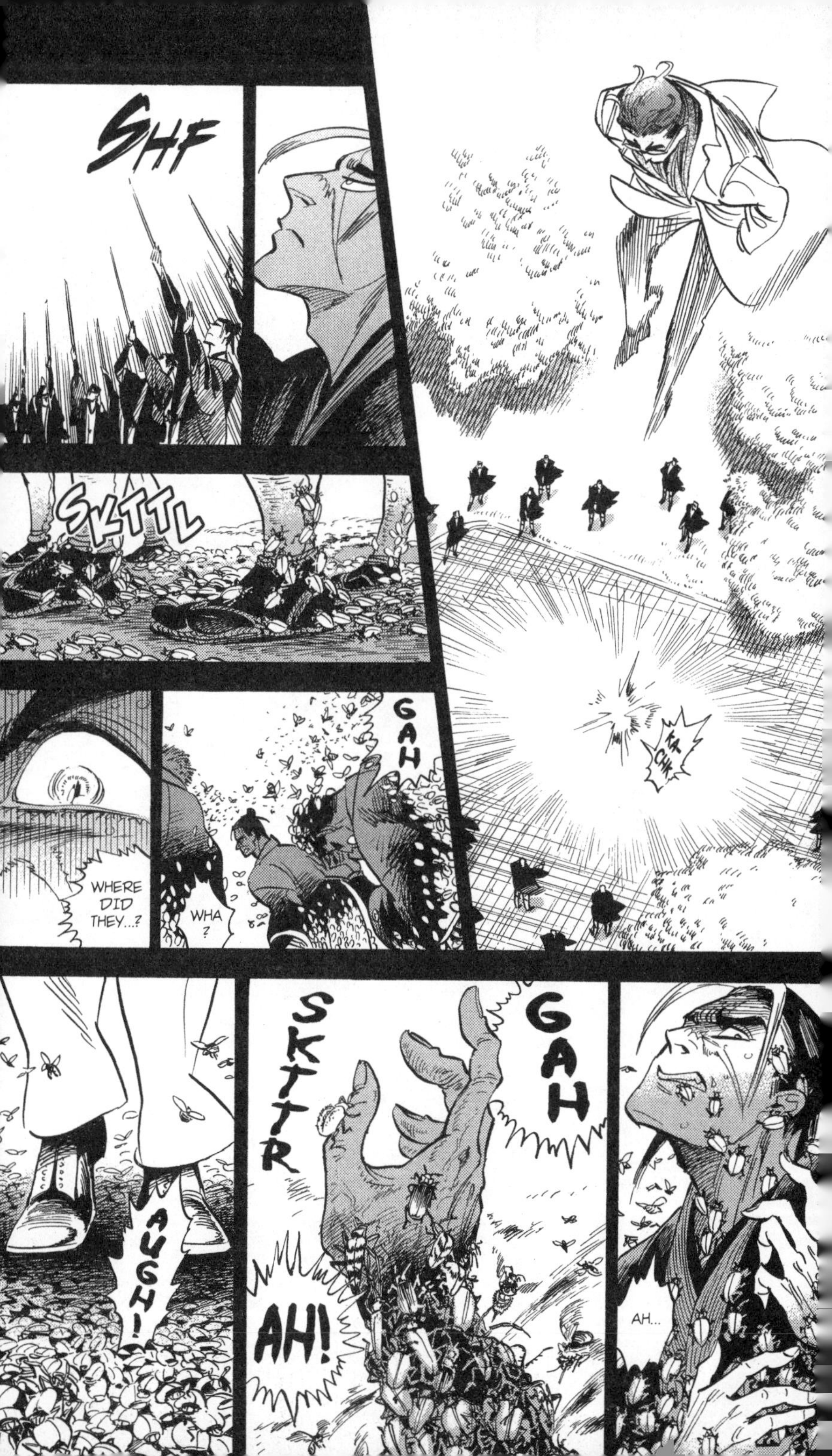
KA CHK
SHF
SKTTL
GAH
WHA?
WHERE DID THEY...?
AH...
GAH
SKTTTR
AH!
AUGH!

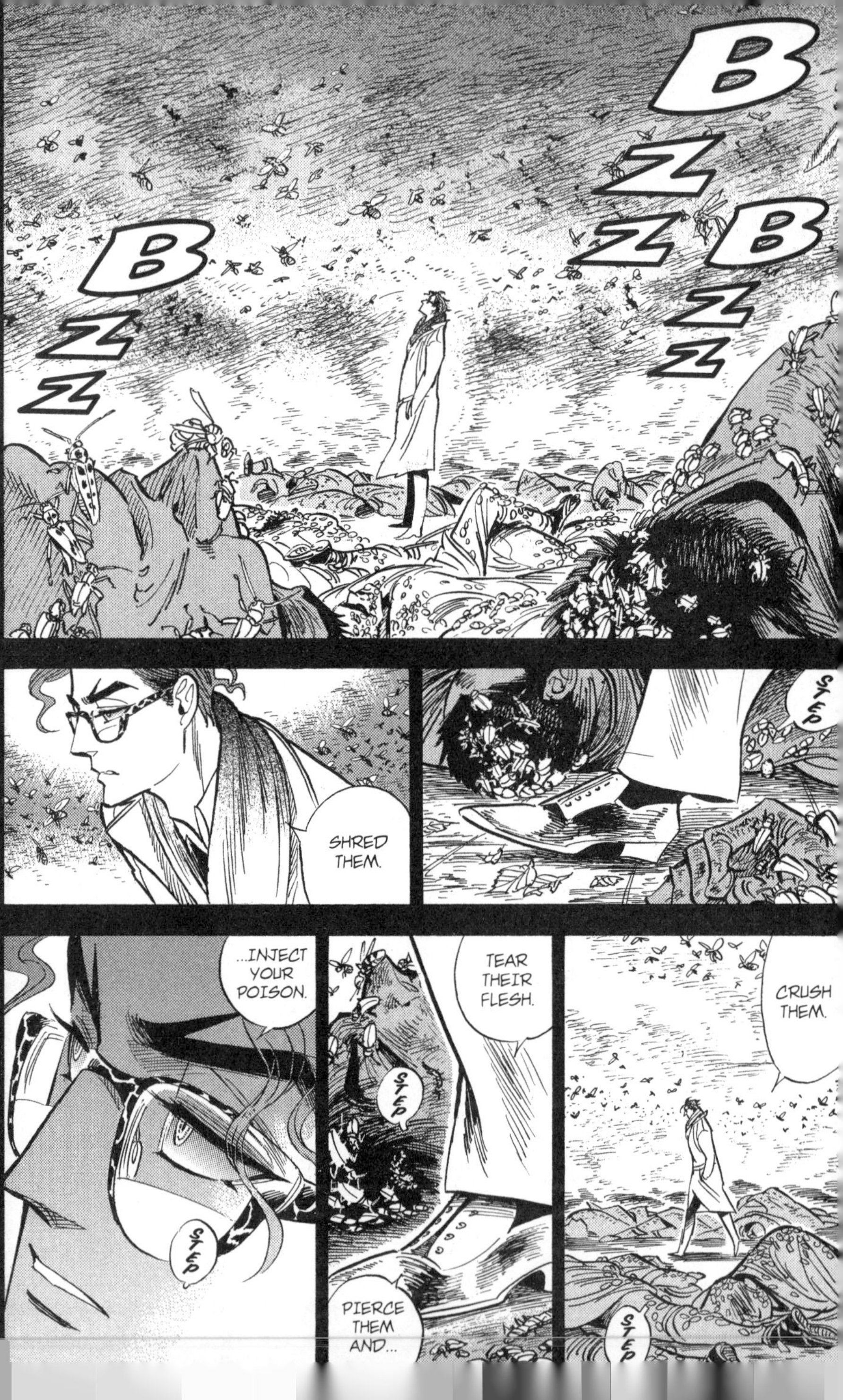
BZZ
BZZ
BZZ
STEP
SHRED THEM.
CRUSH THEM.
STEP
TEAR THEIR FLESH.
STEP
PIERCE THEM AND...
...INJECT YOUR POISON.
STEP

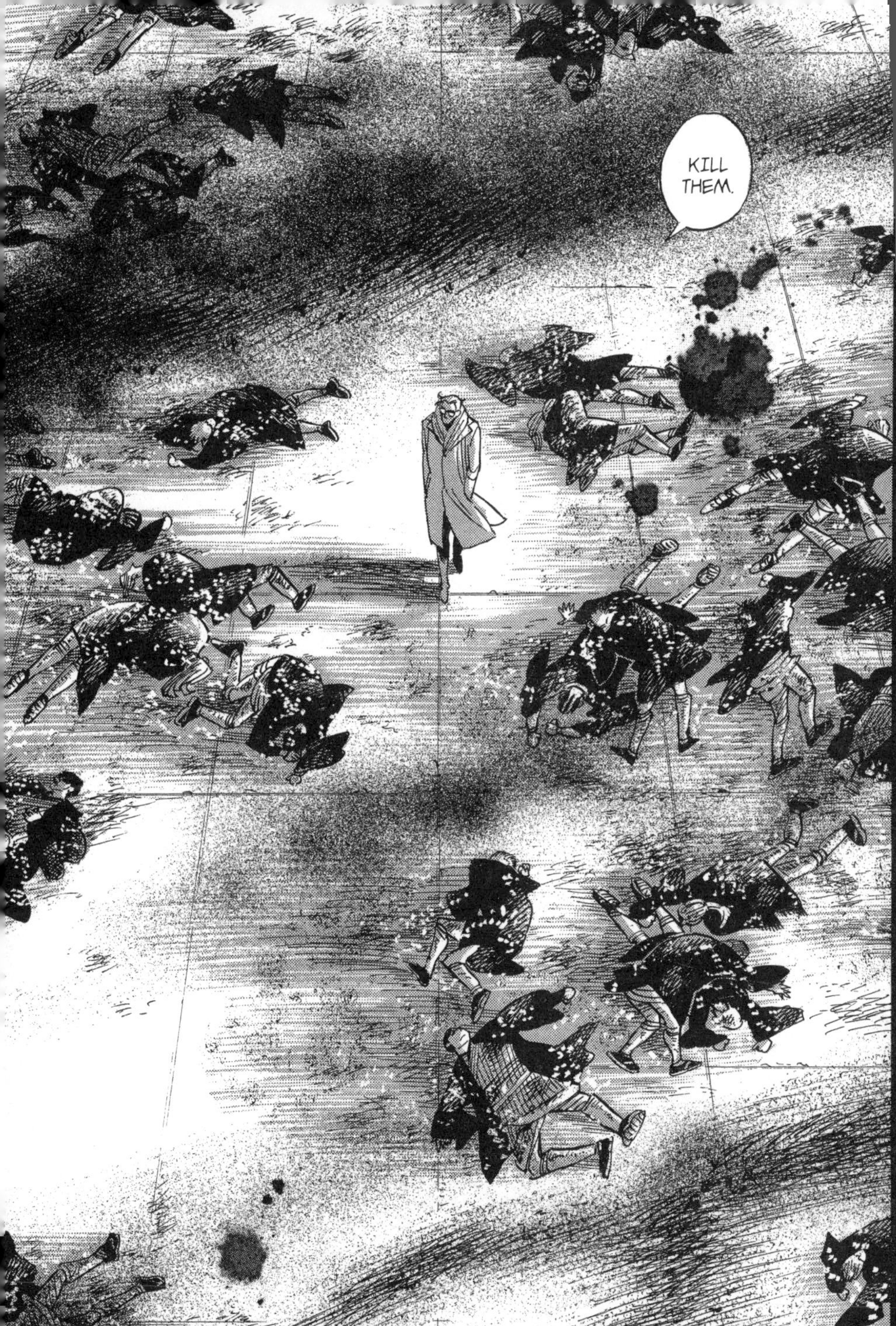
KILL THEM.

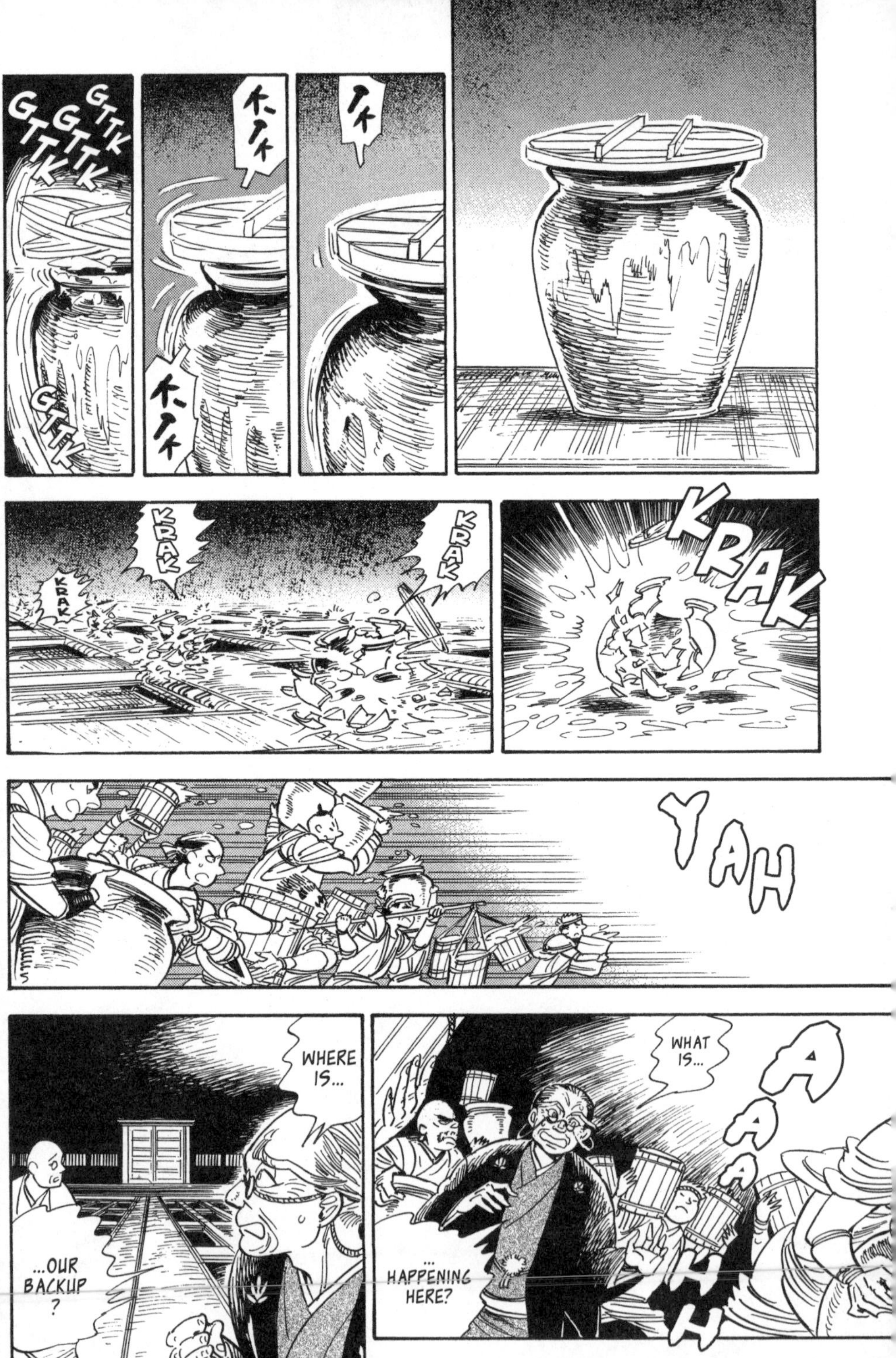
TK
KTK
KTK
GTTK
GTTK
GTTK
GTTK
KRAK
KRAK
KRAK
KRAK
YAH
WHAT IS...
...HAPPENING HERE?
AAAHHH
WHERE IS...
...OUR BACKUP?

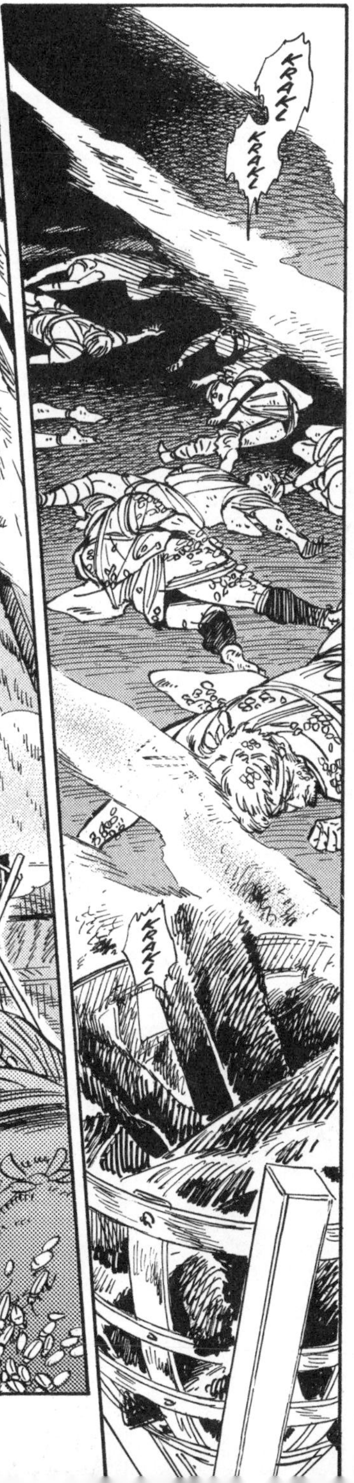
KRAKL
KRAKL
KRAKL

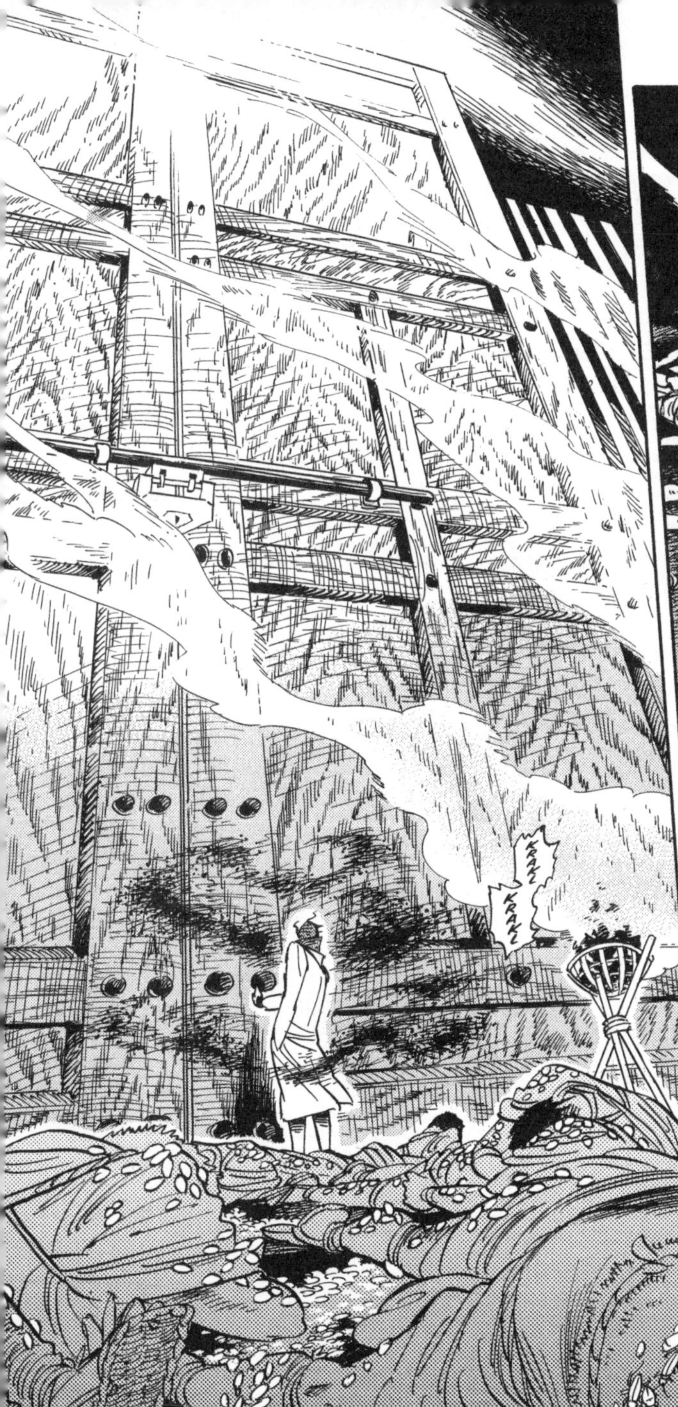
KRAKL
KRAKL

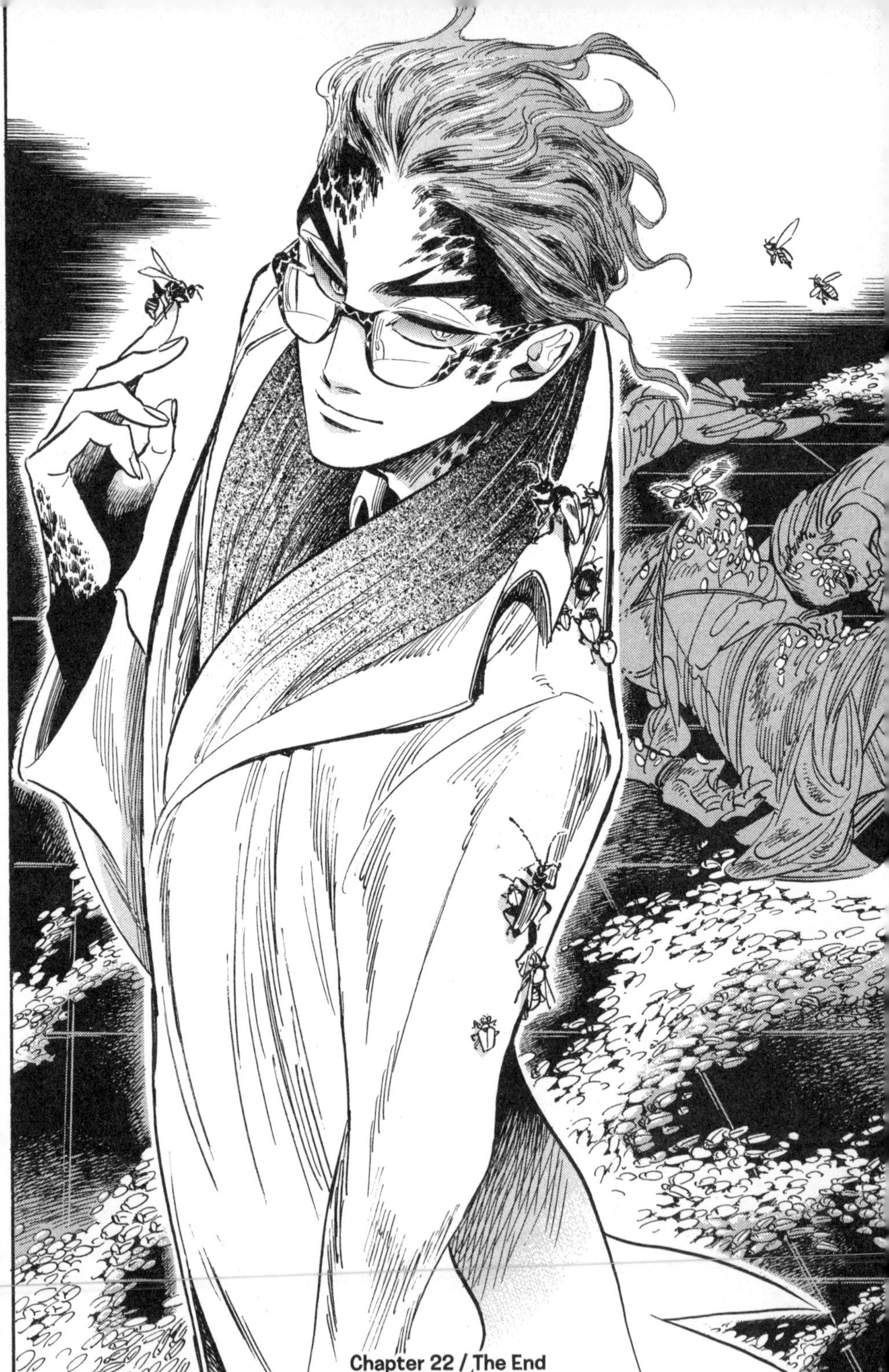

Chapter 22 / The End

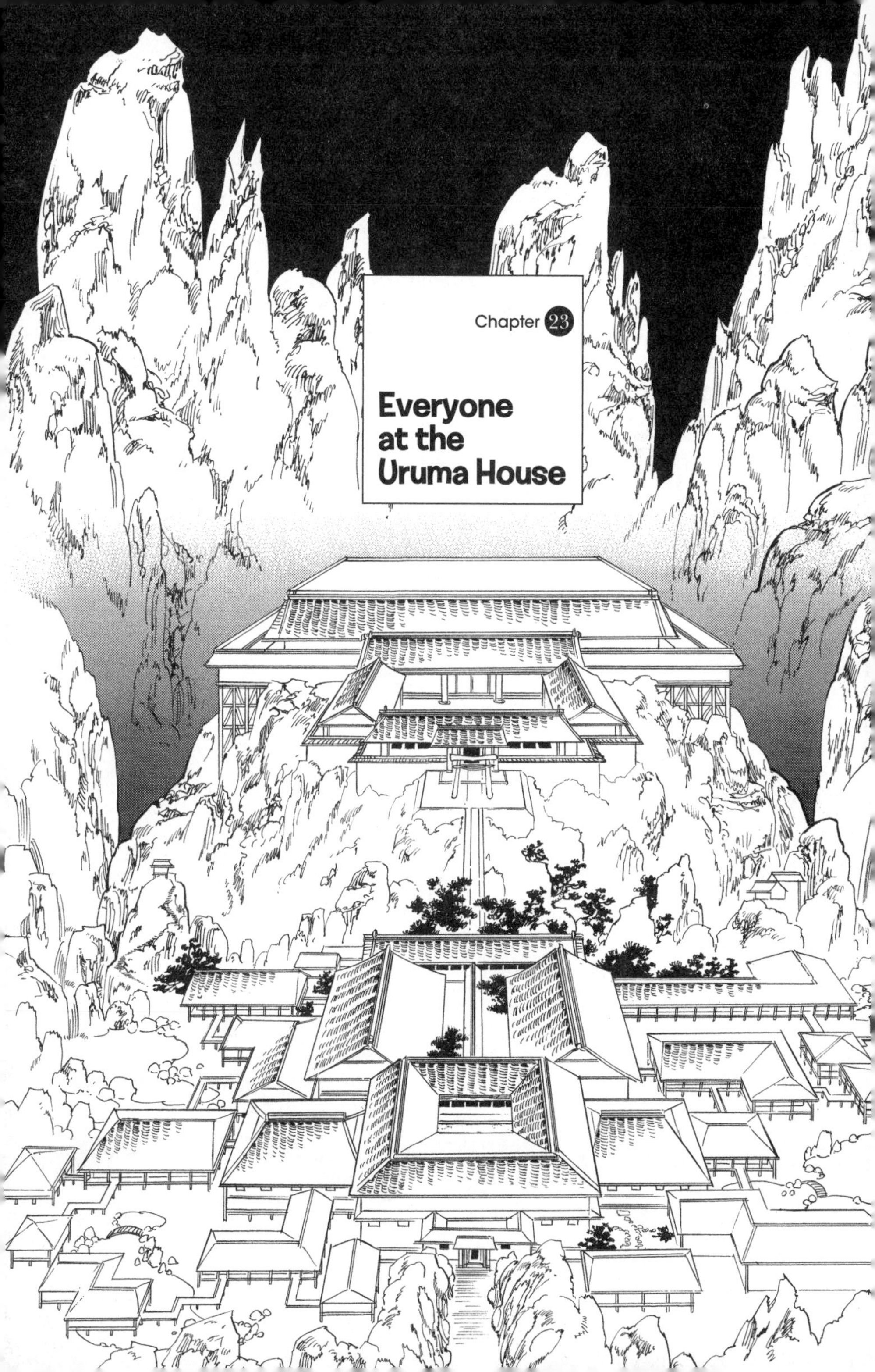
Chapter 23
Everyone at the Uruma House

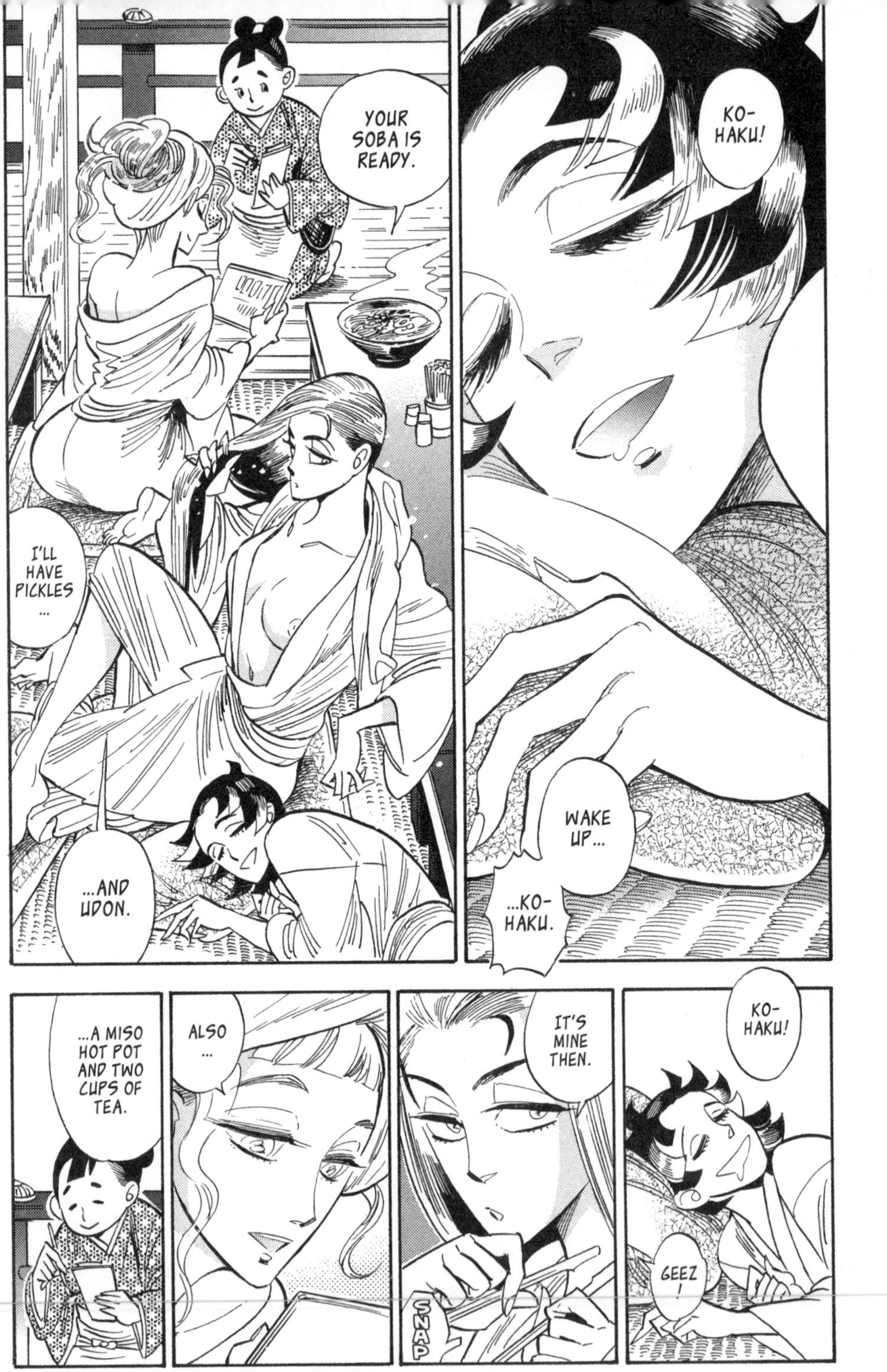
KO-HAKU!
WAKE UP...
...KO-HAKU.
YOUR SOBA IS READY.
I'LL HAVE PICKLES ...
...AND UDON.
KO-HAKU!
GEEZ!
IT'S MINE THEN.
SNAP
ALSO ...
...A MISO HOT POT AND TWO CUPS OF TEA.

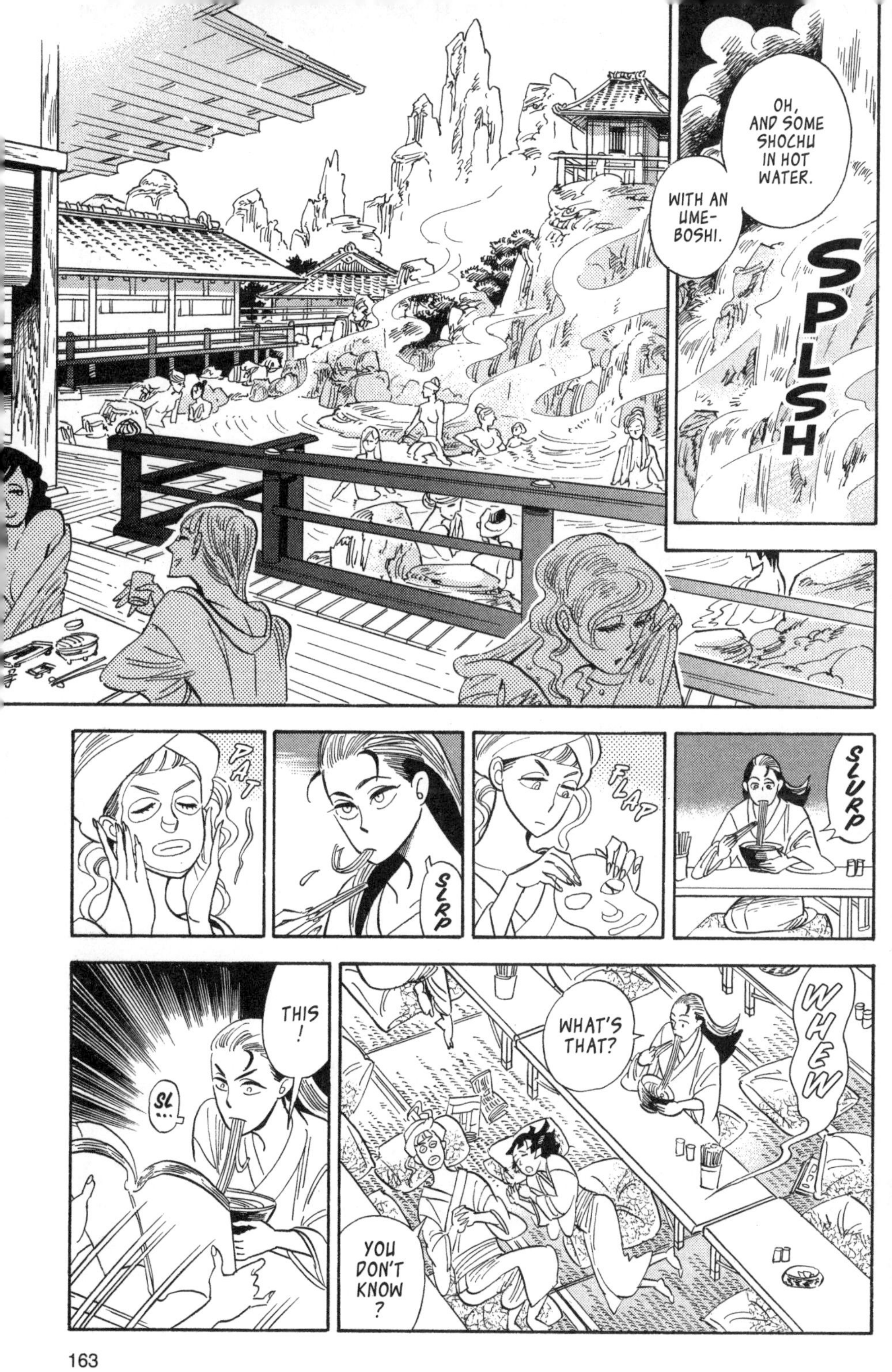

OH, AND SOME SHOCHU IN HOT WATER.
WITH AN UME-BOSHI.
SPLSH
SLURP
FLAP
SLRP
PAT
WHEW
WHAT'S THAT?
YOU DON'T KNOW?
THIS!
SL...

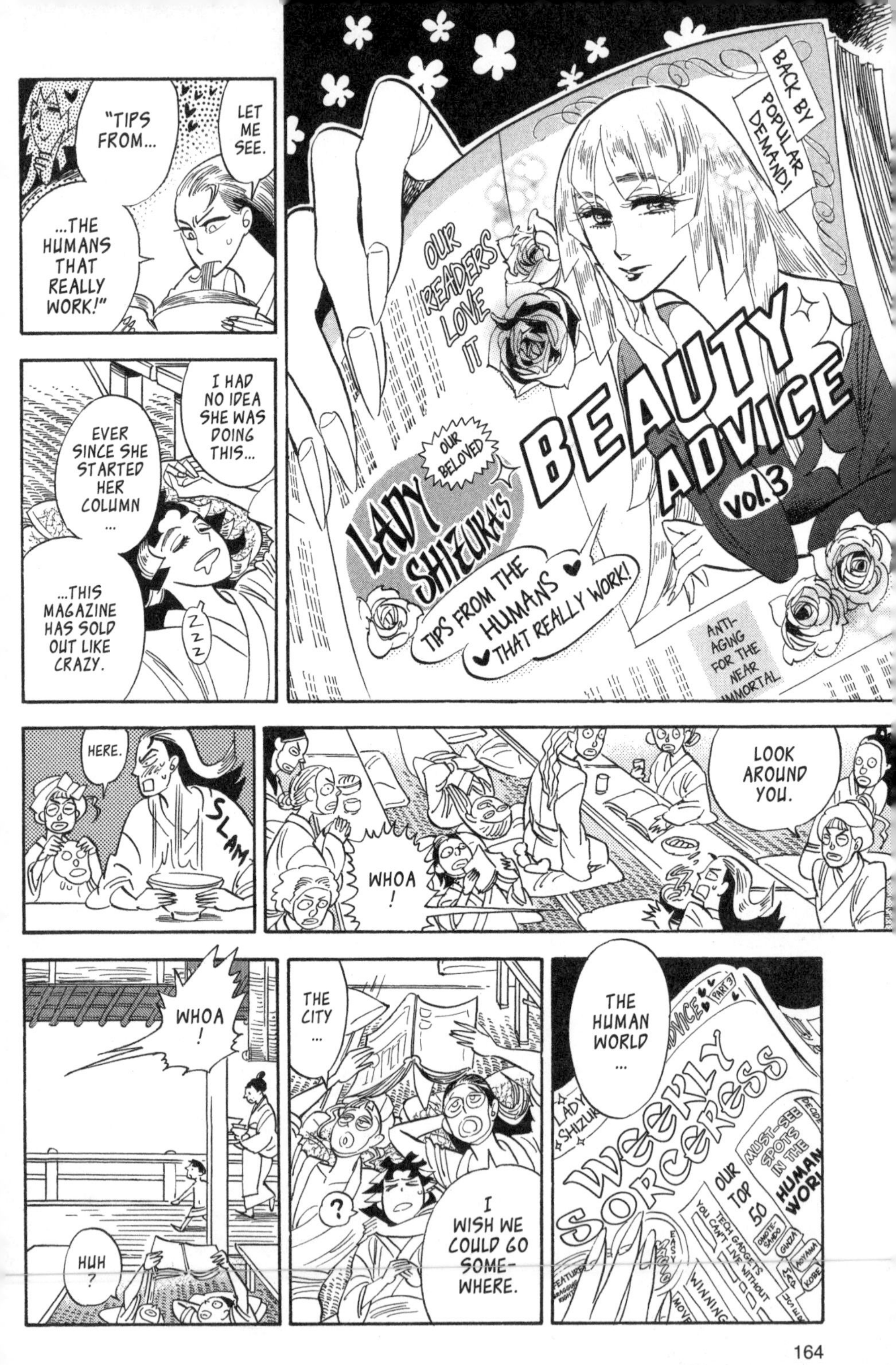
BACK BY POPULAR DEMAND!
OUR READERS LOVE IT
OUR BELOVED
LADY SHIZUKA'S BEAUTY ADVICE vol.3
TIPS FROM THE HUMANS THAT REALLY WORK!
ANTI-AGING FOR THE NEAR IMMORTAL
LET ME SEE.
"TIPS FROM...
...THE HUMANS THAT REALLY WORK!"
I HAD NO IDEA SHE WAS DOING THIS...
EVER SINCE SHE STARTED HER COLUMN...
...THIS MAGAZINE HAS SOLD OUT LIKE CRAZY.
ZZZ
LOOK AROUND YOU.
WHOA!
HERE.
SLAM
THE HUMAN WORLD...
LADY SHIZUKA
ADVICE PART 3
WEEKLY SORCERESS
MUST-SEE SPOTS IN THE HUMAN WORLD
OUR TOP 50
OMOTE-SANDO
GINZA
AOYAMA
KOBE
MAP
TECH GADGETS YOU CAN'T LIVE WITHOUT
WINNING
THE CITY...
I WISH WE COULD GO SOME-WHERE.
?
WHOA!
HUH?

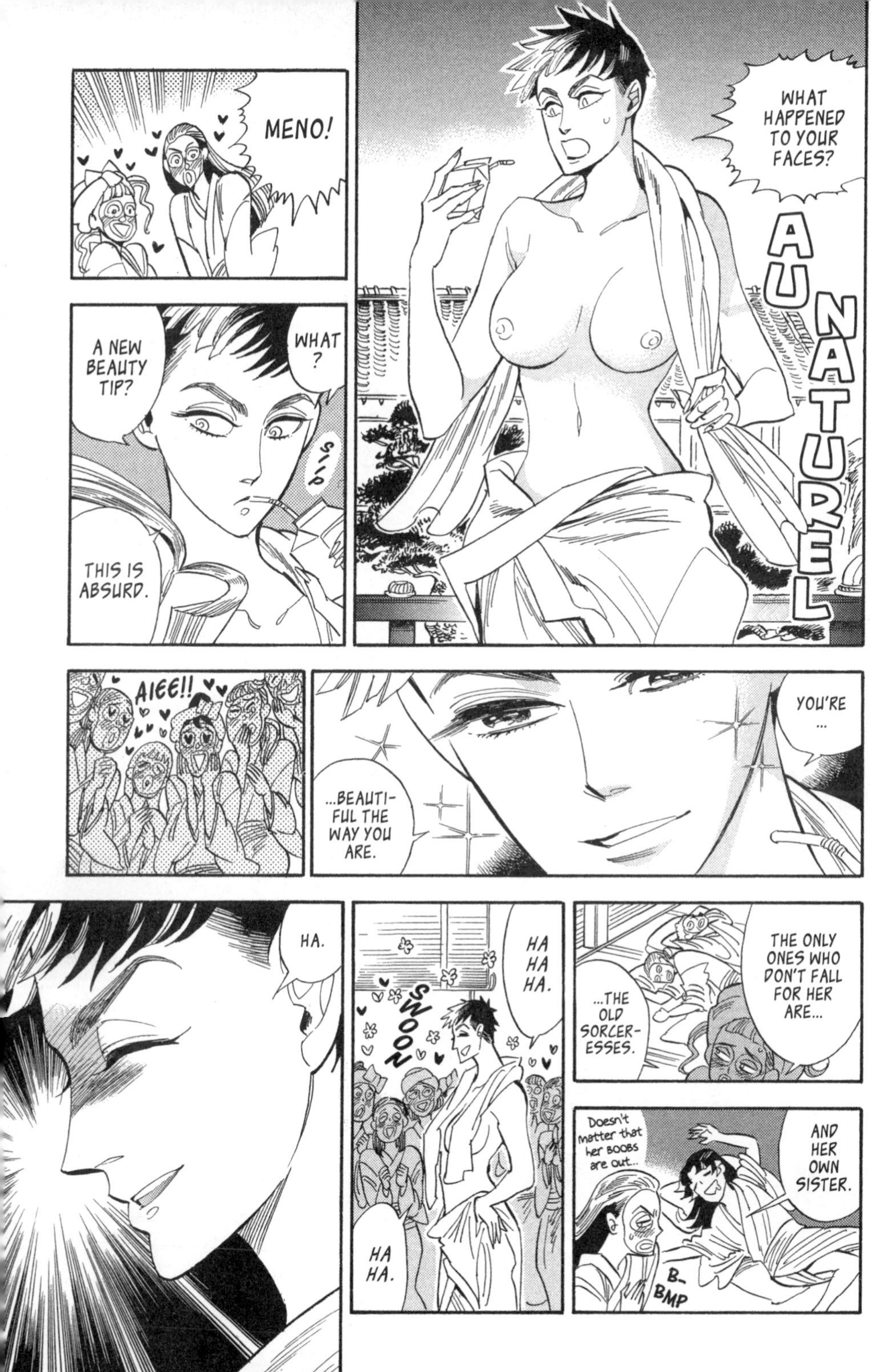
WHAT HAPPENED TO YOUR FACES?
AU NATUREL
MENO!
WHAT ?
A NEW BEAUTY TIP?
SIP
THIS IS ABSURD.
YOU'RE ...
...BEAUTI-FUL THE WAY YOU ARE.
AIEE!!
THE ONLY ONES WHO DON'T FALL FOR HER ARE...
...THE OLD SORCER-ESSES.
AND HER OWN SISTER.
Doesn't matter that her BOOBS are out...
B-BMP
HA HA HA.
SWOON
HA HA.
HA.

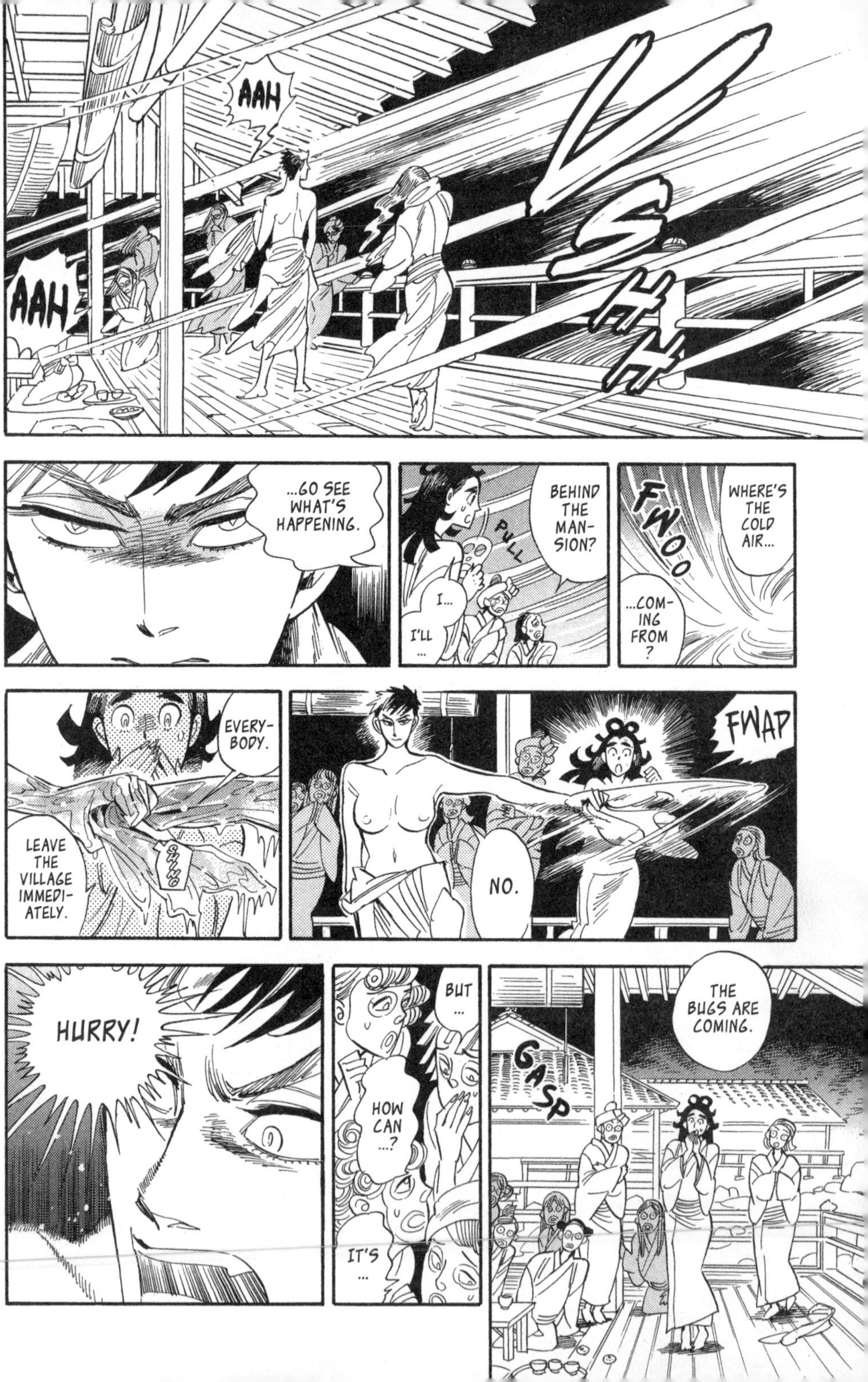
VSHHH
AAH
AAH
FWOO
WHERE'S THE COLD AIR...
...COMING FROM?
BEHIND THE MANSION?
PULL
I...
I'LL...
...GO SEE WHAT'S HAPPENING.
FWAP
NO.
EVERYBODY.
LEAVE THE VILLAGE IMMEDIATELY.
SHING
THE BUGS ARE COMING.
GASP
BUT...
HOW CAN...?
IT'S...
HURRY!

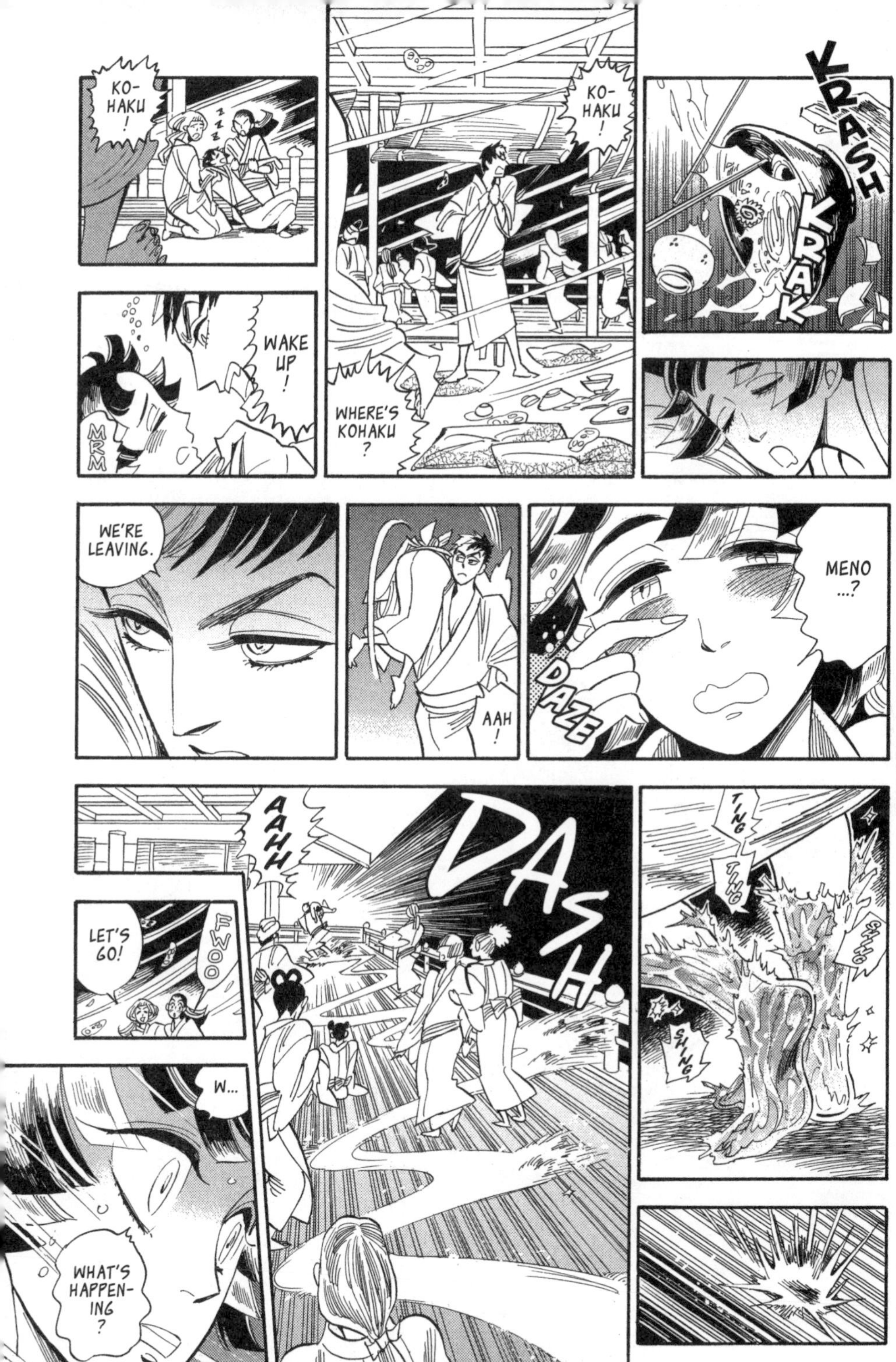
KRASH
KRAK
KO-HAKU!
WHERE'S KOHAKU?
KO-HAKU!
WAKE UP!
MRM
MENO ...?
DAZE
AAH!
WE'RE LEAVING.
TING
TING
SHING
SHING
AAHH
DASH
LET'S GO!
FWOO
W...
WHAT'S HAPPEN-ING?

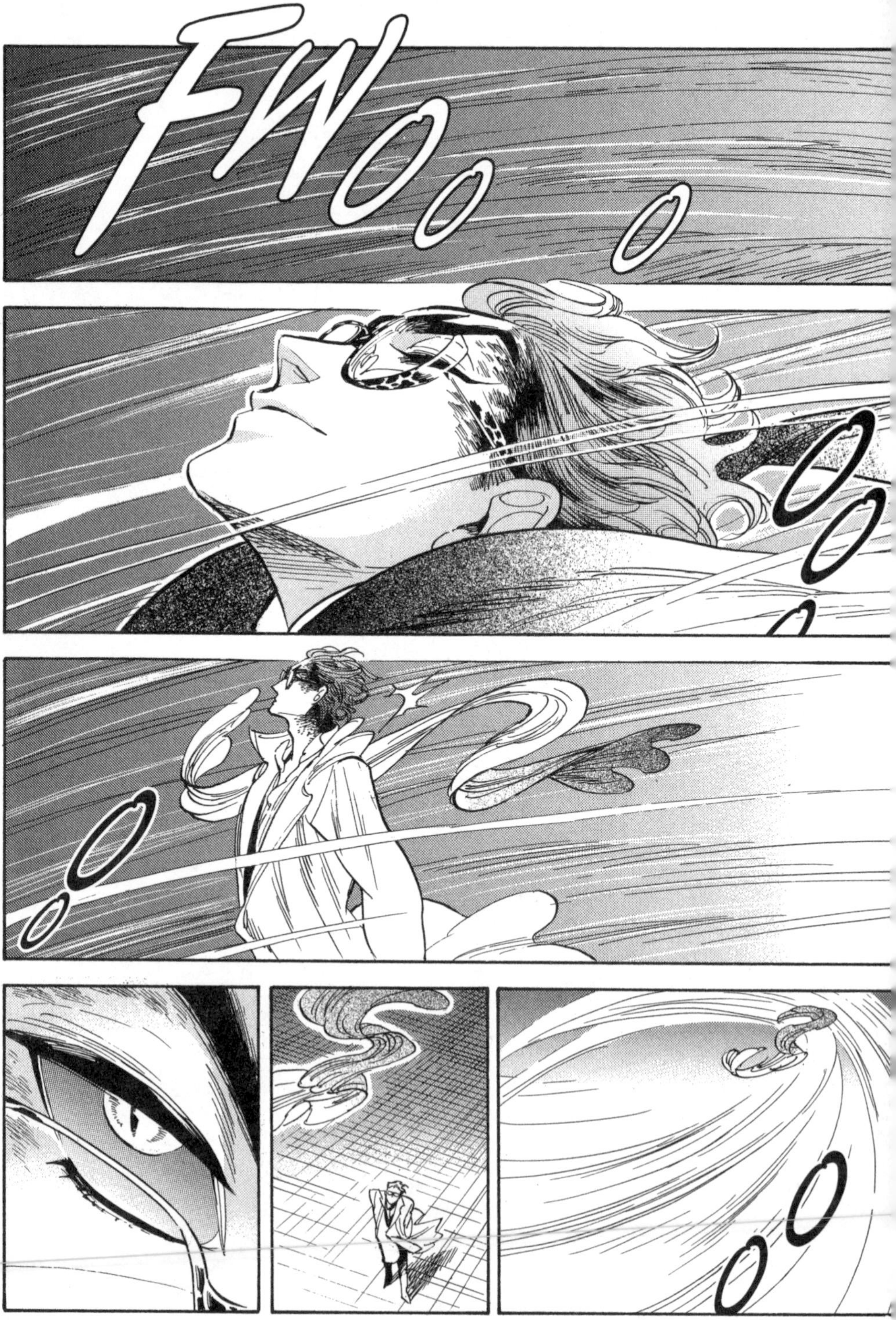
FWOOOO

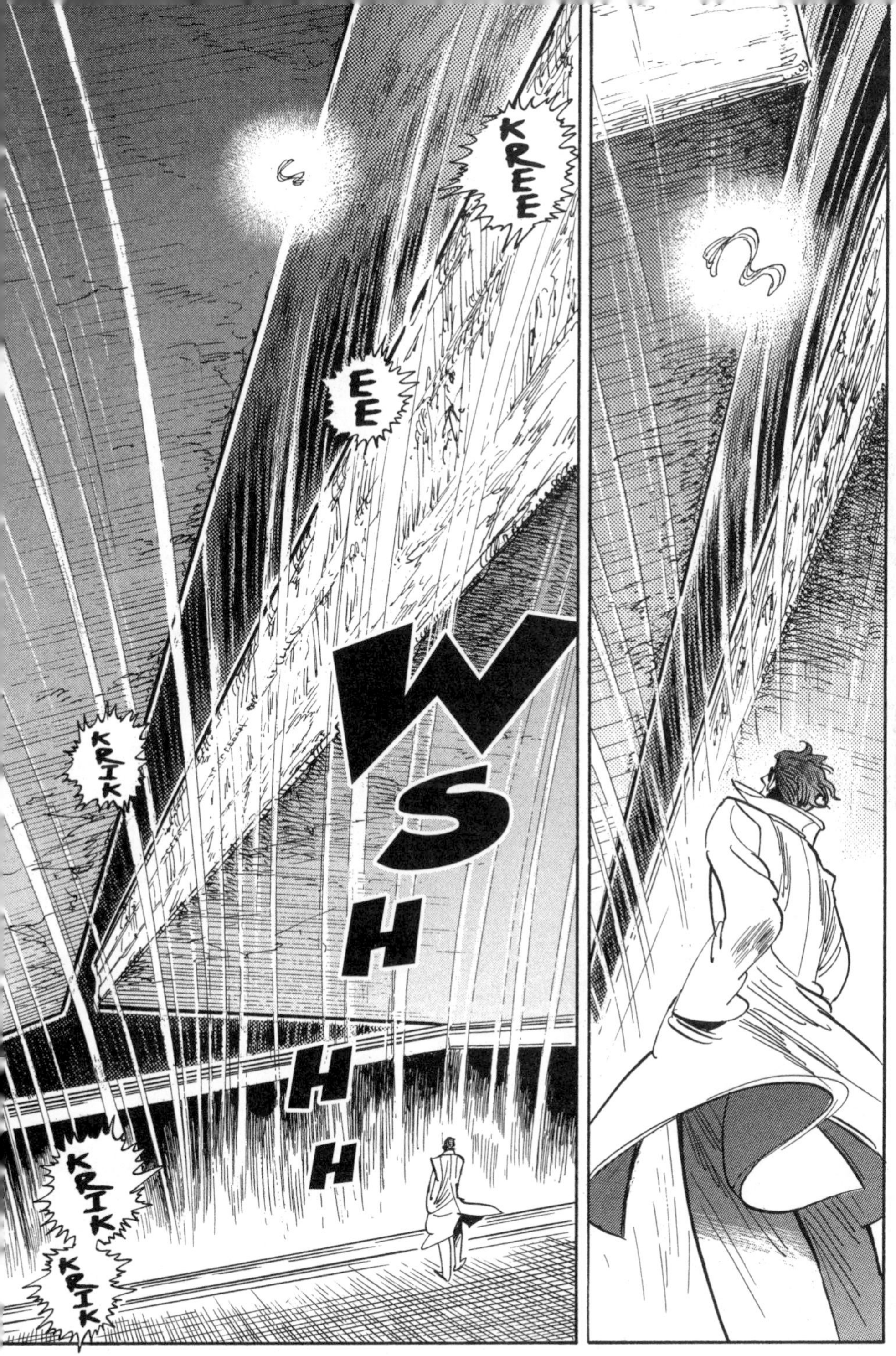
KREE
EE
WSH
H
H
H
KRIK
KRIK
KRIK

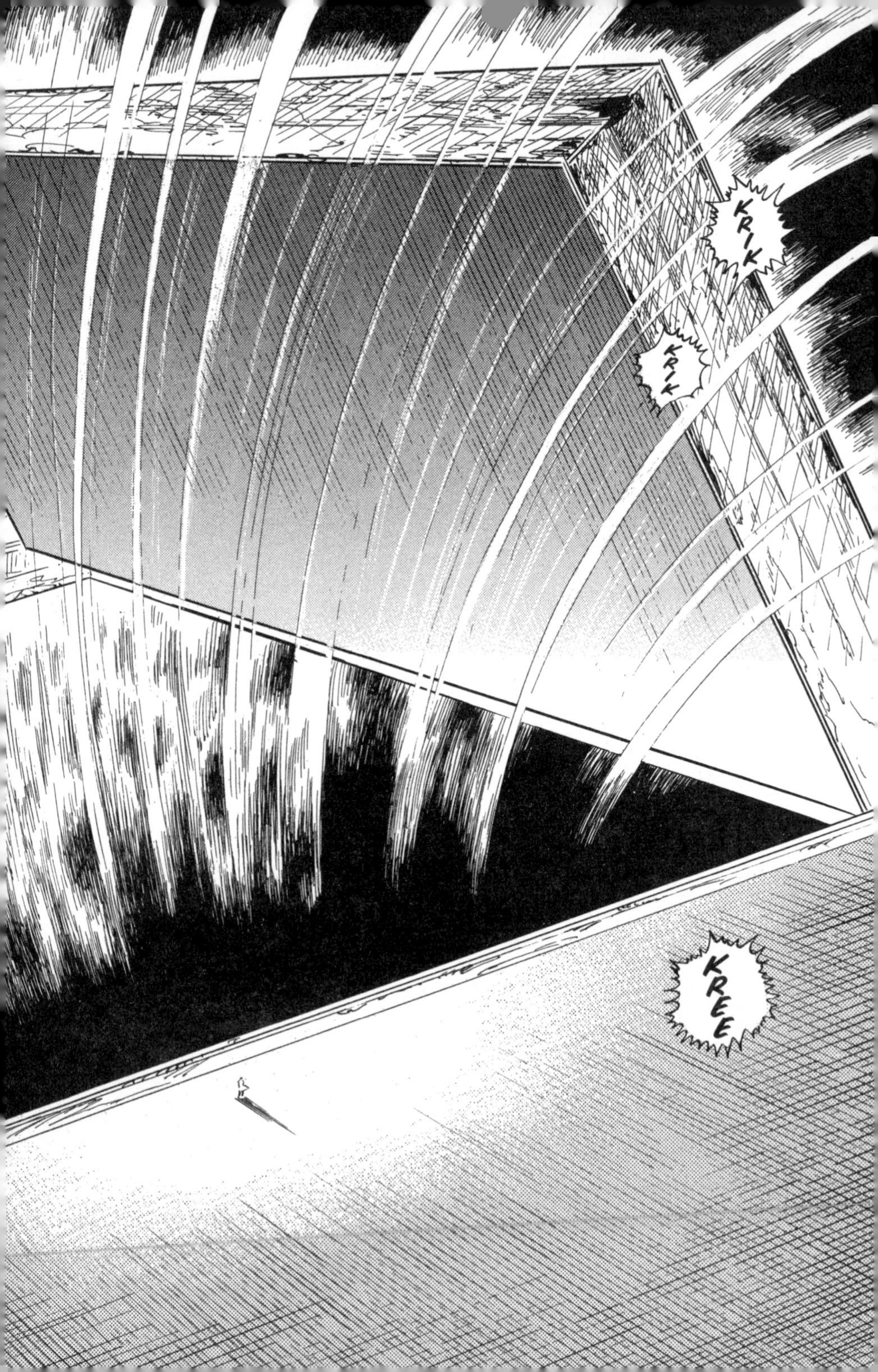
KRIK
KRIK
KREE

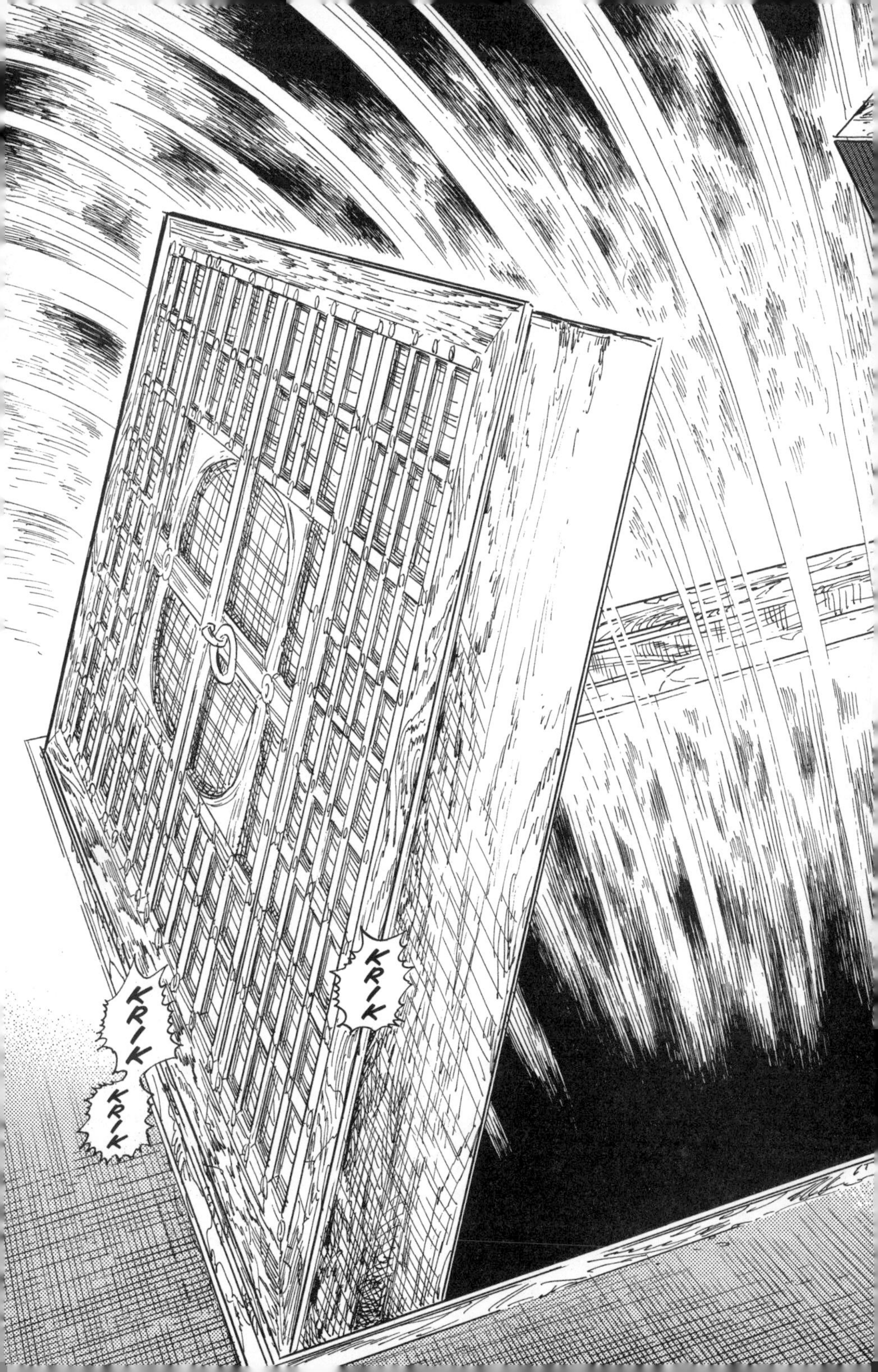
KRIK
KRIK
KRIK

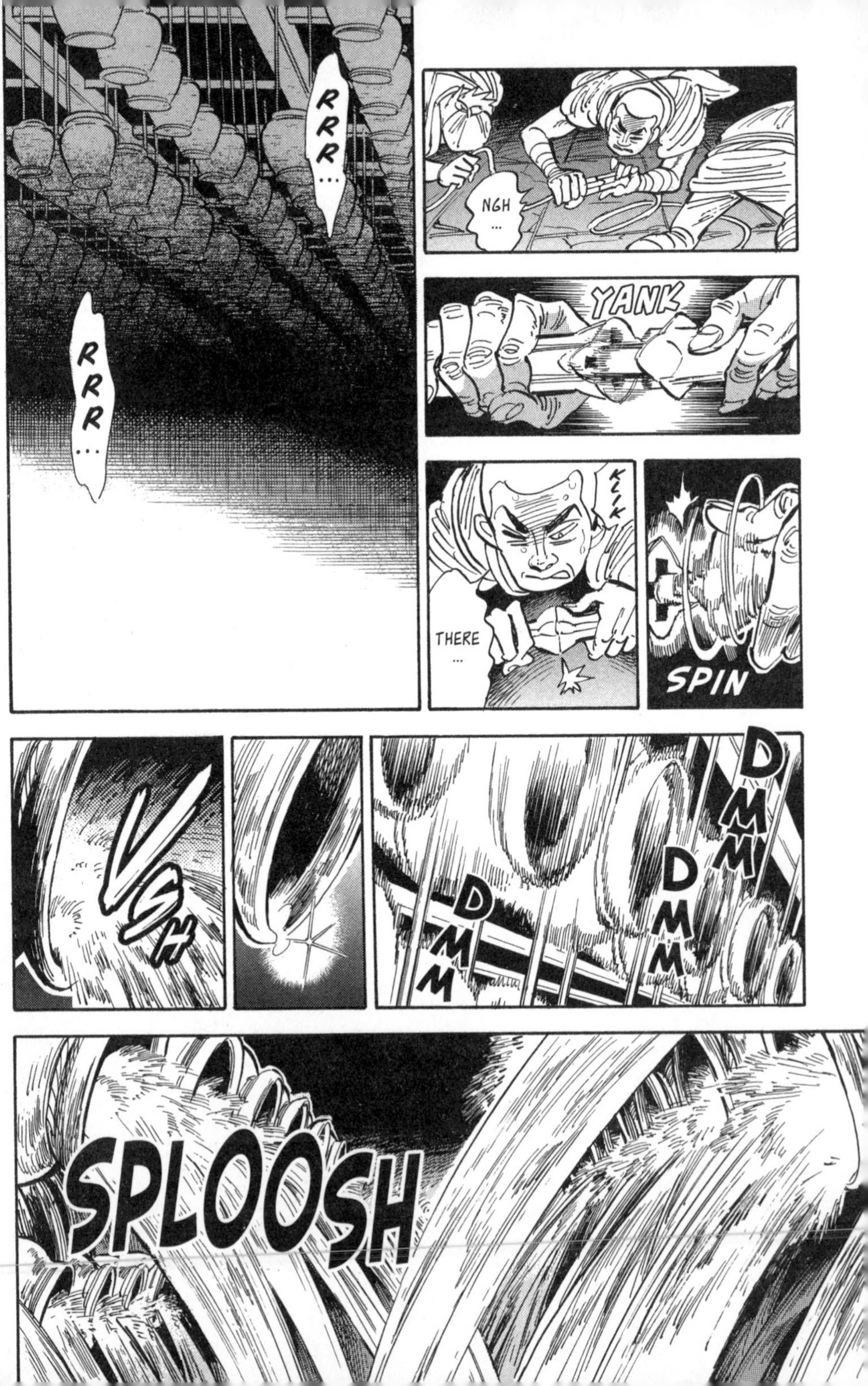
NGH ...
YANK
SPIN
KLIK
THERE ...
RRR ...
RRR ...
DMM
DMM
DMM
VSH
SPLOOSH

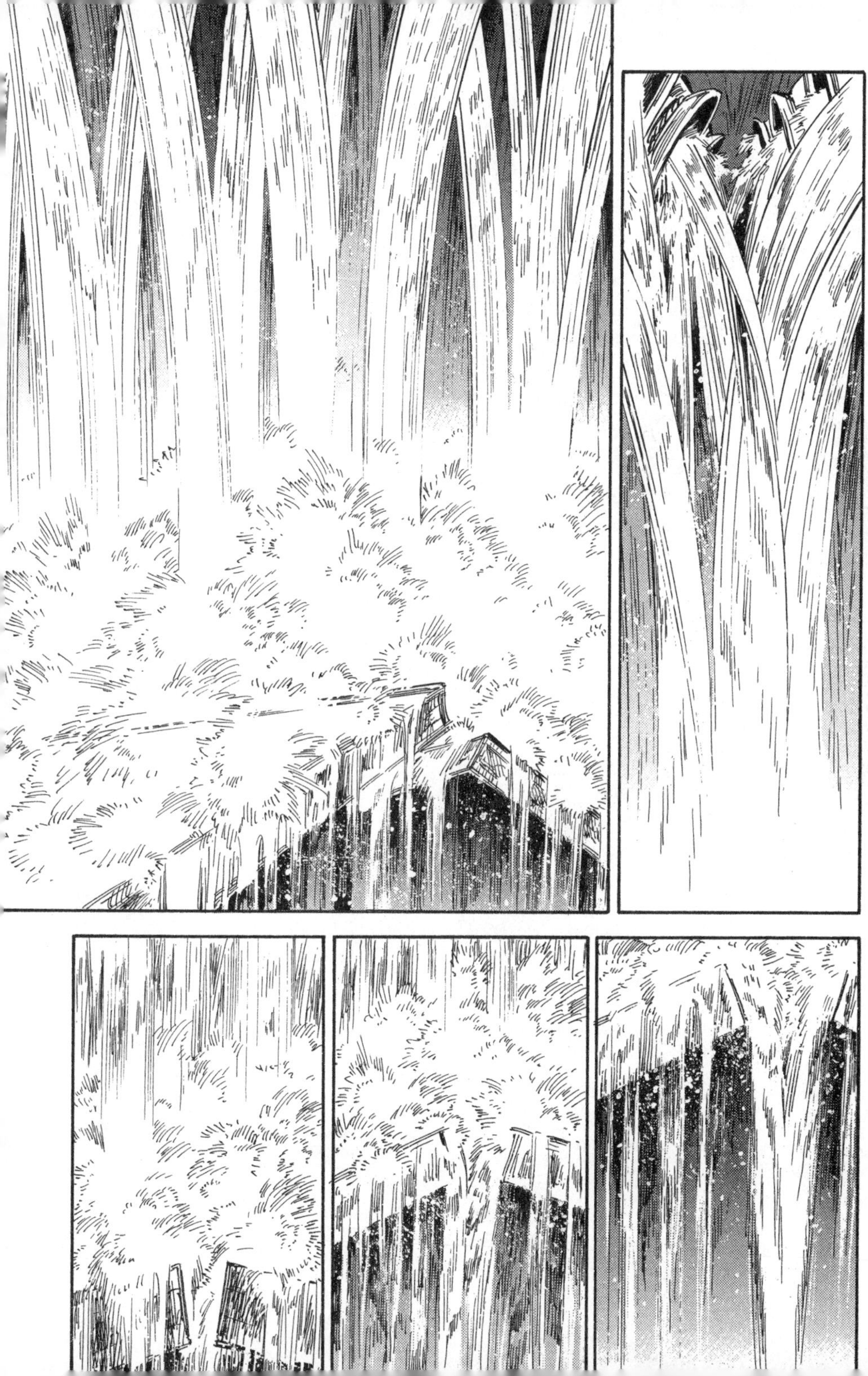

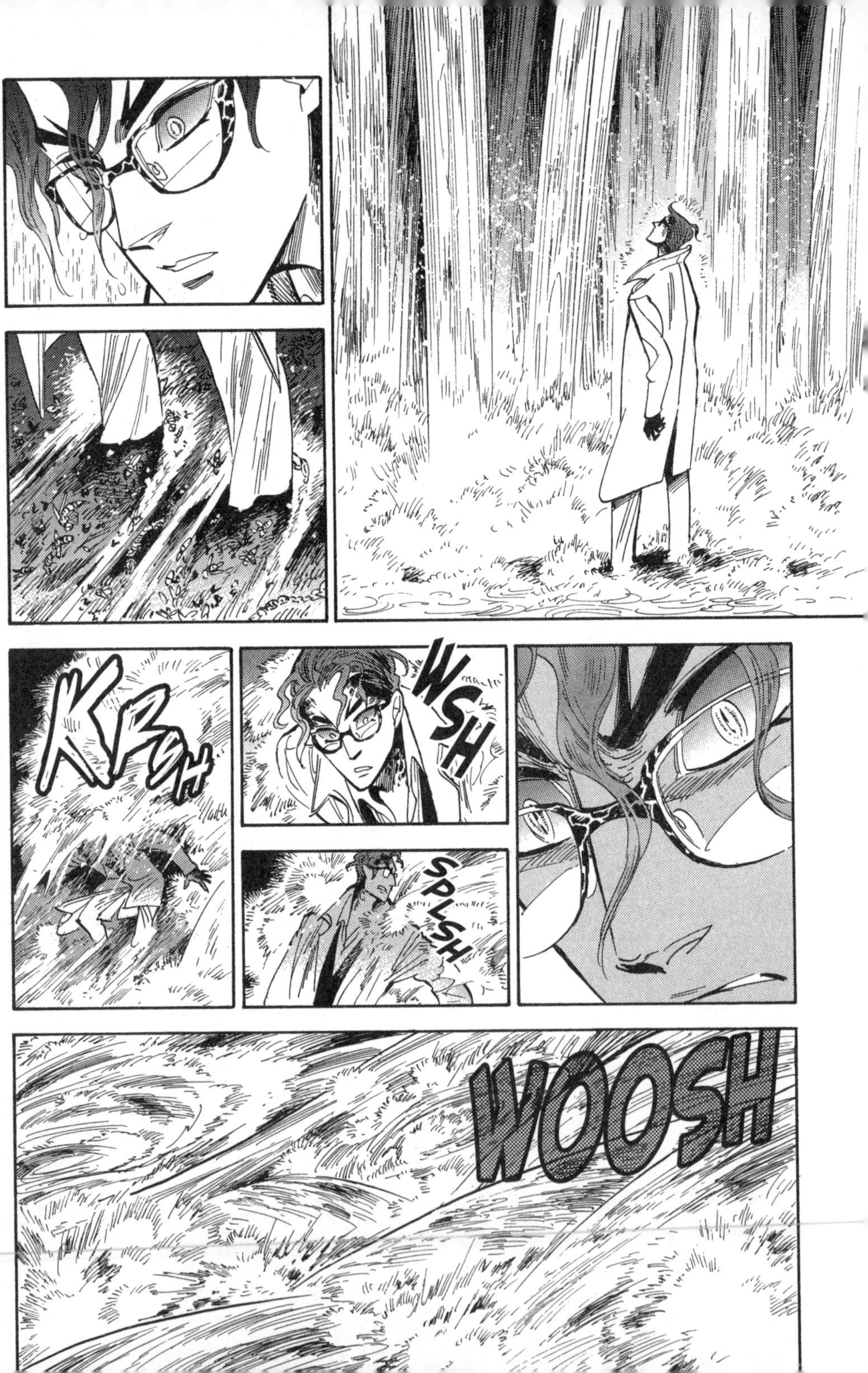
WSH
SPLSH
KRSH
WOOSH

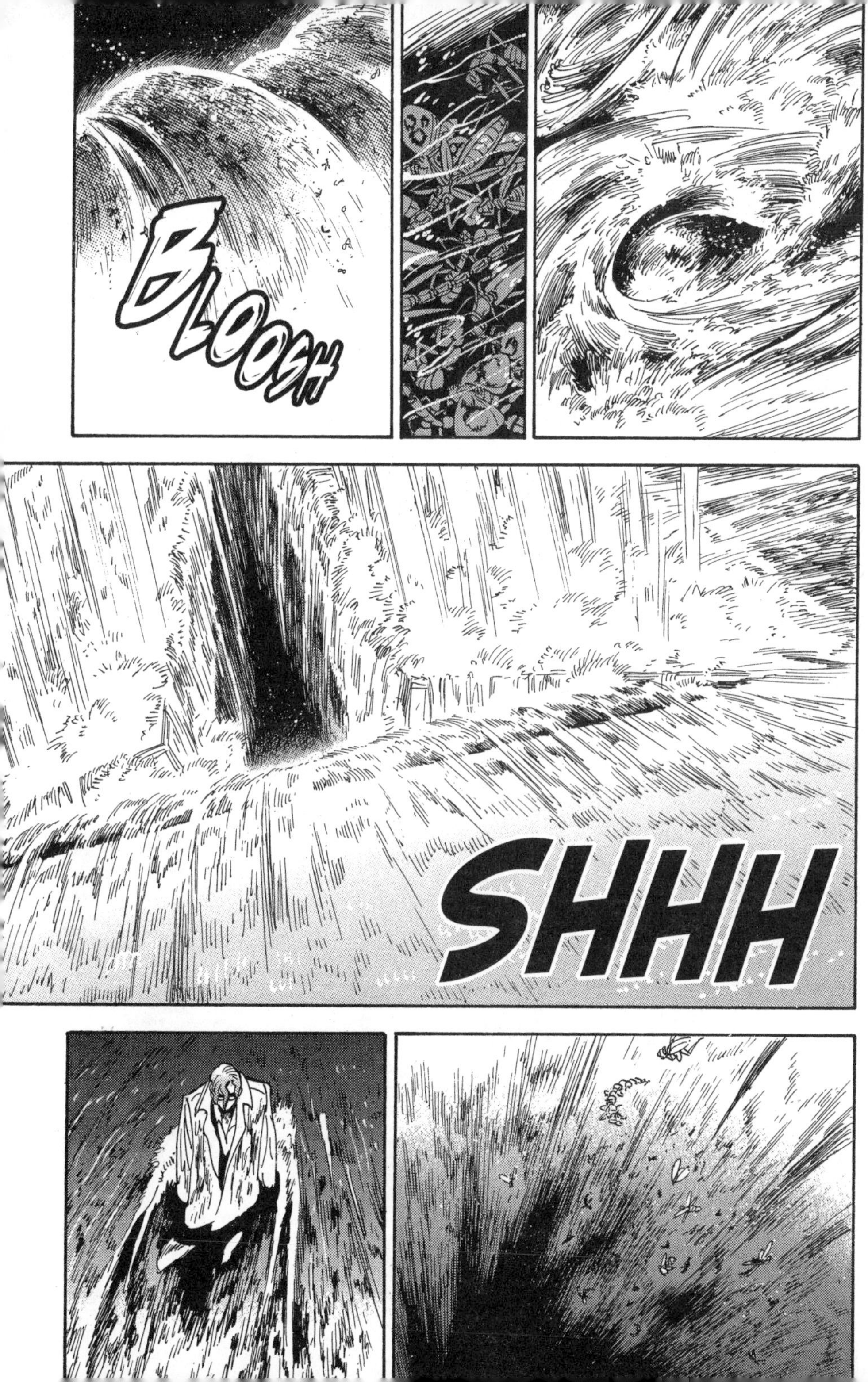
BLOOSH
SHHH

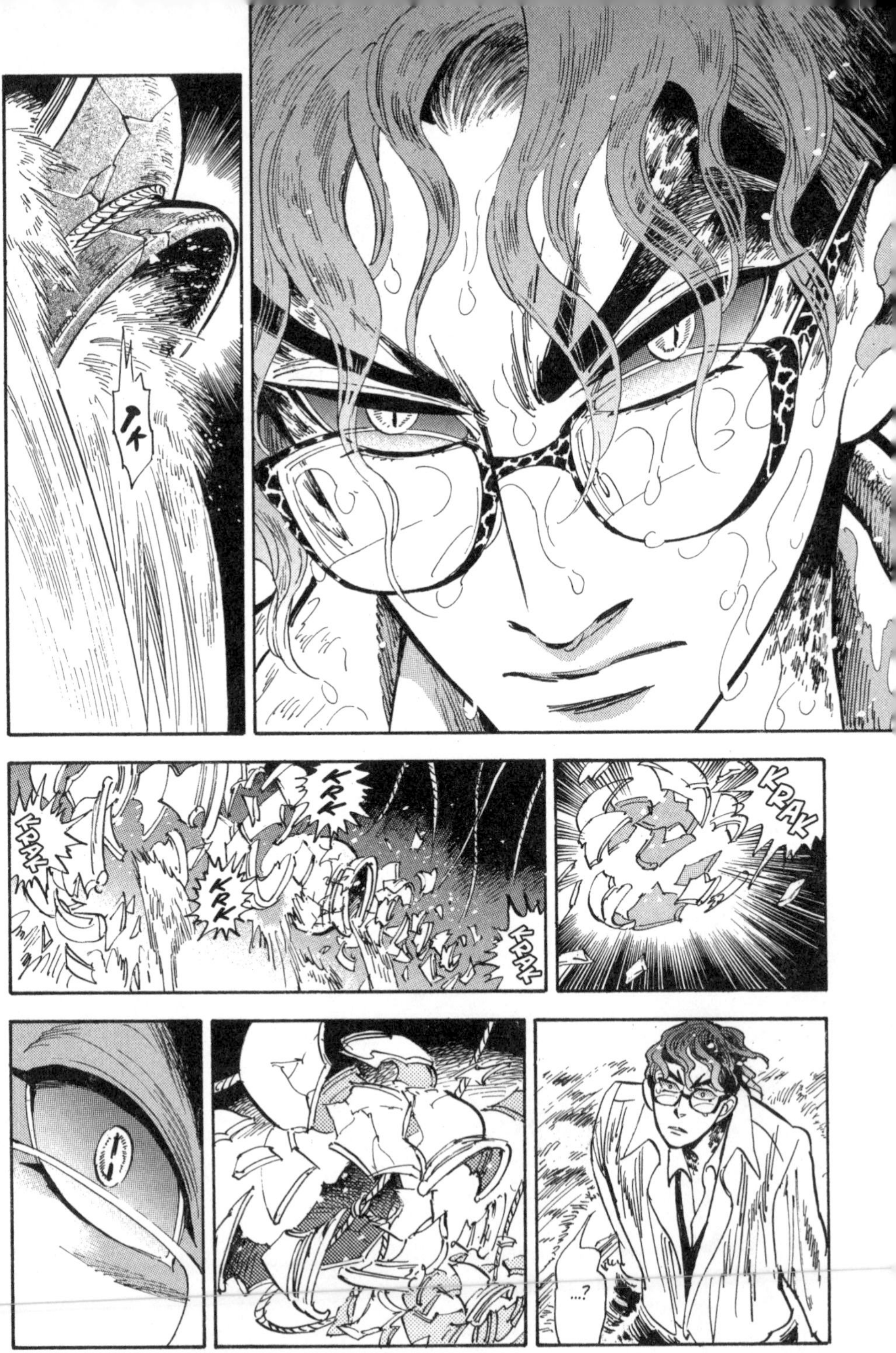
TK
KRAK
KRK
KRAK
KRK
KRAK
...?

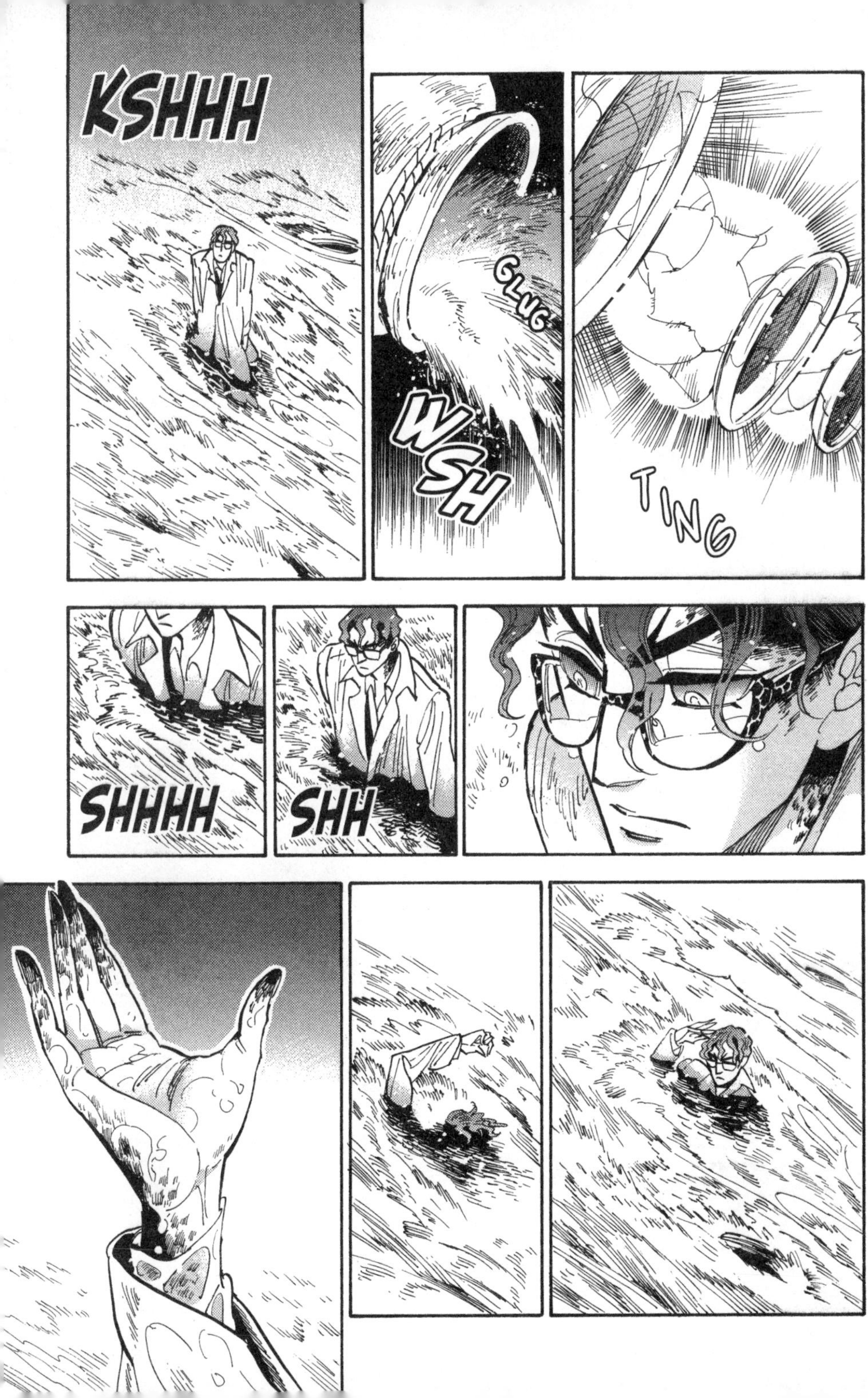
TING
GLUG
WSH
KSHHH
SHH
SHHHH

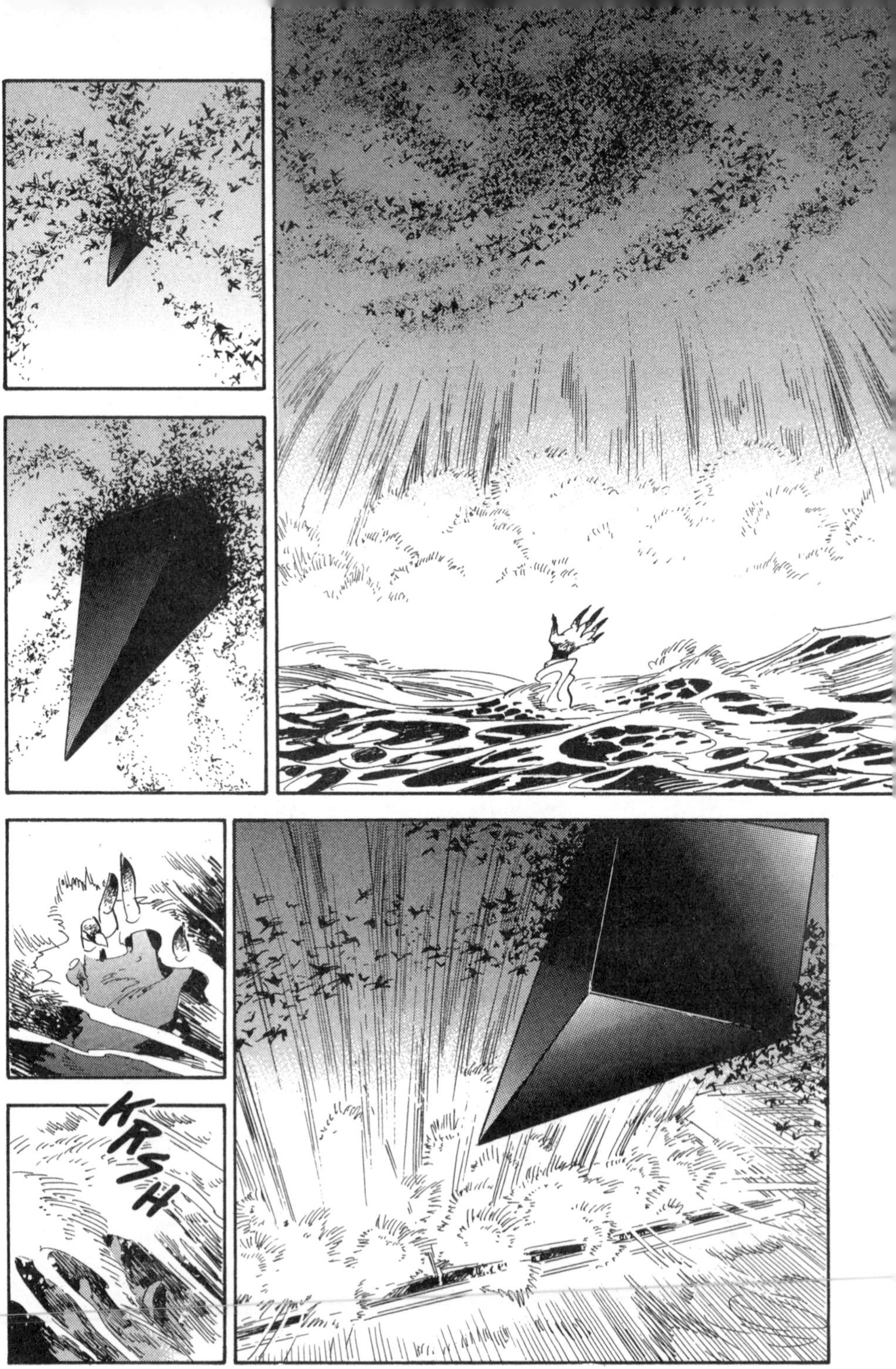
KRSH

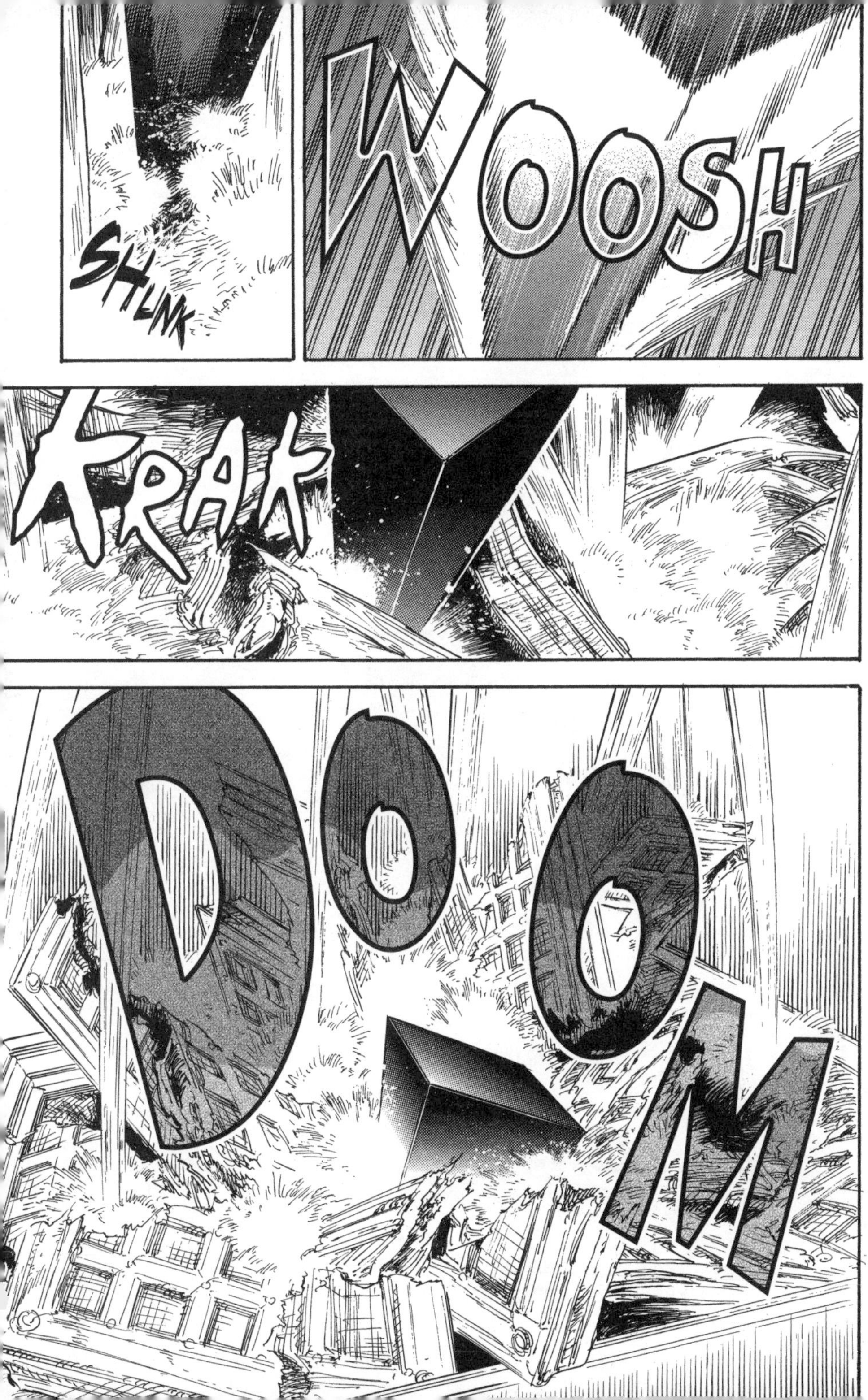
WOOSH
SHLUNK
KRAK
DOOOM

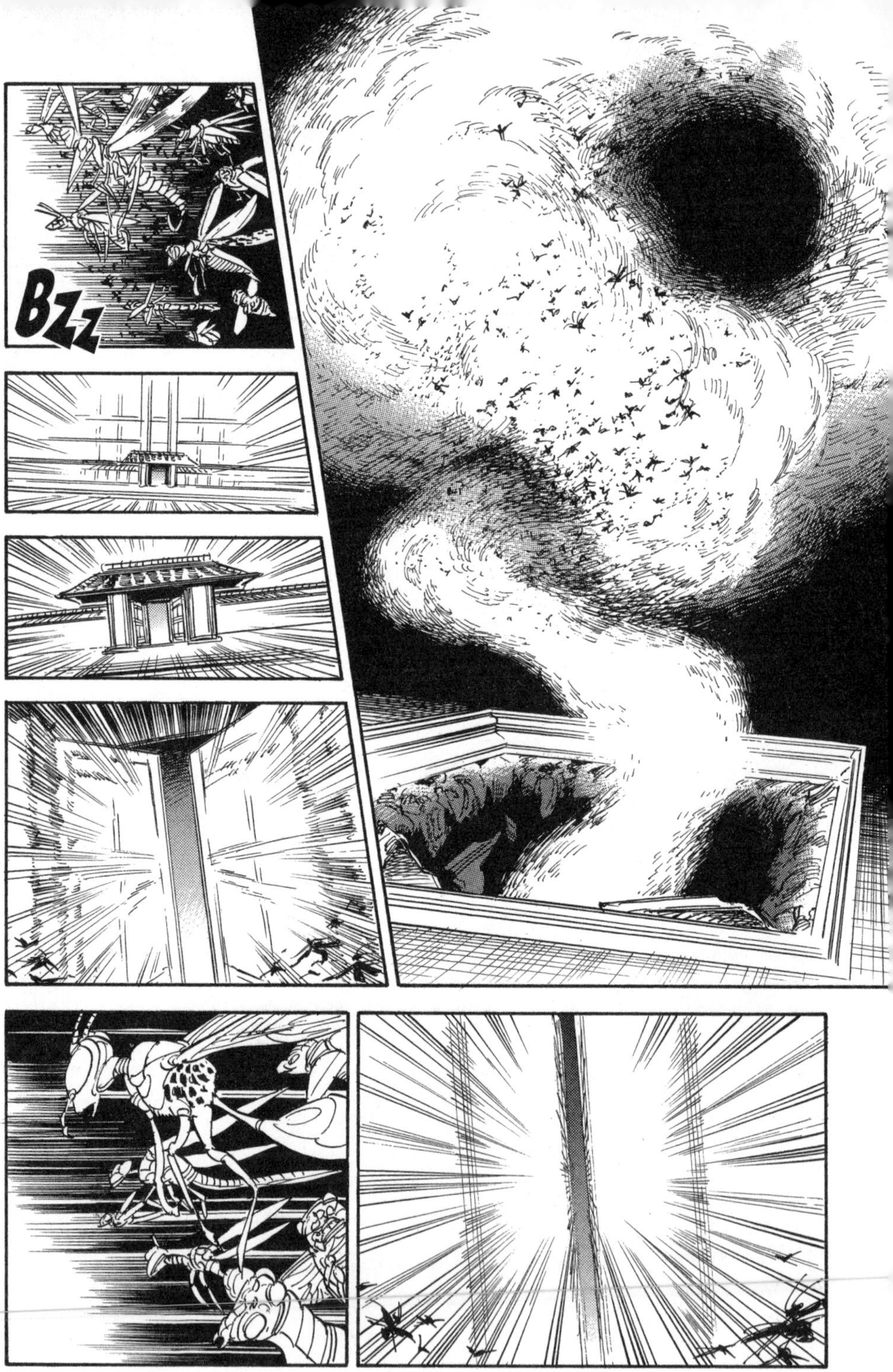
Bzz

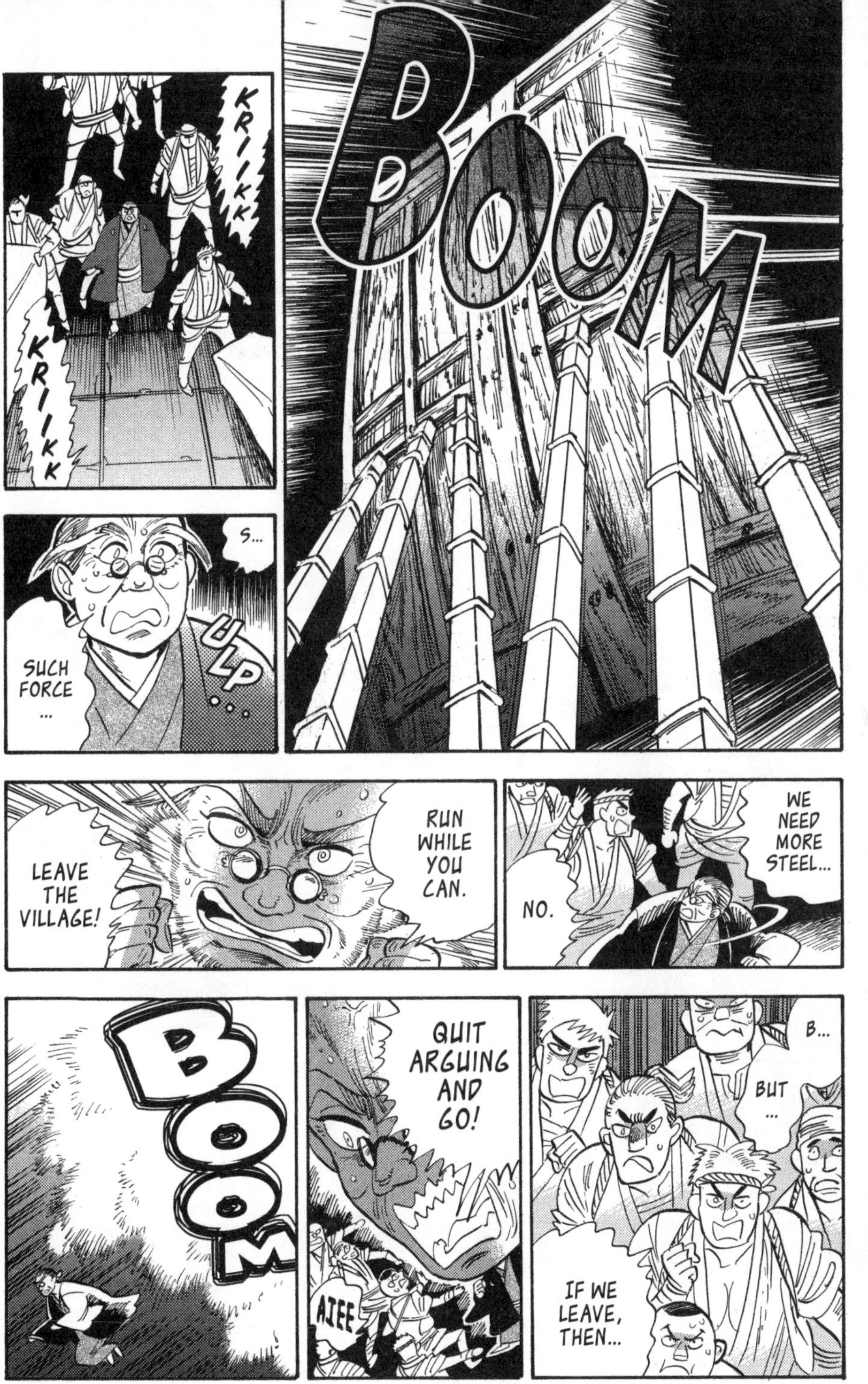
BOOM
KRIIKK
KRIIKK
S...
ULP
SUCH FORCE ...
WE NEED MORE STEEL...
NO.
RUN WHILE YOU CAN.
LEAVE THE VILLAGE!
B...
BUT ...
IF WE LEAVE, THEN...
QUIT ARGUING AND GO!
AIEE
BOOM

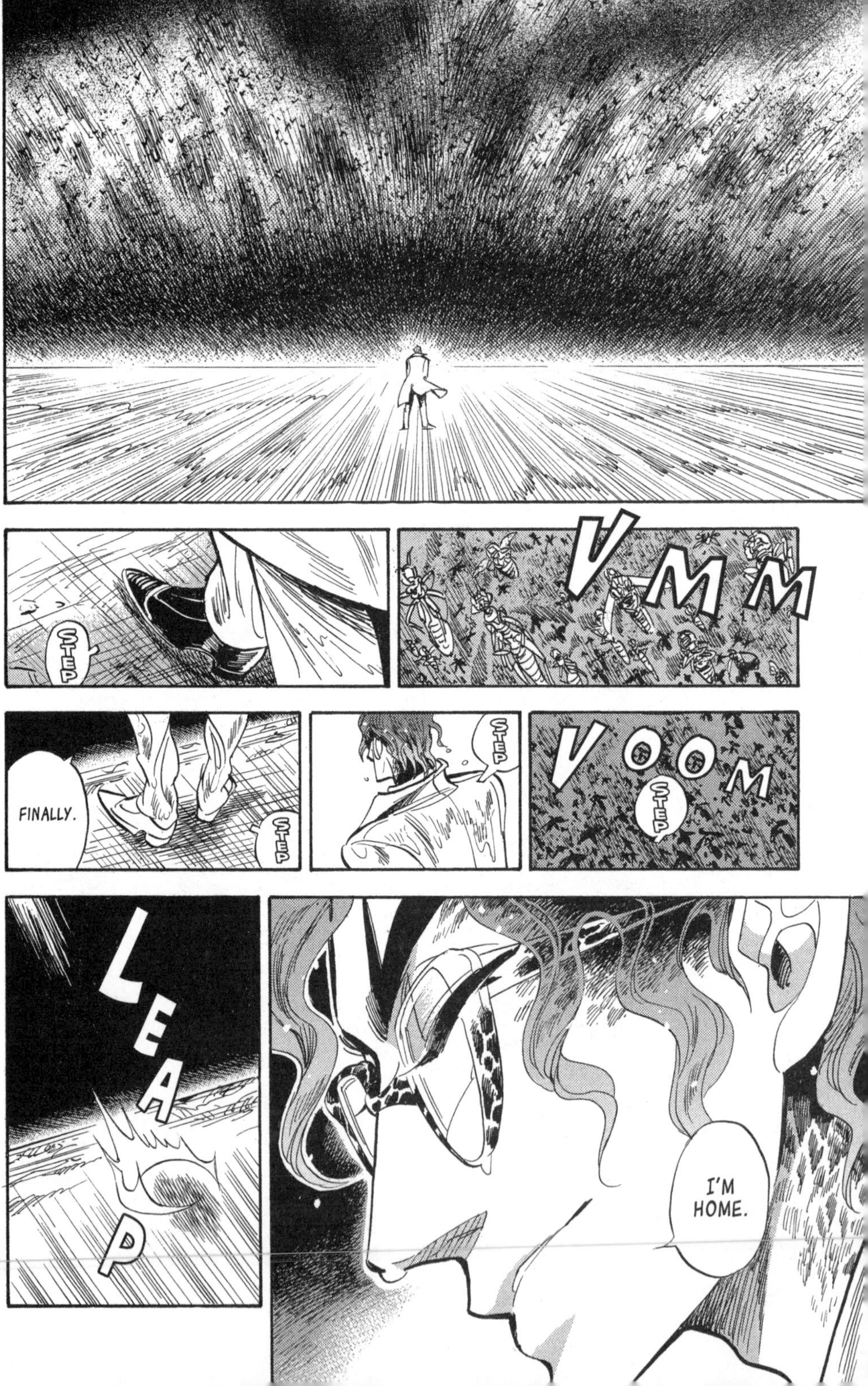
VMMM
STEP
VOOM
STEP
STEP
FINALLY.
STEP
I'M HOME.
LEAP

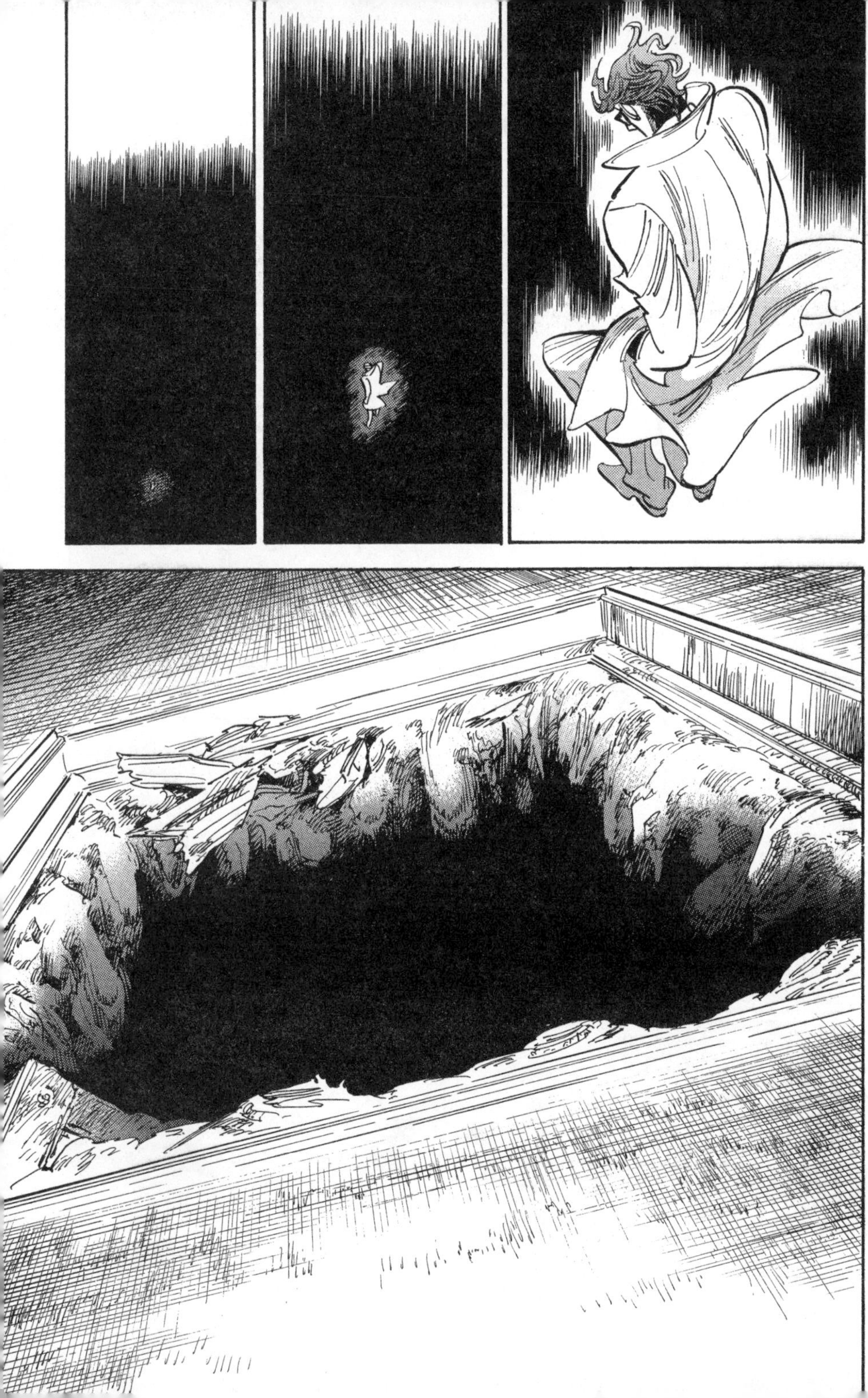

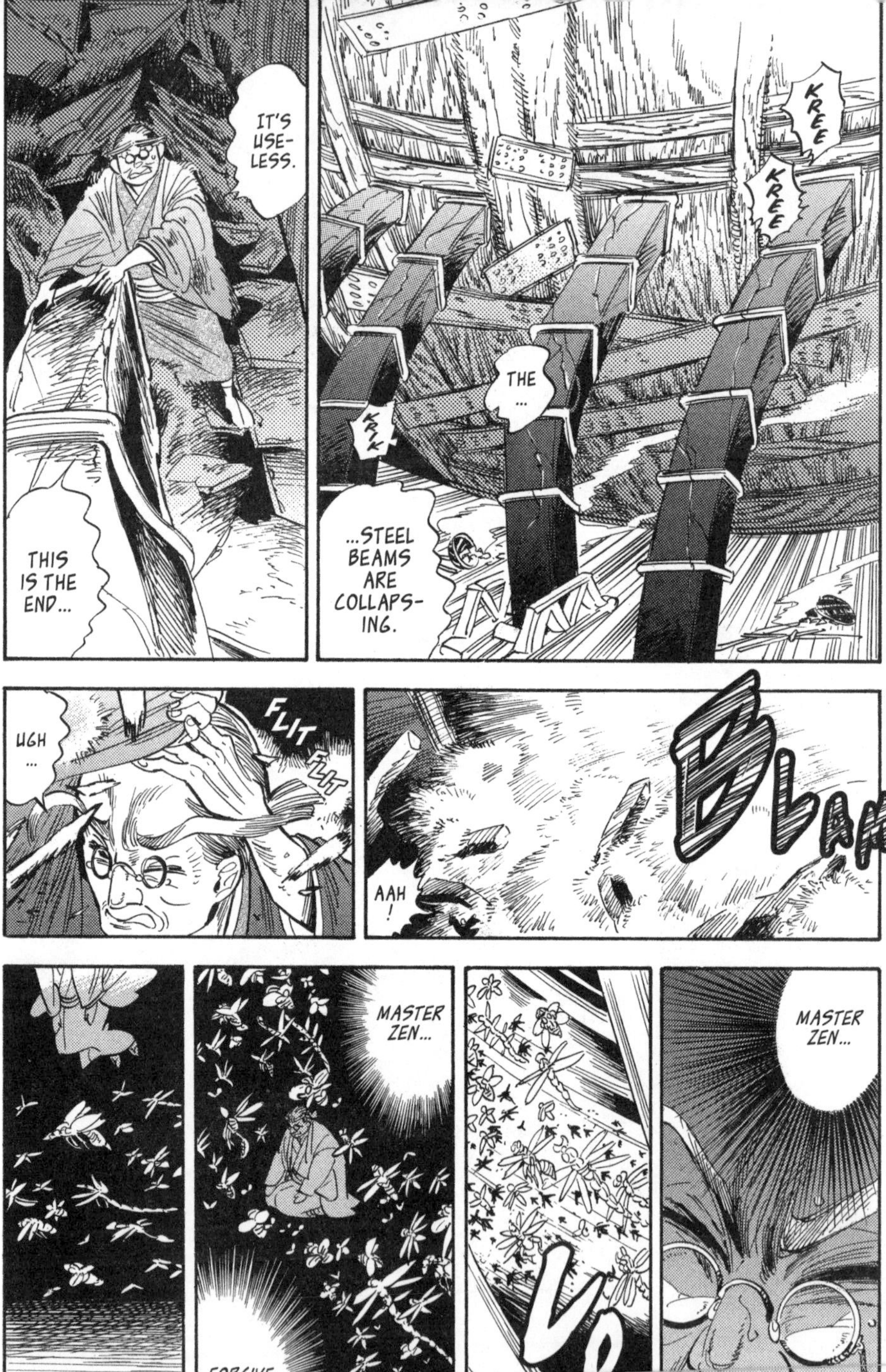
KREE
KREE
THE...
KRIK
...STEEL BEAMS ARE COLLAPSING.
IT'S USELESS.
THIS IS THE END...
BLAM
AAH!
FLIT
FLIT
UGH...
MASTER ZEN...
VOO
MASTER ZEN...
FORGIVE ME.

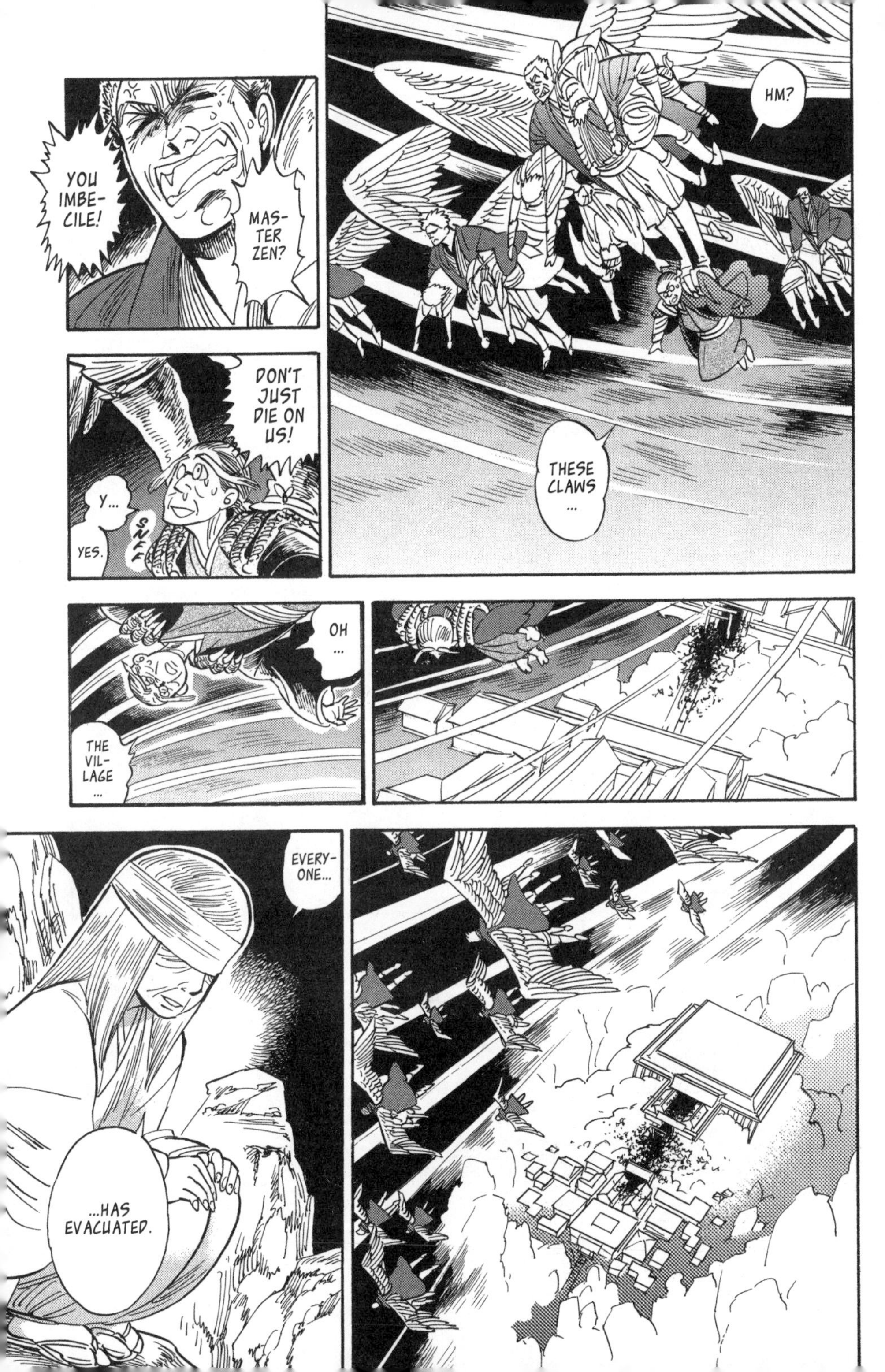
HM?
THESE CLAWS ...
MASTER ZEN?
YOU IMBECILE!
DON'T JUST DIE ON US!
SNFF
Y... YES.
OH ...
THE VILLAGE ...
EVERYONE...
...HAS EVACUATED.

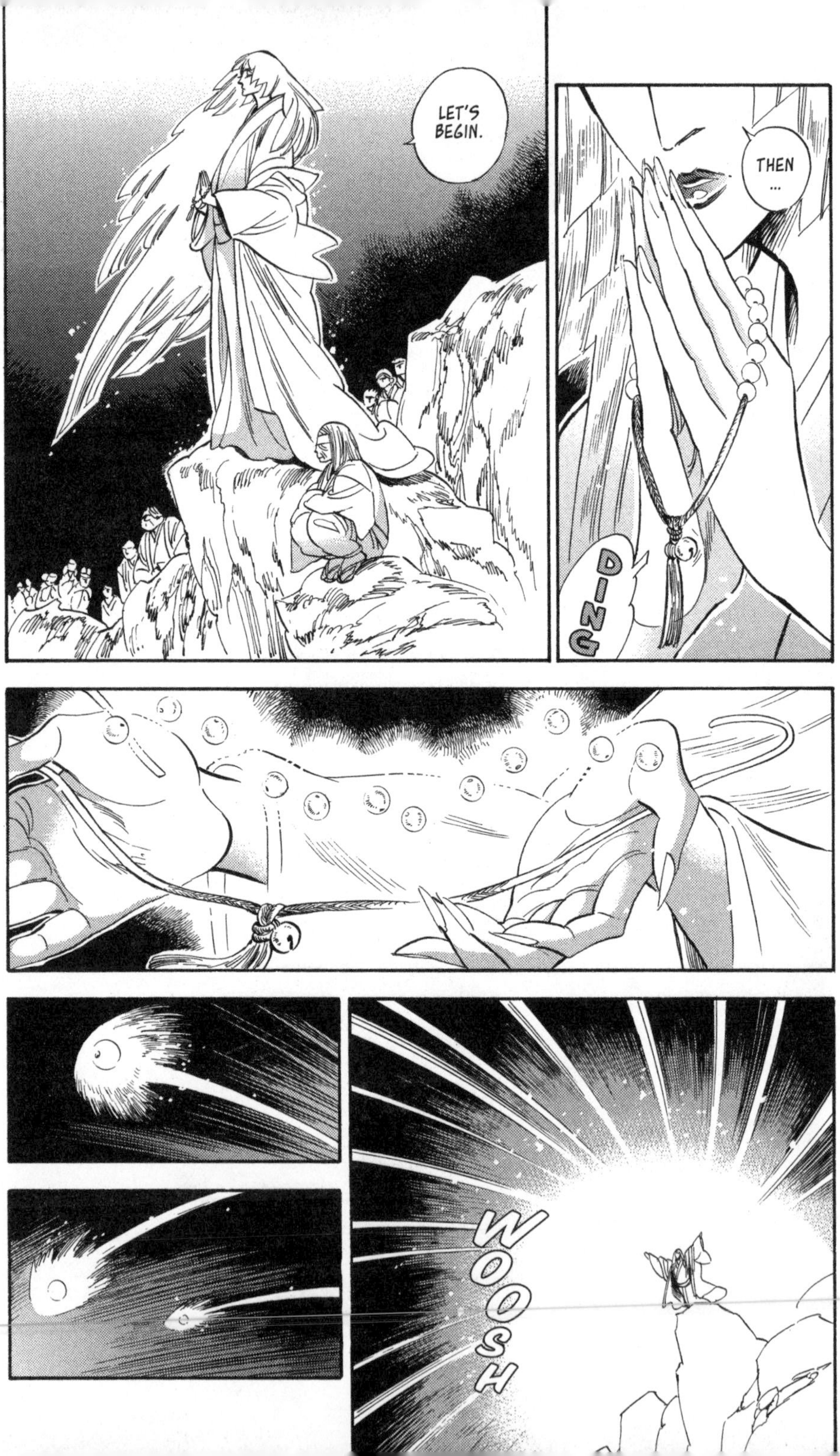
THEN ...
DING
LET'S BEGIN.
WOOSH

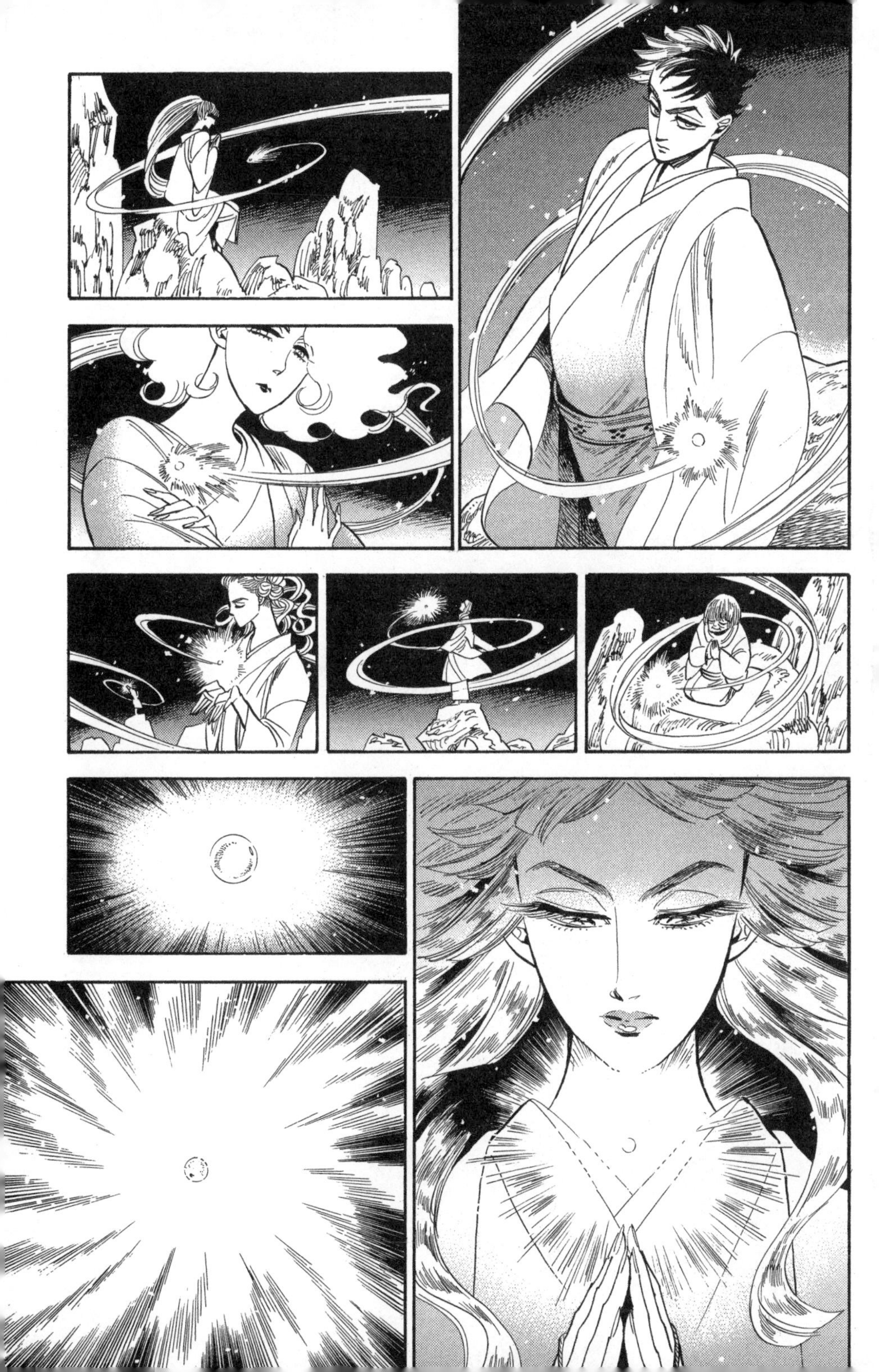

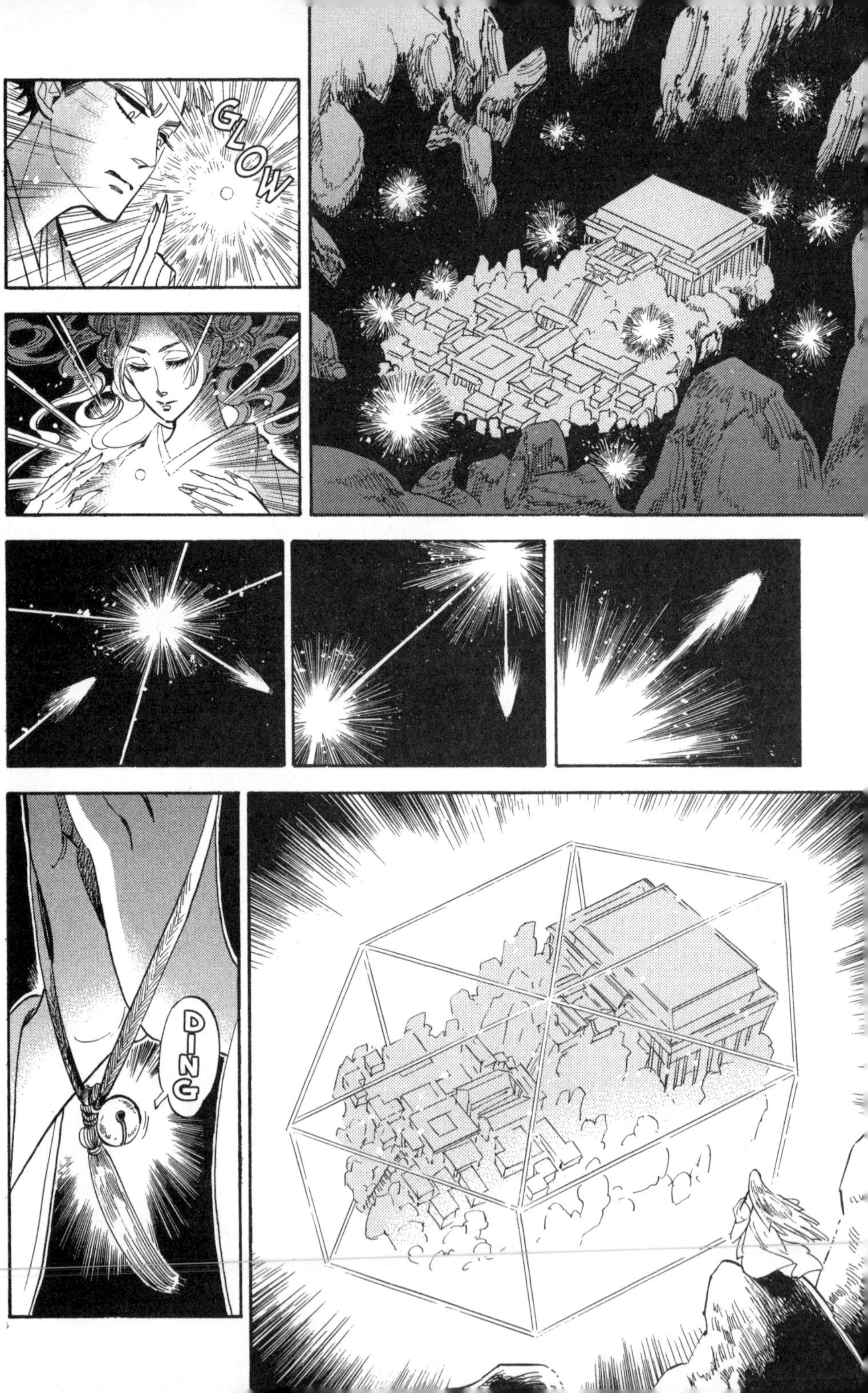
GLOW
DING

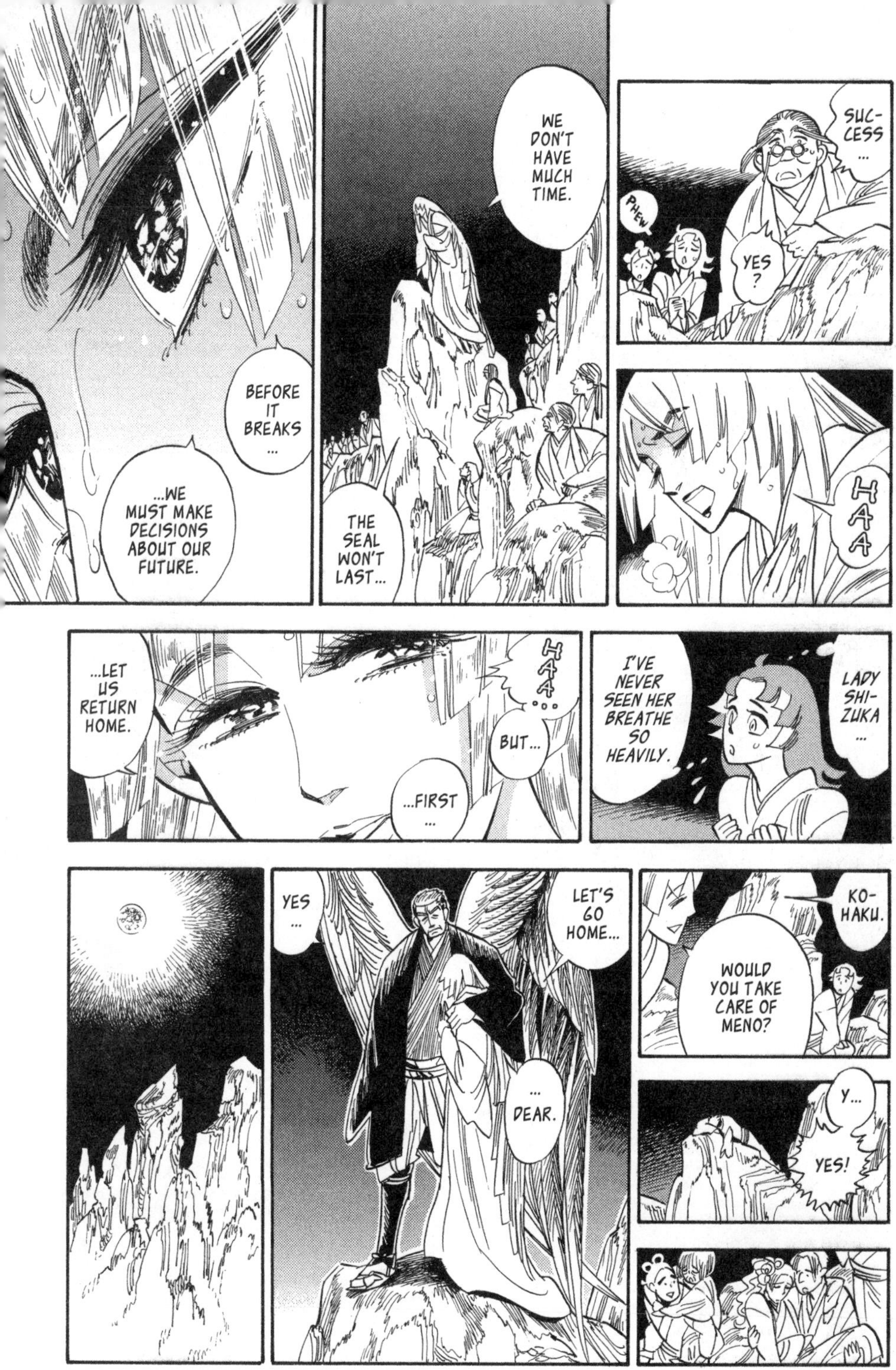
SUC-CESS...
PHEW
YES?
HAA
WE DON'T HAVE MUCH TIME.
THE SEAL WON'T LAST...
BEFORE IT BREAKS...
...WE MUST MAKE DECISIONS ABOUT OUR FUTURE.
LADY SHIZUKA...
I'VE NEVER SEEN HER BREATHE SO HEAVILY.
HAA...
BUT...
...FIRST...
...LET US RETURN HOME.
KO-HAKU.
WOULD YOU TAKE CARE OF MENO?
Y...
YES!
LET'S GO HOME...
YES...
...DEAR.

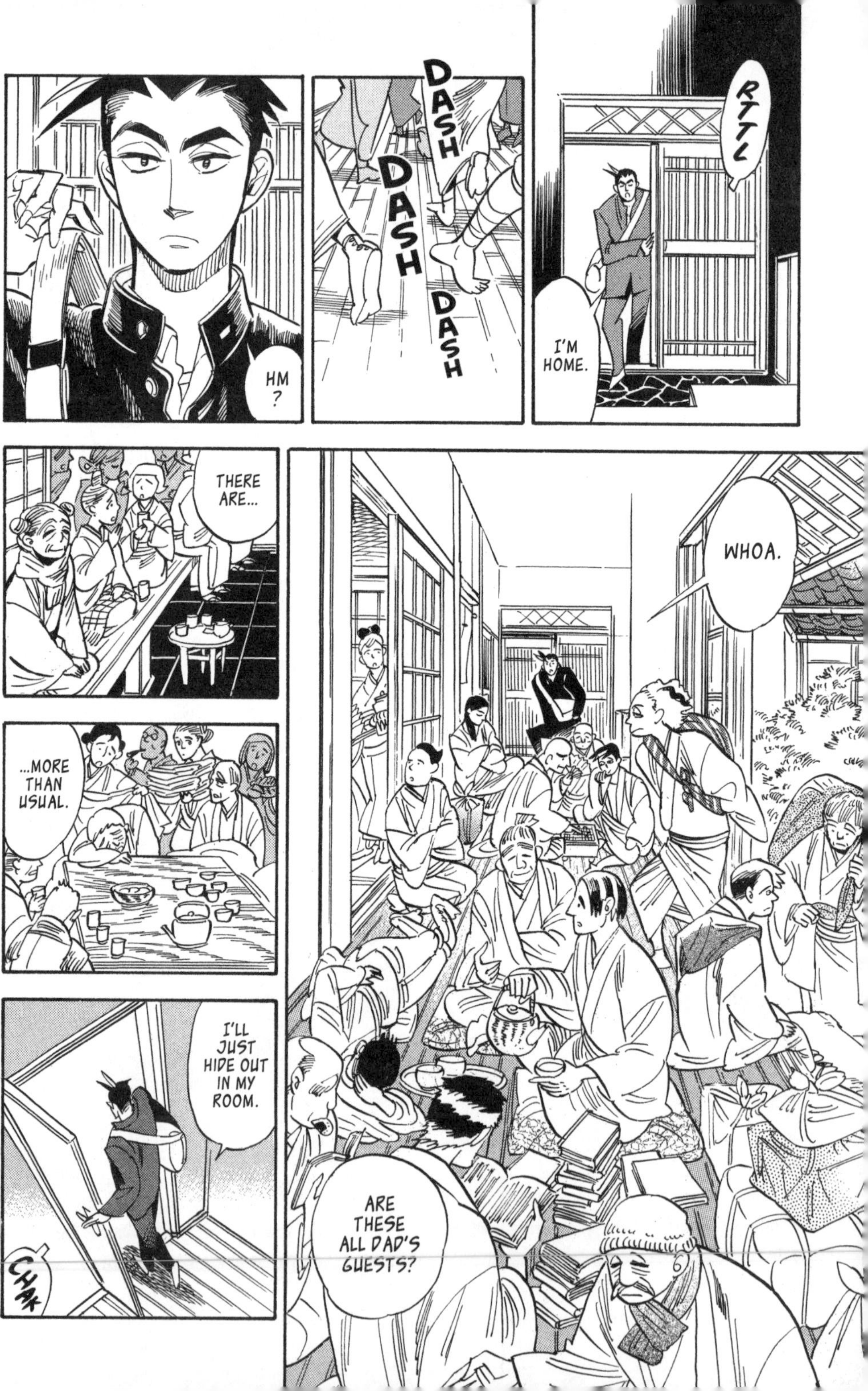
RTTL
I'M HOME.
DASH DASH DASH DASH
HM?
WHOA.
ARE THESE ALL DAD'S GUESTS?
THERE ARE...
...MORE THAN USUAL.
I'LL JUST HIDE OUT IN MY ROOM.
CHAK

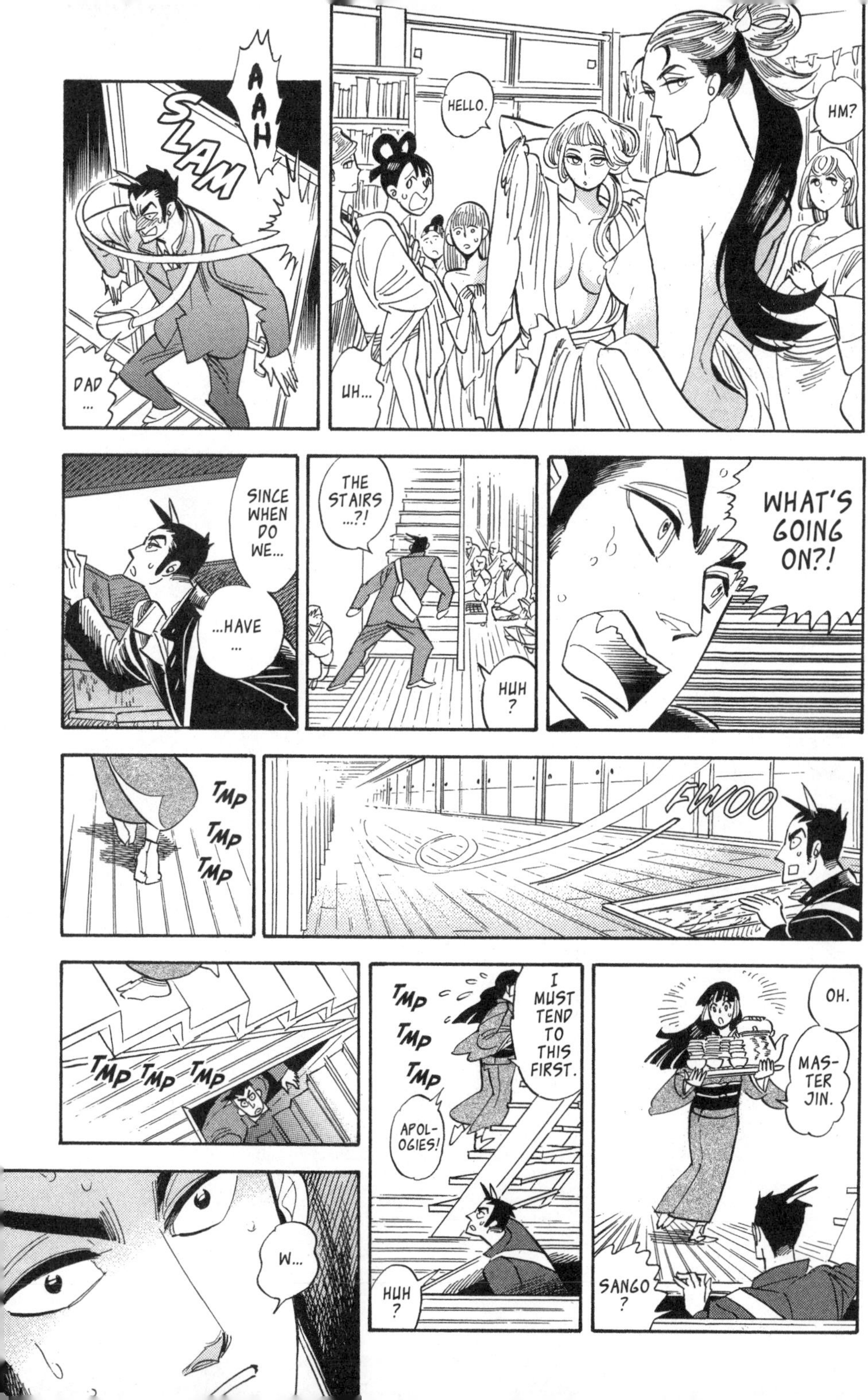
HM?
HELLO.
UH...
AAAH
SLAM
DAD...
WHAT'S GOING ON?!
THE STAIRS...?!
HUH?
SINCE WHEN DO WE...
...HAVE...
FWOO
TMP TMP TMP
OH.
MASTER JIN.
SANGO?
I MUST TEND TO THIS FIRST.
TMP TMP TMP
APOLOGIES!
HUH?
TMP TMP TMP
W...

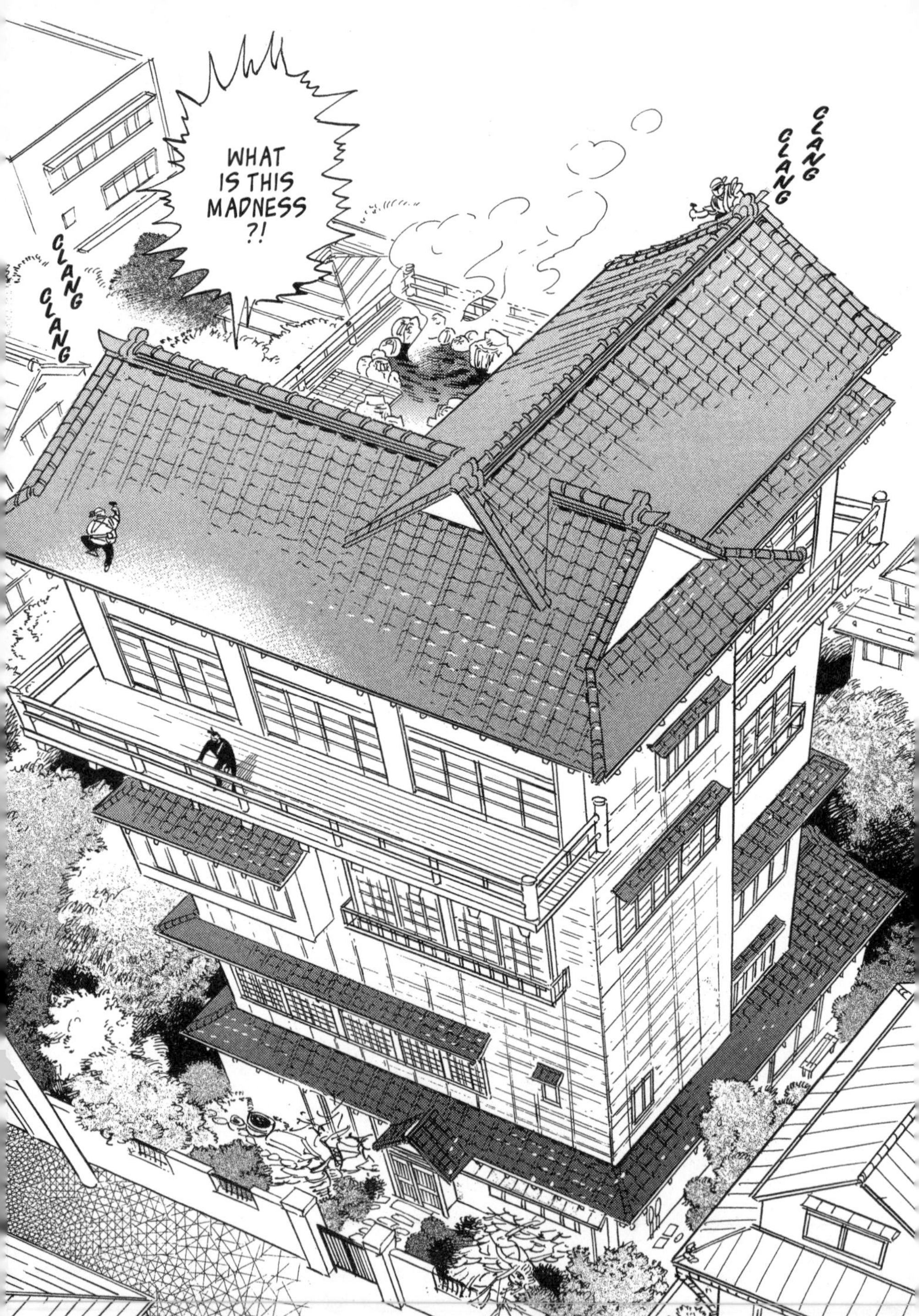
CLANG CLANG
WHAT IS THIS MADNESS?!
CLANG CLANG

Chapter 23 / The End

TO BE
CONTINUED
IN VOLUME 5!

Aki Irie was born in Kagawa Prefecture, Japan. She
began her professional career as a manga artist in
2002 with the short story "Fuku-chan Tabi Mata Tabi"
(Fuku-chan on the Road Again), which was published in
the monthly manga magazine *Papu*. *Ran and the Gray
World*, her first full-length series, is also the first
of her works to be released in English.

RAN AND THE GRAY WORLD

VOL. 4
VIZ Signature Edition

Story & Art by
AKI IRIE

English Translation & Adaptation/Emi Louie-Nishikawa
Touch-Up Art & Lettering/Joanna Estep
Design/Yukiko Whitley
Editor/Amy Yu

RAN TO HAIIRO NO SEKAI Vol. 4
© Aki Irie 2012
First published in Japan in 2012 by KADOKAWA CORPORATION, Tokyo.
English translation rights arranged with KADOKAWA CORPORATION, Tokyo.

Printed in Canada

Published by VIZ Media, LLC
P.O. Box 77010
San Francisco, CA 94107

10 9 8 7 6 5 4 3 2 1
First printing, August 2019

viz.com   vizsignature.com

Ran and
the Gray World